THE FARMER, THE GASTRONOME, AND THE CHEF

The Farmer, the Gastronome, and the Chef

IN PURSUIT OF THE IDEAL MEAL

DANIEL J. PHILIPPON

UNIVERSITY OF VIRGINIA PRESS

Charlottesville and London

The University of Virginia Press is situated on the traditional lands of the Monacan Nation, and the Commonwealth of Virginia was and is home to many other Indigenous people. We pay our respect to all of them, past and present. We also honor the enslaved African and African American people who built the University of Virginia, and we recognize their descendants. We commit to fostering voices from these communities through our publications and to deepening our collective understanding of their histories and contributions.

University of Virginia Press
© 2024 by the Rector and Visitors of the University of Virginia
All rights reserved
Printed in the United States of America on acid-free paper

First published 2024

1 3 5 7 9 8 6 4 2

LIBRARY OF CONGRESS CATALOGING-IN-PUBLICATION DATA

Names: Philippon, Daniel J., author.
Title: The farmer, the gastronome, and the chef : in pursuit of the ideal meal / Daniel J. Philippon.
Description: Charlottesville ; London : University of Virginia Press, 2024. | Includes bibliographical references and index.
Identifiers: LCCN 2024000436 (print) | LCCN 2024000437 (ebook) | ISBN 9780813952031 (hardcover) | ISBN 9780813952017 (paperback) | ISBN 9780813952024 (ebook)
Subjects: LCSH: Food writers—Attitudes. | Berry, Wendell, 1934-—Influence. | Petrini, Carlo, 1949-—Influence. | Waters, Alice—Influence. | Family farms—Wisconsin. | Agriculture—Italy—Piedmont Region. | Women cooks—France—Lyon Region. | Slow food movement. | Food industry and trade—Social aspects. | Philippon, Daniel J.—Travel.
Classification: LCC TX644 .P46 2024 (print) | : LCC TX644 (ebook) | DDC 664—dc23/eng/20240327
LC record available at https://lccn.loc.gov/2024000436
LC ebook record available at https://lccn.loc.gov/2024000437

Cover photo: Fresh fruit at farmers' market, Tuscany. (iStock.com/Yehoshua Halevi)
Cover design: Cecilia Sorochin

TO NANCY

Contents

Preface

This book is about three people—Wendell Berry, Carlo Petrini, and Alice Waters—and their pursuit, over the last fifty years or so, of what I call the "ideal meal," their vision of what a sustainable food system should look like. Each of them pursued that vision from the grounds of their own identity—as a farmer, a gastronome, and a chef, respectively—but they all have one thing in common: each is also a writer. That common thread is what ties this book together, and what sets it apart.

Our food systems currently face a host of threats, from climate chaos to the rise of authoritarianism around the world, and many of our responses to these threats will necessarily come from the realms of science, technology, and public policy. Given this, why should we pay attention to what three popular nonfiction writers had to say about our food futures? Shouldn't we instead be focusing our efforts on developing drought-resistant crop varieties, powering our delivery trucks with renewable energy, and preventing famine through international conflict resolution?

Finding viable, scalable solutions to these and many other global food challenges will be critical to our future in the twenty-first century, of course. But the literary and cultural context for those solutions also matters, since neither science nor policy occurs in a vacuum, and how we feed ourselves in a warming, warring world will depend in part on how we imagine our relationship to what we eat and the wider natural and cultural world from which our food originates. Political and technological solutions are also only one type of solution, and other, less centralized approaches deserve our equal attention.

The Farmer, the Gastronome, and the Chef is the result of my exploration of this broader cultural context off and on over the past ten years, driven by my desire to understand the literary history of the sustainable food movement, especially in the United States and Europe. How has our relationship with food changed since World War II, and why are these three writers responsible for shaping so much of this transformation? More detailed versions of these questions can be found in the introduction, along with some abbreviated answers, while more thorough answers appear in the chapters that follow.

The Farmer, the Gastronome, and the Chef is not only about these writers, however. It's also about my own pursuit of the ideal meal, in both real and imagined forms, as I sought to analyze their work through personal experience as well as close reading. I helped plant and harvest vegetables in central Wisconsin, spoke with growers and food producers in northern Italy, and visited with chefs and restaurateurs in southeastern France. I got my feet wet, my hands dirty, and my taste buds refined, not to mention my brain expanded.

What I found, not surprisingly, is that *it's complicated*. Changing our food systems to produce meals that are healthier and more flavorful, more environmentally friendly, and more socially just is indeed possible, and writing can be a powerful means of initiating and sustaining those transformations. But writing is only one tool in the activist's toolbox, and if there is a single message I took away from my exploration of these writers in these places, it was that *practice matters*: our ideals are intimately bound up with our pursuit of them.

How I came to understand this fundamental truth is both the subject and the method of this book.

Acknowledgments

My pursuit of the ideal meal has required the help and patience of many people, and I am more grateful than I can say for the guidance and assistance they provided.

The seeds of this project were planted when I was a Senior Fellow at the Rachel Carson Center for Environment and Society in Munich, where I developed the chapter on Wendell Berry. I thank Christof Mauch and Helmuth Trischler for their continuing investment in my work, plus the many other friends and colleagues I met in Munich, especially fellow food scholars Michelle Mart, Hanna Schösler, Diana Mincyte, Laura Sayre, Frank Uekotter, Paul Josephson, Rob Emmett, and Hal Crimmel. Thanks also to Kate Clancy and Lisa Heldke for their early guidance on sustainable food systems, and to Scott Slovic, Bill Major, and Serena Chou for their years of friendship and support. Needless to say, this chapter would not have been possible without the insights of Patty Wright and Mike Racette of Spring Hill Community Farm, whose kindness knows no bounds. Thanks to Meredith Cornett and Ethan Perry for encouraging us to join our first CSA so long ago.

My study of Carlo Petrini was made possible by a Fulbright Core Research/ Teaching Award in Italy, cosponsored by Serenella Iovino at the University of Turin and Simone Cinotto at the University of Gastronomic Sciences. I thank them both for their hospitality during my time in their beautiful country. Thanks also to Michael Branch, Rochelle Johnson, and Lee-Ann Kastman Breuch for supporting my application. In addition to the food producers profiled in this chapter, as well as many more whose stories I was unable to use, I am indebted to three Piedmontese locals whose generosity made my exploration of Slow Food's Italian roots possible: Toni Hilton, Christine Townsend, and Paolo Ferrero. (Felice Marino, who briefly appears in chapter 2, unfortunately passed away in May 2017, at the age of ninety-four.) Other members of the Slow Food family who assisted with my research include Cinzia Scaffidi, Alessandra Castelli, Paolo Ferrarini, Silvia Ceriani, and Carlotta Baitone. Carole Counihan offered a valuable perspective on Italian food activism, Marcus Hall helped me make sense of Italian agricultural history, and a public conversation with Fabio Parasecoli at the University of Minnesota's Institute for Advanced Study helped confirm my thinking about Italian food history more generally.

For enabling my reading of Alice Waters in France, I am deeply grateful to François Specq at the École Normale Supérieure de Lyon, where I served as a visiting professor. Lucy Vanel of Plum Lyon Teaching Kitchen gave freely of her time, talent, and knowledge, and I will be forever in her debt. Jennifer Gilbert and Tamiko Kobayashi were equally gracious in welcoming me into their restaurant. Other Lyon friends who helped point me in the right directions include Bill Buford, Rachel Black, and Josh Lund. In Provence, Kermit Lynch and Lulu Peyraud could not have been more generous and accommodating. (Sadly, Lulu passed away in October 2020, at the age of 102.) In Berkeley, I had invaluable assistance from the Bancroft Library and the staff at Chez Panisse.

Portions of my research have been delivered at a variety of scholarly and popular venues, including the Association for the Study of Literature and Environment, the European Society for Environmental History, the University of Illinois at Urbana–Champaign, the University of Turin, the University of Milan, the University of Gastronomic Sciences, the University of Bologna, Lumière University Lyon 2, the École Normale Supérieure de Lyon, Boise State University, the College of Idaho, the University of Wisconsin–Whitewater, the University of Erfurt, the University of Minnesota, the Heinrich Böll Foundation, the Rachel Carson Center for Environment and Society, the Saint Paul Public Library, Mississippi Market Food Co-op, Accenture

Technology, and Spring Hill Community Farm. Portions have also been published in different forms in *American Literary History, Weber: The Contemporary West,* and *RCC Perspectives.*

I am indebted to students in several of my courses at the University of Minnesota who helped refine my thinking, including undergraduates in "Writing from Plow to Plate: Sustainable Food Narratives in the U.S." (EngL 1905), "The American Food Revolution in Literature and Television" (EngL 3071), "Sleeping, Eating, Loving, Dying: The Practice of Everyday Life" (HSem 2025H), and "Food, Clothing, Shelter: The Culture and Politics of Simple Living" (HSem 3025H), as well as graduate students in "Ecocritical Food Studies" (EngL 8090), among other courses. An independent study with Claire Stanford generated helpful ideas early in my research, as did an interview with Michael Pollan. This project is also stronger thanks to feedback from students in the Transatlantic Summer Institute and colleagues in the Environmental Humanities Initiative, the Institute for Advanced Study, the Winton Chair in the Liberal Arts, the University Honors Program, and the Department of English, especially my Minnesota colleagues Charlotte Melin, Tracey Deutsch, Ellen Messer-Davidow, Andrew Elfenbein, and Kathryn Nuernberger. Jo Lee, my research mentor, read almost every word of this book in draft, and I give thanks for her unrelenting encouragement.

Additional thanks to colleagues in the Institute on the Environment, including Jessica Hellmann, my team-teacher in "Seeking the Good Life at the End of the World: Sustainability in the 21st Century" (GCC 3025), and Steve Polasky and Joseph Bump, in whose classes I tried out some of the ideas in the conclusion. I am also thankful for the University of Minnesota's support of this project, which came in the form of an Imagine Fund Annual Award, several research and travel grants, and sabbatical and other release time. The staff at the University Libraries, and especially in the amazing Interlibrary Loan office, were endlessly accommodating. Publication of this volume has been supported by a grant from the University of Minnesota's Myron Allen English Fund. All errors, of course, are mine alone.

At the University of Virginia Press, I am fortunate to have had the assistance of Angie Hogan, the Humanities, Environment, and Science Editor, whose advocacy has been unwavering throughout the publication process. Special thanks to Paul Bogard for introducing us. Ellen Satrom was an outstanding managing editor, and Susan Murray, copyeditor extraordinaire, helped ensure that my style was consistent and my citations complete. I am also deeply grateful to two anonymous reviewers, whose enthusiasm for this project was indispensable in bringing it to fruition, given their deep knowledge of food writing and food studies. Their constructive suggestions have improved this book in ways large and small.

If I learned anything over the years I spent researching and writing this book, it is that I would never have been able to do any of it without the love and support of my family. Although my mother died before the book was complete, both she and my father made substantial investments of time and effort that enabled me to pursue this project, and I will never forget their selflessness in doing so. My daughter, Grace, who appears briefly in these pages, had no choice but to tag along on her father's adventures, but I hope it was worth it, as she is now a fluent German-speaker and student of international culture and politics thanks to our time abroad; I couldn't be more proud. Finally, it is fair to say that this book would not even have begun were it not for the sustained encouragement of my wife, Nancy, and it certainly would not have been finished. Writing it has been a long road, and throughout it all she has been not only my first reader but also my most vocal supporter. In every way this is her book as much as it is mine, and for that reason I dedicate it to her, with my deepest love and gratitude.

THE FARMER, THE GASTRONOME, AND THE CHEF

Introduction

In my long experience as a gastronome, I have given hundreds
of interviews both as a critic and as the president of Slow Food.
In all these interviews, there have been very few occasions
when the interviewer did not ask: "What's your favorite dish?"
or "What's your ideal meal?" . . . The question is an irritating
commonplace which does justice neither to the gastronome's
curiosity nor to the seriousness of the subject.
—CARLO PETRINI, *Slow Food Nation*

THE GOD SHOT

Several years ago, in an effort to raise my coffee game, I decided to invest in a
Gaggia Classic, an entry-level semi-automatic espresso machine, along with
an Ascaso "i-mini" coffee grinder, with steel burrs and a stepless grind-size
adjustment.

For someone who had spent decades perfectly satisfied with the coffee I made in a twenty-dollar French press, figuring out what these things were and why they mattered was kind of a big deal.

To make sure I got the best bang for my buck, I spent hours poring over blogs by coffee nerds, checking out manufacturers' websites, and watching videos from retailers such as "Whole Latte Love" and Seattle Coffee Gear. And once I took the plunge, I still had to make some "mods," or modifications, to the espresso machine, such as lowering the overpressure valve to 9 bar (so that the extraction took about 25–30 seconds) and replacing the steam wand with one from a Rancilio Silvia machine (which makes better microfoam than the stock wand that came with the Gaggia). I have yet to make the jump to using a "naked portafilter" (a bottomless basket that holds the ground coffee) or installing a "PID controller" (a proportional–integral–derivative controller, which regulates the temperature of the water during brewing), but who knows, those days may yet come.

Needless to say, not only did my attempt to master espresso require an investment in both time and money, but it also meant entering the somewhat rarefied world of specialty coffee, which has its own language, values, and spoken and unspoken rules.

Of all the novel espresso terms I came across in my brief dive into (and out of) this world, the one that fascinated me the most was the "God Shot": a shot of espresso said to be so perfectly executed that its consumption is nothing short of a divine experience.

This term gave me something to shoot for, quite literally, because part of the fun of making espresso is trying to ensure that the five basic variables—the beans, the grind, the water, the time, and the temperature—all harmonize to create the tastiest possible result. Since so many things can go wrong (or at least not quite right) when making espresso, the goal is to try to get as many of them as close to perfect as possible, all at the same time. Do that as often as you can, and if you're lucky, one day you might experience the God Shot.

Or so the legend goes.

More than just the holy grail of espresso making (the coffee aficionado's equivalent of pitching a perfect game), the God Shot also embodies many of the concerns I address in this book, which examines three writers who have played central roles in the sustainable food movement.

The Farmer, the Gastronome, and the Chef is an intellectual travelogue of sorts, chronicling a journey in which I set out to understand how Wendell Berry, Carlo Petrini, and Alice Waters sought to make our food systems more sustainable over the last fifty years or so. To do this, I traveled to three different locations—central Wisconsin, the Piedmont region of Italy, and the cities of Lyon and Bandol in southeastern France—with the goal of more deeply apprehending how each of these writers helped readers make sense of three crucial aspects of our food systems—production, processing, and consumption—as agricultural products made their way from farm to fork, or plow to plate.

If this seems far afield, so to speak, from espresso making, consider the following.

Just as the God Shot envisions an espresso so perfect it can't possibly be improved, so too do these writers offer visions of our food future that are nothing if not utopian. In fact, I've subtitled the book *In Pursuit of the Ideal Meal* to signal the importance of this point. In the same way the God Shot implies the existence of a future espresso shot in which all the elements of great coffee come together to make something truly divine, these food writers all tried to show us "what could be": they tried to give us a vision of what an "ideal meal" could look like, if only we could align the features of our food systems with the values we cherish the most. *The Farmer, the Gastronome, and the Chef* is thus a book about pursuing our highest ideals, our utopian imaginations of what our meals could potentially be. (Searching for the perfect meal turns out to be something of a theme in food writing. Compare, for instance, Baxter; Bourdain, *Cook's Tour*; Chin; de Groot; Rayner; Pollan, *Omnivore's Dilemma*; and Stevens.)

It would be easy to dismiss the transcendental vision of the God Shot, and the romanticized view of food it represents, as idealistic in the worst of ways: Sir Thomas More's *Utopia*, after all, was literally *no place*, an imaginary island he created to house his ideal society. But both the God Shot and this book illustrate the power of speculative thinking, or what Carlo Petrini tried to get at when he wrote, "I am convinced that he who sows utopia will reap reality" (*Slow Food Nation* 240). Justin Myers helpfully describes Petrini's vision as a discursive "politics of possibility," in which "conceptual and linguistic framings can open pathways within the practices of everyday life that not only underscore 'another world is possible' but also help facilitate alternative ways of living" (405). And what is true for Petrini is equally true for

Wendell Berry and Alice Waters, though in Berry's case these visions of the future are also intimately tied to his visions of the past, or what I have come to call his "agristalgia."

Taken to an extreme, the activity of positing an ideal might seem to imply a belief in human perfectibility, and thus a denial of our very real and imperfect human selves and societies. But it need not do that. In fact, without ideals—without a vision of some better way to live—we have nothing to live *for*. What we want to avoid is simply taking things too far: positing an ideal way of life that is so far removed from reality that it will never come to pass.

Utopian thinking also implies dystopian thinking, of course, and as hard as these writers worked to paint compelling pictures of better food futures for all of us, they were also reacting against certain food scenarios they disliked, from nightmarish visions of industrialized agriculture run amok to less-than-ideal ways we might prepare the evening meal. But my focus in this book is on these writers' appeals to our better angels—the hope of a God Shot in our future—rather than on any appeals to fear they may make, since all of them seem to agree that positive visions of the future, more than our fears of disaster, are what motivate people to act. (Other aspects of utopian thinking about food and agriculture are examined in Goode; Kelley; Madden and Finch; Stock, Carolan, and Rosin; and Tigner and Carruth.)

For all of the strengths of these utopian reveries, however, there remains the fact that there is no singular ideal meal, no God Shot to end all other shots, as I've now discovered after making thousands of espresso shots over the last few years. In this sense, this book is also a repudiation of the idea of the God Shot altogether—and, by extension, the idea that taste somehow occurs outside of human history and culture.

To put it more concretely, most mornings I make myself a cappuccino soon after I get out of bed. But everything about the espresso shot it requires is unique to me. The beans are usually Peace Coffee's Black Squirrel Espresso Blend, a certified organic, shade-grown, fair-trade coffee, roasted by a local company that delivers their coffee by bicycle to my neighborhood food co-op. (It's painfully virtuous, I know, but it's also damn good coffee.) I grind the beans to the consistency I like, somewhere between table salt and flour; press about 18 grams of the grounds into the portafilter with a 58-millimeter stainless steel tamper; and then extract them with our municipal tap water, most of which is drawn from the Mississippi River. About twenty-five seconds later, give or take a few seconds, I've got about 36 grams of espresso ready to meet my steamed milk.

The point here is that the idea of the God Shot assumes there is such a thing as "food from nowhere," a perfect espresso shot just waiting to be pulled, a mystical experience of oneness with the universe that occurs when your shot finally assumes its ultimate form. Yet this idealized view of reality doesn't reflect the complexities of the real world, which in my experience means that no two shots are ever alike, and all of them have something to offer us.

This is why it was important that I traveled, instead of simply staying in my office, to understand what these authors were trying to say. Just as there is no such thing as "food from nowhere," neither is there such a thing as "reading from nowhere," and I wanted to see what would happen if I put these authors in conversation with certain landscapes that had meaningful associations with what I thought they were trying to say.

As a result, I decided to read the essays of Wendell Berry from the perspective of our community-supported agriculture (CSA) farm in central Wisconsin; to experience firsthand the landscape around Carlo Petrini's hometown of Bra, Italy; and to see Lyon, France, where women just like Alice Waters have been cooking for centuries, as well as the hills of Provence, where Waters eventually found her own culinary inspiration. (I drank plenty of espresso in each of these locations, by the way, and most of these shots— though not all of them—were quite good!)

To put this in slightly more academic terms, the God Shot is not unlike what Donna Haraway calls "the god trick," or the illusory belief that we can see "everything from nowhere" (581). Instead, Haraway argues for what she calls "situated knowledges," which she defines as the "politics and epistemologies of location, positioning, and situating, where partiality and not universality is the condition of being heard to make rational knowledge claims." This, she argues, is "the view from a body, always a complex, contradictory, structuring, and structured body, versus the view from above, from nowhere, from simplicity" (589).

Haraway offers an especially useful point of reference, because she reminds us that the view from nowhere is actually a view from somewhere, and that this "somewhere" is often the "unmarked positions of Man and White," not to mention heterosexual, economically privileged, and human (581). As a white, male, heterosexual, middle-class U.S. academic, I have tried to take special care to be up-front about my position in what follows, given that there are many limitations to my perspective. I recognize, for instance, that in most cases my view arises from leisured reflection, not physical labor, and that my privilege informs my perspective in ways that can both illuminate and obscure my subject (more bougie coffee, anyone?).

More than just a cautionary tale for yours truly, thinking carefully about the "god trick" also means thinking critically about the three writers I examine in *The Farmer, the Gastronome, and the Chef*. To that end, in each section I address several issues of human identity that pertain most closely to each author: for Wendell Berry, the issue of race and the "unbearable whiteness" of sustainable agriculture; for Carlo Petrini, the issue of class and the much-criticized elitism of Slow Food; and for Alice Waters, the issue of gender and the role of women in the professional kitchen.

Haraway's goal of producing "a more adequate, richer, better account of a world, in order to live in it well" (579) is my goal also, which is to say that we are both interested in how our ethics and politics are connected to how we know the world. If there is a take-home message from the chapters that follow, therefore, it is that *there are a plurality of "ideal meals": there is not just one way to imagine what sustainable food production, processing, and consumption should look like.* It depends on *who* is producing, processing, or consuming it; *what materials* it consists of; *where* it is located; *when* it is being produced, processed, or consumed; and *why and how* it is being produced, processed, or consumed that way.

Even though there is no singular God Shot, in other words, there is still plenty of really good espresso out there for all of us to enjoy! And once we recognize this, the world gets a whole lot more interesting.

ON MOVEMENTS AND METHODS

If we lived in a perfect world—God Shots for everyone, all the time!—there would be no need for social movements. But of course, this is not our fate. Instead, we live in a world full of environmental harms, social and economic injustices, and food that could be tastier, healthier, safer, more plentiful, and more equitably distributed, among many other things.

As Wynne Wright and Gerad Middendorf point out, there was a brief, shining moment after World War II when it appeared as if we might actually be living in a food utopia, at least to those who preferred not to look too closely:

> In the postwar era of abundance, food moved to the back burner of the consciousness of many in the industrialized world. For most, it became plentiful, inexpensive, more convenient, and perceived as relatively nutritious. Given a willingness to trust those embedded in our food-provisioning system, we relinquished our civic responsibility for food system oversight to farmers, nutritionists, food corporations, agribusiness, and the state; in other words, we let the experts take charge. Issues of how, where, and by whom food was grown were not generally topics of conversation around the dinner table. In some circles, it might even be considered unacceptable or impolite to ask about the social life of our dinner. (4)

Cracks in the system soon appeared, however. Rural communities were being hollowed out as farms grew larger and more centralized. Lands and waters were degraded by the excessive use of fertilizers, pesticides, and irrigation. Oceans began to suffer from overfishing and the side effects of the aquaculture industry. Animals became nothing more than commodities, raised in filthy, overcrowded conditions, pumped full of antibiotics, and slaughtered on a massive scale with mind-numbing efficiency. Multinational corporations modified the genes of living organisms, patented those innovations, and made seed-saving a crime. Rates of obesity, diabetes, and heart disease began to rise, and reports of foodborne illnesses grew more and more frequent. Millions of people continued to suffer from hunger and malnutrition, while billions of pounds of food went to waste each year. What food was consumed was often prepared in a factory; laden with fat, sugar, and salt; shipped from thousands of miles away; sold regardless of season or cultural context; and eaten in the car, at a desk, or on the run. And hovering over it all was the existential threat of climate chaos.

Bjørn Lomborg, the self-styled "skeptical environmentalist," might call this version of our postwar food system "the Litany," his term for overly pessimistic accounts of our environmental ills that either neglect to consider the benefits that accompany these harms or rely on subtle forms of exaggeration, if not outright lies, for their dramatic effect (3). But whatever debates might surround aspects of each of these claims individually, it became increasingly clear to many that all was not right in the world of food, and as a result the sustainable food movement was born.

In 2010, Michael Pollan described what unified the "big, lumpy tent" of activists working to reform the food system in this way: "The food movement coalesces around the recognition that today's food and farming economy is 'unsustainable'—that it can't go on in its current form much longer without courting a breakdown of some kind, whether environmental, economic, or both." To these activists, the "social/environmental/public health/animal welfare/gastronomic costs" of industrial food production, Pollan said, "are too high" ("Food Movement, Rising").

That movement, now in its second or third iteration since the 1970s, has been called many names: the sustainable food movement, the good food movement, the slow food movement, the local foods movement, the just food movement, the movement for alternative food networks, an alternative agri-food system, and various versions of food democracy and food sovereignty, among other monikers. Sociologists and other social movement theorists have debated whether such a movement indeed exists (most agree that it does), and whether it is a single movement or a collection of smaller movements (the jury's still out on this one), but from my perspective there is little doubt that something is afoot, and for the sake of simplicity I have been calling this the sustainable food movement.

My main question is this: *How did nonfiction writing, as exemplified by the work of these three authors, shape the sustainable food movement?*

In my previous book, *Conserving Words*, I examined how American nature writers shaped the environmental movement, and I argued that they did so by effectively mobilizing discursive frames that enabled individuals and groups to see themselves as part of a larger story. *The Farmer, the Gastronome, and the Chef* addresses a similar issue, but it does so in a different way, and it comes to different conclusions.

As with the environmental movement, part of what brought the food movement into being were writers: eloquent advocates who knew how to frame an argument, tell a good story, get people's attention, and move them to action. This is not so much a book about "food writing" in general, therefore, as it is about a particular subset of that writing: books that have had an influence, writing that has made a difference.

While government reports and other kinds of "gray literature" have undoubtedly shaped the food movement, popular nonfiction writing offers something different: personal responses, emotion, and narration, often rendered in accessible, even eloquent language—features that tend not to appear in the latest white paper on agricultural policy.

Such nonfiction writing takes many forms, including autobiography and memoir, essay, journalism, argument, manifesto, and cookbook, and it is partly through these *forms* that the sustainable food movement came into being (Levine). In a memoir, a reader can see herself in another person's shoes. In a manifesto, he can feel the force of an advocate's passion. And in a cookbook, readers of all kinds can learn how to practice the sort of cooking that aligns with what they and the movement both value. Forms such as these allow a social movement to see itself clearly: they are part of what Evgeny Morozov has called the "intellectual infrastructure" that turns diverse subgroups into a movement and allows its adherents to reflect on what it means to be part of something bigger than themselves (71).

Another way to think about this is that what these texts *do* (their popularity and significance) is closely connected to what these texts *are* (their form and content). If literature is a means to address what Donella Meadows called the "leverage points" needed to change a system, then this diversity of nonfictional food writing may have helped point readers to multiple leverage points in pursuit of systemic change (145–65).

Tracing the relationship of writing to the food movement is further complicated by the fact that this relationship is neither static nor one-directional. Just as these texts shaped a movement, the movement also shaped the texts, particularly as the goals of both changed and evolved over time.

The audience for these writings also mattered, given that the sustainable food movement is not strictly a U.S. phenomenon—although its presence is felt most strongly in Europe and North America. Wendell Berry and Alice Waters are both U.S. writers (one based in Kentucky, the other in California), while Carlo Petrini is an Italian (I read his texts in translation). The subjects of their writing also reflect their location in the Global North, with Berry writing about rural, white farmers in the United States, Petrini concerned with rural Italian producers, and Waters focused mostly on female, middle-class, white, urban and suburban consumers in the United States.

Despite these regional distinctions, these writers unquestionably aimed to be read by, and have an effect on, a wide audience. In some cases, the expectations these authors had about their audience shaped the message of their texts, with Berry proposing particular national policy changes in the United States, for example, and Petrini assuming readers' familiarity with the landscape and customs of northern Italy. In other cases, these authors' focus on primarily European and American readers may have limited their visions to solutions that seemed either familiar or relevant to these audiences. Adam Gopnik observes, for instance, that "all these movements . . . share a sense that the industrialized, Americanized food economy is destructive of small-scale, European, traditional, farm-based eating" (262). Yet Melanie DePuis asks: "Why is Europe presented as the only source of good food and 'the good life'? Why not Japanese or Chinese diets, equally low in saturated fat and high in fiber? What about African American Soul and Southern country cooking meat-and-three-veg diets that are filled with beans and leaves? Why not the bean-and-corn-centered Mexican cuisine? . . . Despite the universality of dietary balance in most cuisines, localist and Slow Food movement actors get caught up in the Mediterranean narrative, which links good food with European sacralization of either peasant rustic or aristocratic, highbrow ways of life" (108).

How did nonfiction writing shape the sustainable food movement, then? The short answer is by changing readers' ideas and behaviors to be more "sustainable," broadly speaking. But this leaves open the question of which ideas and behaviors count as more sustainable, and which do not.

Each of these writers set out to solve specific problems related to food sustainability: Wendell Berry tried to revitalize rural communities, Carlo Petrini sought to improve the competitive position of small producers, and Alice Waters endeavored to connect farms to restaurants and improve the quality of home-cooked food, among other goals. Figuring out *how* to do these things, not to mention how to write about them, is not as easy as these writers sometimes make it look, and the plurality of visions they offer for what counts as "sustainable food" is sometimes bumpy and uneven as a result.

Much of this book, therefore, is about the *conflicts and contestations* between these different visions: the tensions between religion and science in Wendell Berry's thinking about the meaning and purpose of agriculture, between the local and the global in Carlo Petrini's visions for Slow Food, and between art and commerce in the creation of Chez Panisse, Alice Waters's restaurant, and in the cookbooks and memoir that followed it.

In addition, a big part of what I try to do in these pages is to *question dichotomies*: not only between the local and the global, for instance, but also between the industrial and the sustainable, between fast and slow food, between the city and the countryside, between the traditional and modern, between individual choice and structural change, and between the material world and our representations of it. Ultimately, I want to complicate foodie edicts, especially those that distinguish good food from bad food, nature from culture, and local places from the global flows of people, information, goods, and capital that define our contemporary world. My goal is not complexity for complexity's sake but to produce a version of Haraway's "more adequate, richer, better account of a world, in order to live in it well."

Other food studies scholars, such as Richard Wilk and Karen Lykke Syse, have made similar arguments about the perils of binary thinking, but *The Farmer, the Gastronome, and the Chef* is ultimately more grounded in the field of literary studies known as *ecocriticism*, or the study of literature and the environment.

Unlike earlier waves of ecocriticism, which tended to celebrate "nature" while criticizing the excesses of human culture, mine is an ecocriticism in which nature is never separate from human engagement, particularly human engagement through *work*—work in the fields, in the processing plants, and in the kitchen. To this it adds a differentiated understanding of humans (not simply as a single species but as different cultures, ethnicities, and identities). This is also an ecocriticism in which "nature" is always a construction, both as an idea and as a physical reality, and it is always as specific as possible (not simply a singular "nature" or "environment" but specific material aspects of the nonhuman world). It's an ecocriticism in which humans and the rest of the world are engaged in an ever-shifting exchange, a push and pull of influence, in which humans act and nature pushes back, the world shifts and humans respond. Likewise, it sees those individual agents in dynamic relationship with social and ecological systems, part of what I have called (in *Conserving Words*) an "ecology of influence," in which neither the individual actor nor the system takes priority in attempts to explain how individuals and systems interact (5).

It's also necessarily a hybrid ecocriticism, one that need not—indeed, *cannot*—abandon place-based approaches for a placeless cosmopolitanism. Instead, it recognizes the interpenetration of the old dichotomies of the city and the countryside, and the local and the global.

Finally, it takes what ecocritics have called "narrative ecocriticism" on the road, and on the plane, to places near and far, in search of greater understanding. But instead of mixing textual analysis with personal experience of a static "nature," it puts food writing in conversation with my personal experience of specific landscapes—both natural and cultural—in which humans are actively transforming elements of the nonhuman world into something good to eat. (Jane Tompkins, Nancy Miller, and others have termed this type of writing "personal" or "autobiographical" criticism. Similarly, my colleagues Allison Carruth, Chad Lavin, William Major, Michael Mikulak, and Sarah Wald, among others, have all written thoughtfully about food and agriculture from an ecocritical perspective.) For this reason, I hesitate to describe my method as producing a series of "case studies," as that label seems to reduce the lived experience of the people and places I encountered to mere illustrations of some larger and more important "principles" or generalizations. Instead, I would describe it as a form of "field study," in which I test different ideas about these texts in real-world conditions. I want to ensure that our ideas have both people and places in them, and that our knowledge has not only a human face but some nonhuman ones as well.

While I certainly make arguments throughout these pages, *The Farmer, the Gastronome, and the Chef* is less an argument than the narrative of a journey, more an interpretive essay than any kind of rigorous social scientific investigation. My ultimate goal, in other words, is to learn more about food and food writing, and to share that experience with you, not style myself an expert in it or practice anthropology or sociology without a license.

Doing so means adopting a certain kind of reading practice, which I describe as *reading with generosity and curiosity*. It may seem rather superfluous to state something so obvious—isn't this what all reading is about?—but this is not, in fact, what all reading has been about.

Much ink has been spilled over what the literary critic Paul Ricoeur has called "the hermeneutics of suspicion" (Eve Kosofsky Sedgwick and Rita Felski have offered two eloquent responses to the idea), but suffice it to say that I try to approach the authors I examine not with suspicion but with a generous spirit and a genuine curiosity about the motivations and effects of their work. I attempt to do so with precision and specificity, and an appreciation of context and history, but my goal is not to tear these writers and texts down so much as to see what they are trying to accomplish as clearly as I can. Still, despite my focus on these texts as having played a formative role within the sustainable food movement, my purpose is not celebratory but analytic: I consider the assumptions of the movement as open questions rather than received wisdom.

Warren Belasco suggests that people who study food must necessarily be generalists, "people with a decent grounding in science *and* poetry, agriculture *and* philosophy, who are not afraid to question assumptions, values, and methods." The issues surrounding food, he argues, "require that we think about matters political, historical, economic, sociocultural, and scientific *all at once*" (*Food* 7).

As much as I agree with him, a single book cannot do everything, and there are plenty of things this book is *not* about. This is far from a comprehensive literary history of the sustainable food movement, for instance. (Among other things, I am not addressing the literature on urban farming, meat-eating, plant-based eating, genetically modified organisms, obesity, or food waste.) It is not an attempt to be encyclopedic, in other words, so much as representative. Even among the subjects I *am* discussing, there is much I am leaving out. I do not consider Wendell Berry's poetry or fiction, for example, or some of his more recent agrarian essays, given that many of them consist largely of restatements of his earlier thought. I also do not examine Slow Food USA, which Carlo Petrini does not address in great detail, or Alice Waters's *We Are What We Eat: A Slow Food Manifesto* (2021), whose topics I treat elsewhere in this book.

Nevertheless, I have tried to follow Belasco's call toward both holism and accessibility. I have tried to write in an engaging way for as many readers as possible while also trying to "get the scholarship right," as best as I have been able. (For the same reason, I have opted for parenthetical citations instead of endnotes.) But I'm aware that one of the perils of the essayistic critic is to feel caught between the deep immersion of the ethnographer and the superficial insights of the tourist. Nevertheless, I think the payoff in understanding is worth the occasional risk of imprecision, and I hope you do, too.

For readers wishing a sneak peek at what's to come—spoilers ahead—a short outline of the book follows.

Chapter 1 explores the nonfiction prose of Wendell Berry through the lens of the seasons my family and I spent as members of Spring Hill Community Farm, a community-supported agriculture farm, or CSA, in Prairie Farm, Wisconsin. It traces the history and evolution of the farm alongside the development of Berry's nonfiction writing since *The Unsettling of America* in 1977. I compare the spiritualist biodynamic farming philosophy of Rudolf Steiner, upon which many CSAs were founded, to the science-based organic agriculture of Sir Albert Howard, who was a major influence on Berry—and I show how both of these values (science and religion) play important roles in Berry's thought. I also identify some limitations to Berry's agrarianism— especially its reliance on what I call "agristalgia"—while lauding his focus on sustainable communities.

Chapter 2 examines the writings of Carlo Petrini, the founder of Slow Food, from the perspective of the five months my family and I spent living in the Piedmont region of Italy, where Slow Food was born. It tells the story of Slow Food's emergence out of its Italian context, analyzes the Slow Food manifesto and Petrini's early writings on food, explores the changes to Italian agricultural landscapes and traditions since World War II, and demonstrates the significance of Berry's intellectual influence on Petrini. A central portion of the chapter consists of narratives of three site visits my family and I made to Piedmont-based artisan food producers, who Petrini says should be "the center of attention." The remainder of the chapter builds on these site visits to interrupt the dichotomies of fast and slow, big and small, and art and science through an analysis of quality and inequality in artisan production, a discussion of food distribution in traditional outdoor markets versus in Eataly (the Italian food superstore), a consideration of regionalism and authenticity in Italian cuisine, a review of Slow Food's growth as an organization, and a discussion of Petrini's most recent work on food communities.

Chapter 3 reads the writings, cookbooks, and advocacy of Alice Waters from the standpoint of the month my family and I spent living in Lyon, the "gastronomic capital of France," and the area around Bandol in Provence, where Waters found much of the inspiration for her philosophy of food. Waters—whose Berkeley restaurant Chez Panisse helped to usher in America's current love affair with fresh, local, and seasonal food—was deeply affected by her time in France, and this chapter explores the relationship between art and commerce in Waters's life and writings through comparison with the experiences of contemporary female expats working in the Lyonnaise food industry. The chapter also examines the cultural history of the "sustainable kitchen," the role of women in commercial and domestic kitchens in France and the United States, the influence of regional French cuisine on American chefs (resulting in a collection of practices I call "elemental cooking"), Waters's advocacy of garden and kitchen education through her work with the Edible Schoolyard, and the role of cookbooks in helping to advance her progressive vision.

A brief conclusion updates some of the stories I narrate in light of the COVID-19 pandemic and discusses the relationship of writing to social change and ideas to practice. Tracing a chain of causation is difficult in complex systems, I conclude, but change in food systems would likely happen more slowly, or not at all, without the benefit of the written word. I also explore how our ideas and practices are bound up with one another, in the same way the messages of these writers are inseparable from the forms through which those messages are expressed.

ONE

The Farmer

———

Reading Wendell Berry in Wisconsin

Not all of us can live in the country like Wendell Berry.
—NOVELLA CARPENTER, *Farm City*

Much might be done by the promotion of growers' and
consumers' cooperatives.
—WENDELL BERRY, *The Unsettling of America*

THE MAKING OF A MARGINAL FARM

We have a running joke in our family, in which every time we drive to the
farm, I say, "Ugh, I don't want to go to the farm, it's so far away," and every
time we come back, I say, "I'm so glad we did that."

"The farm" is Spring Hill Community Farm, a community-supported

Wendell Berry on his farm in Henry County, Kentucky, December 2011. (Photo by
Guy Mendes; courtesy of Guy Mendes)

agriculture farm located just outside of Prairie Farm, Wisconsin, about an hour-and-a-half drive from our home in Saint Paul, Minnesota.

We've been members of the farm since 2003, when a friend who ran another CSA we belonged to in Prairie Farm decided to call it quits, and we needed a new source for our weekly fix of vegetables. We had been members of this other CSA for three years, and after learning how to cook according to whatever was in our vegetable delivery for that week, it was hard to imagine going back to supermarket produce. Our friend recommended Spring Hill, and the rest, as they say, is history.

One difference between these two CSAs is the member-based delivery system that Spring Hill has had in place since 1992, when the farm began. Our original CSA farmer would make weekly trips to various drop-off sites around the Twin Cities, from which members would pick up their vegetables—a tiresome chore for the farmer, and one of several reasons she eventually decided to stop farming. Spring Hill, in contrast, assigns this task to its members. If you want to get your bag of vegetables every week, you must travel to the farm at least once during the growing season to help harvest, pack, and deliver those vegetables to all the other members, too. It's a clever solution to a challenging labor problem, but it's really much more than that: the system not only reduces the travel burden for the farmers but also keeps members connected to the farm and one another in a direct way. As the software engineers would say, "It's not a bug; it's a feature."

For someone who doesn't like to drive, however, it still seems like a bug—at least until the landscape opens up north of Baldwin, Wisconsin, and we make that final turn down the road toward the farm.

One of my most vivid memories of encountering Wendell Berry's work was seeing the new hardcover edition of *What Are People For?* at the now-defunct Olsson's Books and Records in Georgetown, which to this day remains my ur-bookstore, and to which I attribute a large portion of whatever education I claim to have received at college. I figured that whoever had the daring to ask a question like "what are people for?" must surely have something to teach me. But when a professor I admired scoffed at the title while we were both browsing in the same store, I remember sheepishly returning the book to the shelf and moving on. I continued to admire Berry's book on subsequent visits, but its twenty-dollar price tag seemed hefty at the time, and I never did get around to buying a copy while I was in college. I can still recall its cherry-red cover, though, and the back flap of the copy I now own tells me that the Thomas Hart Benton mural printed on the front is entitled *Politics, Farming and Law in Missouri*. Maybe that's why my professor was so down on the book. Whatever Berry thought people were for, it must have had something to do with farming.

There are really two parts to the story of Mike Racette and Patty Wright: how they came to buy the farm, and how they came to run it as a CSA.

I learned about both parts one sunny afternoon in late April, after spending the morning helping out with the chores.

It finally felt like the beginning of spring that day, with the temperature barely reaching 60 degrees Fahrenheit for one of the first times in months. The trees were still bare, and snow remained in the fields on the way to the farm, but the creeks and irrigation ditches were running high with meltwater, and it felt at long last as if the growing season was about to commence.

Together with Mark Olson, a member of the Spring Hill work crew, Patty and Mike and I pushed zucchini and summer squash seeds into plugs of rich, black humus, made room for our plug-filled flats in the greenhouse, and covered the last two of the hoop houses with plastic sheeting, in anticipation of the tomato and pepper seedlings that were already sprouting in the greenhouse.

After a lunch of hearty burritos and a pot of strong coffee, the three of us sat down in the farmhouse kitchen for about an hour, while Mark resumed the fieldwork.

Of the two of them, Mike has the deeper roots in agriculture, having been raised in a rural community near Montevideo, a prairie town about 130 miles west of Minneapolis. Patty is from Minneapolis, but she too had always been interested in food, having worked at one of the Twin Cities' first food co-ops—coincidentally called Whole Foods, although it predated the existence of the chain by several years.

"I always liked being outside, doing physical labor of some kind," Patty says, "but I never, ever, ever dreamed that I would live in a rural area. It didn't even enter my consciousness. So, yeah, I was in love, I have to say."

"Past tense, I see," says Mike, with a laugh.

After they married in 1984, Patty and Mike decided that they were going to move to a rural community, find a farm, and make their living off the land. "We did not know what that meant," says Patty, "what that was going to look like, but we did have this vision that we were going to farm together in some way, shape, or form."

To try out that vision, they apprenticed for a summer at Pleasant Hill Farm, a blueberry farm in Fennville, Michigan, on the eastern shore of Lake Michigan, near Holland. "We were really inspired by these people that we lived with in Michigan, who had this berry farm, but they were also very much homesteaders," Patty says. "They were milking goats, had a garden, were preserving food, making syrup."

"And yet they also had this commercial enterprise," says Mike, "the first certified organic blueberry farm in the nation."

Upon their return to Minneapolis, they started saving money and looking at properties within an hour-and-a-half radius of the Twin Cities. "We wanted to be able to go in and out in a day without it being a big deal," Patty says.

"We had our things we wanted, which were all about romance," says Patty. "A little water would be nice, maple trees, some woods, some tillable land, a house that was livable, an old barn."

They looked at a lot of farms, but many of the homes had been abandoned, and none of the properties seemed quite right.

"The Midwest was just coming off the farm crisis of the '80's," Mike says, "so land prices were depressed, rural communities were depressed economically, and this area out here was marginal farmland, so it was even more discounted, if you will."

Finally, on a cold day in February 1989, after five years of saving and searching, they came upon an old dairy farm that had been on the market for two years. It was still being used for grazing cattle, and the owner still lived there.

"We were driving down the road, and we went and looked at each other, and said, 'This is it,'" says Patty. "Dead end road, secluded little valley, and the price was definitely right."

"We had no idea," Mike adds, shaking his head.

"Really well-informed shoppers," jokes Patty.

Wendell Berry is known for many things—his fiction, his poetry, and his nonfiction, not to mention his activism—but it is fair to say that his essays on agriculture remain the defining feature of his writing, even after a prolific career of more than fifty years. Many of these writings have been gathered in two anthologies: *The Art of the Commonplace: The Agrarian Essays of Wendell Berry*, edited by Norman Wirzba in 2002, and *Bringing It to the Table: On Farming and Food*, published in 2009, with an introduction by Michael Pollan. Others are scattered throughout Berry's numerous essay collections, and some remain uncollected.

It's both easy and hard to understand Berry's agricultural writing: easy because he's returned again and again to the same subjects throughout his essays, and hard because this thematic consistency masks subtle shifts in argument, emphasis, and style that have occurred over the course of a long career. Even Berry admits that his wife, Tanya, once told him that "my principal asset as a writer has been my knack for repeating myself" (*Art of Loading Brush* 5).

For this reason, it makes sense to start with the book that established Berry's reputation as a leading thinker on agrarianism in the United States: *The Unsettling of America: Culture and Agriculture*, published in 1977.

The Unsettling of America has had an outsized influence on generations of readers concerned with the fate of agriculture. When the Amish farmer David Kline, for example, first read *Unsettling* in 1980, it helped him understand why his father insisted on farming with horses rather than with tractors, and why his father also limited their farm to 120 acres instead of getting bigger. "Wendell took me by the shoulder, turned me around, and led me—with words so profound and powerful that they kept me awake long into the night—to where I could see the whole picture. Here, at last, were answers to the many questions and doubts I had about farming on our scale" (61). Even Berry himself recognized the continuing significance of the book, when he told an interviewer in 2004, "You wish that a book like *The Unsettling of America* would become obsolete, but it's more relevant now than it ever was" (Berger 167).

The Unsettling of America matters so much because it marks the first time that traditional agrarian goals were reformulated as a critique of postwar industrial agriculture. Those goals, in a nutshell, have everything to do with what Kline calls "farming on our scale," or the importance of the small family farm. This is Berry's main argument, which is decidedly Jeffersonian in origin: we need the small family farm because, as Berry quotes Jefferson as saying (in a 1785 letter to John Jay), "Cultivators of the earth are the most valuable citizens. They are the most vigorous, the most independent, the most virtuous, and they are tied to their country, and wedded to its liberty and interests by the most lasting bonds" (145). Almost everything else in Berry's critique follows from this argument: we don't need mechanization or synthetic chemicals; we don't need large farms with absentee owners; we don't need university scientists beholden to an industrial paradigm and corporate interests. In fact, all of these things impede the formation of the very bonds Jefferson held dear, which, according to Berry "were not merely those of economics and property, but those, at once more feeling and more practical, that come from the investment in a place and a community of work, devotion, knowledge, memory, and association" (143–44).

There are good questions to ask about this vision, such as: What makes farmers more virtuous than the rest of us? How realistic is it to expect U.S. citizens to return to rural life, considering that more than 80 percent of the U.S. population now lives in cities and suburbs and less than 2 percent is involved in agriculture? What about all those people who can't afford to buy land, don't want to farm, or think the benefits of industrialism outweigh the drawbacks? And how would changing how we grow food impact the eight billion people around the world who need to eat—four billion more than were alive in 1977?

Berry has refined his argument over time, and in subsequent essays he has tried to address many of the objections to his claims. But to jump right to response and rebuttal would be to do Berry a disservice and to miss the larger point he is trying to make. As he put it in the afterword to the third edition of *Unsettling*, published in 1995, "What we are working for, I think, is an authentic settlement and inhabitation of our country. We would like to see all human work lovingly adapted to the nature of the places where it is done and to the real needs of the people by whom and for whom it is done. We do not believe that any violence to places, to people, or to other creatures is 'inevitable.' We believe that the industrial ideology is wrong because it obscures and disrupts this necessary work of local adaptation or home making" (233).

After Patty and Mike moved to the farm in 1989, they lived and gardened there for three years before deciding to adopt a community-supported agriculture approach. In fact, they had not even heard of the CSA idea when they arrived.

"A friend had given us twenty-five chickens as a housewarming present," Patty says. "We had a couple goats, we had sheep, we were trying lots of different things. And we had maple syrup right from the beginning, we had bees right from the beginning, we heated with wood, we cooked with wood right off the bat." Like the most recent generation of back-to-the-landers in the 1970s, which Dona Brown and others have studied, Patty and Mike were engaged in a great personal experiment, one filled with more than a little idealism, and not a small amount of naiveté.

"We didn't know this community, we didn't know the town, we had no jobs, we spent all our money we had saved on this place, and then looked for jobs," says Mike. Eventually a local retired couple helped them adjust to rural living, and Mike started a full-time job teaching middle-school English in Amery, Wisconsin, about twenty miles to the northwest.

"There were two CSAs that started the year we moved out here," says Patty, "Philadelphia Community Farm and Common Harvest." Both are located in Osceola, Wisconsin, about an hour to the west, and both are still in operation.

"We heard about this idea on the radio," says Mike. "Verna Kragnes from Philadelphia Community Farm was interviewed on Minnesota Public Radio. We heard that story, and we looked at each other, and we said, 'We could do this.'

"Patty came out of a community organizing background, and I had education. And we had both lived in intentional communities in the past: Patty with the Catholic Worker of New York; I had been a volunteer teacher with a Catholic organization in South Texas; we both then came back and worked at Saint Stephen's Catholic Church in South Minneapolis, which is a very progressive, community-oriented place.

"When we heard about this idea of CSA, that there is this community of people who support a farm, and a farm in turn supports them—it just fit with the farm crisis, it fit with our social values, it fit with what we wanted to do, it fit with the economics. There's all these pieces that just jelled in that story at that moment."

So Patty and Mike went to visit Verna, who was very encouraging, and they attended a conference sponsored by the Minnesota Food Association and the Land Stewardship Project, two organizations that have been instrumental in the growth of CSAs in the Upper Midwest. The January 1992 conference featured Trauger Groh (1932–2016), a German who in 1985 helped to start one of the first two community-supported agriculture farms in the United States.

Inspired by Groh's visit, they attended a follow-up workshop for prospective farmers and then joined a study circle that explored the past, present, and future of food and agriculture in the Upper Midwest.

Eventually, they convened a meeting of twelve or so people in the living room of one of their friends to gauge the support for starting a CSA.

"Oh, yeah, let's do it!" was the unanimous response.

And so Spring Hill Community Farm began its first season in the spring of 1992.

At its most basic, farming seems to be a relatively simple endeavor. Want to grow some lettuce? Stick a seed in the ground, water it, and pretty soon you've got yourself a Caesar salad.

Yes, there's the problem of the weather, and yes, there's the labor of weeding and harvesting, but it's not rocket science. In fact, it's not science at all—or at least it doesn't need to be.

Until, that is, you start to think some more about it, and pretty soon you're knee deep into soil science, plant breeding, genomics, entomology, water chemistry, and so on. You've left the farm behind, at least in part, and moved into the laboratory and onto the computer and into the world of abstractions and standardized procedures. You've left *this* farm and started to think about agronomy in general.

And in some sense, this is the challenge for someone like Wendell Berry and for people like Patty and Mike. How much science, and what kind of science, is too much? When is the value of increasing yields—by manipulating the soil and water, by applying pesticides and fertilizers, and by tinkering with the plant itself, either through traditional breeding or genetic engineering—outweighed by other values, such as tradition, community, humility, or environmental quality? And should it matter whether the ends of increasing yields are to make a profit or feed a community?

These are not easy questions, and not surprisingly, they have produced a wide range of answers, from a full-bore embrace of all that science and technology has to offer to a complete repudiation of modern methods and approaches.

Agricultural science as we know it can be dated to the mid-nineteenth century, when Justus von Liebig discovered the role of nitrogen, phosphorus, and potassium (or N-P-K) in fertilizing plants and Gregor Mendel invented genetics by cross-breeding his peas. But even prior to this, farmers sought out alternatives to what could be termed the "mainstream agriculture" of their day. Joan Thirsk, for example, has documented three phases of alternative agriculture in English history, the first of which began soon after the Black Death in the mid-fourteenth century.

Today's alternative agriculture goes by many names, including sustainable agriculture, organic farming, biodynamic agriculture, ecoagriculture, permaculture, conservation agriculture, regenerative agriculture, and agroecology. And although Berry and the CSA movement come out of different traditions—Berry out of agrarianism and CSAs out of biodynamic agriculture—the difference between these approaches begins to muddy, quite literally, once you get back on the farm.

The first season on the farm, a killing frost arrived on June 21, the first day of summer, which was also Father's Day.

"It froze so hard," says Mike, "half of Wisconsin's corn crop was lost that day. I just remember a farm member writing, 'We're farming now.' Right away we started with at least what we still consider to be the core principle of CSAs, which is shared risk."

"People got a lot of cabbage that year," says Patty.

When Patty and Mike went to hear Trauger Groh speak in the Twin Cities, Groh had just coauthored *Farms of Tomorrow,* which was published in 1990, the same year as Berry's *What Are People For?* (A revised edition, *Farms of Tomorrow Revisited,* was released in 1998.) Written with Steven McFadden, the book was the first guide to community-supported agriculture in the United States, and it featured essays by Groh about the CSA concept, portraits of seven kinds of CSA farms, and a collection of documents to help beginning CSA farmers find their footing. Its subtitle—*Community Supported Farms, Farm Supported Communities*—reflected the reciprocal relationship CSAs were meant to create with their members.

For Groh, the "leading concept" of the farms of tomorrow is biodynamic farming. "In the biodynamic approach," writes Groh, "the farm is seen as an organism, and that underlying concept is part of all considerations and actions" (20).

Groh had been a farmer in Buschberghof, near Hamburg in northern Germany, throughout the 1970s and early 1980s, where he had been influenced by the work of Nicolaus Remer, a disciple of Rudolf Steiner. (Groh wrote the foreword for the English translation of Remer's *Lebensgesetze im Landbau* [*Laws of Life in Agriculture*], which was published in German in 1968 but not translated into English until 1995.) After moving in the early 1980s to New Hampshire to join Alice Miller, his new American wife, whom he met on a lecture tour of the United States, Groh worked with Lincoln Geiger and Anthony Graham to start the Temple-Wilton Community Farm (McFadden).

Biodynamic farming grew out of a series of lectures Rudolf Steiner (1861–1925) gave in what is now Kobierzyce, Poland, in 1924, in the year before his death. Steiner was an Austrian philosopher who had also founded the Waldorf schools, and in his lectures to the hundred or so attendees, he proposed a form of agriculture that focused on building the fertility of the soil through manure and compost, rather than through the addition of synthetic fertilizers and pesticides. As Frank Uekötter points out, "The biodynamic method was not actually all that new: it drew on classic humus management practices and a holistic view of the farm as an organism that had been part of the standard repertoire of agricultural science since the late eighteenth century." But Steiner's proposal was also an explicit rejection of the early twentieth-century work of Fritz Haber and Carl Bosch, two German chemists who developed the first practical process for converting atmospheric nitrogen into ammonia, which in turn enabled the production of nitrogen fertilizer on an industrial scale. And, as Uekötter notes, "farmers were sympathetic to this point of view, as investments for artificial fertilizers were among the largest expenditures of farmers in the 1920s" in Germany (50). Although Steiner's lectures were not widely published until 1958, a small number of copies were shared privately among his followers, and these disciples—especially Ehrenfried Pfeiffer, who published *Bio-Dynamic Farming and Gardening* in 1938—developed Steiner's ideas into a more comprehensive approach (Paull).

If Steiner's ideas sound a lot like those used by today's organic growers, they should, because biodynamic farming uses many of the same techniques. For example, among the principles that Groh outlined in *Farms of Tomorrow* are to "aim for a great diversity of plants on the farm in combination with, and as part of, the crop rotation" (31); "recognize that the circulation of carbon, or organic substance, throughout the soil, the plants, and the air is the basis of permanent fertility" (32); restore "the destroyed natural environment," including hedgerows and wetlands (35); and "implement biological weed and pest control" (36).

But biodynamic farming also includes principles that have been variously described by critics as "mystical," "magical," and "pseudoscientific," and *Farms of Tomorrow* includes these, too. For example, Groh says that farmers should exclude "most all mineral or synthetic substances" because "life processes can only be generated out of substances already filled with life" (29); "create harmonious balanced conditions in soil, plants, animals, and landscape as the necessary basis of productivity," including a "polarity of warmth and light substances" (35); and "establish a rhythmical order in animal husbandry and field care that is connected to the rhythms of the earth and its cosmic environment of the sun, the moon, and the other planets" (37).

One needn't embrace all of Groh's biodynamic principles to run a CSA, and in fact most CSAs do not—Spring Hill certainly doesn't. Moreover, most of *Farms of Tomorrow* does not concern biodynamic farming at all but rather the social and economic conditions that can both enable and prevent the creation of healthy food systems.

Still, it's fair to say that at the root of both biodynamic farming and the idea of the CSA is what, for lack of a better term, might be called a vaguely spiritual impulse. Call it what you will, the point is not to leave science and reason behind but to acknowledge that community-supported agriculture is about more than its component parts, whether those parts be soil nutrients or individual people. As Groh tried to articulate in his own way in *Farms of Tomorrow,* the "basic spiritual motivation" of these farms is "that every year life on earth is created anew, so that human beings can be born safely and have healthy bodies that will allow them to live out their individual and collective spiritual destinies" (19).

Regardless of what forms of alternative agriculture they practice, CSAs differ from traditional farms for structural as well as philosophical reasons. There is the obvious benefit of a regular delivery of vegetables, which usually arrives weekly in either a bag (Spring Hill uses a rotating variety of canvas bags) or a box (our previous CSA used brown waxed produce boxes). Another is the idea of "shared risk," as most CSAs ask their members to pay some or all of the cost of the season up front, before their vegetables are only a gleam in the eye of their farmer. If the season is a success, everyone wins and eats well. If it's not—if, say, a killing frost arrives and you lose the tomatoes, eggplant, peppers, summer squash, and basil, leaving you with mainly cabbage, onions, potatoes, carrots, and winter squash—well, you suck it up and make a lot of coleslaw, potato salad, and squash casserole.

A third key piece of a CSA is member involvement, and this is what carried Patty and Mike through that devastating first season.

"You know, it was such a new thing," says Patty. "People were so enthusiastic and committed. I think we were excited about it—it was that community piece."

When the first core group of members was formulating the plan for the farm, says Mike, "the question was: how do members materially participate? And the resolution to that was a member-based delivery system. That started that year: 'We're all going to do this on behalf of each other.' And so, to this day, we still have this system. It's an easy way to put some of those values that we like to think we have into practice."

"I think we were all just very conscious that year that we were somehow . . . pioneers or something. Wendell Berry's idea that 'eating is an agricultural act' wasn't as pervasive then as it is now," says Patty.

The essay in which Berry stated that "eating is an agricultural act" is entitled "The Pleasures of Eating," and it first appeared in book form in *What Are People For?*

Had I bought that book back when it first appeared in 1990, it probably would have saved me a lot of trouble, because "The Pleasures of Eating" was written for the vast majority of Americans who are not actively engaged in agriculture.

"Many times," writes Berry, "after I have finished a lecture on the decline of American farming and rural life, someone in the audience has asked 'What can city people do?'" (145).

The essay is his attempt to provide a more complete explanation than what had become his standard answer: "eat responsibly."

Instead of reading that essay, however, I read *The Unsettling of America*.

For all of the praise that has been heaped upon it, *The Unsettling of America* can be a difficult book to get through, especially now that almost fifty years have passed since its first publication. One thing that makes it challenging is Berry's technique of quoting from and arguing with the authors of now-dated newspaper and magazine articles, as well as with poets and other public figures, often at extended length. Another is the fact that most of the book's 223 pages contain a biting critique of the premises of industrial agriculture, with only five pages outlining what Berry thinks, "in a public or governmental sense, ought to be done" (218). Some readers will also find Berry's assumption of a white, Christian audience to be an obstacle, while others will be put off by the extension of Berry's criticism beyond the "agribusinessmen" and "university experts" he repeatedly assails to ordinary people—particularly city dwellers—trying their best to live within a modern world not of their own making.

Nevertheless, *The Unsettling of America* is unquestionably Berry's most important book and thus deserves our close attention. Written between 1974 and 1977, when Berry was in his early forties, the essays that eventually became *Unsettling* were originally published in such places as *The Nation* and *Co-evolution Quarterly*. One of the things that sets *Unsettling* apart from almost all of Berry's other books, however, is that it functions as an extended argument rather than a collection of essays that are only occasionally related. (The only other books of Berry that offer such a unified approach are *Life Is a Miracle, The Hidden Wound,* and *The Need to Be Whole*.) For this reason, the agricultural ethicist Paul Thompson calls *The Unsettling of America* "the most systematic exposition" of Berry's views ("Land and Water" 471), and Norman Wirzba describes it as "the definitive contemporary statement of agrarian concepts and priorities" (*Essential* 267).

The book's nine chapters, which range from ten to fifty-three pages long, lay out a damning indictment of industrial agriculture that also manages to sweep up much of modern culture along the way. In the book's opening chapter, Berry distinguishes between what he calls two "opposite kinds of mind": the exploiter and nurturer. "I conceive a strip-miner to be a model exploiter," Berry says, "and as a model nurturer I take the old-fashioned idea or ideal of a farmer" (7). In this single sentence, Berry identifies a dichotomy that consistently appears in his subsequent work—that between the industrial and the agrarian—and throws his hat surely in with the agrarian or nurturer. Warning of the "complete deliverance of American agriculture into the hands of corporations," Berry predicts that "husbandry will become an extractive industry; because maintenance will entirely give way to production, the fertility of the soil will become a limited, unrenewable resource like coal or oil" (10).

While this basic dichotomy gives his critique its power, it's clear that Berry does not see the world in black and white. He is too subtle a thinker for this, too aware of the world's complexity, and too intent on linking the social to the personal. "The terms exploitation and nurture," he is careful to note, "describe a division not only between persons but also within persons" (7).

Although in many ways Berry could not be more different from Rachel Carson, in this case he employs the same rhetorical strategy she did in *Silent Spring* (1962), clearly defining an enemy so as to rally the troops against it. Yet for Berry, the enemy is also within us, which both complicates his diagnosis of the problem as well as limits his proposed solutions.

Writing in the context of 1970s environmentalism, particularly the 1973 Arab oil embargo and the beginnings of the farm crisis that reached its peak in the 1980s, Berry argues that the problem is as much individual as it is political. "The basic cause of the energy crisis is not scarcity," he says; "it is moral ignorance and weakness of character" (13). As a result, he argues, "we will not find . . . answers in Washington, D.C., or in the laboratories of oil companies. In order to find them, we will have to look closer to ourselves" (13). He thus celebrates "the idea that as many as possible should share in the ownership of the land and thus be bound to it by economic interest, by the investment of love and work, by family loyalty, by memory and tradition" (13). Setting himself up for accusations of nostalgia that have dogged him throughout his career, Berry then opines, "The old idea is still full of promise. It is potent with healing and with health. . . . It proposes the independent, free-standing citizenry that Jefferson thought to be the surest safeguard of democratic liberty" (14).

In the three chapters that follow, Berry further defines the ecological crisis of the time not only as a "crisis of character" but also as a "crisis of agriculture," the latter of which he also describes as a "crisis of culture." The 1970s language of "crisis" is clear here, but *The Unsettling of America* is notably retrograde in claiming that the appropriate answer at that moment in American history was not more modernity but rather a return to the traditional, agricultural values of European settlers. Though ostensibly a critique of the policies of former secretary of agriculture Earl Butz, Berry's aim is broader than this. Condemning "our almost religious dependence on experts" (34), Berry urges his readers to find the roots of the problem in the idea of modernity itself.

After their first season, Patty says, "it got harder, and then it got easier. When you jump in and you don't know anything, it's all okay. And then as you know more, your expectations of yourselves change."

As their expectations changed, so did the farm. Over the first five years, it grew from eighteen to forty shares. Mike was still working part-time, but after their fifth season Patty and Mike felt confident enough to take the next big step: they decided to double the number of shares. Mike quit his job, and they hired an intern. It was a risk, to be sure, but they had a Plan B. "We felt young enough that if it didn't work, there were jobs to be had."

Decades after that first season, many of the original eighteen families are still members.

"There are a few farms that consistently have high return rates, and we're one of them," says Mike. "And there's a lot better growers out there than us; there are some people who do some amazing things. And there are lots of people far more charismatic than us. But there's something magical that happens when you get a group of people together engaged in the production of food on this place. The physical act of coming here, being on this place, working together, having food together, doing something for all of us, that somehow works. There's something about the place, and frankly I think it can be any place."

According to Berry, one of modernity's principal problems is its retreat from physical labor. Offering a remarkably prescient diagnosis of leisure-based environmentalism's failure to address the idea of work—which the environmental historian Richard White has memorably addressed in "Are You an Environmentalist or Do You Work for a Living?"—Berry observes that conservation "is variously either vacation-oriented or crisis-oriented" (27). As a result, he says, the typical conservationist "has not . . . addressed himself to the problem of use" (28). And this matters because "kindly use depends upon intimate knowledge, the most sensitive responsiveness and responsibility" (31).

A related problem with modernity is that it has led to "the disintegration of the culture and the communities of farming" (41). These two problems are connected, and matter greatly, because if both the value of work and the culture of farming are degraded, little remains on which to build a healthy society, whose basis Berry sees as both literally and figuratively grounded in the soil. Small farms in particular are Berry's priority, not only because they embody Jefferson's vision of a society of independent thinkers but also because large farms undermine that very same vision. "As a social or economic goal," says Berry, "bigness is totalitarian; it establishes an inevitable tendency toward the one that will be the biggest of all. . . . The aim of bigness implies not one aim that is not socially and culturally destructive" (41).

The difficulty of criticizing modernity while also lauding a historical ideal becomes particularly acute in the pivotal fifth chapter of *Unsettling*, which separates the first four overview chapters from the following four chapters, two of which provide a more theoretical framework and two that address issues specific to agricultural research and practice. Chapter 5, "Living in the Future: The 'Modern' Agricultural Ideal," offers an extended critique of the claims made in various articles that Berry has encountered, from *National Geographic*, the *American Farmer*, and the *Louisville Courier-Journal*. Having already risked alienating his readers by arguing in the previous chapter that "from a cultural point of view, the movement from the farm to the city involves a radical simplification of mind and of character" (44), Berry proceeds to condemn the homes of many urban and suburban residents, with seemingly little sympathy for the benefits of modern technology, nor the actual people who might profit from these benefits. "With its array of gadgets and machines, all powered by energies that are destructive of land or air or water, and connected to work, market, school, recreation, etc., by gasoline engines, the modern home is a veritable factory of waste and destruction," he says. "It is the mainstay of the economy of money. But within the economies of energy and nature, it is a catastrophe. It takes the world's goods and converts them into garbage, sewage, and noxious fumes—for none of which we have found a use" (52).

The chapter also features Berry's most rhetorically powerful paean to the past, in which he employs *anaphora*, or the repetition of an initial word at the beginning of successive sentences, to decidedly nostalgic effect: "Once, some farmers, particularly in Europe, lived in their barns—and so were both at home and at work. Once, shopkeepers lived in, above, or behind their shops. Once, many people lived by 'cottage industries'—home production. Once, households were producers and processors of food, centers of their own maintenance, adornment, and repair, places of instruction and amusement" (53). Berry also comes across at his most moralistic in this chapter, sounding more like a Times Square preacher than an essayist seeking agricultural reform. "We must cleanse ourselves of slovenliness, laziness, and waste," he asserts. "We must learn to discipline ourselves, to restrain ourselves, to need less, to care more for the needs of others" (65–66).

Unfortunately, the sometimes severe nature of Berry's rant in this chapter threatens to overpower his most important point: that the "cult of the future" in industrial agriculture threatens to remove both the farmer and nonfarmer from contact with not just "soil" in the abstract but *particular* soils, which ultimately sustain all our lives. And it is this point that makes the following two chapters so penetrating.

Chapters 6 and 7, "The Use of Energy" and "The Body and the Earth," address a range of topics and include some of Berry's most controversial comments about birth control and fertility. He argues, for example, that separating sexuality from fertility is "a profound cultural failure" and that birth control technologies and fertility treatments exemplify our unwillingness to consider "the meaning of restraint" (132). Drawing an analogy between "an infertile woman and an infertile field," he claims that "both receive a dose of chemicals, at the calculated risk of undesirable consequences, and are thus equally reduced to the status of productive machines" (133). These are, to say the least, problematic assertions, and they unquestionably reflect the gendered nature of Berry's agrarianism, as both Deborah Fink and Verlyn Klinkenborg have observed.

But it is Berry's meditations on the place of soil in chapter 6 that interest me the most, because they demonstrate that there is more than one way to farm sustainably, as long as you start with the soil.

Bill McKibben jokes that Berry "rarely writes more than a few paragraphs without mentioning the word 'topsoil,'" and while this is certainly an exaggeration, McKibben's comment gets at the centrality of soil to Berry's worldview ("Prophet in Kentucky" 264).

To understand why this might be, we need to return to the early organic pioneers, like Rudolf Steiner, for whom the soil meant everything.

In his 1924 agriculture course, Steiner described the "the soil of the Earth" as "the foundation of all Agriculture" (Lecture 2, 10 June), and like Berry he observed that "the climate, the conditions of the soil, provide the very first basis for the individuality of a farm. A farming estate in Silesia is not like one in Thuringia, or in South Germany. They are real individualities" (Address, 11 June).

Steiner urged his listeners to "grasp the real connections between what the soil yields and what the soil itself is, with all that surrounds it" (Address, 11 June). In particular, he emphasized what he called the *"astral principle"* in the soil, stressing the "constant and living mutual interplay" between the cosmic forces of the sun, moon, and distant planets and the "inner life of the earthly soil" (Lecture 2). Most famously, he called for burying a cow horn stuffed with manure in the earth, so that "all the radiations that tend to ethe-realise and astralise are poured into the inner hollow of the horn" (Lecture 4, 12 June). But for all of Steiner's astrological speculations ("in due time there will be a science of these things," he predicted), at the core of his recommendations was a recognition that the soil is not mere inert matter but a living, breathing entity. Steiner stressed this point by comparing the Earth's surface to the human diaphragm.

His take-home message? "I am telling you all this to awaken in you an idea of the really intimate kinship between that which is contained within the contours of the plant and that which constitutes the soil around it. It is simply untrue that the life ceases with the contours—with the outer periphery of the plant. The actual life is continued, especially from the roots of the plant, into the surrounding soil. For many plants there is absolutely no hard and fast line between the life within the plant and the life of the surrounding soil in which it is living" (Lecture 4, 12 June).

More than anything, in other words, the founders of the organic movement were concerned that we—in the immortal words of a popular bumper sticker—"don't treat soil like dirt." If *dirt* is the inanimate stuff that bulldozers push around, *soil* is nothing if not alive.

Yet, as Steiner observed, "by prolonged tillage we can gradually impoverish the soil. We are, of course, constantly impoverishing it, and that is why we have to manure it" (Lecture 5, 13 June). In what could be a more refined, biodynamic version of that bumper sticker, Steiner said: "To manure the earth is to make it alive."

Seeing healthy soil as living rather than dead had more than practical significance for the organic pioneers; it also marked their philosophical and religious differences from the scientific understanding of agriculture that was developing at the time. As Philip Conford has observed, "The organicists ... suffered from no dualism of 'spirit' and 'matter.' For them, a sense of the sacred was a prerequisite of genuine materialism" (*Origins* 129). Pushing back against the reductionism that often accompanies scientific materialism, Steiner and other organic proponents argued instead for an understanding of agriculture as an emergent phenomenon that could not be reduced to its constituent parts. As Conford sees it, "A religious philosophy of life was integral to the organic outlook as it developed from the 1920s onwards, in both the biodynamic and mainstream movements" (*Origins* 96). "It would be completely wrong, however, to conclude that they were opposed to scientific development *per se.* . . . From the organic perspective, it was the proponents of industrialized farming who were not proper scientists, since they failed to see the ecological connections of natural phenomena" (*Origins* 97).

Near the end of our kitchen-table conversation in April, I ask Patty and Mike what had changed on the farm since they first saw it on that romance-filled day in 1989.

"We've changed the face of the farm, and I think we've made it a better place," says Mike.

Patty agrees. "We've learned to work with the land we have. If we knew then what we know now, this would not be the place you would buy to grow vegetables. The slope is really not ideal. You'd want a nice, flat, five-acre field. You'd have plots that are the same. We have these little plots that are funny-shaped: this stretch is a three-hundred-foot row; this stretch is a two-hundred-foot row."

"This ground is better suited for melons; we can't grow melons over there," continues Mike, gesturing toward the fields. "The land itself has informed us about how we should grow vegetables."

"We've really learned how to work with this piece of land," says Patty. "Everything's in narrow strips; everything's mulched. As we've grown the fields, we've learned about the soil type, about the contour, about how to play with it."

"We still romanticize farming," says Mike, laughing.

But then Patty grows more animated.

"Yeah, you can romanticize farming," she protests, "but it *is* romantic. You still . . . you walk outside in the morning; you kind of really didn't want to get out of bed; but you walk outside, and the sun hits you and it's like, 'Oh, it's gonna be a good day.' There is still this optimism."

Berry has written admiringly about many of the early advocates of alternative agriculture, including the American horticulturist Liberty Hyde Bailey (1858–1954), the author and conservationist Louis Bromfield (1896–1956), and the practitioners of "permanent agriculture" profiled in F. H. King's *Farmers of Forty Centuries* (1911) and J. Russell Smith's *Tree Crops* (1929). But it is fair to say that no one has had more influence on his thoughts than the English botanist Sir Albert Howard (1873–1947).

It is Howard that Berry was channeling when he wrote "The Use of

Energy," chapter 6 of *The Unsettling of America*. Yet in doing so Berry was also revealing a tension between science and religion that persists to this day in the literature of sustainable agriculture.

"In speaking of the use of energy," Berry writes, "we are speaking of an issue of religion, whether we like it or not" (81). Referencing "the natural cycle of 'birth, growth, maturity, death, and decay' that Sir Albert Howard identified as the 'Wheel of Life,'" Berry identifies the soil as "the great connector of lives, the source and destination of all. It is the healer and restorer and resurrector, by which disease passes into health, age into youth, death into life" (82, 86). As a result, he says, "it is impossible to contemplate the life of the soil for very long without seeing it as analogous to the life of the spirit. No less than the faithful of religion is the good farmer mindful of the persistence of life through death, the passage of energy through changing forms" (86). "Because the soil is alive, various, intricate, and because its processes yield more readily to imitation than analysis, more readily to care than to coercion, agriculture can never be an exact science," Berry declares. But it is, he says, "a practical religion, a practice of religion, a rite. By farming we enact our fundamental connection with energy and matter, light and darkness. In the cycles of farming, which carry the elemental energy again and again through the seasons and the bodies of living things, we recognize the only infinitude within reach of the imagination" (87).

The similarity to biodynamics should be clear, because—as we have seen—Rudolf Steiner made many of the same claims about the irreducibility of the soil back in 1924.

But when Berry first introduced readers to Sir Albert Howard in 1971, in an influential profile of Howard that appeared in *The Last Whole Earth Catalog*, he took pains to distinguish Howard's work from what Berry called "the 'lunatic fringe' of a discipline that demands respect and attention not because it is far out or esoteric or mystical, but because it makes good sense." In what appears to be a direct rebuttal of Steiner and his biodynamic followers, Berry argued that "the principles of organic agriculture are not derived from mystical insight or revelation, but are based upon observation. They have been established in our part of the world in our time by men who were excellent observers, and who were moreover accomplished and respected scientists" (Berry, "An Agricultural Testament" 46).

Howard was certainly a scientist, and much of his appeal to Berry and other organic farmers was tied directly to the respectability that Howard's scientific credentials conferred on the alternative practices he promoted. A Cambridge-educated botanist and horticulturist, Howard traveled to India in 1905 to take a position as the imperial economic botanist at the Agricultural Research Institute in Pusa, near Nepal, where he worked for almost twenty years. In 1924, he moved to Indore, in central India, where he served as the director of the Institute of Plant Industry, until his retirement and return to Britain in 1931, following the death of his wife.

At first, Howard focused on typical "development" goals, such as breeding new varieties of wheat and tobacco, improving irrigation practices, and refining the way fruit trees were cultivated. To give just one example, Howard and his wife, Gabrielle (who was also a scientist), successfully bred several new "Pusa" strains of wheat, which were not only better for milling and baking, but which also substantially increased yields. By 1926, these strains were planted on almost 7.5 million acres in India, resulting in an increased profit of some £5.5 million a year for Indian growers (Louise E. Howard).

But it was Howard's gradual awakening to a more holistic understanding of agriculture that appealed to Berry the most. This understanding is best exemplified in Howard's most prominent achievement, the "Indore Process" of composting. As he points out in *The Waste Products of Agriculture* (1931), Howard's experiments with higher-yielding varieties eventually led him to realize that "the full possibilities in plant breeding could only be achieved when the soil in which the improved types are grown is provided with an adequate supply of organic matter in the right condition." Like Steiner, whose recommendations built on generations of subsistence agriculture in Europe, Howard developed this process based in part on his reading of King's *Farmers of Forty Centuries,* which described traditional agricultural practices in China, Korea, and Japan. In contrast to the West, writes Howard, where "the place of organic matter in the soil economy was forgotten" following Liebig's discoveries, in East Asia "the artificial manure phase had practically no influence on indigenous practice and passed unheeded" (*Waste Products* 22–23). Howard saw a role for traditional East Asian composting practices in India, not only because the peasant farmers there tended to burn their plant waste and dry their animal manure to use as fuel, but also because they could not afford to purchase artificial fertilizer. Composting according to the Indore method was a low-cost solution to the problem of soil fertility that also had the benefit of mimicking natural processes.

In his 1971 profile of Howard, Berry quoted approvingly from *An Agricul-*

tural Testament (1940), Howard's most popular publication, in which Howard developed this holistic understanding even further, resulting in a biting criticism of agricultural researchers who followed the industrial model. According to Berry, "the task Howard set himself was first to understand those processes and interrelationships by which the natural world sustains and renews itself, and then to work out methods by which people could use the land in cooperation with nature" (46). Howard's next step—which became Berry's next step, too—was to reject any scientist who did not share his same orientation. In Howard's words, which Berry quotes in his profile, "Instead of breaking up the subject into fragments and studying agriculture in piecemeal fashion by the analytical methods of science, appropriate only to the discovery of new facts, we must adopt a synthetic approach and look at the wheel of life as one great subject and not as if it were a patchwork of unrelated things." According to Berry, Howard realized that "the specialized analytical approach of 'scientific' agriculture was creating more problems than it solved" (46).

What is implied but not stated in Berry's profile is Howard's parallel rejection of the "unscientific" proposals of Rudolf Steiner. Howard writes in the preface to *An Agricultural Testament* that "some attention has also been paid to the Bio-Dynamic methods of agriculture in Holland and in Great Britain, but I remain unconvinced that the disciples of Rudolph [sic] Steiner can offer any real explanation of natural laws or have yet provided any practical examples which demonstrate the value of their theories" (ix). Five years later, in *The Soil and Health: A Study of Organic Agriculture* (1945), Howard was even more dismissive, describing practices "claiming to be based on esoteric knowledge of an advanced kind" as "a mixture of muck and magic" (212). As Matthew Reed observes in *Rebels for the Soil: The Rise of the Global Organic Food and Farming Movement*, "At a time when the works of Steiner were new and many experimented with a variety of techniques, Howard started to draw rigid lines. At this time most of those in the critical community were experimenting with ideas drawn from those around Steiner as well as their own ideas. Albert Howard, with his insistence on scientific method, offered another path, separate to that of biodynamic farming. Where Steiner had posited hermetic terminology and neo-magical formulations, Howard offered observation and field science more in tune with the dominant ideas of the time" (43–44).

Yet what is most striking to me are not the differences but the similarities between these two men—and between them and Berry, too. Michael Pollan identified one aspect of Howard's spiritual side in *The Omnivore's Dilemma*, when he observed: "Howard's concept of organic agriculture is premodern, arguably even antiscientific: He's telling us we don't need to understand how humus works or what compost does in order to make good use of it. Our ignorance of the teeming wilderness that is the soil (even the act of regarding it *as* a wilderness) is no impediment to nurturing it. To the contrary, a healthy sense of all we don't know—even a sense of mystery—keeps us from reaching for oversimplifications and technological silver bullets" (150). "In Howard's agronomy," Pollan continues, "science is mostly a tool for describing what works and explaining why it does" (151). The philosophy of imitating healthy natural systems—which Janine Benyus has termed "biomimicry"—comes first, in other words, and the science follows from that, rather than imperial science leading the way.

I thought about mystery and all it implies on the drive back from the farm in April, because it can be hard to know where to draw the line when it comes to knowledge. (Plus, the miles pass more quickly when you have something to think about.)

While we were chatting in Patty and Mike's kitchen, I was particularly struck by Patty's observation that maybe there was something to be said for the romanticism about farming that is so frequently dismissed by more hard-headed agricultural types, for whom farming is a demanding and difficult business, with little room for beauty, much less mystery.

And I struggled to articulate this at the time.

"So farming is not just a job, it's not just a lifestyle, . . ." I began to respond.

"No, . . ." said Patty, shaking her head sympathetically.

"This is what I've struggled with in the years of coming here," I continued. "I hesitate to describe it as a sort of 'spiritual' experience, but there's more to this than just feeding your body, more to it than just working the land. There's something else here, some unnamable thing maybe, that makes this worthwhile, or makes this fulfilling. I haven't yet put my finger on it. It's hard to describe. But it sounds like you still feel that, you still experience that, whatever that is."

"Absolutely," said Patty, laughing. "What is 'it'?" she asked me. "What do you think the 'it' is?"

"I don't know," I replied. "The word I've used occasionally is 'holistic.' It's an old word, but it still seems to matter. And until you come here, you can't fully get it. Because you've got the breeze, you've got the quality of the air, the sunlight's coming in a particular way. . . . So I can say 'farm,' but it's not until you come to *this* farm that you say, 'Oh, now I understand.' Is it holistic? I don't know if that's the word, or what the word is. Maybe there is no word."

"I wonder if the 'it' . . . ," began Patty, hesitating briefly, before eventually finding her words.

"We are inextricably a part of this web that is food, that is soil," she continued, "and I think being out here, growing food, walking out the door first thing in the morning is that reminder that we are just one little, insignificant piece of this web, this system. There's something about being reminded of this, however it is that you remind yourself, that is part of the 'it.'"

The final two chapters of *The Unsettling of America* are, respectively, the least and most satisfying of the book.

Chapter 8, "Jefferson, Morrill, and the Upper Crust," combines an extended analysis of a 1976 *Scientific American* article entitled "The Agriculture of the U.S." with a broad-brush indictment of almost all professors of agriculture at land-grant universities. It is an example of Berry's worst tendencies to advance his argument through sweeping generalizations and simplistic dichotomies—a strategy that may rally the troops but usually occasions little sympathy from those best positioned to create change. (Ironically, Berry argues against generalization at the same time as he generalizes!) One may disagree with certain aspects of agricultural research and teaching at land-grant universities without labeling all their proponents as "careerists in pursuit of power, money, and prestige" (147); self-interested, lazy, and lacking conviction (148); and having "no apparent moral allegiances or bearings or limits" (156). This is not the kind of balanced appraisal that inspires confidence in one's argument. Indeed, the same kind of extremist attacks led many agricultural researchers to dismiss Sir Albert Howard's criticism of their work in *An Agricultural Testament*, regardless of the accuracy of his appraisal (Hershey).

Chapter 9, however, "Margins," redeems Berry's diatribe through its specificity, which gives his argument renewed strength and credibility. After an extended example of "sound pre-industrial agriculture" from the Peruvian Andes, Berry identifies what he sees as the characteristics of a healthy farm in the United States. It will, he says, give the impression of abounding life; it will look well maintained; it will have woodlands, orchards, and shade trees; it will have a diversity of species; it will have the right proportion of plants, animals, and people; and it will be, so far as possible, independent and self-sustaining (181–84).

It is hard not to think of Patty and Mike's farm, which embodies all of these characteristics and more.

Perhaps most reassuringly, Berry reminds his readers that "one need not be a specialist to understand the difference between good and bad farming. There is nothing mysterious or obstruse about it. It only requires enough acquaintance with land and people to have some sense of what a prospering farm and what a prospering community ought to look like and the same acquaintance with the signs of greed, hopelessness, neglect, and abandonment" (181).

If there were ever four words that did not apply to Spring Hill Community Farm, they are "greed, hopelessness, neglect, and abandonment."

Berry follows these principles with example after example of healthy farms—from farms in his own Kentucky neighborhood to farms in Iowa and Nebraska, from farms that use draft horses to Amish farms that Berry believes take "exquisite care of the land" in a way "much more sophisticated than orthodox agriculture" (213).

Readers with little interest in the nitty-gritty of agriculture might find these examples tedious, but I find them fascinating, precisely because they are so site-specific. When Berry said, in chapter 3, that "kindly use depends upon intimate knowledge, the most sensitive responsiveness and responsibility," this is what he meant.

The Unsettling of America ends with five pages explaining what Berry thinks, "in a public or governmental sense, ought to be done," after 218 pages of critique (218). As James Montmarquet puts it, "After a very rich plate of social criticism, one must be content with some rather thin gruel, as far as specific recommendations are concerned" (239). Another way to put it is that Berry offers a profoundly declensionist narrative in *Unsettling*, but with few real prescriptions for change. Yet one could also see the sketchiness of these last few pages as a necessary function of Berry's moment, in which the sustainable food movement was still in the process of being born—due in no small part to Berry's own writing.

Moreover, the tentativeness of Berry's recommendations is in keeping with his theme that if change is to come, "it will have to come from the margins"—marginal people and marginal farms—and not from the agricultural orthodoxy. His point throughout this final chapter is an extended religious metaphor: "It was the desert, not the temple, that gave us the prophets," he writes; "the colonies, not the motherland, that gave us Adams and Jefferson" (174).

Of the twelve recommendations Berry offers, one in particular stands out as being more like a prophecy: "there should be a program to promote local self-sufficiency in food." (Though note the passive construction here: who should institute such a program is not clear.) "The cheapest, freshest food is that which is produced closest to home and is not delayed for processing. This should work toward the most direct dealing between farmers and merchants and farmers and consumers. Much might be done by the promotion of growers' and consumers' cooperatives" (220–21).

WHAT THE LAND WILL ALLOW

It's mid-June now, and I'm back on the farm to help transplant some seedlings and walk the land with Patty and Mike. Though I've been out here many times on harvest days—when my wife and daughter and I have been joined by three or four other families eager to haul bags of vegetables back to the Twin Cities—I've never had the chance to talk at length with Mike and Patty about their land, its history, and why they farm the way they do. We've had snippets of conversation in the fields, as we've gathered potatoes or laid onions out to dry, but I've never had an official guided tour, and I'm eager to chat with them at length about their farming practices, unburdened by the demands of actual fieldwork.

But first, I need to fix my shoelace.

I'm wearing an old pair of Lowa hiking shoes, because transplanting is messy work, but they must have been older than I thought, because as soon as I go to tighten the laces, the lace on my right shoe breaks, and I am left holding half a shoelace in my hand before the day has even begun.

After some creative adjustments of the remaining half lace, I join Patty, Mike, and Mark Olson down by the greenhouse on the eastern end of the farm. Everyone is in jeans, T-shirts, and hats, including me—ratty ball caps for the guys and an old straw hat for Patty. Haute couture this is not.

Those seeds we started back in April, along with many others, are now young plants ready for the fields, and it is hard not to think of them as fledglings ready to leave the nest. The process is gradual, with the seedlings moving first from the greenhouse to the hayrack in front of Patty and Mike's barn, where they will "harden off" for a few hours each day, slowly building up their tolerance for direct sunlight, wind and rain, and cooler temperatures. Then it's onto the transplanter, which makes relatively quick work of getting so many seedlings into the ground in time for the growing season.

Today we're doing both of these things: transplanting hundreds of plugs from the hayrack into the soil, and moving additional flats of plants from the greenhouse to take their place on the hayrack. Zucchini and summer squash, watermelon, cauliflower, and green and red cabbage are all taking their first tentative steps into the world today.

We begin by filling up the transplanter with water and loading the ATV with flats of plants.

The transplanter looks like some sort of makeshift launch pad from *Leave It to Beaver*, with two corrugated steel platforms set at an angle on either side of a waterwheel, behind which trail two seats that appear to have been ripped from a junkyard jalopy. Rather than turning from the force of the water, the wheel pokes holes in the ground where the plants will go, while the transplanter delivers a splash of water from the attached tank into each hole. And rather than launching homemade rockets skyward, the angled platforms allow the flats to descend earthward, toward the unlucky operators sitting in those jalopy seats, who take a few plugs at a time from the flats and take turns depositing them into what are now some very muddy holes.

The whole contraption is attached to the tractor, which moves down each row at just a few miles per hour, making it a contest to see who is more unhappy: the driver whose snail's-pace speed makes this seem like the worst amusement park ride ever, or the operators, who must unpack each plug and jam it carefully into the ground before the next muddy hole arrives. Like bagging up vegetables on harvest day, it's a kind of comical version of an assembly line. But unlike the famous candy factory scene in *I Love Lucy*, there are no chocolates to consume along the way.

Nevertheless, it's splendid work, and it makes the connection between the health of the soil and the health of the plants in about as visceral a way as you could want.

For my shift, Mike drives the tractor and I take the jalopy seat on the left, joined first by Mark on the right and then later by Patty. As the morning progresses, we change the planting wheels from a single-wheel of fifteen-inch spacing to two wheels of fifteen-inch spacing, and then finally to two wheels of six-inch spacing, depending on the needs of each crop. It's wet and messy work, and my left foot is soaked by the end of the morning from a loose connection on the water line, which makes me two-for-two for problematic footwear.

What's most noticeable to me, though, is the way each small plant has its own distinctive characteristics, like a schoolroom full of children, each with a different personality. A standard flat (or propagation tray) is about ten by twenty inches and contains about seventy-two plugs (six plugs wide by twelve plugs long), so with two-hundred-foot rows, that's a lot of plugs. As we rumble down the rows, some plugs are easy to remove, while others stick in their trays; some root systems are well established, while others are less so. The result is that some plugs stay together in neat little packages, while others fall apart in my hands, making me worry about the fate of the seedlings I am sending out into the world. Will they survive a strong storm, or an extended drought? Will their roots take hold, despite their crumbling plugs? What if my bumbling unpacking skills result in a lower yield for the crops I was asked to plant?

As if to confirm my insecurities, when we finish out the morning by moving additional flats from the greenhouse to the hayrack, the plastic edge of one of the flats I am carrying splits, and an entire tray of red cabbage seedlings falls upside down, crushed by its own weight. My spirit is crushed along with it: all those carefully tended seeds, now grown into seedlings, destroyed by my own incompetence.

As I scoop up the humus and try to rescue as many seedlings as I can, Patty is surprisingly nonchalant. There was a low germination rate in that flat, anyway, she says, so less than half of the plugs had seedlings. "Don't worry about it," she says, sympathetically. Still, it is painful to see the stems of so many plants broken, their leaves battered and bruised, their root systems exposed for all the world to see.

The first rule of farming really should be: don't drop the cabbages.

After *The Unsettling of America* was published in 1977, reviews of the book fell into roughly two camps.

Some reviews, mostly from other literary writers, praised the book for its passion and vision. The book is "as passionate in its use of fact as in its use of personal experience," wrote essayist Scott Russell Sanders in *The Progressive* (44); Berry is "a prophet of our healing, a utopian poet-legislator like William Blake," said the poet Donald Hall in the *New York Times*; the book, wrote the literary critic Dean Flower in the *Hudson Review,* is "a welcome antidote" (177).

Other reviews, primarily from academic scientists and historians, faulted Berry for his nostalgia, his lack of precision, and his opposition to new forms of agricultural technology. "One wonders if he is aware of what is going on these days in the laboratories and on the field plots of present day agricultural research," asked N. R. "Rick" Richards, former dean of the Ontario Agricultural College, in the pages of *Queen's Quarterly.* Berry, he observed, gives "little attention . . . to the need for growth in food production in relation to foreseeable increasing demands on limited land resources" (139). Calvin O. Qualset, director emeritus of the Genetic Resources Conservation Program at the University of California Davis, voiced a similar concern in *Science Books and Films.* The book's "rather angry style and tendency toward overstatement," said Qualset, "preclude objective evaluation of agriculture and social issues which are of great significance for the maintenance of food production in the United States" (77).

Not surprisingly, Earl Butz—Berry's principal foil in the book—was Berry's most outspoken critic, saying in *Growth & Change* that *The Unsettling of America* "is filled with facts interspersed with fantasy, tilting with straw men, and a nostalgic longing to turn the agricultural clock back by at least a couple of generations." True, said Butz, "we may have lost something in community identity, understanding of nature, and even old-fashioned moral concepts; yet this is a world of trade-offs. We Americans enjoy our widely distributed affluence (and leisure) precisely because our productive modern agriculture has freed millions of us from virtual serfdom on the land. Those who remain on the land live better, too. If the author had recognized this trade-off and had ascribed some good to it, he would have substantially improved his credibility with the scientific community" (52).

Perhaps most telling was an exchange that Berry had with Butz soon after the book was published. Asked to participate in a public debate on the campus of Manchester College in Indiana, Butz argued that "our challenge is not to yield to the nostalgia of yesteryear. Our challenge is not to turn the clock back. Our challenge is not to go back to more inefficient ways. Our challenge is not to put more people back on the land and therefore decrease the efficiency of American agriculture. Our challenge is to adapt to the changing situation in which we find ourselves. We need to evolve a new community structure" (Brand 120). Berry, meanwhile, told Butz, "I don't want to go backward. . . . I think that what we all want to try is the future. It's just a question of how we try and who gets to make the attempt" (Brand 121). When Butz said, "I've got a feeling that Dr. Berry and I haven't met tonight" (Brand 124), Berry responded, "We may never meet, because he's arguing from quantities and I'm arguing from values" (Brand 126). It was an insightful point, emphasized again by Berry near the end of the debate when he said, "I don't think that anybody's going to get to heaven by being efficient" (Brand 127).

This is where we were in 1977, and this is where we remain today: how do we balance the desire for efficiency—to make farmwork easier and to feed more people overall—with the virtues that accompany a life lived in close contact with the soil, for individuals, for communities, and for the soil itself?

After lunch, Mike takes a break from the transplanting to show me around the farm and talk about some of the ways the land has changed over time.

In his review of *The Unsettling of America*, Rick Richards claimed that "the exodus of people from the rural community is not entirely the replacement of men by machines but the preference of people for a shorter work week and the so-called benefits of city dwelling to the dawn to dusk drudgery of the farm" (139). This may sound compelling in the abstract, but it's hard to square with our experience over the next hour, as the noise of the city is for me replaced with the sound of birds singing, crickets chirping, and the crunch of leaves and grasses underfoot as we make our way around the farm. There's no question that the work is physically demanding, but I see more smiles in a few hours on the farm than I sometimes see all day in the city, so this calculus of rural drudgery versus city pleasures is not as simple as it seems. In fact, watching Mark wave to us from the blueberry patch he is weeding, complete with a big grin on his face, makes me wish I could have invited Richards to accompany us on our walk today.

"There are several things that people will *not* be free to do in the nation-of-the-future that will be fed by these farms-of-the-future," Berry warned in that pivotal fifth chapter of *Unsettling*. "They will not live where they work or work where they live. They will not work where they play. And they will not, above all, play where they work. There will be no singing in those fields.

There will be no crews of workers or neighbors laughing and joking, telling stories, or competing at tests of speed or strength or skill. There will be no holiday walks or picnics in those fields because, in the first place, the fields will be ugly, all graces of nature having been ruled out, and, in the second place, they will be dangerous" (74).

Having just spent much of the morning in an extended discussion with Mark about the lyrics to Crosby, Stills, and Nash's "Helplessly Hoping"—complete with requisite harmonizing—I am grateful that Berry's vision has not yet come to pass, at least not here.

Mike and I begin our walk up by the apple orchard, in the southeast corner of the farm, and look out at the valley below us, where most of the farm's fields are located. On a map, Patty and Mike's eighty acres look like two squares stacked on top of each other in classic midwestern fashion, with each forty-acre parcel running for a quarter mile per side, so that the whole farm looks like a tall rectangle, a half-mile high by a quarter-mile wide.

Most of the top square is wooded and located on a steep ridge, so "the farm" as we know it is almost all located in the bottom square, in a valley that runs northwest to southeast through the property. Of the farm's approximately twenty tillable acres, only about six to eight are suitable for vegetables in the style, method, and techniques that Patty and Mike use. To put it another way, only about 10 percent of the farm consists of fields—and for good reason. "There's close to 150 feet of elevation difference between the valley and the ridge top, and it's steep," says Mike. "So we've learned to use the land as it presents itself."

Gazing out across the valley, Mike begins as any proud farmer would, by pointing out the various buildings that have gone up during their time there: a chicken coop, a greenhouse, a pole shed, and a community building, along with four "hoop houses," or high tunnels, which extend the growing season and help to shelter sensitive crops from the weather and harmful insects. Patty and Mike also tore down a variety of other dilapidated buildings over time, including a woodshed, a corn crib, a horse barn, and the original barn, all of which speak to the farm's prior incarnations.

At first, the farm was part of the land grants of the Superior and St. Croix Railroad, which were made after the Ojibwe ceded this portion of Wisconsin to the U.S. government in 1837. Later, Scandinavian and German immigrants arrived, farming wheat and a little tobacco, and then the land eventually became a family dairy farm, which it remained until the mid-1960s. After that, it was converted into a "hobby farm," on which the retired owners grazed beef cattle and made hay, until Patty and Mike bought it in 1989.

"If you were to pick out an ideal vegetable farm, this land would not be it," observes Mike, as we step out of the bright sun for a moment into the shade of the woods. "You'd want really good drainage, you'd want it flat, you'd want a light sandy soil, with irrigation. You put the water on when you want it. However, short of moving, this is what we have, and over twenty years we've made it work, and we've actually built soil, organic matter."

This is not just a generic "farm," in other words. Patty and Mike are doing certain things here, and they're not doing others—all of which depend on what the land will allow them to do.

"There's no way we could be grain farmers here," continues Mike. "There's no way we could really milk cows here. We could probably graze a few animals on a part-time basis, but even that the land wouldn't sustain. You know, twenty acres wouldn't do much. And the other sixty acres of woods, we kind of 'passively manage.' So, yeah, direct marketing of vegetables is actually something that you can have a fairly high return on, on a per-acre basis. You can enter into small-scale vegetable growing with a lot less capital and a lot smaller land base that you would in more conventional farming. And then when you add to it the social component that is the CSA, then it fits for who we are and what we like to do."

Patty joins us as we make our way down into the valley from the orchard, as does Sunny, the farm's resident beagle, now going on fourteen.

"There we go," says Mike, as Sunny lumbers along beside us. "Happy? Are ya happy? Come on, come on," Mike says, encouraging him.

We walk through newly mown grass toward the stream that bisects the valley, which is fed by the eight or nine springs that give Spring Hill Community Farm its name. This little unnamed stream feeds into Vance Creek, just south of the farm, which then flows east toward the Hay River, south into the Red Cedar, and farther south into the Chippewa, which eventually empties into the Mississippi near Pepin. From here south, a twig—or, more significantly, nutrient runoff—can make its way toward the Gulf of Mexico, where a dead zone the size of Connecticut develops each summer from the excess nitrogen and phosphorus that accumulates there.

Unaware of the significance this little stream may hold for the health of

Bubba Gump's shrimp, Sunny immediately bounds into it, seeming now more like a puppy than the geriatric beagle of a moment ago.

Mike picks up a piece of pipe and points upstream to a little pond built by the previous owner, from which he and Patty now draw irrigation water with small Honda pumps. "We knew there were springs when we bought the farm, and we thought, 'cool,'" he says. "But we had no idea that we had this wonderful spring-fed pond that we could irrigate out of."

"Many of the springs on this farm were tiled out years ago, way prior to us," Mike continues, referring to the practice of installing drainage pipes below the surface to move excess water off the land. The previous owners had created a watering system for their animals by tapping into a spring and tiling it out to the stream, then putting a gate valve into the tile so they could close it, which could back the water up into a tank.

"The entire stream bank had also been fenced off by the previous owner to keep the cattle out," Mike says, though he and Patty finally took the fence out this past spring. "So I sometimes think about all these things that we're creating that somebody else is going to have to undo," he jokes.

When Rachel Carson published her landmark critique of the chemical industry in *Silent Spring,* she had already established her reputation as an immensely talented science writer with three best-selling books on the sea. Likewise, when Aldo Leopold concluded *A Sand County Almanac* (1949) with "The Upshot"—four essays explaining his groundbreaking environmental philosophy—he had already spent the first two-thirds of the book establishing his credentials for doing so, through an "almanac" of personal reflections and a series of lyrical travel sketches from "here and there."

Berry's success with *The Unsettling of America* was similar, in that it did not emerge out of nowhere to catch unsuspecting readers off-guard. Berry had already published several novels and poetry collections related to rural life, and his first two essay collections had also directly addressed the culture of farming and the practice of place-making from a personal, autobiographical perspective. As this context makes clear, the success of Berry's *argument* about agriculture was deeply dependent on his *personal experience* as a farmer.

In the title essay of *The Long-Legged House* (1969), for instance, in which Berry describes the reasons for his return to the Kentucky River valley where he was born and raised, Berry meditates on the importance of place to his self-understanding as a writer. "Whereas most American writers—and even most Americans—of my time are displaced persons, I am a placed person. For longer than they can remember, both sides of my family have lived within five or six miles of this riverbank where the old Camp stood and where I sit writing now. . . . For me, it was never a question of finding a subject, but rather of learning what to do with the subject I had from the beginning and could not escape" (140).

Although Berry spent most of the first twenty-four years of his life in Kentucky, where he was born in 1934, he left in 1958 to study and teach creative writing at Stanford University for two years, then traveled in France and Italy for a year on a Guggenheim fellowship, after which he taught English for two more years at New York University. But he eventually returned home to Port Royal in 1964, and the following year moved to Lanes Landing Farm on the banks of the Kentucky River, where he has lived ever since.

Being born in a place does not automatically make one a resident of it, however, as Berry describes later in that same essay. "A man might own a whole country and be a stranger in it," he observes. "If I belonged in this place it was because I belonged *to* it. And I began to understand that so long as I did not know the place fully, or even adequately, I belonged to it only partially. . . . I began to see, however dimly, that one of my ambitions, perhaps my governing ambition, was to belong fully to this place, to belong as the thrushes and the herons and the muskrats belonged, to be altogether at home here" (150).

As Berry's earliest essay collection, *The Long-Legged House* can be self-indulgent at times, as Berry works to establish his bona fides for the moral proclamations he seeks to make at such a young age. And it has a stronger religious cast than some of Berry's later works, with Berry at times sounding more like Rudolf Steiner than he might care to admit. In "A Native Hill," the last essay in the collection, for example, Berry writes: "The most exemplary nature is that of the topsoil. It is very Christ-like in its passivity and beneficence, and in the penetrating energy that issues out of its peaceableness. It increases by experience, by the passage of the seasons over it, growth rising out of it and returning to it, not by ambition or aggressiveness. It is enriched by all things that die and enter into it. It keeps the past, not as history and memory, but as richness, new possibility. Its fertility is always building up out of death into promise. Death is the bridge or the tunnel by which its past enters its future" (204).

Yet the same essay that contains such high-flying theological musings also contains a much more grounded justification for the kind of place-based agriculture Berry thinks we must develop. "Thousands of acres of hill land, here and in the rest of the country, were wasted by a system of agriculture that was fundamentally alien to it," Berry observes. "For more than a century, here, the steepest hillsides were farmed, by my forefathers and their neighbors, as if they were flat, and as if this was not a country of heavy rains. And that symbolizes well enough how alien we remain, in our behavior and in our thoughts, to our country. We haven't yet, in any meaningful sense, arrived in these places that we declare we own" (206–7).

From the bottom of the valley, we walk north along the western edge of the creek, as Patty describes how the fields grew from those first tentative plantings they did as gardeners to the CSA farm they have today, which feeds 150 families per year.

"The first couple gardens started just on the southern slope," she says, turning around, "and then gradually moved down the valley and then across the valley. And we've got the south-facing slopes and the north-facing slopes, so all of our tomatoes, peppers, and eggplant will always be on the south. Melons will also always be on that side, but in soil that's a little bit sandier. Early greens will always go on a south side, because that soil warms up and is workable earlier."

"The north-facing side is really nice for fall brassicas," adds Mike, referring to vegetables like cabbages, cauliflower, broccoli, and Brussels sprouts, "because by then it's dried out. You don't have issues of getting into the ground in a timely fashion like you do early on, and they get a little bit more afternoon shade. They don't get quite so hot."

"And the midseason greens as well," says Patty.

"If I had to choose a side, I'd choose the south," says Mike. "That side has nicer soils, warms up quicker, drains better."

Spring Hill has the soils it does in part because the glaciers spared this portion of Barron County, stopping just to the northwest of here.

"We're right on the edge of the last lobe," says Mike, as we start to make our way up the north ridge toward the woods. "You go right up here, a mile and a half, there's glacial till."

"If you're traveling ever on County Road A," says Patty, "just to the north of us, you'll see: the landscape is flat," thanks to the movement of the glaciers, which last retreated some ten thousand years ago.

The Department of Natural Resources in Wisconsin refers to this region as "Western Coulees and Ridges," and Spring Hill is at the very beginning of this landscape.

The farm was thus spared by the glacier but blessed by its outwash, as the glacier's meltwater carried rocks and other fine particles away in drainage channels, which settled on the land as sediment. What's left now, on top of sedimentary rock, is a soil type known as Hixton silt loam.

"It is a highly erodible soil," says Mike, "so we have learned over the years to be very, very careful about erosion. It's always there for us: how are we going to prevent erosion and build soil."

Some of that soil is sandier, some is more clayey, but all of it has the potential to wash away, just like the soils of Berry's ancestors.

"That's why we do this complete mulch cover system," says Mike, pointing to the rows of vegetables covered with a biodegradable plastic known as bio-mulch. "If we didn't," he says, sweeping his hand down the slope, "whoosh."

Earlier today when we were transplanting, the waterwheel not only poked holes in the ground, it poked holes through the biomulch, so that the rows we were planting looked like someone had just drilled perfectly spaced pot-holes into freshly paved asphalt. Later, Patty and Mike will mulch with hay, a method that keeps the ground covered, builds soil, and prevents erosion—all of which allow them to farm on these hillsides without destroying them.

They first read about this system in *Growing for Market*, a trade magazine for market farmers, which described a farm in Virginia that grows thirty-five acres of vegetables, thirty of which are mulched.

"We always mulched some," says Mike, "but we've really gone heavy toward the mulching in the last, say, five years."

"We were doing it on such a small scale, with square bales," says Patty. "It was so labor-intensive. We loved what it was doing, but we couldn't imagine how we could do it on a larger scale. And then we read about these guys unrolling the round bales."

"Now we'll do anywhere from sixty to ninety round bales a year," says Mike. "So all that organic matter is going into the soil every year. We're really building soil. It's kind of expensive—the biomulch is expensive, the hay is expensive—but we save our soil, and we save on labor later. So once this is done, it's done."

"We realized that the places we had mulched we were seeing, through soil tests, such an improvement in organic matter," says Patty. "Plus, there's no cultivating, no irrigating typically, and the weeding is way down."

"And this is no small thing for me," adds Mike. "Because farm members come here, I want to feel good about what this place looks like. And it looks nice."

After the success of *The Unsettling of America*, Wendell Berry published a new essay collection in 1981, *The Gift of Good Land: Further Essays Cultural and Agricultural*.

While *The Gift of Good Land* builds on *Unsettling* by "presenting a greater number and diversity of exemplary practices" (ix) than Berry was able to provide in his previous book, the book's true antecedent is Berry's second essay collection, *A Continuous Harmony: Essays Cultural and Agricultural* (1972), whose subtitle it references directly.

All three books concern the relationship between culture and agriculture, of course, but whereas *The Unsettling of America* presents Berry's most unified argument, *A Continuous Harmony* and *The Gift of Good Land* do what the rest of Berry's many essay collections do, which is to approach this relationship repeatedly, first from this way and then from that, with the goal of understanding how each of these human activities is dependent on the other. This is unsystematic work, which inevitably leads to some repetition—or, perhaps more appropriately, the plowing of familiar ground—but it is difficult to imagine how else Berry might plumb this relationship, especially when he does so from the perspective of his own personal experience.

Consider this observation from "Discipline and Hope," the central essay in *A Continuous Harmony*: "The fact is that farming is not a laboratory science, but a science of practice. It would be, I think, a good deal more accurate to call it an art, for it grows not only out of factual knowledge but out of cultural tradition; it is learned not only by precept but by example, by apprenticeship; and it requires not merely a competent knowledge of its facts and processes, but also a complex set of attitudes, a certain culturally evolved stance, in the face of the unexpected and the unknown. That is to say, it requires *style* in the highest and richest sense of the term" (94).

This is not the commentary of a disinterested observer but rather the testimony of someone who is himself an apprentice, who knows that knowledge comes from practice—from popping plug after plug out of propagation trays, from setting seedling after seedling in the mud (not too deep, not too shallow), and from carrying tray after tray from greenhouse to hayrack, until one learns which techniques are most appropriate to the task at hand and which are, well, not.

The same might be said of Berry's essays themselves, which more often than not were published as individual pieces before being collected into single volumes—like *The Gift of Good Land,* which gathered essays Berry wrote for *The New Farm* and *Organic Gardening,* both publications of the Rodale Press, for which Berry worked in the 1970s. In a sense, Berry's writing and farming both operate on the same principle: that repeated attention to familiar subjects will yield an outcome of uncommon character.

"Problems must be solved in work and in place, with particular knowledge, fidelity, and care, by people who will suffer the consequences of their mistakes," Berry observes in "Solving for Pattern," an essay from *The New Farm* that appears in *The Gift of Good Land*. "There is no theoretical or ideal *practice.* Practical advice or direction from people who have no practice may have some value, but its value is questionable and is limited" (143).

The Gift of Good Land looks for exactly this kind of practical advice from experts far and near: practitioners of traditional agriculture from the mountains of Peru, the Arizona deserts, and the Amish country of Pennsylvania. From these visits, Berry derives lessons about the virtues of four factors: scale, balance, diversity, and quality (121–23). Of these, scale is clearly the most important.

Looking down at the Andes from an airplane, Berry observes that "the most interesting, crucial, difficult questions of agriculture are questions of propriety. What is the proper size for a farm for one family in a given place? What is the proper size for a field, given a particular slope, climate, soil type, and drainage? What is the appropriate kind and scale of technology?" (43).

Later, Berry answers these questions by reflecting on the ways they are in fact all connected: "In general," he notes, "the steeper the ground, the smaller should be the fields. On the steeper slopes of the Andes, for instance, agriculture has survived for thousands of years. This survival has obviously depended on holding the soil in place, and the Andean peasants have an extensive methodology of erosion control. Of all their means and methods, none is more important than the smallness of their fields—which is permitted by the smallness of their technology, most of the land still being worked by hand or with oxen" (122).

Industrial agriculture, in contrast, "needs large holdings and large level fields. As the scale of technology grows, the small farms with small or steep fields are pushed farther and farther toward the economic margins and are finally abandoned. And so industrial agriculture sticks itself deeper and deeper into a curious paradox: the larger its technology grows in order to 'feed the world,' the more potentially productive 'marginal' land it either ruins or causes to be abandoned" (128).

Good agriculture, Berry concludes, "is virtually synonymous with small-scale agriculture—that is, with what is conventionally called 'the small farm.' The meaning of 'small' will vary, of course, from place to place and from farmer to farmer. What I mean by it has much to do with *propriety* of size and scale. The small farm is defended in this book because smallness tends to be a prerequisite of diversity, and diversity, in turn, a prerequisite of thrift and care in the use of the world" (xi).

Reaching the woods at the top of the ridge, Mike and Patty and I finally wander down to their northernmost field, which this year is planted in potatoes.

"You're seeing lots of fencerows going out right now," Mike observes, speaking of those uncultivated strips of land that would often be found on either side of a farm fence. "As much as anything, that is a reflection of the size and scale of equipment that make it easier just to farm and not have something get in the way."

In contrast, he says, "our vegetable farming style has taken on these really small patches."

We look back down the valley we have just traversed, with all of its "funny-shaped" plots, as Patty called them, with a row of one crop next to a row of another, unlike the endless fields of commodity corn and soybeans that characterize so much of the midwestern landscape.

What do Mike and Patty grow here instead?

"In almost every given year we have an acre of potatoes, an acre of winter squash, an acre of onions, and a little more than an acre of the brassica family. So that's four acres, and then you have the other little odds and ends—the tomatoes, the peppers, the early greens, the things that don't fit into any neat category, like fennel or celeriac—probably another acre, acre and a half. So anywhere from five to six acres in any given year."

Mike and Patty also rotate their crops from year to year and let some fields lie fallow for the season, so as not to exhaust any one of those valuable patches.

Walking around the potato patch, which is just beginning to take shape this year, Mike explains some of the reasons he and Patty space their rows of potatoes so widely, which include increasing airflow between the plants to combat disease and planting a cover crop every fifth row to control erosion.

He also compares his expected yield to that of much larger farms that also grow potatoes.

"Generally speaking, thirty thousand pounds per acre on conventional farms is average production for potatoes. We won't come close to that. Part of it is that our spacing is half of what they do, and part of it is just the organic system. If we get ten thousand pounds, man, we'll all be happy. So if we got nine thousand pounds, and there's 150 shares, that's, what, sixty pounds apiece?" he asks Patty.

"That's a lot of potatoes," I say. No wonder our share bags get so heavy come fall.

"We're kind of in that middling ground between just massive production—monoculture—and gardener," adds Mike. "There's a balance that has to be learned for every scale, I'm sure."

HUMILITY IN FACE OF MYSTERY

One of the most beautiful photographs I have ever received arrived in an email message about three months after my visit to the farm in June.

The message was from Patty, and it contained a single word—"Success!"—to which was attached a photograph of the cabbage patch, post-harvest.

Taken on a hazy, overcast day, the photo shows a row of mature red cabbage plants snaking north up the valley, their broad purple and green leaves open to the sky like upturned palms. And on either side of the plants are the cabbages themselves—hundreds of big, beautiful cabbage heads—freshly sliced from their stems and neatly deposited onto blankets of hay mulch lying on both sides of the row.

It was a beheading worthy of *Macbeth* (and then some), but to my eyes it was a thing of beauty.

Beauty is not the first thing we think of when it comes to agriculture, but maybe it should be. Recall Patty's protest that farming *is* romantic when the sun first hits you in the morning, or Mike's insistence that the farm should look nice for the members when they come to visit.

What if these were not secondary features of sustainable agriculture but central components of it? And what if they were important not only to

Red cabbage harvest at Spring Hill Community Farm, Prairie Farm, Wisconsin, September 2013. (Photo by Michael Racette)

farmers but also to the 98 percent of us who reap the benefits of agriculture without any direct involvement in its pursuit?

The Unsettling of America is almost all about production agriculture, but early in the book Berry gestures toward the other side of the agricultural equation: consumption.

"We are eating thoughtlessly, as no other society ever has been able to do," Berry observed in 1977. "We are eating—drawing our lives out of the land—thoughtlessly" (38).

Thirteen years later he returned to that idea in "The Pleasures of Eating," the essay I wish I had read before *Unsettling*, because it concerns what those of us who do not live on farms should do to "eat responsibly."

In the penultimate paragraph of that essay, Berry offers the following guidance to urban eaters, which may be the most elegant summation of his thinking on the matter:

> The pleasure of eating should be an *extensive* pleasure, not that of the
> mere gourmet. People who know the garden in which their vegetables
> have grown and know that the garden is healthy will remember the beauty
> of the growing plants, perhaps in the dewy first light of morning when
> gardens are at their best. Such a memory involves itself with the food and
> is one of the pleasures of eating. The knowledge of the good health of the
> garden relieves and frees and comforts the eater. The same goes for eating
> meat. The thought of the good pasture and of the calf contentedly grazing
> flavors the steak. Some, I know, will think it bloodthirsty or worse to eat
> a fellow creature you have known all its life. On the contrary, I think it
> means that you eat with understanding and with gratitude. A significant
> part of the pleasure of eating is in one's accurate consciousness of the lives
> and the world from which food comes. The pleasure of eating, then, may
> be the best available standard of our health. And this pleasure, I think, is
> pretty fully available to the urban consumer who will make the necessary
> effort. (*What Are People For?* 151–52)

What strikes me most about this passage, and where I believe it derives its
rhetorical power, is Berry's ability to defamiliarize our notions of pleasure.
Berry insists that no matter how good our meal may taste, or how "gourmet"
it might appear, if its production involved morally questionable practices,
then the pleasure of its consumption should be greatly diminished. Indeed,
any conception of "pleasure" that fails to include broader considerations of
where our food comes from and how it arrives at our table, suggests Berry,
is no longer sufficient in an age of sustainability. As Berry himself indicates,
"there is great *dis*pleasure in knowing about a food economy that degrades
and abuses those arts [such as farming and animal husbandry] and those
plants and animals and the soil from which they come" (151). The philosopher
Lisa Heldke observes that this is in contrast to the industrial view, which
employs a "thin conception of pleasure . . . on which food satisfies so long
as it looks like the box, tastes salty enough, and doesn't take long to prepare" (145). To Berry, eating should be the very opposite of an industrial act.
Instead, as he puts it at the opening of his essay—in a justifiably well-known
remark—"eating is an agricultural act" (145).

Almost as significant, however, is the fact that Berry references not
merely health but beauty as a criterion for the goodness of the sources of
our food: "the beauty of the growing plants, perhaps in the dewy first light of

morning when gardens are at their best" (151). Beauty, notably, is part of what we must consider if we are to have an "accurate consciousness of the lives and the world from which food comes" (151).

Near the end of *In Defense of Food: An Eater's Manifesto*, Michael Pollan makes Berry into a kind of secular saint, and "The Pleasures of Eating" into a modern gospel. Citing lines from the final paragraph of Berry's essay, Pollan writes: "I don't ordinarily offer any special words before a meal, but I do sometimes recall a couple of sentences written by Wendell Berry, which do a good job of getting me to eat more deliberately: 'Eating with the fullest pleasure—pleasure, that is, that does not depend upon ignorance—is perhaps the profoundest enactment of our connection with the world. In this pleasure we experience and celebrate our dependence and gratitude, for we are living from mystery, from creatures we did not make and powers we cannot comprehend'" (196–97).

Back in early July, prior to the cabbage harvest, I spent another day at the farm, helping with some additional chores and managing to sneak in another conversation with Patty and Mike about why they do what they do. With sunny skies, a light breeze, and high of 80 degrees Fahrenheit, the weather seemed as if it had been ordered up just to support Berry's assertions about the importance of beauty as a standard by which we should evaluate the origins of our food.

In the morning, the three of us worked alongside Mark to wrap tomato vines up their trellises, harvest the last of the season's sugar snap peas, and weed the peppers and some newly planted beans before we all broke for lunch. (The fall brassicas were out on the flatbed truck, waiting to be transplanted, but I knew better than to get involved in any more planting schemes.)

After lunch, I joined Patty and Mike at one of the three picnic tables they use for sharing a meal with farm members, in a shady pine grove at the edge of one of the fields, and we talked about their influences, what they would call their style of farming, and the role that science and technology have played in their choices. While we chatted, Sunny lay quietly in the grass beside us— back to acting his age again.

Reflecting on Berry's legacy, Bill McKibben memorably wrote: "I state categorically that I know of no farmer involved in this movement who does not have a well-thumbed copy of *Home Economics* or *The Unsettling of America* or some such on her shelf. I cannot tell you how many bathrooms I have peed in while reading a framed copy of 'The Mad Farmer Manifesto' hung above the toilet. Through sheer power of both rhetoric and example (and without the example the rhetoric wouldn't mean nearly as much) he has touched off this Restoration" ("Citizen of the Real World" 117).

As if to prove his point, the bathroom in the farm's community building—no joke—has a framed stanza from Berry's "Prayers and Sayings of the Mad Farmer" hanging above the toilet.

But, perhaps not surprisingly, it was writers other than Berry who motivated Patty and Mike to turn away from using synthetic fertilizers and pesticides on their farm.

"We were aware of all the Rachel Carson stuff, and the DDT—story after story of concerns of chemicals that proponents would say were very safe but later turned out to be not so safe," says Mike. "And vegetable production on a small-scale organically seemed rather doable."

"One of the books that was very influential was Frances Moore Lappé's *Diet for a Small Planet* [1971]," adds Patty. "That was a book that we had both read early on, before even thinking about moving to the farm."

"That was the first time I really understood the geopolitical aspect of food," says Mike. "And how what we do individually connects to that larger system. And what we don't do."

Mike and Patty are careful not to label their farm as "organic" because that implies a formal certification process—in place since 2000—which legally restricts the use of the term "organic" to only those growers whose practices have been approved by U.S. Department of Agriculture.

So, for that reason among others, says Patty, "we've tried to avoid 'label-y' stuff." Still, she says, "I think we try to farm with a concern toward environmental health and environmental stewardship. I kind of prefer the word 'stewardship,' that it speaks to a relationship between farmer and land."

"I would say, going back to some of the original tenets of the organic movement," adds Mike, "your soil is everything. That's what you focus on. That's what you pay most attention to. That what sustains you over the longest period of time."

At lunch earlier in the day, Mike had told an amusing story about the challenges of asking for organic feed in the local feed mill, where most of the products are sold to conventional farms.

Explaining the significance of this anecdote now, he turns serious.

"There is something about not using the 'organic' label that just removes one more barrier between people who move into a community and those who are there. When one becomes strident about certain things, it's more difficult to build bridges and become part of the community. That said, we still farm the way we do, but labels can sometimes get in the way. And so we've always had a focus on really clean, quality food."

In his introduction to the 2006 reprint of Sir Albert Howard's *The Soil and Health,* Berry took exception to the way the kind of alternative agriculture promoted by Howard has been "seriously oversimplified," not only by parts of the organic movement but also by the regulatory framework that seeks to delimit what does and does not qualify as "organic."

"Under the current and now official definition of organic farming," Berry wrote, "it is possible to have a huge 'organic' farm that grows only one or two crops, has no animals or pastures, is entirely dependent on industrial technology and economics, and imports all its fertility and energy. It was precisely this sort of specialization and oversimplification that Sir Albert Howard worked and wrote against his entire life" (xiv).

Berry was not always so critical of the "organic" label, however, and when he first began farming he was downright enthusiastic about it. As he points out in his introduction to *The Soil and Health,* Berry first learned about Howard's ideas when he returned to Kentucky in the mid-1960s and his editor suggested that he read Howard's work. In "The Making of a Marginal Farm" (1981), Berry recalled his early efforts at living a life consistent with Howard's principles, in which he and his wife, Tanya, built a composting privy and refused to use chemical fertilizers or insecticides (except for a little rotenone, an organic pesticide). In "Think Little," an influential Earth Day speech that was eventually reprinted in *The Whole Earth Catalog* (1970), Berry argued that "a person who is growing a garden, if he is growing it organically, is improving a piece of the world" (*Continuous Harmony* 79). And in a 1972 interview with Gene Logsdon, Berry told Logsdon, "I want to be called an organic farmer. I'm not a purist about organics, but that's where I want to stand" (Logsdon 32).

Yet even when he was advocating for organic agriculture, Berry was defining the word *organic* in relation to Howard's broader understanding of it. In that same interview with Logsdon, Berry made clear that "organics is not just about using chemicals or not using chemicals. That's the narrow view. Organics is talking about a *shift in power*. We want more control over our own *lives*—at the local level" (32). And in a later essay, "Solving for Pattern" (1980), Berry allowed that "once the farmer's mind, his body, and his farm are understood as a single organism, and once it is understood that the question of endurance of this organism is a question about the sufficiency and integrity of a pattern, then the word *organic* can be usefully admitted into this series of standards. . . . An organic farm, properly speaking, is not one that uses certain methods and substances and avoids others; it is a farm whose structure is formed in imitation of the structure of a natural system; it has the integrity, the independence, and the benign dependence of an organism" (*Gift of Good Land* 143–44).

The messiness of "organic" as a term becomes even more pronounced when you compare Berry's (and Howard's) understanding of the farm as organism with the assertions of Trauger Groh, the biodynamic advocate who helped convince Patty, Mike, and many other farmers to adopt the CSA model. "As with any organism," wrote Groh in *Farms of Tomorrow*, "the farm organism needs a strong inner circulation of substances. . . . The condition and the amount of organic matter or carbon substance are decisive factors for the health and productivity of a farm" (21). So while Howard may have wanted to draw "rigid lines" between his own scientific ideas and those of Rudolf Steiner's more spiritual biodynamic approach, this was difficult to do in practice. And nowhere was this more apparent than at Rodale Press, where Berry worked in the 1970s, and whose founder, J. I. Rodale, "attempted to sidestep the internecine quarrel" between Steiner and Howard, according to Philip Conford (*Origins* 101). As Suzanne Peters says of Rodale, "He fused Steiner's esoteric mysticism and Howard's research reforms into a secular and practical mission" (Conford, *Origins* 102).

Over the years, Berry has gradually moved away from advocating for the "organic" label in favor of a focus on both Howard's holistic understanding of agriculture and the sense of mystery that Berry believes underlies it. This can be seen especially well in Berry's essays from the early 1980s that were collected in *Home Economics* (1987), the volume Bill McKibben so often encountered on the shelves of the alternative farmers he knew.

Home Economics opened with Berry's "Letter to Wes Jackson," in which Berry memorably wrote to Jackson that "what I think you and I and a few others are working on is a definition of agriculture as up against mystery and ignorance-based. I think we think that this is its *necessary* definition, just as I think we think that several kinds of ruin are the *necessary* result of an agriculture defined as knowledge-based and up against randomness" (5). But

Berry's advocacy of holism and mystery takes its most fully developed form in his reflections on soil that appear throughout the volume.

One crucial, extended passage from Berry's essay "Two Economies" makes this vividly clear:

> We cannot speak of topsoil, indeed we cannot know what it is, without acknowledging at the outset that we cannot make it. We can care for it (or not), we can even, as we say, "build" it, but we can do so only by assenting to, preserving, and perhaps collaborating in its own processes. To those processes themselves we have nothing to contribute. We cannot make topsoil, and we cannot make any substitute for it; we cannot do what it does. It is apparently impossible to make an adequate description of topsoil in the sort of language that we have come to call "scientific." For, although any soil sample can be reduced to its inert quantities, a handful of the real thing has life in it; it is full of living creatures. And if we try to describe the behavior of that life we will see that it is doing something that, if we are not careful, we will call "unearthly": It is making life out of death. Not so very long ago, had we known about it what we know now, we would probably have called it "miraculous." In a time when death is looked upon with almost universal enmity, it is hard to believe that the land we live on and the lives we live are the gifts of death. Yet that is so, and it is the topsoil that makes it so. In fact, in talking about topsoil, it is hard to avoid the language of religion. (62)

Again and again in *Home Economics*, Berry emphasizes that soil is "too complex for human comprehension" (14) and "a dark wilderness, ultimately unknowable" (140).

In doing so, Berry's goal is clear: the humility that accompanies much religious thought. Later in "Two Economies," Berry claims that "the properties of soil husbandry require acts that are much more complex than industrial acts, for these acts are conditioned by the ability *not* to act, by forbearance or self-restraint, sympathy, or generosity" (66).

Behind "organic," then, is the farm as organism, and behind that organism is unknowable mystery. And our ultimate obligation "in face of mystery," as the theologian Gordon D. Kaufman puts it, is humility.

The wind starts to pick up under the pines, and that's all it really takes to be reminded of how much influence the rest of the world has, not only on the farm but everywhere we humans leave our mark.

It's easy to forget this basic truth. In fact, most days consist *entirely* of us forgetting it—at least for those of us whose lives are largely insulated from direct contact with what, for lack of a better term, we call "nature." Our world is so thoroughly circumscribed by human activities, human desires, and human creations, that our default position is to think and act as if it's all about *us*.

We notice the wind mainly when it is a nuisance: when, as now, it flutters the pages of my notebook and threatens to send my baseball cap flying from my head.

We notice the sun in relation to our own needs: when we miss its warmth in winter, or when we realize we should have put on sunscreen, as I did earlier this morning, after an hour of harvesting peas under a cloudless sky.

And we notice the living creatures in the soil . . . well, we almost never notice the living creatures in the soil, unless a worm washes up on the sidewalk or we need to bait a fishhook.

That it takes a constant, active effort—true mindfulness—to make the nonhuman world present to us, to literally *re-mind* ourselves of our dependence on it, is one of the greatest challenges we face as a society.

Ecologists have taken one step toward doing this by identifying what they call "ecosystem services," those features of our environment that not only keep us alive but also make our lives worth living. They've categorized these into four groups: *provisioning services* that provide us with food, water, medicines, energy, and other natural resources; *regulating services* that maintain our climate, decompose our wastes, pollinate our crops, and purify our air and water; *cultural services* that provide us with recreation, inspiration, and education; and *supporting services,* such as nutrient cycling and soil formation, that make all those other ecosystem services possible (Daily, *Nature's Services*).

What Berry calls "miraculous," in other words, scientists call "ecosystem services."

For all our talk about the farm, I hadn't thought much about the ecosystem services that the woods provide, so I asked Patty and Mike how their woods fit into what they're trying to do here. Although they don't put it in the language of science, their answers turn out to be textbook examples of what ecosystem services are meant to convey.

"The woods were part of the attraction to the farm, and remain so," says Patty, focusing on their cultural services. "The pleasure from the woods is important, even though I don't get there that often. Part of the day's stories are what wildlife we saw: the bear and the bees and the fox coming around. I can't really imagine the farm without the woods."

Mike, meanwhile, speaks of the regulating services the woods provide. "As years go on," he says, "you'll find more and more interesting research relative to how the environment of the woods has a positive impact on the valley and the vegetables. Native pollinators, for example. Bird populations. The heating and cooling, and the wind. All those things that I don't even have a clue about. But they influence what happens in the production aspect, in ways that I can't even begin to comprehend."

One thing that's notable to me about our conversations these past few months is the way so many things that might seem to be at odds in theory— realism and romanticism, preservation and use, scientific abstraction and the particulars of local knowledge—coexist easily in practice on the farm.

Take science and local knowledge.

"Science is huge," says Mike. "We use mostly all hybrids. The biomulch is an industrial product that was discovered, designed, and made possible by extensive scientific research. And the approved organic pesticides that we may use have tremendous amounts of science and research behind them. And then different types of scientific inquiry. So, for example, if you look at insects as problems and you start to look at biocontrols and understanding life cycles of the pests that concern you, that's an aspect of science that is not product-driven but is more holistic."

"It's some interesting marriage between science and scientific studies and really keen observation of what's here," adds Patty. "You can't just read a study about 'this experiment on this farm' and go, oh, this will work great here, because your soil is different, or your climate is different, or each season is different. It's not just transferring knowledge from the lab to the farm."

The same seems to go for technology, which could either be rejected outright or wholeheartedly embraced, but which here seems to exist in balance with the needs of the farm.

Thinking about Berry's decision to farm with horses, I ask Patty and Mike how they decide when to use a certain technology and when not.

"I don't think there's a technology we've avoided for philosophical reasons," says Mike.

"I think it's been sort of interest," says Patty. "Neither one of us is particularly mechanically inclined. We've limited the tractors because, 'How many engines do we want to work on?'"

"How do you want to spend your time?" adds Mike.

"What is pleasant work for you? Is it pleasant work for you to sit on a tractor all day?" asks Patty. (Her question is rhetorical because the answer is so obvious.)

"We recognize where our skills are: what we do best, what we don't do well. And if we have a great tractor that functions really, really well, it doesn't need a lot," says Mike.

"What's appropriate to our scale, and to our landscape as well," says Patty.

If there's a place where Berry goes astray, in tone if not content, it is most certainly in his comments about science and technology.

It is one thing to recognize and humble ourselves before mystery; it is another to equate most scientific inquiry with hubris.

It is one thing to acknowledge ignorance as the foundation of all knowledge; it is another to celebrate ignorance as an ideal, as a state to be desired.

And it is one thing to urge caution in our actions and attention to the consequences of our choices; it is another to reject action altogether, to stifle innovation by demonizing those who dream of creating a better world for ourselves and our children.

Berry does not go quite as far as these examples suggest, but he comes pretty close, and his claims about science and technology not only seem a distraction from his larger argument but also have the effect of clouding his more important points about the value of community and the significance of place.

Recall Berry's attack on agricultural scientists in chapter 8 of *The Unsettling of America*. There he chided careerist and specialist professors for their "transience or rootlessness" and their "inability to respond to local conditions" (147). And he equated their attempt at objectivity with being "shed of the embarrassment of moral and intellectual standards and of any need to define what is excellent or desirable" (149). (In a later essay, Berry acknowledged that "there are many individual professors, scientists, and extension workers . . . whose work has genuinely served the rural home and rural life," but he maintained that "in general, it can no longer be denied that the [land-grant] system as a whole has failed" [*Home Economics* 170].)

In *Life Is a Miracle: An Essay against Modern Superstition* (2000), Berry deepens and extends this appraisal, using the publication of Edward O. Wilson's *Consilience: The Unity of Knowledge* (1998) to launch a wide-ranging critique of science, technology, and the "cult of progress" (69). While Berry claims not to be "proposing an end to science and other intellectual disciplines" (12), he is also not serving as their cheerleader. Instead, he is denouncing what happens when the principles of science—namely, materialism and reductionism—become what he calls "articles of belief" (38). Where materialism leaves no room for mystery, reductionism removes all trace of particulars. But certain things are irreducible, Berry argues, and to treat them otherwise amounts to a form of mechanistic thought that eventually leads to the death of the creature; "we murder to dissect," as Wordsworth would have it ("The Tables Turned"). "The most radical influence of reductive science has been the virtually universal adoption of the idea that the world, its creatures, and all parts of its creatures are machines," says Berry (6). But the world is not a machine, he protests, and "some things are and ought to be forbidden to us, off-limits, unthinkable, foreign, *properly* strange" (76).

Berry believes that we have adopted "a kind of religious faith in the power of science to know all things and solve all problems" and have "conceded to scientists . . . the place once occupied by the prophets and priests of religion" (19). But this new faith is misguided, he says, because "the solutions invented or discovered by science have tended to lead to new problems or become problems themselves" (32). Citing the issues of nuclear waste and the overuse of antibiotics as evidence that "our daily lives are a daily mockery of scientific pretensions" (33), Berry offers a decidedly declensionist reading of scientific progress, in which "nobody seems able to subtract the negative results of scientific 'advances' from the positive" (70).

What Berry wants in place of the "academic hubris" (27) that has resulted in such harm is a sense of "propriety," in which both artists and scientists see their work "as occurring within a larger and ultimately a mysterious pattern of causes and influences" (89). In place of professional norms and standards, he wants a sense of "responsible community membership" (130). And when science must be abstract, he wants its application to respect "the uniqueness of the subject persons or creatures or places, or of their community" (147).

As valuable as such calls for humility and community certainly are, Berry's argument in *Life Is a Miracle* has three problems that I think limit its effectiveness as a guide for understanding the place of science and religion on this or any farm.

For one thing, the book continues Berry's practice of creating dichotomies for argumentative purposes, which he began in *The Unsettling of Amer-*

ica with the dichotomy of the industrial and the agrarian. But whereas that book at times seemed to complicate its foundational dichotomy, *Life Is a Miracle* retains it throughout, suggesting that science and religion are what Stephen Jay Gould once called "non-overlapping magisteria" (NOMA). Berry explains his perspective on the relationship of science and religion this way: "There is no reason, as I hope and believe, that science and religion might not live together in amity and peace, so long as they both acknowledge their real differences and each remains within its own competence. Religion, that is, should not attempt to dispute what science has actually proved; and science should not claim to know what it does not know, it should not confuse theory and knowledge, and it should disavow any claim on what is empirically unknowable" (98).

This is only one way of characterizing the relationship of science and religion, however, and framing the conversation in this way omits other ways of knowing that also deserve our attention. In *When Science Meets Religion,* for example, the scholar Ian Barbour proposed four ways of seeing how science and religion might relate to one another: *conflict* (in which science and religion are fundamentally at odds with one another); *independence* (Berry and Gould's view); *dialogue* (in which science and religion may exhibit similar methods, questions, or analogies); and *integration* (in which religious beliefs either are or could be made compatible with scientific theories). In Berry's view, independence sometimes slides into conflict, and dialogue and integration are almost nowhere to be seen.

A second problem that follows from the first is that Berry generalizes so much that his version of "science" is almost wholly disconnected from actual scientific practice. Rather than talking about individual scientists, specific scientific studies, or particular scientific fields, Berry refers only to "science" in the abstract—which is ironic, given his criticism of the "cold-heartedness of abstraction" (41). While Berry might protest that to do more would be beyond his abilities—he admits that he has "no competence or learning in science" (10)—one longs for examples to support his claims, not to mention counterexamples to contest them.

A third problem with *Life Is a Miracle* is that the book not only simplifies what counts as "science," but it also extends that simplification by regularly linking the practice of science to the abuses of industry and global capitalism. "The abstractions of science are too readily assimilable to the abstractions of industry and commerce," Berry argues at one point (41). "The sciences are sectioned like a stockyard to better serve the corporations," he proclaims at another (123). His critique of science thus becomes a close relative to a wholesale rejection of modernity, which leaves little room for legitimate achievements in the health sciences, astrophysics, mechanical engineering, and a range of other scientific endeavors.

For comparison, consider Berry's statement in an earlier essay ("Preserving Wildness"), in which he says that there are "three questions that must be asked with respect to a human economy in any given place: 1. What is here? 2. What will nature permit us to do here? 3. What will nature help us to do here?" (*Home Economics* 146).

Note that Berry does not ask, "how can we improve on nature?"

What seems like a relatively innocuous idea—asking what nature would allow—in fact avoids the most important question of all: how do we know when science and technology are appropriate, and when they are not?

Philip Conford has observed that "the religious philosophy of belief in a God-given natural order" was "a central feature of the organic movement's early days: an organic farmer is someone who trusts in that order, seeking to understand its workings, and following the rule of return of wastes to the soil" (*Development* 72).

But this assumes that "nature" is always and everywhere good, and that anything "unnatural" is inherently bad. (Philosophers call these "appeals to nature.") That Berry should espouse such a view is not surprising, given its resonance with Christian ideas of a perfect Edenic world from which we have somehow "fallen" as a result of our desire for knowledge.

If we set aside the vagueness of the idea of "nature," appeals to nature are perfectly reasonable in their more modest form, given that the whole of the world is a gift, after all, and last I checked we humans were still unable to perform photosynthesis.

But taken to an extreme, appeals to nature allow no place for scientific or technological innovation (Tucker). Instead, we are left only with the injunction that certain things should be "forbidden" and "unthinkable," to remain ever mysterious by being kept from prying human eyes (Shattuck).

These problems with *Life Is a Miracle* matter because they reflect a more widespread uncertainty about the role of science in environmentalism, in which some opponents see science as the cause of environmental problems, whereas others see science as our potential savior.

In terms of sustainable agriculture, they matter for similar reasons.

On the one hand, Berry's approach to science fails to acknowledge the past: specifically, the tradition of amateur natural history that has captured the imagination of many other nature writers since the eighteenth century. Unlike Gilbert White, Henry David Thoreau, John Muir, Aldo Leopold, or Rachel Carson, Berry has been largely uninterested in integrating science into his agricultural writing, despite the relevance of even such generalist fields as botany, geology, or hydrology. Indeed, by equating science mainly with industry, Berry has lost a valuable opportunity to demonstrate that science is a public good, able to be practiced by anyone—farmers included—who might consider themselves "citizen scientists." While it is true that some might call small-scale agriculture "gardening" rather than "farming," science can happen anywhere, no matter the size of the plot, and one need not be a specialist to participate in scientific research.

On the other hand, Berry's approach also fails to acknowledge the future, especially the significance of agroecology, or the practice of studying farms as ecosystems. Agroecology demonstrates that science need not be so reductionist that it cannot address holism, and it need not be so tied to materialism that all wonder and mystery are stripped from the world. Moreover, it proves that agricultural science, in particular, need not be only about increasing yields.

If we return to the question of whether we can see the woods at Spring Hill through the lens of "ecosystem services," Berry would likely say "no." In *Life Is a Miracle,* Berry asserts that "we have a lot of genuinely concerned people calling upon us to 'save' a world which their language simultaneously reduces to an assemblage of perfectly featureless and dispirited 'ecosystems,' 'organisms,' 'environments,' 'mechanisms,' and the like." Echoing Audre Lorde's 1984 essay "The Master's Tools Will Never Dismantle the Master's House," Berry writes, "It is impossible to prefigure the salvation of the world in the same language by which the world has been dismembered and defaced" (8).

And yet: might not our understanding of community be enriched and enhanced by science and technology? Or must a valuation of the small and the local require that we refute them wholesale?

To be fair, Berry does not seek to banish science and technology from the farmstead, even though his provocations at times seem to lean that way. A more charitable reading might say that Berry seeks to provide a framework for how we might value them appropriately.

Three essays in particular speak to these concerns more directly than *Life Is a Miracle.*

In "Whose Head Is the Farmer Using? Whose Head Is Using the Farmer?" (1984), for example, Berry sounds a lot like Mike and Patty. There, he says: "To the textbook writer or researcher, the farm—the place where knowledge is applied—is necessarily provisional or theoretical; what he proposes must be found to be *generally* true. For the good farmer, on the other hand, the place where knowledge is applied is minutely particular, not *a* farm but *this* farm, *my* farm, the only place exactly like itself in all the world" (28). Understanding how to act, in other words, requires Haraway's "situated knowledge," or what I might call "the practice of place." And there is no better example of situated knowledge than the intelligence shown by the farmer who must respond to hundreds of subtle changes that occur on the farm throughout the growing season. "The good farmer, like an artist, performs within a pattern; he must do one thing while remembering many others," writes Berry. "He must be thoughtful of relationships and connections, always aware of the reciprocity of dependence and influence between part and whole. His work may be physical, but its integrity is made by thought" (28).

In "Renewing Husbandry" (2004), Berry clarifies that he is less interested in the role of science on the farm than he is in making sure that this complex act known as farming itself does not become a science. "When any discipline is made or is called a science, it is thought by some to be much increased in preciseness, complexity, and prestige," Berry writes. "When 'husbandry' becomes 'science,' the lowly has been exalted and the rustic has become urbane. Purporting to increase the sophistication of the humble art of farming, this change in fact brutally oversimplifies it" (*The Way of Ignorance* 98). He contrasts "soil science"—which he says "has tended to treat the soil as a lifeless matrix in which 'soil chemistry' takes place and 'nutrients' are 'made available'"—with "soil husbandry," which he says "leads, in the words of Sir Albert Howard, to understanding 'health in soil, plant, animal, and man as one great subject'" (98). Husbandry need not omit science, but Berry is skeptical that even the science of complexity would be capable of describing, much less understanding, the dense web of connections that makes up a farm. "'Science' is too simple a word to name the complex of relationships and connections that compose a healthy farm—a farm that is a full membership of the soil community. If we propose, not the reductive science we generally have, but a science of complexity, that too will be inadequate, for any complexity that science can comprehend is going to be necessarily a human construct, and therefore too simple" (98).

And in "People, Land, and Community" (1983), Berry clarifies that his unease with technology on the farm ultimately concerns the effect that such technology will have on the farmers themselves. Much like his approach to science, Berry wants to make sure that farmers employ technology cautiously, so it does not end up eclipsing the purpose of their husbandry. As Berry writes, "We would be wrong, of course, to say that anyone who farms with a tractor is a bad farmer. That is not true. What we must say, however, is that once a tractor is introduced into the pattern of a farm, certain necessary restraints and practices, once implicit in technology, must now reside in the character and consciousness of the farmer—at the same time that the economic pressure to cast off restraint and good practice has been greatly increased" (*Standing by Words* 75).

ENVISIONING COMMUNITY

"When you think about your community, how do you envision it?"

That was one of the last questions I put to Mike and Patty as we sat at the picnic table under the pines, and it was a stumper. Or at least it seemed so at first, when an answer was not as forthcoming as most of their others had been.

I tried to clarify.

"Do you feel like you're part of two communities, one being the Prairie Farm community, and the other being the Twin Cities community? Or is this all part of one hybrid community for you?"

The wind continued to blow, the birds continued to chirp, and the sun continued to sparkle through the pines, but we all just sat there, thinking.

Finally, Mike offered up an analogy.

"For me, the most useful descriptor would be a Venn diagram."

"Mmm-hmm," Patty agreed, perhaps grateful that someone had an answer to what was, admittedly, a ridiculously abstract question.

"There's a lot of overlap in a lot of areas, and there's a lot of nonoverlapping areas. But it would be like a Venn diagram with depth, because there's *so many* different aspects to, for example, the community of Prairie Farm."

Patty chuckled as we all tried to imagine what a Venn diagram with depth would look like, but Mike's point was clear.

"Officially, the town itself is four-hundred-and-some people, but you've got the church community, you've got the school community, you've got the transplant community, you've got the Democrats, you've got the Tea Partiers. And there's so many overlapping areas that I don't even know how to begin to describe them, other than to say that I think a Venn diagram would be the easiest."

My question was sparked by the fact that so much of Berry's writing concerns community, especially the community engendered in small farm towns across America. And of course, community-supported agriculture is supposed to be about community. But are those really two different communities, or are they one? Where's the community in community-supported agriculture, in other words?

"There are not two separate fates, urban and rural, but ultimately only one fate that is shared," writes Berry in "A Long Job, Too Late to Quit" (1997). "Ultimately, a city cannot be better than its surrounding countryside, and vice-versa" (*Citizenship Papers* 79). As a result, he says, "We need to do everything we can to encourage urban concern for the fate of the countryside and the country people. We would benefit in innumerable ways from a system of economic alliances between local producers and local consumers" (*Citizenship Papers* 81).

Each year Spring Hill offers at least four opportunities for members to join with other members to participate in the life of the farm: a spring work day, a fall work day, each member's harvest or delivery day, and an annual harvest dinner, usually held on the first Saturday in November.

If you ask members, as Patty and Mike did that year, what they value most about their Spring Hill membership besides the vegetables, the number-one answer—by a wide margin—is the harvest days.

To know why, all you have to do is attend one, as my wife, Nancy, my daughter, Grace, and I did one Saturday in September.

After making the drive out to Prairie Farm, complete with my requisite joke about the distance, we joined three other families to work in the fields and help pack and deliver the vegetables.

We brought work gloves, pruning shears, and a dish to share (a chocolate beet cake this year—yum!) and arrived around 9:30 a.m., just as the work was getting underway.

As we gathered around the packing shed, complete with sweatshirts, sweaters, and fleeces to ward off the morning chill, Patty and Mike assigned us our tasks. One crew would be harvesting pumpkins (both pie pumpkins and carving pumpkins), while another would be prepping vegetables (cleaning onions and shallots and readying—gasp!—red cabbage for delivery). Grace gravitated toward the pumpkins, so while she and Nancy headed to the fields with Mike and a few others, I stuck around the packing shed with Patty and the rest of the team to begin our work prepping vegetables.

Fortunately, none of these tasks is overly complicated, and harvest days are not meant to be physically demanding. Yes, they can involve manual labor, but these sessions are as much a time to meet new people, visit with old friends, and swap stories as they are about accomplishing work. People bring their kids (pets stay at home, for Sunny's sake, among other reasons), and sometimes three generations of a single family will attend together. After a morning of farm tasks, followed by a potluck lunch, the goal is to have all the bags packed and loaded into cars by around 2:00 p.m., so the vegetables will arrive at their pickup sites in Minneapolis and Saint Paul by 4:00 p.m.

"Community" comes from the Latin *communis*, meaning "common," "ordinary," or "commonplace," as well as "public" and "democratic," and that is exactly what harvest days feel like: doing ordinary work together for the sake of the entire community. The farm seems like a true *commons*, shared by the whole membership, and it is easy to think that it is not really Patty and Mike's farm but *our* farm, belonging to all of us. Which, in a very real sense, it is.

In his wonderful book *Rebuilding the Foodshed*, Philip Ackerman-Leist tracks the transition from "community-supported agriculture" to what farmer Josh Slotnick calls "agriculture-supported community." As Slotnick describes it, "It's clear that the education is working when the pronouns begin changing—when the lettuce becomes 'our lettuce,' the tractor becomes 'our tractor,' and we all begin wearing each other's sweatshirts" (113).

And it doesn't hurt that arriving involves a literal breath of fresh air.

Watching as a few latecomers pull into the driveway, I smile as they emerge from their vehicles, breathe deeply, and let their bodies relax into an entirely different rhythm.

They join us as we get started on the onions, cutting off their remaining stalks, trimming their excess roots, and giving their outer skins a good brushing before depositing them into big green plastic tubs for packing. We chat about our jobs, our families, the books we have read and the movies we have seen. But somehow the conversation always eventually turns to the vegetables—the ones we like, the ones we struggle to cook, the ones we could do without. We swap recipe ideas, exalt in successful dishes, and commiserate over failed experiments in the kitchen. This year, I was treated to a welcome lesson on caramelizing fennel, a vegetable whose anise-like flavor I never much liked until I cooked it slowly over low heat with a dash of sugar, and suddenly I had a new favorite topping for pizza.

After the onions were clean, we turned to the cabbage, and I got to see the fruits of my labor—or at least the *surviving* fruits of my labor—up close and personal. Each cabbage was huge, truly the size of a human head, and our task was to peel the dark purple outer leaves away and trim any remaining stalks from the bottom, before placing them, too, into more large green tubs. It was satisfying work, to say the least, and by the time we were done, the bright inner leaves made each cabbage look more like an electric purple bowling ball than anything resembling a human body part.

After Grace and the crew returned from the pumpkin patch, a few of us wandered down to the herb garden with Patty to cut fresh sprigs of sage and thyme to include in the bags, while others picked a few apples from the orchard on the hill.

In all, it was a fine morning, which also happened to mark the end of the growing season. As Patty wrote in the weekly newsletter that accompanied the vegetables we delivered that afternoon, "It's the big letting go. This week summer officially ended at the farm. We've had several light frosts and harder frosts are predicted for both Friday and Saturday night. End of the season frosts are always a mixed bag. First there's the frenzy. The frenzy begins with attempts to 'do it all' followed by, 'okay, we need to set some priorities here' and finally, the big letting go."

This year's frenzy entailed picking boxes and boxes of Roma tomatoes and Japanese peppers from the hoop houses, followed by harvesting four different kinds of squash—butternut, delicata, sunshine, and sweet dumplings—

and piling them in the fields, where they could be covered by tarps to protect them from the cold.

It's one of the curiosities of a CSA that you can usually tell where you are in the growing season by the weight of each week's bag of vegetables, as the light greens of spring transition into the heavy root vegetables of fall. This week's bag, which we packed assembly-line style after lunch, felt more like an extra-large kettlebell than a sack of produce, with its pounds of potatoes, onions, carrots, winter squash, and cauliflower, along with peppers, shallots, some salad mix, and of course a red cabbage and a bunch of the sage and thyme we had just picked.

Each week's newsletter also had a recipe on the back, and this week Patty had given instructions for making braised red cabbage.

Which to me seemed more like a benediction than a recipe.

So there is the community of Prairie Farm, which is diverse in its values but unified by its geography (consisting of roughly thirty-five square miles of land). And there is the community of Spring Hill, which is diverse in its geography (with members scattered throughout the Twin Cities, as well as in Prairie Farm) but unified by its values.

According to a survey that Patty and Mike did of the membership, those values include (in order, in addition to the harvest days), valuing a connection to the farmers, community, meeting other members, knowing where their food comes from, the weekly newsletters, a connection to land, knowing the food is grown in an environmentally sustainable way, supporting a family farm, recipes, cooking videos, the CSA concept, healthy eating, and the hard work of farming.

It may be enough to acknowledge that Prairie Farm (the town) and Spring Hill (the CSA) are two different, overlapping communities, but looking more closely at their connection—at the relationship between Berry's agrarianism and the idea of community-supported agriculture—may help to illuminate that overlap more clearly.

It's no surprise, really, that none of the members of Spring Hill cited "agrarianism" as one of their core values, given that the membership is predominantly urban and also that agrarianism is a messy term with a good bit of baggage.

Like any "ism," it's not exactly clear what "agrarianism" is. Is it a polit-

ical ideology, a social movement, a philosophical system, or a set of practical tools?

In *The Idea of Agrarianism*, James A. Montmarquet defines agrarianism as "the idea that agriculture and those whose occupation involves agriculture are especially important and valuable elements of society" (viii). But that doesn't take us very far, given the breadth of such a definition. More helpful is David B. Danbom's distinction between "rational" and "romantic" agrarians: "Rational agrarians, operating in the tradition of the Physiocrats and Jefferson, stress the tangible contributions agriculture and rural people make to a nation's economic and political well being. Romantic agrarians, following the path trod by Thoreau, emphasize the moral, emotional, and spiritual benefits agriculture and rural life convey to the individual" (1).

Danbom characterizes Berry as a romantic agrarian, but such a distinction fails to fully capture the complexity of Berry's thinking, which concerns the social and economic realities of farming as much as it does the relationship of the individual to the larger community. Danbom gets closer to Berry's outlook when he acknowledges that "agrarianism was—and is—an oppositional and critical point of view rather than a programmatic blueprint. . . . In that role, agrarianism was—and remains—an ideology for all seasons, attractive to great varieties of people who are called upon to share no more than a degree of alienation from modern society" (7).

Berry has addressed agrarianism directly, and at length, in a number of his essays, but the best overview of his thoughts on the subject may come from three essays reprinted in his collection *Citizenship Papers* (2003): "The Whole Horse" (1996), "The Agrarian Standard" (2002), and "Still Standing" (1999).

In "The Whole Horse," Berry contrasts industrialism with agrarianism, which he says "is primarily a practice, a set of attitudes, a loyalty and a passion; it is an idea only secondarily and at a remove" (*Citizenship Papers* 115). He puts it this way: "Whereas industrialism is a way of thought based on monetary capital and technology, agrarianism is a way of thought based on land" (116). Berry spends most of this essay laying out the characteristics of his vision of agrarianism, which should be familiar by now: it is intensely local rather than regional, national, or global; it is concerned with particulars rather than abstractions; it focuses on subsistence economics before market economics; it values independent, small-scale landholders as the bedrock of democracy; and it stresses living within our limits, seeing nature as "the final judge, lawgiver, and pattern-maker of and for the human use of the earth" (117). According to Berry, "The agrarian mind is, at bottom, a religious mind. . . . It prefers the Creation itself to the powers and quantities to which it can be reduced. And this is a mind completely different from that which sees creatures as machines, minds as computers, soil fertility as chemistry, or agrarianism as an idea" (118).

Seeing Berry's agrarianism as more "romantic" than "rational" helps to clarify some of the objections that have been raised to it over the years, which predominantly concern its economic, political, and social aspects, rather than its moral, emotional, or spiritual components. One such objection concerns the applicability of agrarianism to urban settings, as well as the historical hostility Berry and other agrarians have shown toward cities. In *The Unsettling of America*, for example, Berry wrote that "the cities subsist in competition with the country; they live upon a one-way movement of energies out of the countryside—food and fuel, manufacturing materials, human labor, intelligence, and talent. . . . Along with its glittering 'consumer goods,' the modern city produces an equally characteristic outpouring of garbage and pollution—just as it produces and/or collects unemployed, unemployable, and otherwise wasted people" (137). It is one-sided passages such as these (does no good come from cities?) that likely led Novella Carpenter to label Berry "the strident agrarian," whom, she says, "clearly hates cities. . . . But not all of us can live in the country like Wendell Berry" (*Farm City* 60–61).

Over the course of his career, Berry has never focused much of his attention on cities, other than in opposition to the countryside; he has not discussed many of the issues that concern current members of the sustainable food movement, such as urban agriculture, vertical farms, and community gardens; nutrition, obesity, and school lunches; and food deserts, food trucks, and food waste. But that is not to say his thinking has not matured on the subject, or that his recent focus on economics has nothing to say to city dwellers. On the contrary, in "The Whole Horse" Berry clarifies that agrarianism "does not propose that everybody should be a farmer or that we do not need cities" (121). And he admits that "any thinkable human economy would have to grant to manufacturing an appropriate and honorable place" (121). What agrarianism proposes, he argues, is "a revolt of local small producers and local consumers against the global industrialism of the corporations" (122). And as an example of this revolt, says Berry, "I know from friends and neighbors and from my own family that it is now possible for farmers to sell at a premium to local customers such products as organic vegetables, organic beef and lamb, and pasture-raised chicken. This market is being made by the exceptional goodness and freshness of the food, by the wish for urban consumers to support their farming neighbors, and by the excesses and abuses of the corporate food industry" (122).

Interestingly, in making this claim, Berry redefines his 1970s interest in "organic" by saying that "the market for so-called organic food . . . is really a market for good, fresh, trustworthy food, food from producers known and trusted by consumers, and such food cannot be produced by a global corporation" (123). Still, by defining "organic" in this way Berry is very much in keeping with what Philip Conford has called "the most clearly identifiable thread in the organic movement's confused political tapestry: the tendency towards the smaller-scale, the regional, the local" (*Development* 349). It was scale, after all, that Berry saw as a critical feature of Sir Albert Howard's vision of the organic "wheel of life." Berry ended his 1971 profile of Howard by observing that "*An Agricultural Testament* can be read as a confirmation and elaboration of Jefferson's belief in the supreme importance of the small farmer" (46), and in his introduction to the 2006 reissue of Howard's *The Soil and Health*, Berry argued that "only the smaller family farms, such as those of the Amish, permit the diversity and the careful attention that Howard's standards require" (xiv).

As if in direct response to Novella Carpenter, Berry wrote in "The Agrarian Standard" that "in our time it is useless and probably wrong to suppose that a great many urban people ought to go out into the countryside and became homesteaders or farmers. But it is not useless or wrong to suppose that urban people have agricultural responsibilities that they should try to meet" (*Citizenship Papers* 15). Or as he put it in another essay in *Citizenship Papers,* using a memorable turn-of-phrase, city dwellers are all "farming by proxy. They can eat only if land is farmed on their behalf by somebody somewhere in some fashion" (167).

Another objection to Berry's agrarianism concerns its history, which Berry addresses in his essay "Still Standing." Agrarianism has an extensive history stretching back to the ancient Greeks and Romans, the Chinese agriculturalists, and many eighteenth- and nineteenth-century intellectuals. These last thinkers include French Physiocrats such as François Quesnay (who saw agricultural labor as the ultimate source of wealth), Enlightenment philosophers such as Thomas Jefferson and John Locke, and Romantic artists and writers such as Ralph Waldo Emerson and Henry David Thoreau. But the historical figures who had the greatest influence on Berry were the so-called "Southern Agrarians," twelve writers (all white, all men) who each contributed an essay to a landmark volume of southern literature, *I'll Take My Stand: The South and the Agrarian Tradition* (1930). Their values, laid out in an introductory "Statement of Principles," written by John Crowe Ransom, should sound familiar: questioning science and technology, valuing labor, showing humility before nature, and opposing industrialism to agrarianism. According to Berry, the statement's main points "are more obviously true now than they were in 1930. As it stands, I know of no criticism of industrial assumptions that can equal it in clarity, economy, and eloquence" (*Citizenship Papers* 155).

But Berry is aware that the statement and the book are not beyond criticism. He notes that Ransom later dismissed his own statement as "agrarian nostalgia," for example, and subsequent generations of readers began to interpret the book as literature rather than as a serious political argument (156–57). Nevertheless, Berry praises *I'll Take My Stand* for "its astute and uncompromising regionalism," claiming that the Southern Agrarians would agree that an agriculture is good "not by virtue of its universal applicability, but according to its ability to adapt to local conditions and needs. A culture is good according to its ability to provide good local solutions to local problems" (159).

Still, *I'll Take My Stand* is a shaky foundation on which to build a movement, given the book's mythic reconstruction of an agrarian "Old South," made possible in part by the authors' unwillingness to take seriously the role of slavery in shaping the region's social and environmental history. Berry acknowledges that "the reputation and influence of the book have been reduced . . . because it was written during the era of segregation" and "none of the authors at that time had explicitly dissociated himself from racism" (155). But he dismisses as "political correctness" the idea that the authors' racism may have somehow tainted their larger argument about regionalism. "Critical discourse," he argues, "must try to deal intelligently with the fact that people who are wrong about one thing may be right about another" (155).

In mounting such a defense, however, Berry misses out on the larger critique of agrarianism of which segregation is a part. As Julie Guthman has argued, "a romanticized American agrarian imaginary erases the explicitly racist ways in which, historically, American land has been distributed and labor has been organized, erasures that ramify today in more subtle cultural coding of small-scale farming. For African Americans, especially, putting your hands in the soil is more likely to invoke images of slave labor than nostalgia" ("Unbearable Whiteness" 276).

Berry *has* paid more attention to this issue, however, in two other books, *The Hidden Wound* (1970) and *The Need to Be Whole: Patriotism and the History of Prejudice* (2022), published more than fifty years apart.

In *The Hidden Wound*, Berry wrote eloquently about the connection between what he called "the continuing crisis of my life, the crisis of racial awareness" and the treatment of the land. There Berry took white men to task for having "withheld from the black man the positions of responsibility toward the land, and consequently the sense of a legally permanent relationship to it" (103). In so doing, Berry felt, whites abandoned concrete knowledge of the land for abstractions, and left "the thousands of menial small acts by which the land is maintained, and by which men develop a closeness to the land" to blacks (103). "The white man," said Berry, "preoccupied with the abstractions of the economic exploitation and ownership of the land, *necessarily* has lived on the country as a destructive force, an ecological catastrophe, because he has assigned the hand labor, and in that the possibility of intimate knowledge of the land, to a people he considered racially inferior; in thus debasing labor, he destroyed the possibility of a meaningful contact with the earth" (141).

In *The Need to Be Whole*, Berry revisits, deepens, and troubles this claim, so much so that his clarity of focus suffers as a result. Coming in at nearly five hundred pages, *The Need to Be Whole* is Berry's longest book and also his most exhausting, full of numerous digressions and asides, as if Berry, at age eighty-eight, felt he had to fit everything he ever wanted to say between two covers. The book treats his own family's history of enslaving, the Civil War and its aftermath in Kentucky, the effects of post–World War II industrialization, the Ten Commandments, racial slurs, sin and forgiveness, reparations, John Quincy Adams, patriotism versus nationalism, the ideas of freedom, work, and mobility, the value of manual labor, Ernest J. Gaines and Shakespeare, tobacco farming, Paul Krugman and contemporary politics, and globalization and religion, just to name a few of its many subjects. Taken as a whole, *The Need to Be Whole* seems more like two books: one on race and forgiveness, and another on place and industrialism. Berry, of course, would object, as he returns repeatedly to his fundamental claim, that "a society willing to abuse its land will abuse its people, and vice versa" (2).

One clear strength of *The Need to Be Whole* is its extension of an argument Berry began in *The Unsettling of America,* in which he took issue with the process of colonization not only for its effects on indigenous people but also for the "mentality of exploitation" it embodied, which led him to seek a more nurturing kind of inhabitation (7). This was distinct from what the historian Richard Slotkin summarized as the "ideology of agrarianism" Berry inherited from Jefferson, which "only rarely makes mention of the Indian wars, and then as a distant and unpleasant prelude to the real action of history, which involves the clearing and cultivation of the soil by the diligent democratic husbandman" (52). In its place, Berry offered a more egalitarian narrative in which "the members of any *established* people or group or community"—including, eventually, the settlers themselves—"become the designated victims of an utterly ruthless, officially sanctioned and subsidized exploitation" (4).

The Need to Be Whole is unquestionably a complex book, and agrarianism only one of its many subjects, but two points of critique deserve our attention here. First, Berry's "everything is connected" approach tends to discount the significant differences between the topics he seeks to connect. He claims, for example, that "by imposing slavery upon the world, we have enslaved ourselves. Now all of us, rich and poor alike, are living as slaves of Mammon in a sickened world" (485). This is true as far as it goes, but it doesn't go very far, as some slaves of Mammon are doing quite well, thank you very much, compared to the millions of enslaved Africans victimized by a brutal regime of violence in the United States. Second, despite Berry's best intentions, *The Need to Be Whole* suffers from a surprising lack of empathy, especially for people other than Berry and his friends, whether those "others" be enslaved persons in the antebellum South or proponents of the views Berry dismisses, again, as little more than "political correctness" (41). Berry says that he "tried to write what I could honestly consider my part of a conversation" (448), but the result is a decidedly one-sided conversation for a book about prejudice, and I long to hear the reasoning of those who might cheer the removal of Confederate statues or be less sympathetic to the situation of Robert E. Lee than Berry.

The flip side of these critiques is that Berry can also be quite effective when he writes out of his own experience and thus makes connections that others might miss. Being a resident of rural America gives him an uncommon insight, for instance, into how the food movement's urban bias toward *consumption* has distracted it from the problems that industrial food *production* creates on the land itself:

> I supposed for a while that a significant urban agrarianism, and thus an effective urban lobby for sustainable agriculture, might grow from the "food movement," but that so far has failed to happen. I welcomed the food movement. In principle and in general I approve of it. On its own terms, it fails only when it fails to control production, and thus, as of old, throws individual producers destructively into competition with one another. But the acreage protected by the food movement—I mean by organic farming, community-supported agriculture, and the local suppliers of food stores, restaurants, and farmers' markets—is too small to be ecologically significant, or to affect the national food economy, let alone the national economy. Its *political* significance so far has been to distract attention from the enormous acreage still under the dominion of industrial agriculture. The surviving few critics of our "normal" food economy are regularly confronted by objectors who call their attention to the farmers' market of some large city. This is bitter irony. The food movement, which the agri-industrialists would not have started and could not approve, now charmingly masks their continuing aggression against rural America. This sort of thing, and the great ignorance it comes from, account for the failure after many years of effort to establish a regional food economy for Louisville. (423–24)

Berry's observation is similar to that of the philosopher Olúfẹ́mi O. Táíwò, who coined the term "elite capture" to describe how "the advantaged few steer resources and institutions that could serve the many toward their own narrower interests and aims" (22). But in voicing his disappointment with the efforts of urban activists to attend more carefully to rural problems, Berry misses an opportunity to consider how just as much blame might be put on the forces of Big Food itself, which have expertly co-opted agrarian rhetoric to their own industrialized ends (Pollan, "Big Food Strikes Back"; Singer, Grey, and Motter 6). In this case, an even greater focus on urban efforts to achieve food justice might have served Berry's goal of reconciling people and the land better than the rural resentment that fills too much of *The Need to Be Whole.*

One unfortunate effect of Berry's Confederate sympathizing in *The Need to Be Whole* is that it will likely only feed the fire of those who diagnose agrarianism with an incurable case of what I have come to call "agristalgia," or the wistful affection for an ideal preindustrial world that never truly existed and thus can never fully be recaptured. As Paul Thompson points out, "the very idea of a 'return' to agrarian morality is deceiving, for much of the world's land has been farmed as large, landed estates and plantations for several centuries. And while the agrarian emphasis on stewardship may have been a serviceable ethic for land use, its emphasis on place, prosperity, and loyalty to one's fellow citizens fed xenophobic and insular attitudes toward other peoples. Agrarian moral arguments have been handmaidens to racism and fascism in their application" ("Land and Water" 469).

It's unfair, of course, to suggest that Berry's agrarianism even remotely involves anything like the blood-and-soil nationalism of Nazi Germany, but the critiques of Carpenter, Guthman, and Thompson all point to a central question with which contemporary forms of agrarianism must continue to wrestle: how inviting does agrarianism appear to people outside its inner circle, whether they be urban, suburban, or historically disenfranchised? To put it another way, who is part of the agrarian community and who is not, either by design, omission, or neglect? Is it possible for agrarianism to be inclusive enough to become a mainstream movement?

The question of inclusiveness is related to the fact that Berry tends to minimize the more unpleasant aspects of small-town life, or what Bill McKibben describes as "the unnecessary feuds . . . that derive from some forgotten insult three generations back, or the mean prejudices and claustrophobia that so many people move to the city to escape" ("Prophet in Kentucky" 272). As a result, observes Greg Garrard, "While it is not impossible to imagine an urban equivalent of Berry's neo-Jeffersonian utopia, it is somewhat easier to imagine escapees from oppressive rural communities, be they female, black, gay, Jewish, short on piety or keen on anonymity, wanting none of it" (115). Cities and suburbs can harbor equal amounts of prejudice and oppression, to be sure, but they tend not to be cast in quite so positive a light.

Janet Fiskio has also pointed to the ways in which the agrarian framework "reinscribes the marginalization of migrant, undocumented, tenant, and temporary workers," noting that "an account of agricultural ethics stem-ming from the experience and perspective of the settled landowner excludes the agency of many who engage in agricultural labor today" (308).

As a final complicating factor, consider the place of women and gender in Berry's agrarian imagination.

If that seems difficult to do, it may be because women do not appear much in Berry's nonfiction, and the gendered aspects of farm life and domes-tic work receive little comment from him. Some of this is the result of the autobiographical nature of his essays, but that is no reason not to address gender more directly. Kimberly K. Smith has argued that Berry's engagement with issues of gender is "deeper and more pervasive than most critics recog-nize" (642), but she turns to Berry's fiction at least as much as to his nonfic-tion for evidence to support her case. While I agree with Smith that Berry demonstrates a "complex relationship to feminism" (623), his nonfiction all too often either fails to address the role of women in agrarianism or reflects the traditional gender roles so often found in rural America.

As William H. Major has observed, "Agrarian ideology is historically patriarchal. It has neglected to include the labor and ideas of women within its fundamental frameworks, mostly because women's labor has been associ-ated with, and confined to, the home" (150). Major argues that agrarianism needs to develop "new visions of domesticity, one in which gender roles for both sexes are more fluid" (150), and he admits that it is hard to know what Berry might say about "gay and lesbian domesticity, or whether such forms of domestic life can provide other alternative economic arrangements" (164). But it is clear that whatever the future of agrarianism may be, it will need to grapple much more thoroughly and thoughtfully with what sustainability would look like for a community that is not merely, or even principally, white, male, straight, and rural.

Ever since we've been members of Spring Hill, the annual harvest dinner has been held in the basement of St. Frances Cabrini Church in Minneapolis. The farm isn't affiliated with the church in any way; it's simply big enough to hold all the members, and like many large churches, it has a kitchen in the base-ment that makes food service for a crowd that much easier.

Last Tuesday we received our last bag of vegetables for the season— pie pumpkins, delicata squash, turnips, celeriac, onions, garlic, carrots, and cabbage—and now it's time to celebrate!

The harvest dinner is a potluck, so I've spent much of the afternoon making one of my favorite dishes, the humble-sounding "Rice and Winter Squash Gratin" from Deborah Madison's *Vegetarian Cooking for Everyone*. But don't let the uninspiring name fool you; this dish would better be named "Not-to-Be-Forgotten Gratin." It's time-consuming to prepare, and it ain't low-cal, but my, my is it good. You sauté the winter squash with sage, mix it with garlic and fresh parsley, and then combine it with rice, Gruyère, and a rich béchamel sauce. I triple the recipe, but every time I bring it somewhere, it always disappears.

Here in Minnesota, this is no "casserole"; it's a "hot dish." So we load up our official hot dish carrier, along with some plates, cups, and utensils, and make our way across town to the church.

Down in the basement there's a big box of extra garlic heads to take, some bottles of Wisconsin maple syrup to purchase, and a table of name labels, for assisting aging memories as well as meeting new friends.

After adding our gratin to the long row of dishes releasing enticing aromas, we slowly make our way through the crowd, chatting with friends we have known for years, with people we have met at our harvest days, with our site hosts (from whose house we pick up our weekly share), and of course with Patty and Mike, the most popular people in the room.

Many of the faces are white, but that doesn't tell the whole story, as members of the farm are young and old, male and female, gay and straight, single and coupled, with and without children, well off and just getting by, urban and suburban, and many other permutations of the markers of human identity.

Following a few words of thankfulness, dinner is served, and it's a mad rush to the tables, now overloaded with platters and pots, most containing Spring Hill vegetables in one form or another. There are multiple variations on coleslaw, a veggie lasagna, scalloped potatoes, trays of roasted root vegetables, and bowls full of carrot salads, shredded Brussels sprouts, and peanut noodles with broccoli. It's a feast worthy of a king (and queen), but it's exactly the opposite of aristocratic: it's food democracy in action.

It's perhaps appropriate that the harvest dinner takes place in the basement of a church, because religious communities have something important to tell us about communities in general—namely, that they involve both beliefs and practices.

Critics often take issue with a particular religion's beliefs: those doctrines, myths, and ethical systems that define a community to itself and to others. (Think of Berry's reflections on the Ten Commandments in *The Need to Be Whole,* for instance.) But as the scholar Ninian Smart has observed, religions also involve practices: rituals, personal experiences, social organizations, and the objects or places through which beliefs are made manifest (*World's Religions*). It is in practice that we act out our beliefs, and it is fair to say that any beliefs not made visible through practice would hardly qualify as strongly held. The connection between beliefs and practices is so important, in fact, that when our actions contradict our beliefs, we are called out for our hypocrisy.

We become a community, therefore, through practice, through the familiarity that comes from repeated interaction. But interaction alone is not enough without shared commitments—the commitment to learning that takes place in a classroom setting, for instance, or the commitment to free speech, a free press, and the freedom of religion, among other things, that defines the United States.

Berry celebrates communities of place for this very reason: they enact their beliefs through public and private rituals, and the sustenance of the land is dependent on the sustenance of the community. In his 1983 essay "People, Land, and Community," Berry wrote, "Without community, the good work of a single farmer or a single family will not mean much or last long. For good farming to last, it must occur in a good farming community— that is a neighborhood of people who know each other, who understand their mutual dependences, and who place a proper value on good farming. In its cultural aspect, the community is an order of memories preserved consciously in instructions, songs, and stories, and both consciously and unconsciously in *ways*" (*Standing by Words* 72–73). What Berry calls "ways," I'm calling practices.

Communities of interest (such as Spring Hill) are not meant to undermine communities of place (such as Prairie Farm), therefore. In fact, they are mutually beneficial. In *Sharing the Harvest: A Citizen's Guide to Community Supported Agriculture,* Elizabeth Henderson suggests that "perhaps we need to think about community differently, as a sharing of values and a commitment to act on those values, even in very modest ways" (161). Citing Berry's 1995 essay "Conserving Communities," she contrasts Trauger Groh's vision of an "associative economy," in which spirituality prevails, with Berry's more political vision, in which, Henderson says, "CSAs and our more conservative rural neighbors" might join together in opposing "the forces of neoliberalism and neocolonial globalization" (22).

Berry says as much himself in "Conserving Communities," observing that "the old opposition of country and city, which was never useful, is now more useless than ever. It is, in fact, damaging to everybody involved, as is the opposition of producers and consumers." The proper opposition, according to Berry, is between what he identifies as "the party of the global economy" and "the party of the local community" (16).

Yet this dichotomy, too, may be inadequate. Consider that in the first edition of her influential book *Agrarian Dreams* (2004), Julie Guthman seemed to agree with Berry on the importance of this opposition, concluding that what is most striking about CSAs "is how the transformative agronomic methods, the *reworking of nature* that occurs on such farms, are clearly driven by the decommodification of food *and* land, which opens up an economic space where social divisions can be eroded rather than accentuated. This is an alternative agriculture of substance, because it provides an alternative not only to production inputs and method but to the entire system of industrial farming" (185). Or, as Laura DeLind has put it, CSAs "raise food, not commodities. They feed people—people they know—not distant markets" (194).

But in the revised edition (2014), Guthman was more circumspect, given the ways in which even CSAs cannot escape the problems inherent in the agrarian ideal, including the question of who is included as part of the community. Finding particular fault with agrarianism's erasure of farmworkers, despite its glorification of the family farmer, Guthman suggests that the focus on alternatives may itself be the problem, as many such alternatives "rely on exclusions to be effective" (225). Whereas in 2004 she used the CSA idea as a starting point for what she calls "a utopia of process" (a term she borrowed from the geographer David Harvey), in 2014 she refined her central argument that the food movement should value *process* over *form*. "Rather than focusing on the forms that the worst of industrial agriculture takes (whether big, global, corporate, or otherwise) and trying to create new forms in putative opposition (e.g., small, local, independent), it may be more productive to focus on the processes of exploitation and intensification and work to reverse those while imagining processes more kind to nature and humans" (225).

It's an important point, though I'm not convinced that form and process have nothing to do with one another, particularly when it comes to community. Spring Hill tops out at around 150 families for a reason: beyond that, it becomes a different kind of farm, and Patty and Mike become different kinds of farmers. Moreover, the community loses whatever sense of itself it may have. Malcolm Gladwell makes a similar observation in *The Tipping Point* about what he calls the Rule of 150, which says that "congregants of a rapidly expanding church, or the members of a social club, or anyone in a group activity banking on the epidemic spread of shared ideals needs to be particularly cognizant of the perils of bigness. Crossing the 150 line is a small change that can make a big difference" (182–83).

Nevertheless, Guthman's invocation of utopia as a process is a good one, not unlike Adrian Shirk's assertion in *Heaven Is a Place on Earth* that "whatever value there may be in engaging utopian thought must be about process, not progress; experiment, not end result" (5). Or, to put it in more Berry-like terms, "Utopia-making is a practice rather than a program; it's action and not theory, or it's the dissolution of that dichotomy" (8).

Throughout my conversations with Mike and Patty, we often came back to the CSA idea, whether we were discussing what made them begin to farm in this way, how they made decisions about what crops to grow, or how they envisioned the future of the farm. And as we did, Mike repeatedly returned to the question of whether the CSA idea could survive its growing popularity.

"The genesis of the CSA movement in the Twin Cities area was certainly movement-based," he said. "It was driven by a set of social values and economic conditions in rural America that were really on everybody's plate at the time. Over time, as CSA became kind of a culturally accepted form of growing produce and engaging in agriculture, some of those early social aspects have become less important to a lot of people, in my opinion. It's more of an economic model, a marketing model.

"My concern for the CSA movement as a whole is that right now, with the emphasis on the marketing, on the economic aspect, we lose those pieces, we lose the community piece, and sooner or later, someone can do this more cheaply, with better quality, and more conveniently than we can. And, given the nature of capitalism, somebody will do that. And so what is it that is going to hold farmers and members together over time?"

"When it works," he added, "the CSA model can be a socially transformative model. And in that Jeffersonian sense, when you have all of these small farms in a community, the community benefits as well."

Mike is not the only one who has expressed concerns about what happens when the CSA idea is put into practice. Dan Imhoff, who has written widely about industrial agriculture and its alternatives, has catalogued some of the many issues that have arisen as CSAs have become more and more mainstream. According to Imhoff,

> it is easy to wax optimistic and idealistic about the CSA model, and wild claims have appeared, citing revolutionary overhauls of the small-farm scene. CSAs continue to cater mostly to well-to-do city dwellers rather than rural residents; the same people who can afford to buy microbrews can now purchase handcrafted fruits and vegetables and feel good about them. Viewed even more skeptically, these farms-in-a-box schemes could be seen as just another form of entertainment, in this case for people who have the time and tools to prepare high-quality meals. Critics also argue that low-income families and farmworkers are shut out of the movement because of the hardship of paying cash at the beginning of a growing season—or even in any given week—and that these people as much as others are in need of fresh, healthful food. Others point to CSA arrangements in which members have little connection to the work at all, other than writing a check and reading weekly newsletters. Many farmers still live on low incomes, and relationships among farming couples are sometimes as strained as ever. Member attrition can be problematic. And even successful farms struggle with undercapitalization. (24)

Spring Hill hasn't solved all of these problems, but it's certainly doing everything it can to address them. It offers on-farm pickup, and a number of its members live in and around the Prairie Farm area in Wisconsin. It provides resources for members who need help preparing their vegetables, from recipes on the back of each week's newsletter, to a twentieth-anniversary cookbook, to cooking videos produced by an enterprising farm member. It has a sliding fee scale, which few CSAs offer; it features several different kinds of payment plans, including a month-to-month option; and site hosts donate unused vegetables to local food shelves. It has ensured that Patty and

Mike receive health insurance and contribute to a retirement plan, and it has regularly increased the wages of both the farmers and their hired workers. The member-based delivery system gets people out on the land, and the farm has an exceptionally high return rate. And while I can't speak to the state of Patty and Mike's relationship, all the evidence suggests it's as strong as any I've ever seen.

Of all the interpretations of Wendell Berry's work that exist (of which there are many), the one I like the most comes from David Orr, who says, "To dismiss Berry as simply nostalgic . . . misses the point. He ought to be read as much as a futurist describing better possibilities as someone looking back to what once had been" (176).

Berry himself has said that "one easy (and silly) way to dismiss my argument is to call it nostalgic. There are indeed things in the past that I look back upon with love. But I know that the past does not return. I have been a steadfast critic of the past and certainly of my own inheritance from the past. History demonstrates certain possibilities, both good and bad, that we had better not forget. But my argument will stand or fall by the validity of its concern for the preservation of necessary things. I've tried to learn from the waste or destruction or ruin of some things that we might have inherited from the past, and that we need now" ("Toward" 121).

Orr describes Berry as a "futurist," as someone who is positing an ideal world, but I think describing Berry as an "idealist" gets even closer to the truth of his approach.

Two of my initial questions about Berry's vision in *The Unsettling of America* point us toward how Berry's critique of social and economic structures is wrapped up in his moral idealism.

One question I asked about Berry's vision was: how would changing how we grow food impact the eight billion people around the world who need to eat? Bill McKibben, for example, notes that "any rapid retreat to a saner but less productive method of agriculture might well mean famine in the nations that depend on America's surplus" ("Prophet in Kentucky" 267–68). McKibben answers this question by claiming that "Berry's argument is not a purely or even chiefly scientific one: he is a moral critic" ("Prophet in Kentucky" 268). But what does this mean, exactly?

It means that Berry is, at root, less interested in the scalar implications of his argument than he is in getting people back in touch with the land—with that soil he writes so much about—and the effect this would have on each individual. Which raises another interesting question: does the validity of an argument rest upon its ability to be scaled up to the largest possible implications, or can an argument be valid on a smaller scale even if, writ large, it would be difficult or even dangerous to put into practice all at once?

A second question I asked was: what makes farmers more virtuous than the rest of us? Paul Thompson has mounted a similar critique of Jeffersonian agrarianism generally:

> The idea that agriculture has to serve as a moral example seems pretty old-fashioned in today's world. What is more, the patience of today's farmers, agricultural researchers, and agribusiness employees must wear thin when they are told they must be moral saints, exhibiting virtues of solidarity, self-reliance, stewardship, faith, hope, and charity in an economic environment that is very much like that of any other business. Understood as moral duties that the rural folk must perform for the salvation of our urban population, the Jeffersonian ideals are absurd. Yet the key point is that acquiring this set of virtues can still be understood as a social goal, even as a component of sustainability. (*Agrarian Vision* 191)

In both of these cases, what becomes clear is how deeply the "rational" agrarian critique is entwined in the "romantic" one for Berry. An excellent place to see this is in Berry's comment that "hovering over nearly everything I have written is the question of how a human economy might be conducted with reverence, and therefore with due respect and kindness toward everything involved" (*Imagination in Place* 15). What at first appears to be an assertion about economics ultimately becomes a statement about morality: about the moral virtues of reverence, respect, and kindness. Does it matter that the economic structures in which such virtues are most fully embedded are not easily scalable? In the end, I think not.

Recall Berry's point about the importance of the margins, which suggests that his goal is not to "scale up" his vision to address global hunger or reform industrial agriculture in its current state. In fact, such an attempt at reformation might only lead to the dissolution of Berry's vision, much like the rise of "industrial organic" (recounted by Michael Pollan in *The Omnivore's Dilemma*) could be seen as an attempt by the center to absorb the subversive forces of the margins.

Instead, I think Berry's goal is to have every farm become a marginal farm, have every landscape become a home landscape, and have every person reconnect to the sources of their food in a literal, physical way. His goal, in short, is not to scale up his ideas or reform the center. His goal is to do away with the center altogether.

If Berry sees himself as a visionary, mapping an agricultural ideal for future generations, his use of the essay as a means to articulate that vision (in addition to his fiction and poetry) has both enabled and constrained his moral idealism in important ways.

Eric Freyfogle has observed that "throughout his writing Berry makes use of the literary technique of synecdoche, drawing upon the specific example and circumstances of his life to illustrate larger principles and claims. His skilled use of the technique helps make his writing vivid, exact, and appealing. It also accounts, though, for his dismissal by readers who assume that he is offering his own life as the one and true way to dwell" (*Conservation* 229).

This is more true for Berry's early essays than for his more recent ones, which rely less on autobiography and more on argument, with the notable exception of *The Need to Be Whole*. While many of Berry's early essays are autobiographical (such as "The Long-Legged House," "A Native Hill," and "The Making of a Marginal Farm"), fewer more recent ones include autobiographical details, with some other exceptions being "An Argument for Diversity" (1988), "Economy and Pleasure" (1988), "Nature as Measure" (1989), "Renewing Husbandry" (2004), and "It All Turns on Affection" (2012). (Janet Goodrich surveys Berry's early autobiographical impulse in *The Unforeseen Self in the Works of Wendell Berry*.)

Nevertheless, the degree to which any of Berry's essays—even the ones that are not explicitly autobiographical—are persuasive depends not only on the quality of his argument (or what Aristotle called "logos") but also on Berry's character (or his "ethos"). In fact, it is not too much to say that much of the moral authority Berry seems to convey is the consequence of his own personal story. He is never just an "essayist"; he is always a "farmer-writer."

This usually works to his advantage, but not always, such as when he attempts to speak about subjects of which he does not have direct experience, like one of his rare commentaries on the position of women (*The Unsettling of America* 113–16). Verlyn Klinkenborg has been particularly critical of Berry on this point, noting that "Berry derives his strength as a writer from contact with the earth, the more immediate, the better. . . . But he can also make you feel like you're warming yourself at a bonfire of straw men and women. All too often I'm disturbed, to the point of physical unease, by the involuted, strangely patristic way his writing and thinking move, the grandeur of his modesty."

Part of the unease Klinkenborg feels is likely the result of Berry's infrequent appeals to his reader's emotions (or "pathos"), although this technique is much more present in his fiction. Indeed, Berry's essays generally lack not only emotion but also irony and humor. Although he shows occasional flashes of humor, and sometimes cheekiness, for the most part Berry is a moralist—even a scold—and this can be off-putting to readers looking for a more sympathetic perspective. As Freyfogle puts it, "In much of his writing, Berry speaks with a moral certainty that strikes many readers as smug and didactic. In a literary culture that honors moral ambiguity—or at least is uncomfortable with the appearance of dogma—Berry's light is focused too sharply. Even admirers can wince at his tendency to heavy-handedness" ("The Dilemma of Wendell Berry" 384).

What can get lost in considering the strengths of Berry's *arguments,* however, is that he is not trying to be a systematic thinker. This is not to say that he is not a *consistent* thinker or a *careful* thinker, but it is to say that he is an essayist, with all that the genre of the essay implies. This is clear in many ways: in his use of epigraphs from Montaigne, the originator of the form, whose *Essais* (1580) reflect the French *essayer,* "to try" or "to attempt." It is clear in his use of different essayistic forms: letters ("A Letter to Wes Jackson"), lists ("Six Agricultural Fallacies"), propositions ("Out of Your Car, Off Your Horse"), fragments ("Paragraphs from a Notebook"), and prose poems or lyric essays ("Damage" and "Healing"). And it is clear in his frequent use of phrases such as "What I have been trying to do," "What I am working toward," and "What I have been preparing to say." (Jeffrey Bilbro explores the "sustainability" of these forms in *Virtues of Renewal.*)

Scott Slovic has described Berry's prose style as "steady, subtly modulated, more like plowing a field or floating downriver with the current" (118). But this suggests perhaps a bit too much direction to Berry's prose, which at its best is much more uncertain—which may seem like a strange thing to say of a moral idealist but is true nonetheless. Even Berry has observed this fact in the various collections he has issued over the years.

In *The Unsettling of America*, for instance, he admits, "I have been writing what my experience has made it possible for me to say—with the understanding that it must then await confirmation, amplification, or contradiction from the experience of other people" (160). In the preface to *Home Economics*, he observes, "Such an argument is necessarily an *essay*—a trial or an attempt. It risks error all the time; it is in error, inevitably, some of the time" (ix). And in the preface to *The Way of Ignorance*, he says, "I hope my readers will recognize what an ad hoc affair my essay writing has been. As a writer on agriculture, I have of course been under the influence of other writers, but what I have written has also been influenced immensely by the instruction, conversation, and example of farmers I have known, and by my daily work on my own small farm. I am a small writer as I am a small farmer" (x).

Such comments could, of course, be interpreted as mere rhetorical posturing, the essayist's more elegant version of the standard disclaimer, couched as an acceptance of responsibility, "All errors are my own." (See, for example, the acknowledgments to this book.) But I think not, as the essays themselves sometimes bear out the truth of Berry's admissions of imperfection.

Like Aldo Leopold, whose most powerful essay ("Thinking Like a Mountain," in *A Sand County Almanac*) contains an admission of guilt for having improperly understood the role of predators in the landscape, Berry's most memorable essay (for me, anyway) involves a scene in which he inadvertently destabilizes a hillside by digging a pond into it, an error requiring more than six years of expense and effort to correct ("The Making of a Marginal Farm"). In this small moment, relayed in two short paragraphs, are embodied all of Berry's finest qualities as an essayist: he draws on his direct experience, displays a dry sense of humor, and underlines his moral idealism with a deep sense of his own humility:

> A small hillside farm will not survive many mistakes of that order. Nor will a modest income.
>
> The true remedy for mistakes is to keep from making them. It is not in the piecemeal technological solutions that our society now offers, but in a change of cultural (and economic) values that will encourage in the whole population the necessary respect, restraint, and care. Even more important, it is in the possibility of settled families and local communities, in which the knowledge of proper means and methods, proper moderations and restraints, can be handed down, and so accumulate in place and stay

alive; the experience of one generation is not adequate to inform and control its actions. (339)

Somewhere around 2010, Patty and Mike created their own version of a collapsed hillside, except in their case they did it on purpose. Taking advantage of a cost-sharing program with the Soil and Water Conservation Department, they installed a swale to better manage water runoff at the southern end of the valley.

"We hadn't really had these same issues with water early on," says Patty. "Because we were getting heavier rains, it seemed we were seeing water running in places it hadn't run before. Over time, we were getting these five-inch rains or seven-inch rains."

Climate change had come to Spring Hill, and Patty and Mike needed to adapt. So the Soil and Water Conservation Department did the engineering, and Patty and Mike hired contractors to install the swale, hoping to slow the runoff from these large rain events and increase its infiltration into the soil.

Digging a swale is one thing, but dealing with the effects of climate change on agriculture is another.

"Here's the hard part with climate change," says Mike. "When you get erratic patterns, you can't just simply go, 'Oh, okay, we're going to have a monsoon season every spring, better get used to it.' Then you can adjust, you can develop a system. But you can't develop a system very well for chaos. And that's what's really hard."

Recently, Patty and Mike also installed a solar array on the roof of the packing shed, which will be able to generate all of the farm's electrical needs for the year, thanks to community contributions. It won't stop climate change, but it's another step in the right direction, by reducing the farm's reliance on electricity generated by fossil fuels. (Berry's Lanes Landing Farm has a solar array as well.)

This is the kind of long-term, multigenerational thinking Berry was encouraging as a result of his own failed efforts at improving his hillside back in 1974.

When I asked, gently, what Patty and Mike were thinking about with regard to the future of the farm, Patty was adamant in her response: "I do not want to be the overseer of this farm's demise. I want to continue to build it and work it and then hand it over to somebody else who can carry that on."

Despite having three children, at the moment none of the kids have an interest in taking over the farm, so its future is still uncertain.

"We're having this conversation daily," says Mike.

And the two of them have also reached out to the farm's core group, which Nancy and I eventually joined, to help imagine what the farm might look like after Patty and Mike are no longer able to work the land.

"Our best decisions have been made in community," explains Patty. "It's a way to gain the wisdom of that group, but it's also the pattern, the legacy, the history of this farm."

"I think that's been the key to the farm's success all along," agrees Mike. "That's it's been this larger group of people engaging in and identifying the questions. What is Spring Hill? Is it this place? Is it this set of relationships? Is it a commitment to an idea?"

"As we have continued to live on and from our place," Berry writes in "The Making of a Marginal Farm," "we have slowly begun its restoration and healing. . . . A great deal of work is still left to do, and some of it—the rebuilding of fertility in the depleted hillsides—will take longer than we will live. But in doing these things we have begun a restoration and healing in ourselves" (334).

Spring Hill isn't the abused land of Berry's ancestors, nor the worn-out farm that Aldo Leopold restored near his beloved "shack," about two hundred miles southeast of here near Baraboo, Wisconsin. And even calling what Patty and Mike are doing here "restoration" seems a stretch, since they're not exactly "restoring" anything—not returning the land to some pre-Columbian state, or attempting to re-create one of the previous farms that existed on this site years ago.

In fact, there's no easy label to attach to the kind of relationship Patty and Mike have developed with this land, short of more common terms like "caring" and "love." But perhaps we don't need fancy labels, don't need to market our feelings for a place with a special kind of term. Instead, to paraphrase the poet Mary Oliver, we may only need to let our soft animal bodies love what they love ("Wild Geese").

Perhaps Berry has been right all along: it really does all turn on affection.

TWO

The Gastronome

———

Reading Carlo Petrini in Italy

To study material culture, get to know about it, and spread
that knowledge. This is the movement's principal theoretical
and behavioral guideline: namely, that it is pointless to sing
the praises of fine wine or the smell of good bread if you don't
know how they are produced.

—CARLO PETRINI, *Slow Food: The Case for Taste*

It is not a matter of choosing the right cheese, but of being
chosen. There is a reciprocal relationship between cheese
and customer: each cheese awaits its customer, poses so as to
attract him, with a firmness or a somewhat haughty graininess,
or on the contrary, by melting in submissive abandon.

—ITALO CALVINO, *Mr Palomar*

Carlo Petrini at Identità Golose in Milan, January 2010. (Photo by Bruno Cordioli)

FROM THE FOOT OF THE MOUNTAINS

In 2003, the same year we joined Spring Hill Community Farm, I chanced upon a rather curious book in the food section of our local bookstore. A slim volume, published by Columbia University Press, with a foreword by Alice Waters, the book argued for the value of gastronomes, *osterie,* and *convivia,* and referred throughout to the Ark of Taste, the Presidia, and the Salone del Gusto. It might as well have been a book from outer space, as far as I was concerned, so unfamiliar were these terms and so unlikely to take hold in the popular imagination.

Shows you how much I know.

The book, of course, was the English translation of Carlo Petrini's *Slow Food: The Case for Taste,* and today the Slow Food network he founded counts more than one hundred thousand members in about 160 countries, not to mention hundreds of thousands of people who claim to practice some less formalized version of "slow food."

How did this happen? What exactly does it mean? And how does Slow Food address the vast and complicated space between what's harvested in the field and what ends up on our plates—the processes, in other words, that turn agricultural products into food?

Even though almost forty years have passed since its founding in 1986, Slow Food began as an Italian-directed association, as Geoff Andrews has observed, "and the cultural and regional context in which food cultures thrive there has continued to shape the movement" (viii).

Or, to put it in more food-specific terms, "Petrini's eco-gastronomy . . . has a specific *terroir* of ideas and historical experiences," as Serenella Iovino has insightfully written (*Ecocriticism and Italy* 147).

Which means that to fully understand Slow Food, you need to know something about the Piedmont region of Italy, where Slow Food was born, and where it continues to thrive today.

So in the spring of 2012, after almost ten years of eating Spring Hill vegetables, Nancy, Grace, and I headed to the Piedmont for five months to learn more about where the rest of our food comes from, as well as what Slow Food has to say about that admittedly messy process in between "farm to table."

The first thing we noticed were the lizards, *Podarcis muralis.* They scattered as we walked up the gravel path to our vacation rental, disappearing into nooks and crannies in the cement retaining walls that lined the driveway.

They popped out of tiny drainage pipes when we least expected it, scaring the bejeezus out of us when we approached the garden. And they were the source of most, if not all, of the mysterious rustling sounds we heard as we passed by the rocky borders of our yard. They were simultaneously cute and disconcerting, about the size of a finger—if your finger had legs, a slender tail, and a rapidly flicking tongue.

Our house was located in the Basso Monferrato region of Piedmont, Italy's largest northwestern province. Piedmont means "at the foot of the mountains" (*a piè dei monti*), and on a good day we could see all three ranges of the Alps: Swiss Alps to the north, French Alps to the west, and Ligurian Alps to the south. On a map, the Alps frame Piedmont like an arcing letter "C," with the city of Turin at its center and the Po River valley opening onto the Lombardy plains to the east. Its other major river, the Tanaro, flows northeast from the Ligurian Alps to meet the Po near Lombardy, passing the cities of Pollenzo, Alba, Asti, and Alessandria on its way.

Slow Food was born in what's known as the Langhe, a hilly area that rises southeast of the Tanaro, but the Basso Monferrato lies north of that, between the Tanaro and the Po, and I'd like to think this gave me a little bit of a distance—both physical and critical—from which to reflect on the movement and its charismatic founder.

"If you ask what Slow Food is, you may get ten different answers," one Slow Food staff member warned me when we spoke in Turin, and he wasn't kidding.

Even published attempts at definition can't seem to agree upon an answer. *Slow Food Nation's Come to the Table: The Slow Food Way of Living* (2008), includes seven possible meanings of the term:

1. An alternative to "fast food."
2. A descriptive phrase for food that can be traced to its source, esp. food that is produced without chemical and/or other industrial processes.
3. A celebration of food traditions, emphasizing seasonal and regional qualities.
4. A description of the fundamental human activity of preparing, eating, enjoying, and sharing healthy, flavorful food.
5. A global food initiative seeking to counter the industrialized food system's environmentally and culturally unsustainable methods and their consequences.

6. A relationship with food that centers on the values of "good, clean, and fair": healthy and delicious ingredients, produced with ecologically sound and humane methods, on a fair economic model.

7. Any delicious snack or meal, simple or elaborate, from real ingredients. (Heron)

This lack of precision can be a strength, as it enables a wide range of people to identify themselves as practicing one form or another of "slow food." But it can also be a source of confusion, as it blurs the line between the official pronouncements of the Slow Food organization and the everyday activities of people the world over—potentially diluting the distinctiveness of Slow Food in the process.

This confusion is compounded by the fact that the organization itself has been changing over time, beginning with a focus on educating people about the pleasures of regional cuisine, expanding to encompass a range of ecological concerns, and, most recently, adding an appreciation that social justice must be part of any understanding of what constitutes sustainable food. Today, that evolution is embodied in Slow Food's belief that food should be "good, clean, and fair":

1. GOOD: a fresh and flavorsome seasonal diet that satisfies the senses and is part of one's local culture

2. CLEAN: food production and consumption that does not harm the environment, animal welfare, or human health

3. FAIR: accessible prices for consumers and fair conditions and pay for small-scale producers ("Our Philosophy")

One of the first things that critical distance taught me, therefore, was that it's not easy to separate the Slow Food organization from the idea of "slow food" and its accompanying "movement," and the Italian landscapes, cultures, and culinary traditions out of which the organization, the idea, and parts of the movement have grown.

If we turn to the works of Carlo Petrini for clarification, we may emerge slightly more perplexed, given the quirkiness of their structure and the fact that each of them was originally published in Italian before being translated into English.

Petrini has published four nonfiction collections in English since 2001: *Slow Food: The Case for Taste* (2001 Italy; 2003 US); *Slow Food Nation: Why Our Food Should Be Good, Clean, and Fair* (2005 Italy; 2007 US); *Terra Madre: Forging a New Global Network of Sustainable Food Communities* (2009 Italy; 2010 US); and *Food and Freedom: How the Slow Food Movement Is Changing the World through Gastronomy* (2013 Italy; 2015 US). A fifth book—*Slow Food Revolution: A New Culture for Eating and Living* (2005 Italy; 2006 US)—constitutes a collection of interviews Petrini did with Gigi Padovani, later issued in an updated Italian version as *Slow Food: Storia di un'utopia possibile* (2017).

All of the titles are, to varying degrees, loose mixtures of journalism, essays, and diary entries that are highly self-referential, and occasionally self-aggrandizing. They also happen to be unapologetic promotional vehicles for the Slow Food organization, leading the reader to wonder where the man ends and the organization begins, so tightly are the two bound together in these pages.

That these books are also the product of Petrini's close collaboration with Carlo Bogliotti, a central figure in Slow Food's publishing ventures, only complicates the matter. But since it is ultimately Petrini's name that appears on the spines of these volumes, I consider him the primary author, however much the "other Carlo" may have contributed to the creation and presentation of their contents.

Carlo Petrini—known affectionately as Carlin—was born in 1949 in the town of Bra, which is located about an hour south of Turin, on the western edge of the Langhe. As with most leaders, Petrini owes his success to a happy combination of personal magnetism and fortuitous circumstances.

"He was charismatic and creative from the start," says Irene Ciravegna, a childhood friend. "Carlo and his friends, Ravinale and Azio, were characterized by their activism, and also by their playfulness" (Sardo).

"Ravinale and Azio" are Giovanni Ravinale and Azio Citi, two of Petrini's closest friends, and together they embarked on a series of actions in the 1970s and 1980s that eventually culminated in the founding of Slow Food.

Much like in the United States, the 1970s in Italy were shaped by the events of the 1960s, including the May 1968 uprising in Paris and Italy's "Hot Autumn" of 1969—both of which began as student protests but widened into strikes by disaffected workers, and eventually became a social rebellion that continued through the next decade and beyond.

As Alison Leitch has observed, however, the 1970s in Italy was "a period in which the radical ideals of the student movements of the late 1960s had ended in disillusionment. While some members of this generation had turned in frustration to the power of bullets, others abandoned revolutionary ideals for alternative forms of transformational cultural politics. . . . Alongside his collaborators, Petrini came of age within younger leftist critiques of the Italian Communist Party, which at this time was itself in crisis" ("Virtuous Globalization" 46).

In 1974, after graduating with a degree in sociology from the University of Trento, Petrini helped his friends publish a left-wing newspaper, *In Campo Rosso* (In Red domain), modeled after *Il Manifesto*, the radical leftist newspaper that grew out of the Italian Communist Party in 1969. The following year, they started a pirate radio station, Radio Bra Onde Rosse (Radio Bra Red Waves), to contest the monopoly held by Italy's state-owned broadcasting company. The police shut it down after a month, but the station eventually returned to the air, after Dario Fo and Roberto Benigni campaigned on its behalf. Petrini and company also opened a bookstore, the Cooperativa Libraria La Torre (Tower Book Co-op), and a grocery store, the Spaccio di unità popolare (Store of Popular Unity), which featured local products. And if that wasn't enough, they got Petrini elected to the local town council.

As Irene Ciravegna's comment about their playfulness indicates, however, Petrini, Ravinale, and Azio were far from dour revolutionaries. They called themselves the "Philoridiculous" group, and their cultural politics were delivered in the same comic spirit that Jon Stewart has delivered the news on *The Daily Show*. They were theatrical, and they seemed never to take themselves too seriously, even if their message was ultimately quite important. For instance, they performed a kind of cabaret show as part of the Club Tenco musical festival in 1978, and in 1979 they created a five-day folk music festival, Cantè i'euv (Singing for Eggs), that attracted thousands of young people to Bra for three years running.

Food had always been an important part of Petrini's life, but it wasn't until the 1980s that it assumed a more central place. Part of the political activism in Bra involved a desire to preserve the Langhe's distinct identity, and since the Langhe is home to some of the region's best-known red wines—Barolo, Barbera, and Dolcetto—and its legendary white truffles, it made sense that food would ultimately become a part of those politics. In 1981 Petrini joined with other wine aficionados to form the Free and Praiseworthy Association of the Friends of Barolo, a group dedicated to promoting and developing the region's wine industry. And in 1984 he helped to open a local tavern, Osteria del Boccondivino (the Divine Mouth), which remains one of Bra's most popular restaurants, still located next to the Slow Food headquarters.

But while Bra's comic revolutionaries may have seen little contradiction between their left-leaning politics and the celebration of food and wine, not all the members of the Italian Communist Party agreed with them, and the ensuing controversy was the first sign of a tension that has dogged Slow Food since its inception. Like many Italian leftists, Petrini and his friends were members of a group known as ARCI (Associazione Ricreativa e Culturale Italiana, pronounced "AR-chee"), a network of cultural clubs formed by members of the Partito Comunista Italiano (PCI) in 1957. After complaining about the quality of the food at one of the ARCI clubs in Tuscany, Petrini engaged in a public debate about the role of food in the PCI, and its role in politics more generally. On one side were PCI traditionalists, who believed that food and wine were elitist pleasures, at odds with their revolutionary goals. On the other side was Petrini, who—like other believers in the power of cultural politics—argued that "the personal is political" and that the personal should include an appreciation of food and wine. As Geoff Andrews has put it, Petrini saw that "the pursuit of pleasure was everybody's concern, and was not to be left to hedonists and elitists" (9).

Petrini eventually won this battle, as he was later asked by the national council of ARCI to open an ARCI section of the Friends of Barolo, which later became Slow Food. But the most common criticism of Slow Food remains that it is an elitist organization, more concerned with fine dining than with economic justice for food system workers and other such issues.

In the short term, though, part of what turned the tide in Petrini's favor was a series of environmental scandals and food scares that made Italians think twice about the safety of the food and water they consumed. The first and most immediately damaging was the "methanol scandal" of March 1986, in which a series of Italian winemakers began illegally boosting the alcohol content of their wines by adulterating them with toxic methanol. Two men in particular—Giovanni Ciravegna and his son Daniele, from the Piedmont province of Cuneo—were arrested for distributing Barbera with up to a 5.7 percent methyl alcohol content, which far exceeded the legal limit of 0.3 percent. In a preeminent example of the dangers of short-term thinking, the winemakers were motivated by the fact that the price of wine is tied in part to its alcohol content: in general, the higher the alcohol content, the greater the value of the wine. Methyl (or wood) alcohol occurs naturally in wine at very low doses, but at high doses it can cause blindness and death, and by the end of the scandal twenty-three people had died from methanol poisoning, and many more were hospitalized. As a result, exports of Italian wine fell by more than a third, and total revenues declined by more than a quarter ("Poison Plonk"; Petrini, *Food and Freedom* 10).

The following month, in April 1986, the Chernobyl disaster created widespread fear about the radioactive contamination of food in northern Europe—from fresh vegetables and milk to wild mushrooms, berries, and meat (Suro). And beginning in June, municipalities throughout Italy's Po Valley banned the consumption of tap water due to its contamination by atrazine, a water-soluble herbicide that had infiltrated the region's permeable soils and accumulated in the underlying aquifer (Cori, Faustini, and Settimi 250). When Petrini and friends assembled in the town of Barolo in July 1986, therefore, to form ARCI Gola (later "Arcigola"), the forerunner of Slow Food, the time was ripe for a new approach to food.

In keeping with Petrini's playful spirit, "Arcigola" was a play on words: it signified a new Langhe section of ARCI, but also the affiliation of many founding members to the monthly magazine *La Gola* (1982–89), which explored the culture of food and wine from a variety of disciplinary perspectives. The name "Arcigola" also implied that the sixty-two founding members displayed an "archappetite" or "archgluttony" (*la gola* means "throat," as well as "appetite" or "gluttony" in Italian), which did little to counter critics' belief that this was a society devoted to the pursuit of gustatory pleasure.

When Petrini was unanimously elected president, he became the standard-bearer for a movement that, in retrospect, had yet to find its true purpose (Petrini and Padovani).

Slow Food has not been helped by the fact that its name is somewhat of a misnomer, suggesting that the organization exists in binary opposition to fast food and that "slowness" is its primary modus operandi. As with the name "Arcigola," the name "Slow Food" may have seemed appropriate in the early years of the organization, but it seems less so now—although a case can be made that "Slow Food" has now become more like a brand, one whose literal meaning has been eclipsed by the multiplicity of other meanings with which people now associate it.

In the early years, though, "Slow Food" did indeed mean the opposite of fast. This was perhaps best exemplified by Arcigola's signature demonstration to protest the opening of a McDonald's in the Piazza di Spagna, below the Spanish Steps in Rome, in which protestors were armed with bowls of penne pasta. It was there that the name "Slow Food" was coined, leading to the publication of the Slow Food manifesto in November 1987, and later, in December 1989, to the launching of the International Slow Food Movement at the Opéra Comique in Paris.

In their analysis of the Slow Food manifesto, Wendy Parkins and Geoffrey Craig describe "slowness" as "an overdetermined signifier which is constantly interrogated and redeployed within the movement in response to factors such as a diversification of aims and projects and the increasing heterogeneity of membership" (52). In other words, "slowness" is so pliable a term it can come to mean almost anything, which has worked well as the Slow Food movement has grown far beyond its dedicated core of supporters in Piedmont.

But the manifesto itself reflects the Manichaean logic of Slow Food's origins, in which the fast/slow binary eclipses a range of more complex understandings of food's past and futures in the modern world.

Written by founding member Folco Portinari (notably, not by Petrini), the manifesto is brief enough to reprint in full:

> Our century, which began and has developed under the insignia of industrial civilization, first invented the machine, and then took it as its life model.
>
> We are enslaved by speed and have all succumbed to the same insidious virus: Fast Life, which disrupts our habits, pervades the privacy of our homes and forces us to eat Fast Foods.
>
> To be worthy of the name, *Homo Sapiens* should rid himself of speed before it reduces him to a species in danger of extinction.
>
> A firm defense of quiet material pleasure is the only way to oppose the universal folly of Fast Life.
>
> May suitable doses of guaranteed sensual pleasure and slow, long-lasting enjoyment preserve us from the contagion of the multitude who mistake frenzy for efficiency.
>
> Our defense should begin at the table with Slow Food. Let us rediscover the flavors and savors of regional cooking and banish the degrading effects of Fast Food.

In the name of productivity, Fast Life has changed our way of being and
threatens our environment and our landscapes. So Slow Food is now
the only truly progressive answer.

That is what real culture is all about: developing taste rather than demean-
ing it. And what better way to set about this than an international
exchange of experiences, knowledge, projects?

Slow Food guarantees a better future. Slow Food is an idea that needs
plenty of qualified supporters who can help turn this (slow) motion
into an international movement, with the little snail as its symbol.

Parkins and Craig helpfully point to Janet Lyon's *Manifestoes: Provocations of the Modern* (1999), which identifies three characteristics of the manifesto genre, and which in turn allows us to understand the Slow Food manifesto as emblematic of its form. Parkins and Craig note that the manifesto (1) "deploys a selective and condensed version of history which has led to the present moment of crisis"; (2) enumerates a list of grievances or demands, constructing a struggle against oppression through the use of a dichotomy; and (3) employs declarative rhetoric to challenge the enemy "while uniting its audience in a call to action" (53–54).

In short, the manifesto offers a simplified vision of the world that can act as a rallying cry for more complex forms of politics to follow. (Subsequent Slow Food manifestos, such as the "Manifesto on the Future of Food," Michael Pollan's *In Defense of Food: An Eater's Manifesto,* and Alice Waters's *We Are What We Eat: A Slow Food Manifesto,* are longer documents that offer more complex arguments.)

The original version of the manifesto, which was longer than the final, official one, was more explicit about its generic heritage. "Since the dawn of the century," it proclaimed, "many manifestos have been churned out and declaimed, with speed being the main ideology." Filippo Tommaso Marinetti's "Futurist Manifesto," for example, published in 1909, declared that "the splendor of the world has been enriched by a new beauty: the beauty of speed" (Petrini and Padovani 71).

More troubling than the manifesto's dichotomy of fast and slow, however, is the way its language likely reinforced the perception that Slow Food was more committed to creating a society of snobbish gourmets than advancing a social and cultural revolution through food. As Parkins and Craig point out, "It could be argued that the manifesto is by its nature not only a genre lacking in rhetorical subtlety but anti-democratic, denouncing the status quo from an implied position of truth/superiority to those who need to be exposed or enlightened: it is not a dialogue or an exchange among equals" (55). For all the talk of rediscovering "the flavors and savors of regional cooking," therefore, there is an equal amount of "developing taste" among "qualified supporters" to combat "the contagion of the multitude."

Today, when I think of the spread of Slow Food around the world, it is hard not also to think of the spread of Italian food, which has conquered the globe in its ubiquity. Pizza can be had as far afield as Durban, South Africa, and Los Angeles, California; it can be found as easily in Tokyo as it can be in Rio de Janeiro.

Yet I also think of another analogy, one less well known but perhaps equally compelling, at least in my mind.

In 1951, a ten-year-old boy named George Rau was visiting northern Italy on vacation, much as my eight-year-old daughter Grace was doing on our trip there. As enraptured by the European wall lizards as we were, he decided to bring some home with him, so he stuffed six lizards in a sock and carried them back to Cincinnati, where he lived.

"My plan was always to release them," he told a reporter for the *Cincinnati Enquirer* in 2011. "The climate was almost exactly the same (as in northern Italy) and I thought it would be fun to see them climbing on the rock walls where I grew up" (Dennis).

His plan worked all too well, and the lizards began spreading throughout the neighborhood. Locals soon began calling them "Lazarus lizards," since Rau was the stepson of Fred Lazarus III, the well-known owner of the Lazarus department store chain, now part of Macy's.

Today, hundreds of thousands of Lazarus lizards can be found throughout the Cincinnati region, from north of Columbus to the neighboring states of Kentucky and Indiana. Colonies have also been spotted as far away as New York City and Vancouver Island, British Columbia.

According to University of Cincinnati biologist Ken Petren, the lizards have not spread uniformly throughout the region but in isolated pockets, because they prefer rocky terrain or crumbling walls on southern-facing slopes—just like the crumbling walls that lined our Piedmontese driveway. "It's a very patchy environment where they can make it through the winter," Petren said (Dennis).

That didn't stop other people from replicating Rau's initial introduction, however, and fifteen people admitted to Petren that they had intentionally transferred the lizards to new areas (Dennis).

The analogy is not perfect, of course, as there are considerable differences between European wall lizards and the Slow Food movement! But it is instructive, I think, to remember that ideas are also living organisms, which require a certain habitat in which to flourish and enthusiastic partisans to assist in their migration. And, like so many species, sometimes they must adapt or die.

The idea that there is one "Slow Food Story" is complicated by the fragmentary nature of Petrini's writings, as well as the fact that there are multiple Slow Food stories—or "stories that underlie the story," as Rebecca Solnit would have it.

Nevertheless, recognizing that Petrini is as much a philosopher as he is an activist can also help us to understand his books in a different light: rather than just a random collection of his thoughts on food, Petrini's books in fact constitute a multivolume intellectual autobiography—fragmentary and anecdotal, to be sure, but one that tracks not only the evolution of his own ideas but also the evolution of the Slow Food movement as a whole.

And while this intellectual aspect of Petrini can make his writing seem dry and uninspiring to some readers, as a number of critical reviews on Amazon.com attest, Petrini's books are still worth our time and effort, as they are more than mere manifestos: they are portraits of a movement in action.

Understanding Petrini's books, however, also requires two other types of Slow Food stories: stories of the producers who are at the center of everything Slow Food is about, and stories of what Petrini has come to call "co-producers" (that is, consumers, like me), who perform "the final act of the production process" (*Slow Food Nation* 165).

As Petrini himself has written, "One can talk about any place in the world simply by talking about the food that is produced and consumed there. In telling stories about food, one tells stories about agriculture, about restaurants, about trade, about global and local economies, about tastes, and even about famine. . . . When one comes into contact with these stories, one understands more and more clearly that food is the primary means of interpreting reality, the world around us. Food reflects the complexity of the present-day world and of past history, the intertwining of cultures, and the overlapping of different philosophies of production" (*Slow Food Nation* 37–38).

A LANDSCAPE OF CONTRADICTIONS

It's not every day you get to spend five months in Italy, so when we learned we would be able to do so, thanks to a Fulbright grant, we decided to make the most of it.

Figuring out what "making the most of it" meant was harder than it seemed, however, because we constantly felt torn between wanting to embrace every last stereotype about the good life in Italy, and knowing that these stereotypes exist for a reason—namely, that they were manufactured to capture the imagination of people just like us.

Stephanie Malia Hom neatly summarizes some of the romantic expectations surrounding Italy in *The Beautiful Country: Tourism and the Impossible State of Destination Italy*:

> Italy is publicized as the land of quaint medieval hill towns rather than of sprawling suburbs; the producer of handcrafted leather goods, not mass-produced schlock; and the purveyor of locally grown, kilometre-zero cuisine that stands against all forms of fast food. The fact that the Fascist regime (1922–43) completely refurbished a number of those quaint Tuscan hill towns, that illegal migrants make many of those "Made in Italy" leather goods in sweatshops outside of Florence, or that Italy ranks tenth in the world in the number of McDonald's restaurants by country is hardly ever brought to light. In such ways, destination Italy becomes linked to ideas of tradition and authenticity that have been invented and staged primarily for tourists.
>
>   This patina of tradition and authenticity dissociates destination Italy from the messiness of globalization. It structures the fantasy of an Italy that does not fully take part in, say, the growing inequality between rich and poor or the escalation of environmental catastrophes related to climate change—two direct consequences of globalization and its underpinning ideology, neoliberalism. In this fantasy, destination Italy remains a

country of *piccole industrie* (small industries) and family-based capitalism
in which the social relations between people trump the economies of
scale. The natural landscape is all cypress groves, vineyards, and olive
trees unaffected by global warming. Urban areas stand free of cookie-
cutter sprawl and slick architectural eyesores. (10)

So what did we do? We rented a four-hundred-year-old stone house in a
quaint medieval hill town, ate as much locally grown, kilometer-zero cuisine
as we could find, and spent much of our time visiting family-based *piccole
industrie* situated among vineyards and olive trees. And we did it all with a
huge dose of self-consciousness and more than a little bit of irony.

But Hom's point is well taken: in fact, it was a big part of what motivated
our visit in the first place. Are ideas of tradition and authenticity really a
"patina" that "dissociates destination Italy from the messiness of globalization," or can these ideas effectively function as instruments of resistance,
helping to enable a food system in which social relations between people
really do trump economies of scale?

Although we were well aware that most Italians lived in cities and sprawling
suburbs, we chose to live in Villadeati, a tiny hill town in Monferrato, because
we already lived in a city in the United States, and why should we do abroad
what we already did at home? Moreover, we wanted to experience the Piedmont landscape firsthand—its history, culture, and geography—rather than
from a book. We wanted to know what it was like to live and eat in one place
for more than a week's vacation. We wanted to watch the seasons change from
winter to spring and summer, and we wanted to change along with them.

Romantic stereotypes notwithstanding, this turned out to be a very
good idea.

For starters, just because we lived in a medieval hill town doesn't mean that
globalization passed us by. Instead, it existed—and continues to exist—in an
uneasy tension with the histories and traditions that define the region and its
culinary identity.

For example, we did our food shopping at markets and vendors across
the size spectrum: we shopped at bigger supermarket chains (Esselunga and
Famila) in the larger towns; we frequented local butchers, a produce shop,

and a smaller supermarket chain (Dimeglio) in a neighboring village; and at least once a week (sometimes more often) we visited the outdoor markets held in the main piazza of towns throughout the region.

Even at the weekly markets, which you might imagine would be bastions of tradition and authenticity, you are just as likely to find bins filled with plastic trinkets from China and racks of the latest "fast fashion" from Bangladesh as you are to come across a wheel of fresh robiola cheese or some locally made *paste di meliga* (cornmeal cookies), both of which are typical of Piedmont.

Traveling from town to town also required a leased car and plenty of diesel fuel, not to mention nerves of steel for rounding blind curves and navigating the narrowest of passageways. Public transit existed, but you could spend half your day getting where you wanted to go—and arrive just in time to watch the shops close for the *pausa*, or three-hour lunch break, that's still widely practiced throughout the region.

Perhaps most noticeably, while the rolling hills framed by snow-capped Alps make for a nice picture postcard, the reality is a bit noisier and smellier, as is the case with almost every working landscape. Imported tractors, leaf blowers, and Weedwackers were hard at work on almost any given day, and the scent of burning brush was an almost constant companion, making us wonder whether anyone in Italy had ever heard of a woodchipper or a compost pile. Radio, television, and *telefonini* (cell phone) towers also dotted the landscape, and the local electronics retailers (Trony and Media World) sold every kind of digital gadget imaginable. That our newly installed Wi-Fi had trouble passing through the foot-wide stone walls of our centuries-old farmhouse perhaps best encapsulated globalization's uneasy entry into the farthest reaches of Italy's history and geography.

The landscape of Slow Food's origins, therefore, is a landscape of contradictions—or, at the very least, a landscape of considerable complexity.

One need not venture far into Carlo Petrini's books to see that this is the case. In the first chapter of *Slow Food: The Case for Taste,* for example, Petrini introduces the origins of Slow Food by speaking not of *il bel paese* (the beautiful country) but of the industrial pollution generated by the leather-tanning industry that defined Bra during the late nineteenth and twentieth centuries. He quotes the poet Giovanni Arpino, whose "Cronaca Piemontese" declares:

Our town was ringed
by a belt of factories
where blackened men scraped and hung hides;
in the April sun the air smelled of leather.
We its citizens, every one, leaving here
bear within us a heaviness of stone
of thick fog and extracts of tannin.
[Bra] has a heart that's been tanned
and left to dry in the sun
beneath the gaze of old gardens. (1–2)

Although Petrini observes that the age of tannin helped to create "a history of workers' cooperatives" and "a strong tradition of joining organized groups," he primarily uses the tanning industry as example of the mark left on Bra by industrial production, particularly (in Velso Mucci's words) "the great morbid stink of rotting scraps of hide" and "the acrid sulphurous whiff of chemical tanning agents" (2). All in all, says Petrini, speaking of Bra in the years prior to the arrival of Slow Food, "we are not talking about a gastronomic capital" (3).

Similarly, in the first diary entry of *Slow Food Nation,* Petrini reflects on the experience of driving on SS 231 (SS stands for *strada statale,* or state highway), which links Bra and Alba, and which I, too, traveled on a regular basis. The road is "notorious for its inadequacies as a thoroughfare," Petrini says, and "runs along a long string of factories, suburban shopping centers, and big-box stores that are among the worst architectural horrors that could possibly be imagined." It is a "depressing experience," he continues, "to drive through such squalid surroundings, especially as the slowness of the road always gives you plenty of time to meditate at length on 'development' and its effects" (7).

Not exactly words from the tourism bureau. Yet Petrini is notable for his honesty, his lack of pretension, and his unwillingness to turn away from the less appealing aspects of the Piedmont landscape, which are not merely aesthetic but what Stacey Alaimo calls "trans-corporeal"—interpenetrating with our bodies through the air, the water, the soil, and, most intimately, the food we eat (Alaimo 2).

Petrini is not the only Piedmont resident to have spoken of the region's ecological challenges, of course. Serenella Iovino has gone so far as to describe the landscape of the Po Valley, which begins in the Piedmont Alps, as a "necro-region" rather than a "bio-region," in order to call attention to its "long and deeply compromised" ecology, the result of "decades of uncontrolled industrial development and urban sprawl" that left it in "a detectable state of cultural and ecological abandon" ("Restoring" 102).

Yet both Iovino and Petrini seek to make this region whole again through stories: Iovino by imagining future stories that might reanimate our relationship with such places, and Petrini by calling attention to food stories that have either been lost or ignored for too long.

In the introduction to an atlas of the agro-food products of the Po River, prepared by students at the University of Gastronomic Sciences, Petrini was heartened by the number of food products the students identified. "The Po Valley is not dead," he declared. Like every great river, he acknowledged, the Po has been a victim of "exploitation, degradation, and abandonment," but these setbacks do not negate "the liveliness of the productions that are found there." An atlas such as the students produced, Petrini observed, will prove an "invaluable tool" for future projects that want to revitalize places and landscapes in all their ecological, cultural and social complexity (Introduction [my translation], n.p.).

Looking out at this landscape from the balcony of our house, which we did as often as we were able, it wasn't hard to bracket these contradictions and complexities and merely breathe, letting the undeniable beauty of the place wash over us like in a dream.

What made it beautiful wasn't one thing in isolation, but the way all the different elements of the landscape worked together: the variety of small farm fields, the undulating hills (some forested, some not, towns creeping up the sides of others), the squat farmhouses with their tile roofs and colored stucco walls, the snow-capped Alps rising in the distance, mingling with the clouds on a sunny day, and the way the light would alter the scene from one day to the next, so that every day was a new adventure.

The trouble is, our senses—especially our vision, the most dominant of our senses—can take us only so far. They can help us be present in the moment (no small feat, that), but they can't provide the context we need to really know a place in depth: to understand its history, its traditions, its culture, and its ecological functioning. They can't, in other words, answer one of the more important questions we can ask about this place: why does the landscape look this way?

For that we need another sort of knowledge, culled from histories, works of art, and humanistic and scientific studies.

Were I to ask this question back home, in the midwestern United States, my answer would be different and somewhat more straightforward. Although North America has been inhabited for at least thirteen thousand years, and its landscape altered through fire, hunting, and other human activities, the survey system that gave the Northwest Territory its distinctive grid pattern is less than 250 years old, the result of Jefferson's Land Ordinance of 1785.

In Italy, the history of agricultural land use is longer, and much less uniform. Emilio Sereni's *History of the Italian Agricultural Landscape*, a classic of environmental history, begins with the Greek colonization of Italy in the first century BCE and chronicles centuries of land use, in which Roman roads and aqueducts enable medieval clearings and plantations, followed by the construction of Renaissance villas and enclosures, and the transformations that accompanied the railroads and mechanization of the Industrial Revolution.

We need not go that far back, however, to understand how the vista before us is connected to the social relations of the past—and present.

Whereas the drive to Prairie Farm involves passing acres of corn and soybeans, what distinguishes this Piedmont landscape is the smallness of its parcels and the diversity of crops they support. Here you might pass a vineyard of Barbera grapes, followed by a field of wheat, and another planted in lavender, all opposite a hazelnut orchard. Around the bend you might come upon some pastureland bordered by rows of poplar trees and neighbored by a field of sunflowers. It's a patchwork quilt, rather than the uniformity of monoculture, one punctuated by a similar diversity of architectural forms, from farmhouses and villas to stables, warehouses, and barns.

Some of this is due to geography, certainly, as cropping huge rotations of corn and soybeans requires a large expanse of relatively flat land, which is hard to come by here (though parts of Piedmont do lend themselves to limited forms of monoculture, including corn, grapes, and rice, as we will see). Some is also due to the variety of natural habitats that permit or restrict the cultivation of certain plant varieties, including the same kind of features at work in Prairie Farm, such as microclimates and soil types.

But what has also shaped it, and any agricultural landscape, are a range of socioeconomic factors that can be difficult to discern at first glance. These include things like who owns or rents the land, whether inheritance laws encourage or prevent its fragmentation, how much capital and ability the owners or tenants have to invest in its improvement (through purchasing equipment, erecting and maintaining buildings, buying seeds, and so forth), whether the necessary number of workers can be found to plant and harvest the crops, whether markets exist for certain crops and how easily farmers can reach them, and what government and trade policies (regulations, subsidies, and quotas) may affect the choice and price of certain crops.

In the case of Piedmont, however, another factor was hiding in plain sight; it just took me forever to see it.

Unlike in the United States, where memorials commemorating the World War II veterans who fought "over there" are located in places largely unaffected by the war, Italy has monuments and memorials to the resistance movement (1943–45) in situ around the country, and this is especially true for rural Piedmont.

As Adriano Balbo observed in his diary on the resistance in the Langhe, "Fascists are in the cities; there is no fascist in the hills. Just peasants awaiting the end of the war" (Balbo 32; quoted in Armiero 158).

What may seem to be merely markers of political history, however, could equally be considered markers of environmental history, I realized, given the significance of World War II to the region's demographics, and thus its landscape.

Mauro Agnoletti puts the importance of this period in its full historical context:

At least until the second postwar period, much of the country's rural landscape was still strongly influenced by traditional agro-silvo-pastoral models developed during the previous century, and sometimes going all the way back to the Etruscan period and Greek civilization. The following decades, however, witnessed deep transformations. Due to demographic growth and the expansion of agriculture into mountain areas, the rural landscape attained the peak of its development in the decades between the late nineteenth and early twentieth century. The resulting landscape was one of great complexity, enhanced by the stratification of the prints left by so many civilizations on the land, and the country's complex orography and climatic variability. In the second postwar period, however, we observe a gradual simplification and homogenization of the rural landscape. (12)

We certainly saw this as we made our way from town to town, with some towns clearly vibrant and others seeming all but abandoned.

Throughout the twentieth century, our own town's population had been declining, from a high of more than two thousand people in the early part of the century down to around five hundred when we were there. We could sense this on our evening *passeggiata,* as we strolled up and down the Via Roma that exists in almost every Piedmont town, with many shutters closed and locked, and every other house used only occasionally by people whose permanent residence was elsewhere, usually in the city. Most of all, though, we experienced this decline on a daily basis, as we were forced to drive everywhere for our provisions, since no shops or services remained in the town, save for the post office, which itself was open only a few mornings a week.

This, I finally realized, was the central context for Petrini's establishment of Slow Food: a recognition that the industrialization of Italian agriculture and the changes to rural life that have occurred since World War II have not been all for the good.

As David Moss has observed, "In the past half-century, the place of agriculture in Italian society has been utterly transformed. Many of the practices, values and social relations of a rural world less than two generations away have been dispatched into history by the combined forces of the industrial economic miracle, massive emigration from the countryside of the South and Northeast, the impact of the European Union's Common Agricultural Policy, and contemporary agribusiness" (12–13).

Petrini observes as much in *Slow Food: The Case for Taste,* noting that in the beginning of the twentieth century, rural agriculturalists in Italy accounted for more than 60 percent of the labor force, but in 2001, they represented less than 7 percent (80). "At a time when the application of the industrial model to agriculture has reached a point of no return," he asserts, "the only feasible solution is the revival of traditional models of farming that respond to the new demand for quality and respect for the environment" (63).

It's undeniable that a sense of loss for the preindustrial landscape is part of what motivated Petrini, but this heartache is coupled by a desire not merely to preserve the region's disappearing food cultures and traditions but also to build an economic model that will enable those cultures to flourish long into the future.

That this sounds a lot like Wendell Berry should come as no surprise, because Petrini has made no secret of Berry's influence on him.

Berry's influence becomes most clear in *Slow Food Nation,* in which Petrini writes, "An interest in agriculture, its evolution, and its changes should be a priority for everyone who eats: 'Eating is an agricultural act,' in the magisterial definition of Wendell Berry, the Kentucky farmer, poet, and essayist" (66).

But this was not always the case for either Petrini or Slow Food, as Petrini indicated in an interview he conducted with Berry for the newspaper *La Stampa* in 2004 (later reprinted in Petrini's edited collection of interviews, *Loving the Earth: Dialogues on the Future of Our Planet*). Slow Food, Petrini admitted, "was born as a gastronomic movement" but has evolved "more and more towards the issues concerning the production of food and therefore agriculture." It combined "the pleasure of eating well" with "the responsibility for promoting sustainable production techniques and respect for local cultures" (606–9).

At a July 2003 meeting on globalization at the estate of San Rossore, near Pisa, which Petrini also attended, Berry reflected on the impact that Italian agriculture had on his own thinking about agrarianism more than forty years prior. His experience was hauntingly familiar:

> In 1961 and 1962, my wife and daughter and I spent several months in Florence, learning in the process to speak a dialect of tourist-Italian that I cannot now reproduce. We lived in a cottage that once had been the barn of a monastery south of the Arno. . . . From our windows we could see farmers at work with their teams of white cattle on a terraced slope on which crops of grain stood among olive trees and grape vines. Reeds and willows growing along the waterways provided stakes for the vines and osiers with which to tie the vines to the stakes.
>
> I had never imagined such farming as this was. I studied it carefully and with excitement. It was a way of farming that was lovingly adapted to its place. It was highly diversified. It wasted nothing. It was scaled to permit close attention to details. It was beautiful. I began to understand that probably the supreme works of art in Tuscany were its agricultural landscapes.
>
> Another thing I understood was that this great, still contemporary, daily-working work of art was very old. The terraced slopes and small valley fields had been farmed in essentially the same way by essentially the same people for many centuries. Through all that time, these people had

performed a continuous act of fidelity to the land, to the seasons, to their crops and animals, and to human need. They had maintained their work and their faithfulness through hardships of every kind.

And so my first visit to Tuscany taught me something of the appearance, the practical means, the meaning, and the value of a way of farming developed in a long association between a local community and its land. I have not ceased to think of these things in the years since. (*Citizenship Papers* 175–76)

When Berry returned for a second visit in the fall of 1992, however, he found that "the traditional agriculture I was so fortunate to see only thirty years before had all too expectably given way to industrialization." He was careful not to lapse into a nostalgia for the premodern: "I am not saying that the old is all good and the new is all bad. Nor am I saying that there is something invariably destructive in the use of industrial machinery in agriculture." But he labeled "the substitution of industrial standards for agrarian standards . . . a costly mistake" (176).

Reiterating what he has said elsewhere, Berry claimed that "industrialism damages agriculture by removing the cultural, economic, and technological constraints that assure propriety of scale. When the scale of work is appropriate to the place where the work is done, then attention, memory, and affection have a consequential power, and our limited human intelligence can be used without extreme or permanent damage. But limited intelligence minus traditional restraints plus unlimited funds equals unlimited damage. Only an appropriately-scaled, locally-adapted, locally owned economy can make a commonwealth of a 'natural resource'" (177).

The conclusion Berry presented to this gathering on globalization, while predictable, is notable for its consonance with what Petrini was also coming to realize. "The global economy is no more discerning than any other weapon of mass destruction," Berry proclaimed, speaking just a few months after the 2003 invasion of Iraq. "That is why many of us are working now to develop local economies, partnerships of local producers and local consumers, which are the only effective answer to great concentrations of wealth and power" (179).

While Berry has always been primarily concerned with the opposition of industrial agriculture and sustainable agriculture, Petrini found himself more and more focused on the opposition of industrial production methods and artisanal production methods—though it is clear that agricultural and artisanal production are closely connected in his mind.

In *Slow Food: The Case for Taste,* he offers a paean to a vanished world of pre–World War II food communities, which those memorials to the resistance movement so vividly came to signify for me:

> Clearly the changed relationship between contemporary man and food derives from the slashing of the umbilical cord that once bound the world of the peasant farmer to the world of consumption, the producer of food to the diner. In today's society, almost no one procures their daily wine directly from a trusted vine dresser/winemaker anymore, or goes to a farmstead to pick up a week's supply of eggs, a chicken, or a rabbit. Almost no one is personally acquainted with the baker who makes the bread she puts on the table, or the sausage maker who personally takes part in the butchering of pigs and the preparation of salami and other meat products, or the cheese maker who prepares cheese from the milk of his own sheep or goats. The small food stores and the *osterie* that were once to be found in even the smallest villages, and to which people went not only to get their provisions but to keep in touch with village life and meet their neighbors, closed their doors one by one, and in the cities the spread of the supermarkets (which now control 40 percent of the food retail business) is inexorably smothering the small retailers, with all that entails in loss of human rapport, direct selection of merchandise, and exchange of information and acquaintance. . . .
>
> In this way we have lost touch forever with an immense heritage of wisdom relating to the cultivation of fruits and vegetables, the raising of animals, and the preparation of artisanal specialties and even traditional local dishes. (67–68)

Petrini argues instead that "food producers ought to be at the center of attention, to make up for the low esteem they have hitherto enjoyed, and rewarded for their work in rescuing a species of livestock, a fruit or vegetable, a variety of cured meat or cheese. This isn't just an Italian problem; it is the same in many other countries around the world, each of them a treasury of local specialties and individual traditions, a specific 'heritage'" (51).

Looking back on Slow Food's origins, Petrini acknowledges that "by emphasizing small-scale artisanal production and entrepreneurial capacity that respects the environment while ignoring the large-scale food industry that does, after all, exist, we ran the risk of shutting ourselves up inside a snail shell." But the fact is, he claims, "none of us believed in the 'good old days of yore.'" Rather than "a rearguard action," he insists, Slow Food should be seen instead as "an avant-garde response to the minefield of modernity that we have to traverse" (86).

Nostalgia, Petrini ultimately contends, is "the one sentiment I am unable to feel" (111).

That the story of Italian agriculture is not simply one of decline was brought home to me one rainy afternoon in June when I walked up the hill to talk with our neighbors, Edoardo "Dino" Carelli and his wife, Stefania, who lived with Dino's brother Carlo in the house next door. Dino and Stefania had shared some of their *genuino* (homemade) wine with us, along with a harvest of lettuce from their garden, and as a thank-you we had brought them the results of our own experiments with *torta di nocciole* (hazelnut cake) and good ol' American chocolate chip cookies.

All three of them were then retired, but Dino's family had lived in Villadeati for many years, and Dino—then in his eighties—enjoyed reminiscing about the past. As we sat on their veranda, the rain echoing off the roof, Dino filled in some of the gaps in my knowledge of the town, with the help of my friend and translator Toni Hilton.

Villadeati's most prominent landmark, for instance, is the castle that sits atop the hill (and which is now owned by the Feltrinelli family, a leading Italian publisher). Dino's grandfather had been the administrator of the castle's lands, and in exchange for helping the owner sell off some of those lands in the most profitable way possible, he was given the house in which Dino now lives, along with four hectares of land. Dino remembers the town at its liveliest, when there was a school, a grocery store, and a fabric store, for the women of the town to make clothes.

Before the war, Dino said, "somebody could live on a hectare of land. Every house had a stall, and a wine cellar, and a chicken coop. If you didn't have much, you had a cow. The ones who were well-off had two cows. A little wine, a little wheat, and a little to sell. You ate a bean soup for lunch, or pasta and beans, an omelette with herbs. Occasionally a piece of boiled beef on Sunday—and those were well-off. The rest did the best they could, the *contadino,* the small shareholders. They had to be content with what they had."

The war, however, changed everything. "Between Italians and Americans there were fifty years of difference," Dino said. In 1946, he observed, it took six workers a whole day to plant a row of grape vines two hundred meters long. (Because the soil was hard from being so high in calcium, they had to work it with hoes rather than with a horse and plow.) But in 1948, a farmer in the village bought a tractor that had been used by the U.S. military for transporting artillery, and he added a plow. As a result, he was able to plant the same row of vines by himself in about thirty minutes.

Although Villadeati, in the Monferrato region, was only about fifty kilometers from the Langhe, where Carlo Petrini was raised, the differences between the two areas could not be more striking.

"In the Langhe area, they were so much farther from the city," Dino pointed out. "To transport from the Langhe was much more difficult because of the hills, and you only had horses up until the war. Here, Villadeati was always in a better position because you're starting at the top, and you go down, and then you've got a straight road to Turin, a flat road. So Villadeati was wealthier and was advantaged because of that. With the horses, it was an important thing, going up and down hills. Then, with tractors and trucks, it became much less important; our advantage diminished."

Nevertheless, Dino used that advantage to *his* advantage, while it lasted. His wife, Stefania, was one of seven children from a farm family outside of Alba, in the Langhe. They were sharecroppers, and when Stefania was twelve, she moved to Bra with her father, who took a job in a tannery. Because of the situation with transport, the people in the Langhe were miserable, Dino said, whereas the Monferrini were rich, because they were favored by their topography.

"I had to go all the way over there to get a wife, because she appreciated Monferrini. I was trying to help the Langhe out," Dino joked.

"We were very snobbish about the people over there, because they were poor; they dressed miserably. And so she obviously fell for the first well-dressed, good-looking Monferrino that crossed her path," he said with a laugh.

Dino admitted that the Langhe brought something else exceptional into his life: Stefania's gnocchi, which she learned to make from her mother and her aunts in Alba.

"The gnocchi she makes are unbelievable," Dino said. "She makes these little pillows of potatoes, only with certain potatoes. And I plant the right potatoes so she can make the gnocchi. These potatoes have to be at just the right age, because it has to do with moisture. They have to be the right kind, at the right moment. One teaspoon too much of flour, and you can throw it all away."

"I would make you gnocchi, but now is not the moment," Stefania added. "In fifteen days, it will be. If it was only ten days, I would stretch it. I wouldn't trust potatoes of other people. And absolutely not those bought—you don't know where they come from."

In an important section of *Slow Food Nation*, Petrini's follow-up to *Slow Food: The Case for Taste*, Petrini reflects at length on the metaphor of the "umbilical cord" connecting producers and consumers, agricultural and gastronomic acts, and places near and far.

> There was a sort of umbilical cord that was guaranteed by the proximity between agricultural practice, processing, and consumption. Many activities of this productive cycle were the appanage of the consumer himself, who was thus in effect a *co-producer*. This was not just a prerogative of the rural world; in the town, the same thing happened—whether it was a legacy of recent life in the country, contact and the exchange of knowledge and information between the producer and the townsman was manifested in the shops and markets.
>
> Nowadays, that umbilical cord has been cut, and dramatically so. Opening a packet of pasta in sauce, which we only need to heat up for a few minutes in a saucepan, makes us forget, neglect to think about what kind of pasta we are eating, what tomatoes were used in the sauce, what other ingredients went into that dish and what their history has been. . . .
>
> This is not to say that we should all go back to living in the country or to producing our food ourselves, but the severed umbilical cord must be repaired—through the search for information, through a commitment by the producers to provide information about their processes and their transportation of raw materials, through a willingness on the part of the large-scale distributors to redesign their system to achieve greater localization, through us and our desire to become co-producers again as we once would have been as a matter of course, and through our efforts to set

up new food communities, in which the new gastronome is simply the final
link, but an essential one in the whole chain. Food communities should
unite producers and co-producers where both parties feel, and operate, as
new gastronomes. (167–68)

Berry's intellectual shadow looms large over this section of *Slow Food
Nation,* so much so that at times it seems as if Petrini is simply Berry in
a well-cut Italian suit. The term "co-producer" seems to be an original
invention of Petrini's, but much of the rest of his argument—particularly
the importance of food communities and local adaptation—unquestionably
comes from Berry.

Reiterating his earlier claim about Berry's importance, Petrini generously
acknowledges his influence:

Wendell Berry, fine poet that he is, has condensed into a single phrase the
whole meaning of being a co-producer: "Eating is an agricultural act." We
should adopt these words and make them our motto, for they condense
the whole awareness that, by our choices as the final consumers in a long
process that starts from the land, we influence production, the styles of
management of the earth and the environment, as well as the future of
farming communities. It also conveys all the solidarity, the sense of *community,* almost of belonging, that we should feel toward the producers of
our food. Bringing them closer to us, physically and also psychologically,
is a mission for the new gastronome. But the sense of community must be
shared by the producers, with awareness and through the most complete
openness. To paraphrase Berry, therefore, one might also argue that "cultivating, stock-raising, and processing must be a gastronomic act." (169)

It was one thing to spend a season trying to understand how a community-
supported agriculture farm works—something Petrini also mentions promi-
nently in this section, as an example of Berry's principle of "local adaptation."
But it is another entirely to try to understand food processing as a "gastronomic act," particularly in a foreign country. How do you start? Where do
you even begin?

Fortunately, the good people at the University of Gastronomic Sciences
in Bra—otherwise known as the Slow Food University—had a few tips for

me, which I augmented with some of my own discoveries. The result was that Nancy, Grace, and I spent much of our five months in Piedmont visiting a host of chefs, distributors, and producers of rice, olive oil, cheese, beef, chicken, wine, beer, flour, and chocolate. (I know, I know—somebody had to do it!)

Throughout all of these visits, I was motivated by one simple question: what could I learn from these producers with "gastronomic aims"? (175). I hoped to learn about Slow Food, certainly, but also about the Piedmont, about the process of getting food from "farm to table," and, perhaps most importantly, about the food itself. And I hoped that, ultimately, my education in these subjects would help me better understand Petrini's writing and the impact it has had on the sustainable food movement.

Each of these visits was different, but some common themes ultimately emerged, and I've chosen three of them to illustrate some of the important lessons I learned during our time in Italy:

1. Quality matters more than anything.
2. "Organic" and "natural" do not necessarily equal quality.
3. History and tradition matter, but so do technology and innovation.

SLOW FOOD STORIES

1. QUALITY MATTERS MORE THAN ANYTHING

About fifteen minutes south of Canelli, Italy, lies the little town of Cossano Belbo, in Cuneo province. And down a steep hill, just off the main road, lies Mulino Marino, a natural stone mill that's been operated by the Marino family since 1955.

Mulino Marino doesn't look like much on the outside: it's a series of stucco and steel buildings, with several loading docks, a few delivery trucks, and a bright-yellow forklift for moving pallets of flour around. But, as with so many things in life, it's what's on the inside that counts.

We traveled to Mulino Marino one sunny afternoon in the spring to meet Fulvio Marino, whom Corby Kummer and Susie Cushner first introduced to American readers in *The Pleasures of Slow Food,* published in 2002. At the time, Fulvio was only sixteen years old, and Kummer and Cushner marveled at the young man's energy. "He's the most charismatic kid I've ever met," Cushner said.

I was curious how much Fulvio might have changed over the years, but as he bounded across the pavement to meet us, his energy level seemed not to have diminished one iota. He remained a bundle of good cheer, constantly in motion.

After eager handshakes all around and the requisite apology for his imperfect English, Fulvio led us into the packing room, where his grandfather Felice was busy preparing small bags of flour for shipment. It's a testament to Italian hospitality that as soon as we were introduced, Felice asked Grace if she would like to help him, and for the next few minutes Grace eagerly worked alongside Felice, wrapping short pieces of string around the tops of the bags, while Nancy and I learned more about the mill from Fulvio.

It turns out that a water-powered mill had existed in Cossano Belbo as early as the year 1280, and since that time many other mills had sprung up in the region. When Felice was a young man, he lived on a farm in the town of Mango, just a few kilometers away, and he brought grain to the mill in Cossano Belbo on a regular basis. When World War II came, Felice joined the resistance, helping British paratroopers fight the Nazis and fascists. After the war ended, he decided to buy the mill he worked at when he was younger, and now it's the only one left in the area. Like many small businesses in Italy, it remains very much a family affair, with three generations of Marino men working alongside one another at the mill. And all of their names, notably, start with the letter "F": there's grandfather Felice; Fulvio's father, Ferdinando; and uncle Flavio; and Fulvio's brother Fausto and cousin Federico.

The war had an effect not only on Felice but also on the context in which the mill operated. "During the war," said Fulvio, "everyone ate whole grains. After the war, the white flour was [seemed like] a better flour, because it was the flour of the rich, like white sugar, and it would last longer [not go rancid as quickly as whole grain flour]." As a result, when Felice first bought the mill, he produced mainly white flour, and he did so in a cylinder mill, because a stone mill can't produce the highly refined flour used today in many pastas, cakes, and pastries. In the 1980s, however, when interest in whole grains returned, Felice and his sons decided to grind more of their flour using traditional methods. They still use the cylinder mill for some soft wheat flours, but now most of their flours are whole grain, ground on granite millstones imported from France.

Fulvio was eager to show us the process in action, so we walked next door into a small room where much of the stone milling takes place. The cylinder mill and other modern equipment are housed in a building across the courtyard, but this room holds two sets of Mulino Marino's signature millstones: one set for cutting corn, and another for grinding wheat. (A third set of millstones housed elsewhere produces flour for people with food allergies, including flour made from spelt, rye, buckwheat, kamut, chickpea, barley, and chestnut.) Here in this mill room, the two sets of stones sit on a raised wooden platform at the back of the room, in housings that look like giant wooden barrels that have been cut in half. Inside each housing, the bottom stone (or bed stone) remains stationary, while the top stone (or runner stone) rotates slowly over it—never quite touching the bottom stone, but coming close enough to break the grains into their various parts. Because the top stone moves so slowly, the flour does not get as hot as it does in a cylinder mill, which helps preserve more of the nutrients, aromas, and flavors of the grain.

The mill was cutting corn today, so we watched for a moment as the dried corn kernels fell from a pipe in the ceiling into a large wooden hopper, then descended into a hole into the center of the top millstone, were ground against the solid bottom millstone, and finally fell from the front of the mill in a gossamer veil of polenta, steadily but gently, until it landed in a rectangular steel bin on the floor.

Being lovers of polenta, we were fortunate to visit during the corn-milling process, because Mulino Marino doesn't use just any kind of corn. They use *mais ottofile*, or "eight-row maize," which makes the most flavorful polenta we know. Though we had purchased some *mais ottofile* flour to keep in our cupboard at the house, we had never seen the cobs themselves, so Fulvio grabbed a handful from the office and showed us how they differed up close. Unlike modern varieties of sweet corn, which can produce more than one ear per plant, each containing fourteen to eighteen rows of kernels, *mais ottofile* produces only one ear per plant, and that ear contains only eight rows of kernels—thus its name, "eight-row maize." It is also known as "the King's maize," because it is said to have been a favorite of King Vittorio Emanuele II of Italy, and it was grown throughout the Piedmont in the nineteenth and early twentieth centuries. *Mais ottofile* was all but abandoned in the mid-twentieth century, however, in favor of the higher-yielding, hybrid varieties of corn developed in North America. A few peasants continued to plant it for polenta, but *mais ottofile* takes longer to cook, and who has time for that? Now, however, as more and more people have come to appreciate its sweet flavor and rich yellow-orange color, not to mention the philosophy of "slow food" it embodies, *mais ottofile* is again being grown in the Alta Langa region, where Mulino Marino is located.

But *mais ottofile* isn't the only heirloom grain the mill uses, and seeing our interest in this traditional variety of corn, Fulvio couldn't wait to introduce us to something we didn't know anything about: namely, Enkir. Enkir is a trademarked variety of einkorn, a grain whose Latin binominal is *Triticum monococcum* (you can see why they named it Enkir). Einkorn is the parent grain of durum and soft wheat and is considered the "father of cereals." It was first domesticated in the Near East around ten thousand years ago, and some varieties still grow in Turkey, Iran, and other areas of the Fertile Crescent. The Marinos became interested in Enkir in the 1990s because its characteristics were a good match for the Alta Langhe. As Fulvio explained, historically this hilly region had been good for only "*prato* and potatoes" (meadow and potatoes), but with so few animals in pasture now, it made sense for the region's farmers to plant Enkir, because the grain grows well in poor soil and doesn't require pesticides, herbicides, or fertilizers. Working with Coldiretti, the Italian farmer's union, Mulino Marino was able to bring Enkir to the Alta Langhe—and, in the process, to build relationships with local growers that went beyond simply paying for their products. "We can speak with the farmer," Fulvio says. "We know the grain and the soil." Best of all, by planting Enkir right in its own backyard, just like *mais ottofile,* the mill could make its supply chain "kilometer zero," or what Americans would call "zero food miles."

Mais ottofile and Enkir are good examples of how Mulino Marino has tried to carve out a niche for itself as an artisan producer. "We are a little mill in front of a big mill," says Fulvio, speaking of Barilla, the Italian milling giant. (Fulvio is careful to point out that he means no disrespect to the company: Barilla "is fine," he says, "but is different.") If Mulino Marino can't compete with Barilla on price, it can compete on quality. "We are not an industrial mill," says Fulvio. "We can't produce many, many tons of flour, but we can produce quality flour. We have only one way, and this way is quality."

Fulvio was certainly right about Barilla: it *is* a big mill. We made a lot of bread during the time we spent in Italy, because Italian bread often leaves a lot to be desired. In fact, it's kind of an open secret that while Italians may make the world's best pasta, their bread can be pale, dry, and tasteless. Germany: great bread, wonderful fragrant loaves of rich, hearty rye to dip in soups and slather with butter. France: fantastic bread, baguettes to die for, with beautiful golden-brown exteriors that crackle when you rip into them, revealing the softest, most tender interiors you can imagine. Italy: not so much. We tried loaf after loaf of Italian bread before we finally gave up and made our own every other day, using an Emeril Lagasse recipe we found on the Internet. As a result, we also bought a lot of flour in Italy, and Barilla was our staple: *Farina per tutte le preparazioni* (flour for all preparations), *di grano tenero tipo* 00 (soft wheat, type double-zero, ground exceptionally fine, almost like baby powder). This flour is everywhere, and for good reason: it's cheap, reliable, and makes a solid batch of pasta, a crispy crust for pizza, and a sturdy loaf of bread. What it's not, however, is distinctive.

Mulino Marino is distinctive not only for how it mills its flour, and for the kinds of grains it mills, but also for three other things. First, in 1994, the mill went all organic. Fulvio talks about *controlla la farina,* the rules of organic, which his mill greatly exceeds by running many, many tests to ensure the integrity of its product. "We go beyond organic," he says. "Organic for us is a very good start. But organic does not always mean a good product." Second, the mill produces all of its flour using only solar power. "In this moment," Fulvio says, acknowledging our global sustainability challenges, "it is important for us" to do this. Finally, the Marinos hammer their granite millstones by hand, a delicate process called "dressing the stones" that involves recutting the grooves on the face of each stone, so that an optimum grinding surface is achieved. "Everything we make is made by hand," says Fulvio.

"For us," Fulvio points out, "Slow Food is very important. As a little artisan, we have a big problem—the problem is communication. Slow Food helps us to explain to the masses why our flour is better. It is very difficult; it is not simple to tell the story." In other words, you can't tell a whole story on a label, so you need to build a market for your product person by person. As Fulvio puts it, "We create the customer." The Marinos educate people by having them taste their flour directly; by selling bread made with their flour in Eataly, the Italian food superstore; and by making pizza with their flour at the Salone del Gusto, the biennial Slow Food gathering held in Turin. "Fortunately," says Fulvio, "the smell and the taste of the flour is different."

This communication problem is especially acute in the contemporary economy, when people do not have as much money to buy their products, yet it costs a lot of money to ensure the quality of those products. "Now is a difficult moment, but a good moment," says Fulvio. "The difficult moment is to have the money from the customer. We have to reinvest in the company." The mill needs to buy the solar collectors that power its grindstones; it needs to maintain the optical grain reader that picks out the damaged grains before milling; and it needs to pay for the analysis to keep its organic certification. Moreover, the Marinos find it hard to compete with companies that claim to be artisan but are not—the ones that say they have "natural" or "stone-ground" flour but that use artificial stones to mill it. But now is also a "good moment" for the mill, because Mulino Marino's products are becoming much more widely known. Although most of its customers still live in the Piedmont, its flour can now be found throughout the world, including at Eataly in New York, Formaggio Kitchen in Boston, and Zingerman's in Ann Arbor. In fact, it was Corby Kummer who introduced the Marinos to Zingerman's at the Salone del Gusto in 2006, Fulvio says.

We got a final taste of what it means to be an artisan producer when Fulvio invited us into the mill's kitchen for some espresso and a taste of Enkir beer. Yes, Enkir *beer*. Birra del Borgo, an Italian artisan brewery, began making a beer from 55 percent Enkir, milled right here at Mulino Marino. Fulvio grabbed a bottle on our way inside and had poured us a glass before we even got in the door. It was a dark-blond brew, with a substantial head, a fruity depth, and an exceptionally smooth mouthfeel, and we drank as much as we felt we could, knowing we would soon be getting back on the road. On the way into the kitchen, Fulvio pointed to the rest of his family in pictures and news clippings that were on display in the office, and several of the Marino men and women stopped into the kitchen to say *ciao* while we were there. While Grace munched on some grain-cakes made from puffed Enkir, Fulvio served us the best coffee we had in Italy, made in a well-used moka pot on the stovetop, and he also showed us the sourdough starter he kept in the refrigerator, testament to his deep appreciation for the wonders of fermentation. As we spoke about the changes the mill has gone though over the last fifty years, I couldn't help but be impressed by how well grounded this young man seemed to be. "We live in a moment—in the economics of Facebook and Google—but I am satisfied," he said. "To make a real product is a good thing. I touch the grain when I begin, and then I make flour. I am a miller."

2. "ORGANIC" AND "NATURAL" DO NOT NECESSARILY EQUAL QUALITY

If you stop at the tourist office in Alba—the principal town in the Langhe, about a half hour northwest of Cossano Belbo—you would be hard-pressed to find any travel guides trumpeting the virtues of the region's flour production. What you would discover, however, are innumerable books, maps, and brochures informing you about the Piedmont's best-known agricultural products: hazelnuts, truffles, and wine.

And if, on another lovely spring day, you were to follow the Langhe's notoriously windy roads east out of Alba, passing vineyard after vineyard planted with Barbera and Nebbiolo, Piedmont's most successful native grape varieties, you would come fairly quickly to Rizzi, the eighteenth-century estate of Ernesto Dellapiana. Located near the top of one of the region's steeply sloping hills, the estate provides a commanding view of the ridge to the south and the valley below, through which you would have just traveled.

But if you expected to encounter some fashion-forward vintner roaming the premises, you might be sorely disappointed. Instead, you might find—as we did—Ernesto's son Enrico, dressed in gym shorts, a beat-up pair of Addias running shoes, and a dusty T-shirt proclaiming him an "Official Taster" of Tito's Handmade Vodka from Austin, Texas. Yet another Italian stereotype bites the dust.

No sooner did we arrive than Enrico took us on a fast-paced tour on the gravel paths that surrounded the farmhouse, walking and talking as if we were in some viticultural version of *The West Wing*.

"In the past," Enrico says midstride, "there was much more fields" here; now it is almost all grapes. In the past, he continues, gesturing toward the nearby hills, "all persons have a small piece of soil. All people have a small vineyard. But in the last ten to twenty years, some properties get bigger and bigger."

The Rizzi estate is no exception. In 1973, Enrico's father sold a paper-making business in Turin and returned to his family farm, which at the time was about ten to fifteen hectares large. With the purchase of a vineyard from his brother and the addition of other neighboring farms, the family since came to own thirty-five hectares (or about eighty-five acres) and became one of the largest wine producers in the Barbaresco area. Today, says Enrico, one hectare of land in Barbaresco can cost five hundred thousand euros or more. And in Barolo, about twenty minutes south of here, the price can reach upward of one million euros per hectare.

Maximizing profit, however, is not Enrico's goal. Although he produces sixty thousand bottles, and eventually would like to produce one hundred thousand bottles, Enrico has consciously limited the amount of growth he thinks the vineyard—and his family—can sustain. "With thirty-five hectares, I can produce three hundred thousand bottles," he says, but he doesn't want to do that. "If I get bigger, I have to have other persons. I have to work harder if I get bigger. If I become bigger, I lose some part of the process." Perhaps most important, Enrico adds, this is not some niche idea that only a few people hold; it is a much broader cultural ideal in the Piedmont. "I think that's the richness of our region: small, small," he emphasizes. "That's the beauty of our richness, and also our uniqueness. How the human work changes the landscape."

Enrico stops from time to time to prune the vines as we speak, taking some of the leaves off with his hands and kicking others off with his feet. As I watch Enrico's well-worn running shoe make repeated contact with such highly valued grapevines, I am reminded that winemaking is a competitive business, and grape growing is no place for the timid.

Grabbing a handful of the newly formed fruits, Enrico explains how environment matters. It was a cold spring this year, so the grapes flowered at the end of May rather than the start of May, as they had in previous years, and this basic fact shapes the cycle of work on the vineyard. Come fall, he will use twelve to fifteen harvesters, who will labor from the end of August to the beginning or middle of October. "Our roof is the sky," he says, and the weather helps determine which grapes are harvested when.

Rizzi's grapes, Enrico tells me, range in age from nine to sixty years old: the youngest vines are the Nebbiolo, planted nine years ago; in the middle are the Chardonnay, planted in 1972 and 1994, and the Moscato vines are the oldest, planted in the 1950s and 1960s. Each variety also has its own preferred orientation: the Nebbiolo does best on south- and southwest-facing slopes, while the Moscato and Chardonnay prefer north-facing slopes. "The vineyard, the vine, is like a person," Enrico observes. "The wine is like children." In other words, you need to give them your personal attention, you need to be mindful of what makes them happy.

I look back at my daughter, Grace, trying to keep up as we hurry around the vineyard and think, "There's a gelato in my future, I just know it."

Like Mulino Marino, Rizzi works hard to produce a quality product and to do so in a sustainable way. The Dellapianas put solar panels on the roof, becoming the first winery in the Piedmont to rely entirely on solar power, and they have tried to make the bottles in which they store their wine as light as possible to save energy during transport, while still preserving the integrity of the product. Enrico allows plants (he calls them "herbs") to grow between the vines to prevent soil erosion, and he says that for twenty years his father never used chemical treatments in the fields. Today, they use only minimal pesticides. "We work here, too," says Enrico. "We don't want a lot of chemicals."

It would be easy to say that the philosophy at Rizzi is somehow less "pure" than that at Mulino Marino, but to do so would be to miss the differences between grain milling and wine making, as well as the similarities between the producers in terms of their commitment to quality. "Natural," "organic," "biological": these are problematic terms, says Enrico, as we move from the vineyard to the tasting room. "If my wine is 'natural,' the other wine is not?" he asks, incredulously. "Too many producers use the word 'natural' not because they believe it, but because they want to sell wine." There is no point to having a "natural" wine that is bad, he stresses. "I'm happy that it's natural, but it's no good. The wine has to be good, and you have to respect the soil and the place where you live."

Enrico grows animated as he pours us each a glass of last year's Chardonnay. The wine glows in the afternoon light like the captured sunshine it is, radiating onto the varnished wood table where we sit.

"Organic," Enrico says. "What's that mean, 'organic'?" It's hard to understand the boundary between "organic" and "sustainable," he observes. "There are many factors to sustainability," not just organic, and a good winemaker needs to consider all the tools at his or her disposal. "The technology exists, the chemicals exist," he insists, putting his hand on the table for emphasis. But that doesn't mean that anything goes at Rizzi. Behind every decision in the vineyard is a person—whether Enrico, his father, or Enrico's sister Jole—

who lives and works in *this place* and values quality above all else. "I control everything," he says. "I'm honest with myself, with my conscience. I want to produce great wine, and I want people to ask for my wine. I like *passaparola*" (or word of mouth), he says, not advertising.

"The idea of Slow Food is a very good idea," he continues. "Slow Food tells the story of the wine, the cheese. People need to know something more" about where their food comes from. The product, he points out, is not only the wine—it is all that is behind the wine.

As if to prove it, he pours us glass after glass of some of the finest wine we had in the Piedmont. A sparkling wine, using the traditional, Champagne method. A Stërbu, or "cloudy wine," in the Piedmontese dialect. A Barbera, a Dolcetto, and two different vintages of Barbaresco, from 2007 and 2008. "I change always," Enrico says. "It's difficult to get to perfect" with so many variables in the field each year. "I like very much the complexity of the wine—the balance between sugar and acidity, the alcohol and the tannins. Always balance—in the wine, in the life, in everything."

3. HISTORY AND TRADITION MATTER, BUT SO DO TECHNOLOGY AND INNOVATION

If wine is Piedmont's most iconic food product, and flour one of its most invisible, rice lies somewhere in between—obvious once you think about it, but surprising if you don't. Rice? Like, the grain?

Yes, rice. Or, as it's better known in its most iconic Italian form, *risotto*.

While rice cultivation may bring to mind the rice paddies of Southeast Asia, where the majority of the world's rice originates, rice is grown throughout the world, including in the Piedmont—just not in the wine country of the Langhe.

To find it, we must travel an hour and a half north, through the Tanaro River valley, over the gently rolling hills of the Basso Monferrato, and down into the Province of Vercelli, where the floodplain of the Po River extends as far as the eye can see. There the landscape changes dramatically, flattening out into a shimmery sea of silver and green, where rice plants emerge from the flooded paddies as if poking through the sky itself.

Here, about fifteen minutes north of the banks of the Po, is Tenuta Torrone della Colombara, the Colombara Estate, which rises from the landscape like a low brick fortress in the distance. It is a Saturday in early summer, and the only sounds we hear, as we walk down the long entrance road to the estate, are the barking of a dog in the background and the occasional passing car on the road. But even these sounds gradually diminish the closer we get to the estate, and eventually we are left with nothing but the crunch of our shoes on the raised gravel path and the plopping of frogs into the paddies that surround us. We are thousands of miles away from Japan, yet this may be the most Zen-like experience we've had during our time in Italy.

Once we reach the courtyard, we are greeted by Cris Arantes, our translator, and Piero Rondolino, the owner and creator of Acquerello rice—quite possibly the finest risotto rice in the world. Piero resembles nothing less than the Laughing Buddha of rice: playful, happy, and with a boyish grin that instantly puts us at ease. Cris may need to translate, but Piero's smile would be understood anywhere in the world.

Rice first came to this part of Italy in the late fifteenth century, and the church across the street from the farm became the center of rice growing in the region in the 1600s. Piero's father, Cesare, bought the farm in 1935, and Piero joined him as a rice producer in the 1970s. During this period, the farm increased to some 600 hectares, and the farm philosophy followed the industrial model of maximum yield. In the 1990s, however, Piero and his son Rinaldo took a different path, shrinking the size of the farm to 140 hectares; transitioning to all-organic production methods; and planting only one variety of rice, Carnaroli, which has a lower yield but which makes up for that difference in quality.

Whenever we made risotto in the past, we would use Arborio rice, which yielded a creamy, chewy, and somewhat sticky dish, almost like an oatmeal made of rice. After living in Italy, however, now we use Carnaroli, because its grains keep their shape better and have a firmer bite to them, even after the long cooking time risotto requires. Arborio may have a higher yield, which is why many producers prefer it, but Carnaroli remains the top choice of chefs the world over. And for Thomas Keller of Per Se and the French Laundry, and Heston Blumenthal of the Fat Duck, among many other fans, Acquerello is the Rolls Royce of Carnaroli.

There is a saying in Italy that "rice is born in water but dies in wine," and as far as I knew, there wasn't much more to it than that: you grow the rice, you harvest it, and then you cook it. But that was before I met Piero. Piero plants his rice by early April, and harvest is done in September or October. But it's what happens *after* the harvest that matters for Acquerello.

Piero uses twenty different machines in the production process. First, a mechanical dryer reduces the moisture content of the rice from 25 percent to 14 percent. It takes Piero three days to do this—a step that other producers rush through in thirty minutes. Next, a machine with rubber surfaces cleans the rice, removing the outer husk and preparing it for subsequent stages. A helix then whitens the rice by tumbling the grains against one another in a downward spiral so that the bran is gradually rubbed away from each kernel. This method is slower and more expensive than others, but fewer grains are broken in the process. After this step, a set of lasers read the grains by color, weight, and size to make them all uniform. And finally, the rice gets vacuum packed, boxed, and ready to ship.

Although many other rice producers employ versions of these same steps, two other aspects of the production process set Acquerello apart. The first of these became clear as Piero asked us to follow him up a steep metal staircase and onto the perforated walkway of the drying room, several stories above the ground. There we found him grinning from ear to ear, as we looked out over container after container filled with aging, unhulled rice. Unlike other producers, Acquerello ages its rice in temperature-controlled silos, and this additional step helps the grains absorb more water and retain more of their vitamins, proteins, and starch during the cooking process. As a result, the final product becomes more flavorful, more nutritious, and more like risotto should be, with large, firm kernels of rice that don't stick together.

All Acquerello rice is aged for at least one year, but some is aged even longer, and tags hanging above the tops of each silo told us the year each container of rice was harvested. Many tags said 2011, since 96 percent of the rice is aged for one year. But some said 2006, for the 3 percent that is aged for seven years. And one particular tag, which was closest to us, said 2003, for the less than 1 percent of the rice that is aged for nine years—and this exclusively for the Chinese market.

"Oooo, Mommy," said Grace, spying this last tag. "2003—that's the year I was born!"

At this, Piero motioned for Grace to climb on top of this towering pile of nine-year-old rice and sit under the tag, which of course she did in a heartbeat. But as she heaved herself up onto a pile of rice as old as she was, I couldn't but help think that this was probably not what those wealthy Chinese diners had in mind when they pictured their Rolls Royce of Carnaroli. Fortunately, there were still plenty of steps between this unhulled rice and the risotto that appears on our plates.

One of these steps, in fact, constitutes the other aspect of the production process that is specific to Acquerello—a step so unique, it's patented. This is the reintegration of the rice germ (which was removed in the helix) back into the rice kernel at the end of the process. Piero is the only producer who separates the germ of the brown rice from the bran, and the only one who then reintegrates that germ back into the whitened rice. He does this by melting the germ at 40 degrees Celsius and then slowly mixing it back into the white rice, so that the germ both penetrates and coats the refined kernels. Piero first started doing this a few years ago, so that the rice could be enriched by the valuable nutrients in the germ, which are usually lost in the refining process. And because the germ constitutes 3 percent of the original rice kernel, Piero adds an equivalent amount of germ back into the kernel at the end. Now that's precision.

But as impressive as all these technologies are, and as much time as Piero's process seems to take, I was beginning to wonder how well these two aspects of Acquerello's philosophy—futuristic technology and old-fashioned slowness—really worked together. So I asked him.

"The past, present, and future are all here," Piero said, referring to the place of technology on the farm: old technologies like the helix, modern technologies like the laser, and future technologies that find more use for the rice germ. (Although the helix was invented in 1975, the technology behind it has existed for more than a hundred years.) "Good technology preserves the product," he said. "It can be old technology, or it can be new. Aging is a tradition, but it is not possible without a technology. They go all together, side by side."

"Slow Food is not against technology," he continued. "If it wasn't for Slow Food, we would forget about the past. Slow Food helps keep it alive. It's very important to learn from the past in order to be able to build the future. And where I work," he said with a smile, "is a library."

He wasn't kidding about that last part. He really *does* work in a library—or at least a museum.

Before we left, Piero led us across the rice fields under the hot summer sun to a low brick building we had been admiring in the distance. This was the sleeping quarters of the *mondina*, or "rice weeders," made famous in Giuseppe De Santis's 1949 neorealist film *Riso amaro* (Bitter rice), starring Silvana Mangano. The *mondina* were the seasonal workers who transplanted the delicate rice seedlings and weeded the rice paddies in late nineteenth- and early twentieth-century Italy. Their work was exceedingly difficult and consisted of standing in sometimes knee-deep water for hours, bending constantly to pull up the weeds that invaded the rice paddies, all while battling the mosquitoes and other biting insects that thrive in such aquatic environments. Not surprisingly, women who lived in dormitories such as this initiated the first strike in Italian history and went on to create regulations that put in place the first eight-hour workday.

As a tribute to these women, Piero has re-created their dormitory just as they left it, with sheets on the rickety old cots that line the walls, their skirts and stockings hung up to dry, and their sun hats and leather suitcases ready for when they depart. And in case the connection between technology and history was lost on me, Piero reminded me that—thanks to technology—fourteen people now do the work that used to require thirty entire families to accomplish.

Piero also took us to another part of the farm that housed old workshops and farm implements, as well as additional living quarters, and the school where the workers' children were educated. But as much as this history fascinated me, it was the future of the farm that concerned me most, and I asked Piero about this as we stopped to admire the network of canals that feed the rice paddies and have made this complicated system of agricultural production possible over the last five hundred years.

The land on which the Colombara Estate sits is part of a much larger landscape, whose elevation gradually declines as you move southeast from the Alps to Pavia, south of Milan. And the watershed that feeds the farm depends on the Dora Baltea River, a tributary of the Po that begins near Mont Blanc. The Dora Baltea also happens to be fed by glaciers, and if the glacier melt that feeds the river diminishes because of climate change, this will disrupt the entire ecosystem on which the farm depends, not to mention the marriage of nature and culture that Acquerello embodies.

As we ended our time together, and Piero loaded us up with plenty of containers of Acquerello rice, I asked him about Thomas Jefferson, who in 1787 smuggled pocketfuls of unhusked rice out of this part of Italy—a crime punishable by death at the time—in order to assist the fledgling rice industry in the United States. Could Piero's passion for technological innovation, which he shares with Jefferson, ultimately help us solve the climate crisis? Piero was cagey about Jefferson, perhaps still smarting from this long-ago slight to his countrymen, but he did allow me this one parting bit of Italian wisdom: "The best ideas come to the hungry people."

QUALITY AND INEQUALITY

You know we've reached "peak artisanal" when the *New Yorker* publishes a cartoon spoofing the idea, almost every year since 2003, for more than a decade. But you also know the term's touched a nerve.

What is it about "artisanal" that so grates on us? Could it be the insufferable self-righteousness with which all too many people use the word? (As more than one wag has observed, you can't spell "artisanal" without "anal.") Could it be how quickly the term has been co-opted—not only by corporate food marketers but by almost anyone selling anything even marginally "handcrafted"? Could it be the ease with which "artisan" has been so emptied of meaning that even McDonald's can offer an "Artisan Grilled Chicken Sandwich"? Yes, yes, and yes.

And yet the term lives on, in part because it still manages to retain enough of its original meaning—signifying some degree of craft, skill, and art involved in the production of food—to function as a useful foil to modern, mechanized, industrial food production.

In *The Life of Cheese: Crafting Food and Value in America,* Heather Paxson observes that "artisanal cheese is inescapably defined against the industrial: it is made more by hand than by machine, in small batches compared to industrial scales of production, using recipes and techniques developed through the practical knowledge of previous artisans rather than via the technical knowledge of dairy scientists and industrial engineers. Indeed, the question of what counts as artisanal cheese only becomes significant in an era of industrial processing" (128).

There's processing, in other words, and then there's processing.

Mulino Marino, Rizzi, Acquerello, and thousands more artisanal processors like them aren't huge corporations cranking out what Carlos Monteiro has called "ultra-processed foods." Instead, they are small, usually family-run operations processing ingredients to be later used in home cooking, or making foods and beverages that the average person can't easily make at home. They are supporting engagement with one's food, and building connections between producers and consumers, rather than undermining these things as large-scale industrial food processors often do, however unintentionally.

Yet there is as much danger in romanticizing small producers as there is in ignoring their many virtues.

We might ask of Mulino Marino, for example, what are the implications of trademarking Einkorn as Enkir®? Is it a step toward or away from the industrialization of food? Alison Leitch has observed a similar tension in one Italian community's attempt to trademark the name *lardo,* or pork fat, noting that "this is a story not of the 'invention of tradition' but of its commodification" ("Politics of Pork Fat" 448). In the case of Enkir, the trademark seems more like an attempt to further distinguish Mulino Marino in the marketplace, but we might view this strategy equally critically, given Pierre Bourdieu's reflections on the idea of "distinction."

In *Distinction: A Social Critique of the Judgement of Taste* (1979), the French sociologist argued that food is an important signifier of class and social status, much like clothing, music, or art. Thus one's "taste" for certain foods is not merely about the flavor of these foods or their perceived "quality" but also about the role they play in social life, reinforcing the status of either the ruling class or the working class. "Social subjects . . . distinguish themselves by the distinctions they make," Bourdieu claimed, noting the differences between what he called "the taste of necessity," which favors the functions food plays in life (food that is filling and inexpensive is therefore valuable), and "the taste of luxury," which favors the style in which food is presented and consumed (6).

Yet Bourdieu also saw that income (or economic capital) was only one factor in explaining "taste," and that education (or cultural capital) was also needed to fully understand how food functioned in society. This lead him memorably to chart what he called "the food space," in which, for example, the food preferences of French teachers were opposed to those of the nouveau riche. Whereas the teachers, "richer in cultural capital than in economic capital, and therefore inclined to ascetic consumption in all areas, pursue originality at the lowest economic cost and go in for exoticism (Italian, Chinese cooking etc.) and culinary populism (peasant dishes)," the *nouveau riche* "have the economic means to flaunt, with an arrogance perceived as 'vulgar,' a life-style which remains very close to that of the working classes as regards economic and cultural consumption" and therefore favor salty, fatty, strong, and rich food (185).

The result was much like *New York* magazine's "Approval Matrix," but thirty years earlier, and much more French.

In an inspired and humorous (though admittedly unscientific) updating of Bourdieu's food space for *Gastronomica* in 2012, illustrated by Leigh Wells,

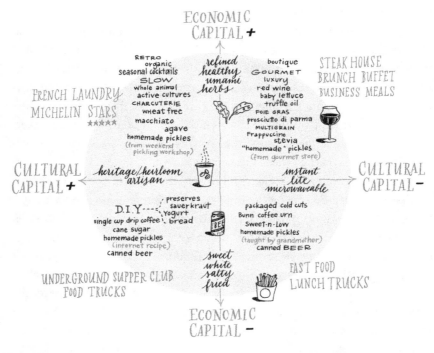

Bourdieu's food space, 2012. (Leigh Wells and Molly Watson; courtesy of Leigh Wells)

Molly Watson showed how Slow Food and its various artisanal relatives signified the presence of both economic and cultural capital, as opposed to, say, canned beer and packaged cold cuts, which signified the absence of both.

What matters here, and this returns us to Mulino Marino, is that the features that make the mill distinctive from Barilla—its granite millstones, heritage grains, organic certification, and solar power—also make it exclusive, in both the economic and the cultural sense, which is true for many "artisanal" foods, not to mention Slow Food generally. (That the artisanal polenta we made from their *mais ottofile* was once the food of the poor in northern Italy, leading to an outbreak of pellagra, only adds to the complexity of this story.) Can artisanal food be democratized enough to build a good, clean, and fair food future for all?

Bourdieu suggests not, or at least not easily, given the way that "taste" functions to reproduce inequality, often below the level of conscious awareness. Thus, not only does "good taste" require cultural and economic capital to acquire, but the idea of "taste" itself tends to reproduce the very class divisions on which it depends. Through such distinctions, says Bourdieu, "the social order is progressively inscribed in people's minds. Social divisions become principles of division, organizing the image of the social world. Objective limits become a sense of limits, . . . a 'sense of one's place' which leads one to exclude oneself from the goods, persons, places and so forth from which one is excluded" (471).

But distinction is not the only concept we must keep in mind when trying to understand artisanal food production and its place in Carlo Petrini's vision of Slow Food. We must also address the issue of scale—particularly the relationship of quality and size.

Almost inevitably, no matter whom I talked to in Piedmont about food, one word was bound to appear at some point in the conversation, and that word was "quality."

As an American, I found it hard not to think of the J. D. Powers Initial Quality Award every time this word was mentioned, given how pervasive this award has been in television advertisements for new cars. In part because of this, the meaning of "quality" has always had something of a negative connotation for me, implying that the default production standard for new American cars was so low that someone had to create an award for when a car was not automatically a lemon. (The J. D. Powers Initial Quality Study, which began in 1987, measures car quality by analyzing problems reported by owners in the first ninety days of ownership.)

For Italians, however, "quality" does not automatically call up visions of automotive defects leading to endless recalls. Instead, it means something akin to "excellence," but not as measured in relationship to other things as much as measured in relationship to the intrinsic possibilities of the thing itself. Thus, when Petrini expressed disappointment about the quality of the food at the ARCI club in Tuscany, his complaint was not just that better food could be had elsewhere, but that the Tuscan food did not live up to its own potential.

For those of a certain literary bent, mentions of "quality" may also bring to mind *Zen and the Art of Motorcycle Maintenance* (1974), Robert Pirsig's philosophical novel, in which the narrator claims that the term "quality" is undefinable, and there is something of this at work in Italian understandings of quality, as well. Given this, my own skepticism about claims of "quality" products may not be wholly misplaced, since who can say what constitutes quality?

Geographer Amy Zader calls this dilemma "the politics of quality," and she has demonstrated that it functions similarly in Chinese society. What makes "quality" rice, she wondered? Is it the taste of the rice, the location in which it was grown, its protein content, or some other variable? "In the case of high quality japonica rice in China," she observed, "we find competing ideas of what constitute[s] quality rice between scientists, consumers, and farmers. The idea of quality food is interpreted and translated in different ways. What is evident, however, is the idea that the quality of rice is worth attaining" (54).

I certainly found the same to be true in Italy, and Zader's conclusions about how "quality" functions in Chinese food systems can help us understand its role in Slow Food as well. "The economy is not simply about supply and demand, but is shaped by specific cultural conditions that project 'quality' on a product," says Zader. "Quality is a combination of the interactions between people and rice at various stages of production to label this rice as such" (57). And the lack of government regulation about what constitutes a "quality" product in China only increases the importance of how the meaning of this term is negotiated through discourse.

For Enrico Dellapiana of the Rizzi estate, as well as for many of the other artisan food processors I interviewed, quality has as much to do with size as it does with adherence to "organic" certification or claims to produce a "natural" product.

In *The Gift of Good Land,* Wendell Berry put it this way: "If you sell all you grow, you want to sell as much as possible; your interest, then, is in *quantity.* If, on the other hand, you intend to eat at least a part of what you grow, you naturally want it to be as *good* as possible; you are interested, first of all, in quality; quantity, important as it is, is of secondary importance" (10).

When I met with the brewmaster and the marketing manager of Baladin, Italy's first and largest craft brewery, for instance, they both stressed the importance of scale. "We are the biggest, but we are not so big," said Fabio "Moz" Mozzone, the marketing manager, echoing what Fulvio Marino said about Barilla. One year's production of Baladin is equivalent to one day's production of Heineken Italia, so Baladin is still considered a small brewery in comparison to its industrial counterparts. And like Rizzi, Baladin has vowed: this far and no farther. "We fixed a limit to the brewery," said Paolo

"Palli" Fontana, the brewmaster. "We have already chosen where we want to arrive." Producing about one million bottles when I met with them, Baladin only wants to grow so much. "After 1,600,000 bottles, we can't assure the quality," said Palli. Plus, Moz added, "We want to sustain ourselves." That is, they want to have time for family and friends, and they also want to consider all eight people who work in the brewery. "They have to keep up with the growth," said Moz. "The goal was to make all of the people who work here happy," said Paolo.

Another way to think about this is to consider that "slow food" is something of a misnomer.

There's no question that Petrini shares many of the concerns about speed that Folco Portinari articulated in the first Slow Food manifesto. In *Slow Food Nation*, for example, Petrini celebrates that "the Slow Food movement has made slowness its watchword" (182) and observes that the quest for slowness "begins as a simple rebellion against the impoverishment of taste in our lives" (180).

Yet he also acknowledges that "the contrast should not be between slowness and speed—slow versus fast—but rather between attention and distraction; slowness, in fact, is not so much a question of duration as of an ability to distinguish and evaluate, with the propensity to cultivate pleasure, knowledge, and quality" (183). In fact, Petrini writes, "Perhaps the limit is the cipher of slowness; if you know its meaning, you are safe from the perils of speed" (184).

The idea of *limits*, then, whether to speed or to size, is central to the idea of slow food. Bill Buford addressed the idea of limits to size in his memoir *Heat*, in which he apprentices himself to a range of charismatic experts on Italian food, suggesting that "slow food" might better be termed "small food":

> As theories go, mine is pretty crude. Small food—good. Big food—bad. For me, the language we use to talk about modern food isn't quite accurate or at least doesn't account for how this Italian valley has taught me to think. The metaphor is usually one of speed: fast food has ruined our culture; slow food will save it (and is the rallying manifesto for the movement of the same name, based in Bra, in northern Italy). You see the metaphor's appeal. But it obscures a fundamental problem, which has little to do with speed and everything to do with size. Fast food did not ruin our culture. The problem was already in place, systemic in fact, and began the moment

food was treated as an inanimate object—like any other commodity—that could be manufactured in increasing numbers to satisfy a market. (299)

Artisan (or "small food") producers, in other words, are more likely to enable the quality of attention that Petrini values, whereas large-scale enterprises ("big food") are more likely to undermine it, or ignore it altogether in favor of a relentless focus on profit. In this sense, size and speed are closely connected: if maximum productivity is one defining feature of "fast" culture, then "slow food" might best be seen as a positive term for a lack of efficiency.

When Piero Rondolino told me that "Slow Food is not against technology," he might as well have been channeling Petrini, who makes much the same point in *Slow Food Nation*. But of all the aspects of Petrini's thought, this one may be the least well developed, mostly because it is so abstractly rendered. Walking from Acquerello's state-of-the-art processing plant to its museum of agricultural technology, it is easy to see how "technology" is not so much an idea as a bunch of actual *things*—the material embodiments of innovation— and how difficult it is to speak of technology without reference to specific technologies.

Nevertheless, artisan producers clearly have a complicated relationship with the various technologies they employ, so it makes sense that Petrini would want to articulate an overarching vision to help guide that relationship.

In *Slow Food Nation*, Petrini describes his vision as a "dialogue between realms"—one realm being science and technology, the other being traditional knowledge. "Quantitative and reductionist thought are not in themselves the problem," he argues. "The scientific method, though it denies that some senses are useful to the interpretation of reality, is not in itself the problem. It is the distortions of these modes of thought and their predominance over everything else that have created an unsustainable situation" (179).

Equating those "distortions" to speed, Petrini then posits that *slowness* provides one means of access to traditional knowledge, which he says exists on what Berry called the "margins" of modernity. "By slowing down in comparison to the world," Petrini writes, "you soon come into contact with what the world regards as its 'dumps' of knowledge, which have been deemed slow and therefore marginalized. By exploring the 'margins' of slowness, you encounter these pockets of supposedly 'minor' culture that are alive in the memories of old people, typical of civilizations that have not yet become frantic" (180).

(Notably, "you" are not marginal.) One of the aims of Slow Food, Petrini suggests, must be to catalogue, preserve, and reanimate traditional knowledge,
so that the "different scientific methods" of country people can be accorded
"equal dignity and authority" as modern science and technology (181).

> In short, my wish is for a food industry that enters into dialogue with the
> methods of processing and with traditional cooking; a modern agro-
> nomic science that enters into dialogue with agroecology and traditional
> knowledge; and a scientific research that does not only go in the direction
> of productivism but places itself at the service of the producing commu-
> nities and of small-scale agriculture, combining their respective skills.
> There must be no predominant plan, and equal authority: neither of the
> two realms is called upon to demonstrate the validity of the other. It is
> sufficient that they communicate and put their knowledge at the service of
> good, clean, and fair food, and of the happiness of us all. (182)

Although Petrini's claims about science and technology certainly demonstrate Wendy Parkins and Geoffrey Craig's point that slowness has become
"an overdetermined signifier," they also reflect the maturation of Petrini's
thinking beyond the binary logic of the original Slow Food manifesto. Moreover, the form of *Slow Food Nation* allows Petrini to address his critics at least
partially—not only those who would fault him for the abstractness of his
vision but also those who would question whether the "quality" of artisanal
food is enough to address the host of structural inequalities seemingly baked
into the global food system.

While there is no lack of criticism of Slow Food as a movement, there is less
direct criticism of Petrini as a writer—although what criticism does exist is
not particularly complimentary.

In a blistering 2004 review of *Slow Food: The Case for Taste*, the food historian and self-identified "culinary modernist" Rachel Laudan calls it "an
infuriating book—pompous, self-congratulatory, long on rhetoric, short on
argument, and shorter yet on evidence" ("French" 135). Asking "whether a
gastronomic movement like Slow Food, founded to stimulate culinary tourism, can deliver on the much grander ambitions of its advocates to correct
or replace Culinary Modernism," Laudan says that Petrini's book provides
"nothing to suggest that it can" (139). She particularly faults Petrini for pro-

moting a "romanticized version of history" that "simply glosses over much of what made Italian food what it is today. . . . He offers a country without supermarkets, a country without its own fast food chains. There is no Food and Agriculture Association headquartered in Rome supporting the study of peasant means of food production worldwide, no World Trade Association with General Agreements on Tariffs and Trade and no CAP, the Common Agricultural Policy of the European Union" (139). In short, Laudan claims, "Petrini's is an Italy as artificial as a Maui beach resort with its trucked in sand and palm trees or a Disney Magic Kingdom with its oversized Mickey and its undersized castle. Instead of white sand and Mickey, we have tiny rural restaurants that offer up wonderful food, shops that offer artisanal bread, cheeses and salami" (139–40). Full of "sonorous but vacuous" paradoxes, *Slow Food*—and by extension Slow Food—ultimately "has nothing to say about the plight of the hungry worldwide" and thus serves as a rejection of what Laudan sees as culinary modernism's principal goal: "affordable, decent food for all" (142–43).

In 2009, Laudan posted an article on her blog by Luca Simonetti, a lawyer in Rome, who, Laudan says, "was moved to write . . . by the increasing political clout of Slow Food in Italy" (Laudan, "Italian Critic"). The following year Simonetti published a book-length version of his argument in Italian as *L'ideologia di Slow Food*, and a shorter version of his article in English appeared in the *Journal of European Studies* in 2012.

Although Simonetti admits in a comment on the blog post that "Petrini is by no means the devil," he certainly makes Petrini seem like one. Among other things, Simonetti claims that Petrini's Slow Food is—deep breath now—"anti-progressive, antiscientific, worshipping the traditional societies, fond of the little, stratified and perennial communities in which the place of each is eternally fixed and immutable, uncaring and ignorant of history and of the reality of the relations of production, and thus incapable of seeing the inextricable contradictions and historical fictions which build up this vision" (25). As insightful as many parts of Simonetti's analysis can be, the article as a whole reads very much like a prosecutor making his case, which is not surprising considering Simonetti's profession. Lost is any sense of generosity— that Slow Food may have some redeeming qualities, for instance, or that Petrini, like the rest of us, may be a well-meaning but imperfect messenger for his organization. Much of Simonetti's critique tracks Laudan's closely: "We are dealing, in sum," he says, "with pure rhetorical exercises, void of substance: idealizations of an imaginary past, of which one selects only the appealing features, systematically forgetting all others" (19).

In a 2011 master's thesis on Slow Food's "exclusionary rhetoric," Garrett Michael McCord builds on Laudan's and Simonetti's critiques to explore how Petrini's ideological positions are connected to his rhetorical choices. These choices include his failure to address opposing arguments, his acceptance of binary formulations, his romanticized portrayal of rural food producers, his use of religious symbolism, and his appeals to naturalness, guilt, and fear. Like Simonetti's, however, McCord's analysis itself tends to be one-sided, and his relentless quest to catalogue all the ways that Slow Food is "exclusionary" eventually becomes tiresome. Nevertheless, McCord is one of the few people to comment, if only in passing, on Petrini's use of diary entries in *Slow Food Nation*, which McCord simply says help Petrini "establish credibility through experience" (89).

To my mind, these diary entries are central to Petrini's purpose, and they are also what make *Slow Food Nation* the most compelling of his four books. Yes, there are flaws in Petrini's arguments, and no, his vision is not nearly as democratic as he thinks it is. But Petrini's diary entries demonstrate that the man is *human*, not some kind of argumentative robot, and certainly not the devilish character his critics make him out to be. The diary entries are in fact a large part of how Petrini makes his case, and as a result they also illustrate—in one high-profile example—how Petrini's missteps can become Slow Food's missteps. As Justin Myers observed in a 2013 article, while "Slow Food as an organization" and "Slow Food as Carlo Petrini's alternative imaginary . . . are two very different animals," problems with Petrini's vision can quickly become Slow Food's problems.

Slow Food Nation is the most important of Petrini's four essay collections in part because it most fully articulates his vision that food should be "good, clean, and fair." While *Slow Food: The Case for Taste* introduces readers to the Slow Food movement in general, and Petrini's subsequent books (*Terra Madre* and *Food and Freedom*) extend the Slow Food idea to a global network of food communities, *Slow Food Nation* develops the core concepts that remain at the heart of Slow Food's mission, and it does so in a structure unique among Petrini's books.

All of Petrini's collections group his essays into sections that roughly correspond to each book's major themes, but only *Slow Food Nation* interrupts its five sections with seventeen first-person "diaries" that provide important context for Petrini's arguments. Petrini explains the reason for these diaries in a brief prefatory note:

> I have included them because these episodes provide concrete examples of the various theories I shall try to develop in this book, and because I find that a compelling subject like gastronomy must also make use of firsthand knowledge, of traveling, and of direct contact with other cultures or with one's own roots. You cannot become a gastronome simply by reading books: you need to put your theories into practice; you must be curious, you must try to read reality with your senses, by coming into contact with as many different environments as possible, by talking to people, and by tasting. You cannot become a gastronome simply by eating in restaurants; you must meet the small farmers, the people who produce and process food, the people who strive to make the production-consumption system fairer, to render it sustainable and enjoyable. (6)

Although these entries disrupt the flow of the text, they also add to it by grounding Petrini's theories, concepts, and ideas in the stories of particular people in particular places, including Petrini himself. The diaries toggle between his home landscape of Piedmont and locations around the world, including Mexico, the United States, Scandinavia, France, and India, and they address a wide range of subjects: his search for the now-rare "square" pepper of Asti, profiles of some of his most influential teachers, a working group meeting on the future of food held in Florence, an illness that compromised his liver, a visit to the Stone Barns Center for Food and Agriculture, and so on. Early in the book these entries are grouped into sets of three—at the start of the book and in the second part on gastronomy—but in the last three parts they are scattered throughout the text, appearing after almost every other entry in a kind of antiphony.

If, as I have suggested, Petrini's books can collectively be read as a kind of intellectual autobiography, these diaries are critical components of that common text, because they almost always show Petrini actively learning. They demonstrate his childlike curiosity about the world around him— and his frequent surprise at what he discovers: he is "dumbfounded" (9), "immediately fascinated" (177), and "astonished" (211) on a regular basis. His experiences do not end with this amazement, however, but go further by becoming key moments in his gastronomic education: he says he "learned a great deal" (34), has "come to understand" (53), and "realized" (198) many things through these encounters. Of his discovery of the work of Sir Albert Howard, for instance, Petrini writes: "Learning about the ideas and techniques described by this great British scientist and seeing how he approached the Indian cultures and farming practices, drawing lessons from them, made a strong impact on me" (177). As testaments to the transformation of ignorance into knowledge, these diary entries do more than simply establish Petrini's credibility; they also demonstrate his character as someone who is always learning, someone who actively seeks out new people and new experiences in the hope that they will have something to teach him—which they inevitably do. As Petrini himself explains, "these episodes are like phases in a journey through life and through thought" (6).

The degree to which this is true can be seen most clearly in Diary 10, "Green California," which caused a very public dust-up during a visit Petrini made to San Francisco to promote *Slow Food Nation* in 2007.

One of the longer diary entries in the book, "Green California" recounts a day Petrini spent in California as part of an earlier visit to the state in the fall of 2003. The entry appears within part 3 of *Slow Food Nation*, which is devoted to explaining the ideas of good, clean, and fair as "the three essential preconditions which must be met before we can say that a particular product is a quality product" (93). Each of these ideas receives its own chapter, preceded by a diary entry. The section explaining "good," for example, is preceded by a diary entry recounting Petrini's memories of his earliest tastes, illustrating how taste requires both flavor and knowledge. Likewise, the section on "clean" is preceded by a diary entry about prawn farming in India, illustrating how environmental damage and social upheaval can go hand in hand. And the section on "fair" is preceded by the diary entry entitled "Green California," supposedly illustrating how quality food must involve social justice, particularly for small farmers. Except that's not quite the way this section was received, at least not in California.

The entry unfolds chronologically, with a morning visit to the Ferry Plaza farmers' market in San Francisco with Alice Waters; an afternoon trip to the University of California, Berkeley, to speak with agroecologist Miguel Altieri; and a brief evening reflection about the connections between these two experiences. Given that the bulk of the controversy concerned his comments about the Ferry Plaza market, it is worth reprinting these in full:

Morning. The cool morning began quite early: if you are going to the market it is best to be ready by seven o'clock at the latest. The sun was not yet warm enough when, in the company of my chef friend Alice Waters, I entered an elegantly refurbished area of the docks; pretty little coffee shops were serving warm mugs of excellent organic fair-trade coffee; sumptuous bakeries were putting out all sorts of good things, spreading the fragrant aroma of some wonderful kinds of bread. Oil and wine producers were offering samples in marquees, while hundreds of open-air stalls were selling excellent products: fruit and vegetables, fish, meat, sausages, and even flowers—fresh, healthy-looking food, all carefully marked *organic.*

One could have easily spent a fortune there. The prices were astronomical, twice or even three times as high as those of "conventional" products. But how hard it is to produce things so well, and what costs are involved in obtaining certification! I am convinced that the farmers' intelligent productive efforts deserve to be paid for generously, so I was not too scandalized by the prices, even though they were those of a boutique. Yes, a boutique: for I soon realized I was in an extremely exclusive place (bear in mind that this is one of the oldest and most important farmers' markets in town, *la crème de la crème*). The amiable ex-hippies and young dropouts-turned-farmers greeted their customers with a smile and offered generous samples of their products to a clientele whose social status was pretty clear: either wealthy or very wealthy.

Alice Waters introduced me to dozens of farmers: they were all well-to-do college graduates, former employees of Silicon Valley, many of them young. Meanwhile, their customers, most of whom seemed to be actresses, went home clutching their peppers, squashes, and apples, showing them off like jewels, status symbols.

Two of the producers in particular struck me: a young man with a long beard and a man who was selling oil. The former, with long hair and a plaid flannel shirt, held his lovely little blond-haired daughter in his arms and told me, in a conspiratorial tone, that he had to drive two hundred miles to come and sell in that market: he charged incredibly high prices for his squashes, it was "a cinch," and in just two monthly visits he could earn more than enough to maintain his family and spend hours surfing on the beach.

The latter, who wore a tie, extolled the beauties of his farm: it consisted of hundreds of hectares of olive trees, stretching as far as the eye could see, and nothing else. While I was tasting his excellent organic oil on a slice of bread which reminded me of Tuscan bread—absolutely delicious—I was thinking of what he must have uprooted and cleared away in order to grow all those plants, each one of them impeccably *organic*. (130–31)

Petrini's afternoon conversation with Miguel Altieri serves as a useful foil to his morning excursion with San Francisco's moneyed, organic elite—at least in Petrini's telling. Although Petrini characterizes Ferry Plaza as "the marvelous farmers' market," it is clearly the antithesis of Altieri's work. Petrini listens "spellbound" as Altieri tells him of his work developing sustainable agricultural systems in South America. And he pays close attention as Altieri takes issue with the expansion of organic agriculture in California: its vast monocultures (of which the vineyards of Piedmont are another example, Petrini acknowledges) and its armies of poorly paid immigrant workers from Mexico, who literally cannot afford to eat the fruits of their own labor. According to Altieri, organic agriculture in California is "facing the same problems as conventional agriculture . . . the concentration of production, the exploitation of the work of ethnic minorities, monocultures, the reduction of biodiversity, and prices determined by a free market which is not sustainable" (133).

Petrini's comments in the final "evening" section summarize the message about organic agriculture he takes away from his day in California: "Organic farming is undoubtedly a very good thing; it is an excellent alternative to agroindustry, and I do not like to find fault with people—my friends of that morning—who sell products that are so naturally good. But perhaps it is better to have doubts. Reality is complex and resists labels. There is a risk that technocratic thought, when it is deeply rooted, may shape and influence even those tendencies that are opposed to the system, thereby creating other anomalies" (134). Yet Petrini does not seem to see the mismatch of ending his day with a "memorable dinner" at pricey Chez Panisse in the same entry in which he takes issue with the excesses of capitalism in agriculture. Instead, the only contradiction he observes is that he is served "the best *agnolotti* I have ever eaten" in Berkeley rather than in Piedmont. "Green California . . . *vive la contradiction!*" he writes.

It is clear from the surrounding context—of both the book as a whole and the diary entry itself—that what Petrini calls "the luxurious and very important Ferry Plaza farmers' market" (130) is meant to play a very specific role in *Slow Food Nation:* that of the organic movement gone awry. Unsurprisingly, however, the vendors of Ferry Plaza did not take too kindly to being cast in a role for which they did not audition. When Petrini was scheduled to sign copies of *Slow Food Nation* at the Ferry Market—who thought *that* would be a good idea?—the signing was canceled and a meeting was called between Petrini, the vendors, and representatives of the Center for Urban Education about Sustainable Agriculture (CUESA), which runs the market ("Showdown at Slow Food").

In a series of blog posts about the incident, Steve Sando was quick to take Petrini to task, and he did not hold back. Sando is the founder of Rancho Gordo, a Napa Valley–based producer of heirloom beans, and he says Petrini's account of his visit contains "a number of disturbing suggestions and some flat-out lies" (Sando, "Part 1").

First, Sando takes issue with Petrini's focus on the market's prices, which Sando admits can be high but which he says can also be low, depending on

Steve Sando vs. Carlo Petrini, 2007. (Graphic by a Rancho Gordo customer; courtesy of Steve Sando)

the item. Sando also claims that "it's downright irresponsible to bring up price without mentioning what it takes to bring a 69 cent head of romaine to a grocery store," and he accuses Petrini of hypocrisy, given Slow Food's sixty-dollar membership fee (Sando, "Part 1").

To be fair, Petrini regularly talks about paying more for quality products in his diary entries: he blanches at "paying a considerable price—but a fair one, all things considered" for a set of authentic Laguiole knives (16), and he describes his scheme to sell a thousand capons (a variety of chicken) at twice the market price, because "the added value of these quality products deserved to be recognized" (164). Petrini is also certainly aware of the externalities involved in bringing conventional produce to market, and the whole point of his following section on "fair" food is to argue for economic sustainability. "It is not possible for one liter of olive oil to cost less than seven or eight dollars," Petrini claims. "If that does happen it can only mean that the farmer is not being paid a fair amount, that production costs are higher than the final price, and that somewhere along the food production line unfairness must have occurred" (138). But Sando's overall point about price—that it is hypocritical for Petrini to criticize the Ferry Market for its elitism when Slow Food is nothing if not elite—is certainly not far from the mark.

At the same time, Sando's more important point, to my mind, has to do not with price but with prose: namely, that Petrini's diary entry was dishonest. According to Sando, "these two farmers who left such an impression on Petrini simply don't exist. He made them up as a way to illustrate his points." Although Sando says the "surfer farmer" may have been based on Joe Schirmer of Dirty Girl Produce, Schirmer is "an innovative farmer" who "works like a dog and sleeps in a tent on the beaches of Mexico" rather than someone who is "gouging the customer in order to go surfing." As for the olive oil farmer who Petrini thinks may have displaced a more biodiverse landscape to cultivate his trees, Sando says, "Since this farmer and this grove of olives don't exist, it is hard to say what was uprooted, but if it's in Northern California, there's a better chance that this olive grove prevented more suburban sprawl rather than destroy native habitat" (Sando, "Part 1").

Petrini eventually sent a letter to CUESA, apologizing for "any offense caused by this passage, whether to your organization or the many farmers who are your members and collaborators." In the letter, Petrini says "that the translation of this passage was, unfortunately, not as accurate as it should have been," and he admits "that this specific passage may be vulnerable to misunderstandings when judged outside of the context of the chapter in which it resides, not to mention the book in its entirety." Of the latter misunderstandings, he says, "I can only apologize for the imperfections of my own writing, in my attempt to explore some of the contradictions that exist within the highly relative concept of sustainability" (Sula). Although Petrini closed his letter by calling for "a dialogue where we face these issues with an open mind and a generous heart," his letter seems not to have been circulated among the vendors until after their meeting, which unfortunately turned into a shouting match between Petrini and Sando (Sando, "Part 2").

What Petrini did not acknowledge in his letter are the dangers of the diary form, which is meant to be improvisational, incomplete, and experimental. In this entry, as in several others, he seems to have sought to make some sense out of his experiences, to craft a coherent narrative rather than simply document those events as they occurred. He may, in other words, have written himself into a corner, and the only way out was to emphasize those aspects of the market that fit the story he needed to tell. Whether he misremembered the farmers he portrayed or described them as he wanted them to be, the result was a story that didn't ring true to the people for whom it mattered most: his subjects.

Says Sando: "My impression is that Petrini has a certain amount of disdain for America, justified or not. His disdain is based on impressions, not facts. He's only interested in his own output, not in taking in anything beyond the cliches he's already learned. He needs us to be greedy, foolish, over the top or stupid so Poppa Petrini can come in and save us. He won't be happy until we follow his model to the letter. And the funny thing is, there are lots of problems with this market, and a lot of other farmers markets as well, but they're not the problems Petrini describes. Language and cultural bias are going to keep him from understanding what they are and what we should do about them" (Sando, "Part 2").

As Sando's comment suggests, the issue was ultimately one of dueling impressions. Whether you agree with Sando's impression of Petrini or not, it's clear that the problems with Petrini's impressions of Ferry Plaza were neither problems of translation nor problems of context; instead, they were problems of narration.

Food journalist Tom Philpott also took Petrini to task for what he saw as his "gross distortions, overstatements, and questionable assumptions" and lamented that "for all its heat, the Ferry Plaza affair had generated very little deep discussion, within the food community or elsewhere, of food and class." Instead of taking the opportunity to "write a truly provocative commentary on the California scene," Petrini had "lapsed into easy caricature" ("Ruminations").

As necessary as a more nuanced consideration of class dynamics might have been, the problem seems more basic—less about structural inequality, that is, and more about literary structure. Knowing he would discuss "fair" food in the subsequent section, Petrini may well have felt that this diary entry was not the place to address that subject in depth, so he opted instead to use his visit to the farmers' market as a kind of "local color" introduction to his more substantive conversation with Miguel Altieri about organic agriculture. That Petrini eventually included the entire interview with Altieri in his edited collection *Loving the Earth: Dialogues on the Future of Our Planet* suggests that this conversation was his primary purpose that day—and that Ferry Plaza, despite coming first in the narrative, was really of secondary importance.

Finally, the shock that Petrini expressed at the quality of the *agnolotti* at Chez Panisse should not be cause to dismiss him as unconcerned with issues of class, considering that *agnolotti* (meat-filled pasta) are so distinctively Piedmontese: they are typical, ubiquitous, and almost universally delicious, no matter where in Piedmont you find them. Finding a better version in California, therefore, was absolutely worthy of note.

If Ferry Plaza surprised Petrini with its high prices and exclusivity, it may be because Piedmont's markets offer exactly the opposite: competitive pricing and widespread appeal.

Outdoor markets are everywhere in Piedmont, and we visited them every chance we got.

The largest is Turin's Porta Palazzo (Palace Gate) market in Piazza della Repubblica, open every weekday morning, as well as all day on Saturday. It offers a dizzying selection of fruits and vegetables and is said to be one of the biggest open-air markets in Europe. Wandering through its stalls for the first time, we had to keep close watch on one another, lest we get lost—or lose each other—amid the overwhelming amount of produce and people crammed into that impressive space (R. E. Black, *Porta Palazzo*).

A close second is the outdoor market held twice weekly in Asti's Piazza Alfieri and Campo del Palio, which we visited as often as we were able, since we lived about a half hour north of town. Like Porta Palazzo, it pulses with energy, especially on the fourth Sunday of every month, when Asti's antiques market takes over the rest of the city center.

But the real gems for us were the weekly markets that rotated from town to town and ended up structuring the rhythm of our days.

The first time we visited Bra, which we did very early in our time in Italy, we unknowingly arrived just as the city's weekly market was closing, and this certainly whetted our appetite for more. Watching as the last of the vendors discarded their empty vegetable crates and disassembled their stalls felt like missing a train the moment it pulled away from the station. From then on, we went to every market we possibly could, so as to never again feel like we lost out on such an experience.

Of all the weekly markets we visited, our favorites were the Monday market in Murisengo, our neighboring village, and the Thursday market in Moncalvo, about twenty-five minutes away by car. The Moncalvo market is the larger of the two, and it had the added benefit for Grace—okay, for all of us—of being right around the corner from a gelateria. But the Murisengo market was the first market we saw after we missed our chance in Bra, so it holds a special place in our hearts, not to mention being only ten minutes away.

As in every town, market day in Murisengo starts early, around 8:00 a.m., and lasts until about 1:00 p.m. It occupies roughly a quarter mile of the town's main drag, Via Umberto I, from Piazza Boario on the south to Piazza della Vittorio on the north.

Piazza Boario hosts the farmers' market, featuring products from the province of Alessandria, of which Murisengo is a part, and promoting farmers who are affiliated with Campagna Amica, a foundation devoted to local, sustainable agriculture.

Between there and Piazza della Vittorio are what I came to think of as the "mushroomers": vendor after vendor whose stands seemed to pop up like mushrooms after a rainstorm, their nondescript white vans and trucks expanding in an instant into portable storefronts. The sides of their vehicles would open up and out, awnings would unfold like umbrellas, and display cases would appear as if by magic, the street suddenly awash in colorful products from every corner of the globe. Most of these consisted of cheaply made clothing, shoes, and other knickknacks, but there was also the occasional houseware item that would endure more than a season of use. Then, as quickly as they appeared, they would be gone, the street returned to its normal state, completely clear, as if nothing had ever happened.

At the top of the street are more food vendors, who turned Piazza della Vittorio into a veritable gastronomic bazaar every market day, their trucks teeming with a variety of preserved foods, fresh and dried pastas (including *agnolotti*, of course), and fruits and vegetables from around the European Union and the world. These are mostly resellers, who buy their products on the wholesale market and resell them here, rather than the farmers of Piazza Boario. But whereas the farmers' market is relatively tame, the resellers' market is a riot of colors, sounds, and smells, at least to my eyes and ears: the rows of wooden crates, plastic bins, and wax-coated cardboard boxes, heavily laden with every kind of produce imaginable; the animated vendors, communicating with their customers in bursts of fast-moving Italian; the customers jostling and jockeying for position, hoping to be the next in line; the hastily handwritten signs, shouting their prices from whiteboards and colored poster paper jammed into plastic sheaths to protect them from the rain; the smells of olives, anchovies, salami, and cheeses all mixing with the scent of ripe fruits, fresh meats and seafood, and whatever blew in with the morning air.

Best of all, the market changes all the time, depending on the weather, the seasons, the vendors, the customers, the goods on offer, and the subtle interactions between all of these elements. We make the market together, humans and nonhumans, in a kind of collaborative, public performance.

To experience a market such as this—in some ways similar to an American farmers' market but in other ways quite different—is to come face-to-face with another important piece of the Slow Food puzzle: distribution.

It is one thing to advocate for sustainable agriculture, for artisan food production, and the value of good, clean, and fair food. But these things mean nothing if that food cannot make it into the hands of the consumer, particularly if that consumer (or coproducer, in Slow Food's terms) is not a member of a CSA or other cooperative venture.

Thinking about distribution systems is not quite as sexy as working alongside a talented farmer or learning from an accomplished chef, but it is just as important, because of what use is quality food if it rots in the field or never makes it into the kitchen?

Near the end of *Slow Food Nation,* where Petrini calls for the creation of a "virtuous food network" of producers, intermediaries, and coproducers, he turns to the question of creating a fair and sustainable distribution system.

The current global distribution system has certain advantages, he admits, "if one thinks of products of mass consumption such as tea, coffee, or cocoa, which are consumed globally but can be grown only in certain areas, or the provision of food for those large sections of the world population (about half of it) who live in urban areas where food is more difficult to produce" (227).

But the modern system also has numerous problems: it has forced farmers to "abandon crops in the face of a flood of competition"; it has relied upon a system of transportation that has had "a devastating impact on the environment"; it has led to a centralization of power in the hands of "a few big operators who draw strength from their financial structure and supranational operations"; and it has helped to "increase even further the distance between producer and consumer" (227).

In response, Petrini proposes a project of "alternative distribution" that calls on traders to adopt "the new concept of sustainable quality as an essential prerequisite to any operation" (228) and encourages consumers and chefs to adopt a "healthy localism for all those kinds of food which can be grown, raised, and processed near their areas of consumption" (231). In some cases, Petrini offers specific proposals, such as the creation of online directories of quality products, but in general this section is focused more on articulating overarching principles than proposing practical solutions.

Still, one paragraph stands out, for either its prescience or its lack of candor, depending on how you look at it. "Most of all," Petrini writes, the current conception of trade "excludes from the circuit the highest-quality producers, who find themselves outcasts with no market at all for their wares or, in the more fortunate cases, a market described as 'niche'—that is to say, an elitist, exclusive outlet incapable of generating real wealth and development. Reevaluating trade also means rejecting that continual refrain that the gastronome is always having to cope with: 'Quality is expensive, it costs too much, it is not democratic'" (229).

With Slow Food's involvement in Eataly, which was already in development when the Italian version of *Slow Food Nation* appeared in 2005, that reevaluation of trade faced its biggest test.

THE ELEPHANT IN THE ROOM

If you're an artisan producer intent on staying in business, you need to have enough income to offset your expenses, just like anyone else using a balance sheet. That means having enough customers buying your product, or having high enough prices on a smaller amount of product, to pay for your labor costs (including your own salary), your materials, your overhead expenses (lighting, heating, rent, etc.), any marketing and promotion you do, and so on. And all of that happens in a competitive environment, in which other producers or distributors are attempting to keep prices low to attract more customers, while the cost of expenses almost inevitably continues to rise.

So even if you completely agree with Petrini's reformulation of quality food as good, clean, and fair, you still need to stay in business, and that means you need customers. For this reason, a big part of the Slow Food mission has been to expand the markets for artisan products from the local to the global and everywhere in between.

But recall Bill Buford's point in *Heat*: "Fast food did not ruin our culture. The problem was already in place, systemic in fact, and began the moment food was treated as an inanimate object—like any other commodity—that could be manufactured in increasing numbers to satisfy a market" (299). Thus, the elements of agristalgia in Slow Food for a preindustrial world in which commodity production was not the norm and market relations did not determine the value of our food or ourselves. Petrini himself puts it this way: "Food today is more a product to be sold than to be eaten. Reducing our relationship with what we eat almost exclusively to a series of market operations is both the cause and effect of a system that has removed value from food and meaning from our lives" (*Terra Madre* 47).

But Petrini is also not naive, and he knows that most of us do not live in such a world, whether that be a subsistence economy or some form of socialism. Instead, we live in the capitalist marketplace, where goods and services are subject to the laws of supply and demand. As a result, Petrini does not suggest that we abandon this world altogether in order to create an alternative. "It is not a question of completely rejecting the present system or of repudiating the figure of the trader or the role of trade," he says. "Rather, it is a question of exploiting the system's potential" to make it more fair and sustainable (*Slow Food Nation* 228).

The question is, how best to do this?

No matter where I went in Italy, it seemed that every time I started to talk with someone about Slow Food, the conversation inevitably turned to Eataly, the Italian food superstore that opened its first branch in Turin in January 2007.

Students I talked to at the University of Turin said Eataly was intimidating: it requires financial ability and culinary knowledge and expertise. A chef I spoke with in Murisengo said, "Eataly for me is like IKEA: 'You buy my food, and you share my philosophy.'" An independent grocer in Casale Monferrato said that whereas Eataly can have a thousand or so producers represented in its stores, he does not have the space to carry so many products, so he tries to select alternatives to the products featured in Eataly.

Again and again, I found that Eataly was the elephant in the room when it came to Slow Food, because no one seemed able to separate the two.

Which meant, of course, that I needed to pay Eataly a visit.

Late July in Piedmont yields some stunningly beautiful days, with temperatures approaching 80 degrees Fahrenheit and the sky a remarkable shade of cerulean blue—the perfect weather for an outdoor market. Which made it all the more difficult for Nancy, Grace, and me to step through a set of automatic doors and enter the air-conditioned gastronomic pleasure palace that is Eataly Lingotto.

At the time, Eataly had stores in eleven countries, including seventeen in Italy, five in the United States, and three in Japan, but this store was the first, constructed in an old Carpano vermouth factory just north of the Lingotto complex, which used to house Turin's legendary Fiat factory.

After browsing through some of the books on display near the entrance, including several published by Slow Food, we were met by Jennifer Telfeyan, Eataly's chief food buyer and export manager, along with her intern, Lauren Kelleher, who took us on a tour.

Eataly Lingotto is, by any measure, a gorgeous store, due to a combination of clever architecture and savvy marketing. Portions of the store are three stories tall, with balconies, brick-lined walls, and an impressive glass ceiling, so it feels much like an outdoor market tucked between two buildings—though a market whose rougher edges have been smoothed down, not unlike a Disneyland version of Main Street. Here there are no smells of rotting fruit, no exhaust fumes from delivery trucks, no crowded aisles, and no shouting vendors. Instead, there are clean tile floors, tidy displays, and sparkling steel ventilation pipes, ready to carry any offending odors away.

In the central part of the store, vegetables, fruits, and other fresh items are stocked on faux vendor carts with colorful striped awnings, as if the farmer had just stepped away for a moment but would be right back to help you with your produce. Off to the sides are eat-in counters devoted to different categories of foods, including vegetables, salami and cheeses, pizza and focaccia, pasta, coffee, and, of course, gelato. Downstairs is an extensive wine cellar, a beer house, a cheese cave (with the requisite wheels of parmesan stacked on wooden shelves), and a charcuterie chamber, while the rest of the store features many of the typical components of a supermarket, such as refrigerated cases, shelving for dry goods, and counters selling meat, fish, and fresh pasta.

According to Jenn, the original philosophy was, "You can shop here, you can eat here, and you can learn." In other words, the in-store restaurants serve foods you can buy, and both your eating and your purchasing help you learn about those foods and the people who produced them. Or at least that's the idea. Thus, the large banner welcoming customers to the store that quotes Wendell Berry: *Mangiare è un atto agricolo* (Eating is an agricultural act).

At the same time, "We wanted to make it like a normal grocery, where you can do all your shopping," said Jenn. Eataly's motto, she added, is "high-quality products at sustainable prices for everyone." But surely this is no normal grocery store.

Jenn is a graduate of the University of Gastronomic Sciences, and when we spoke, she had been working at Eataly for about two years, doing the purchasing and exporting for Eataly's New York store, which opened in 2010 in partnership with the Batali & Bastianich Hospitality Group. As a result, much of our discussion focused on the differences between the two stores, as well as the problem of scale more generally.

So what's the difference between Eataly and a normal grocery store? In Italy, Jenn says, "it's the artisanal products" (more smaller producers, less industrial production), but in New York, it's that the products are Italian. Whereas the Turin store is "more rooted in the idea of simple food," in New York "there's a different perception of Italian food. It's a foreign cuisine; it's a luxury product." Jenn also noted that "in the US, everything is so extreme," meaning that consumers want to know why all the produce is not organic, when the more important fact may be that it comes from small producers.

As we made our way around the store, our little tour group stopped for a moment in front of something you would never see in the United States: a raw milk vending machine, from which you could dispense full-fat, unpasteurized milk into your own glass bottles. Written in large black letters, a sign on the machine read, *In vetro il latte è più buono* (In glass the milk is better).

While next to it, in smaller red letters, a government-mandated warning sign read, *Prodotto da consumarsi solo dopo bollitura* (Product to be consumed only after boiling), which few people do, because why would you? That defeats the whole point of raw milk, which tastes like it just came from the cow, complete with the beneficial bacteria, vitamins, and enzymes that are destroyed in the pasteurization process. There are dangers to raw milk, of course, which are that it may also contain harmful bacteria—such as campylobacter, E. coli, and salmonella—that can cause a range of foodborne illnesses. But the risk of such an outbreak is quite small, particularly because most raw milk producers are themselves artisan producers who do not use concentrated animal feedlots, where pathogens can spread more quickly.

Jenn asked if Grace would like to try some, and while we don't drink raw milk in Minnesota (where it is illegal), we decided that the benefits outweighed the risks in this case and gave our blessing. Jenn opened the stainless-steel door of the machine, inserted an Eataly-branded paper cup, and filled it to the rim with frothy, cold, raw milk. According to the sign on the machine, the cows had just been milked earlier that day. After a tentative sniff, Grace took a healthy glug and broke out in a big smile. The verdict was in.

On our way back to the main part of the store, I asked Jenn what it was like working with small producers for the American market, given the differences between the two countries in terms of regulations, not to mention their different cultural attitudes about food.

"The producers need to do a little bit of investment to be in the American market," she said, whether those be investments in packaging, labeling, or increased volume of production. But she also noted that it's a risk for Eataly, given that the store buys the food outright from the producers before reselling it to consumers, not unlike the resellers in Piazza della Vittorio. "It's an investment for them, and a risk for us," she said, since Eataly can't know if the products will sell until they reach the store.

Standing in such a beautifully appointed space, so distant from the sources of production, it was hard not to wonder how much the relationships that exist in a thriving food community—such as those on display at a farmers' market—get "outsourced" to Eataly by its customers, like environmentalists who send checks to the Sierra Club in the hope that someone else will do the hard work of lobbying, protesting, and fighting on their behalf.

Talking with Jenn, it also occurred to me that although the *stories* of artisan production that Carlo Petrini shares in his books may travel well, the products themselves can have a harder time of it.

"They're not always geniuses about the paperwork," Jenn says of some of the smaller producers with whom she has worked over the years. When one producer was asked to put a barcode on every product destined for export to the American market, for example, the products all arrived with the word "barcode" written on them in magic marker. As the renegade farmer Joel Salatin memorably wrote to Michael Pollan in *The Omnivore's Dilemma*, "Greetings from the non-Barcode people" (241).

These problems are not unique to Eataly, of course, and could be said about any food retailer, such as Whole Foods or a community co-op, that attempts to bridge the gap between producer and consumer.

But there is one significant difference: Slow Food has not endorsed them.

In the beginning, says Sebastiano Sardo, the Slow Food consultant to Eataly, "there was this perception that this was the Slow Food store, or Eataly has bought Slow Food. But I think the problem has decreased because Eataly has become more famous than Slow Food," he says. "There is still some confusion, but it has decreased."

I am sitting in a conference room above Eataly Lingotto, chatting with Sebastiano beneath a poster of Oscar Farinetti, the founder of Eataly.

Sebastiano might just as well have said that Farinetti has become more famous than Carlo Petrini, because Farinetti's name came up at least as often as Petrini's when I spoke with people throughout the region.

Born in Alba, Farinetti gained fame as the founder of UniEuro, a chain of consumer electronics stores. After selling the chain in 2003 for about $350 million, he eventually returned to the original family business, which was running a grocery store. Farinetti had known Petrini for many years, he shares Petrini's socialist background, and he has given generously to the University of Gastronomic Sciences.

None of these connections seemed to matter to Farinetti's critics, however, who felt that Slow Food's involvement with Eataly was "the definitive sellout," as Corby Kummer has described their reactions ("Supermarket").

"In the beginning, there were big, big doubts" among Slow Food staff about the arrangement with Eataly, Sebastiano tells me. "They were questioning the identity of Slow Food" and worrying about Eataly being called the Slow Food superstore.

The confusion is understandable, since signs throughout the store feature the Slow Food logo and describe the organization's efforts on behalf of endangered foods.

"While Eataly is a business, Slow Food is a consultant," Sebastiano explains. "Slow Food is trying to improve the selection for Eataly. In Italy, the quality foods are defined as 'niche,'" a word that Petrini hates. (Recall Petrini's definition of a niche market as "an elitist, exclusive outlet incapable of generating real wealth and development.") When Farinetti approached Slow Food about serving as a consultant to Eataly, "Slow Food was enticed and intrigued because we wanted to 'de-niche' quality food. We didn't want quality food to be only for elite consumers. We wanted it to be more democratic."

Slow Food thus agreed to function as a "bridge" between small producers and the large company, helping Eataly make connections that would otherwise have been impossible. "It was crucial for Eataly to have the support of Slow Food when it started," he explains.

Eataly is trying to achieve a "difficult balance" between price and quality, Sebastiano admits, between making quality foods available to as many people as possible. And this has not been without controversy.

"We know there are problems," he says, particularly in terms of scaling up artisan production. "For some producers, the business is too big. For others, it's a huge opportunity."

One of the more interesting aspects of our time at Eataly Lingotto was the fun we had identifying the products made by the artisan producers we had visited.

A whole wall was devoted to Mulino Marino's flour, including its *mais ottofile*. Rice from Acquerello had a prominent place on the shelves, as did nougat from D. Barbero and cheese from Beppino Occelli, two other producers whose facilities we toured. And a huge photo of Baladin's founder, Matterino "Teo" Musso, loomed over the beer taps. (Teo was part of the start-up team for Eataly, and he helped identify other breweries to be included.)

Given just how many artisan producers are represented in Eataly—the store started with eighteen and at the time of our visit featured more than two hundred—it's hard to think of a better example of the complexities of scale that Petrini addresses in his writing (Sebastiani, Montagnini, and Dalli 480). Which is why it's surprising that no references to the store appear anywhere in his books.

Whatever the reason for this omission, it's undeniable that the case of Eataly can help us better understand this central question about Slow Food: can artisanal food scale?

It's worth acknowledging, first of all, that while Eataly may share some features with large European food halls (such as Harrods in London or KaDeWe in Berlin), two of its practices with regard to scale help distinguish it from some of the large supermarket chains (such as Aldi and Whole Foods) with which it could also be compared.

Unlike Aldi, Eataly does not require its suppliers to sign an "exclusivity" agreement that restricts them from selling the same products elsewhere. According to Silvia Massa and Stefania Testa, such agreements could ultimately harm the small producers Eataly has pledged to support, as they could drive prices downward and prevent these suppliers from entering other lucrative markets (116–17).

Likewise, Eataly does not feature any "private labels," such as Whole Foods' 365 Everyday Value® products, which are manufactured for Whole Foods by other companies but sold under its own brand. Although private labels could provide higher margins and help Eataly build its own brand, the store has chosen not to adopt them, because they could undermine the producers' own brands, as well as make those producers seem "anonymous" to consumers, which is precisely the opposite of what Eataly is trying to achieve (Massa and Testa 117).

Even with these values-based practices, however, Eataly elicits different reactions from different producers, depending on whom you ask. When we visited La Granda, a meat cooperative based in Genola, for instance, we saw some of the ways in which a partnership with Eataly could help support the kind of agriculture Petrini promotes. Before touring La Granda's new processing facility, we met with Elena Mazzone, an elegant, fast-talking Italian whose sharp white dress, round black glasses, and black beaded necklace were as stylish as the co-op's sparkling new digs.

La Granda was founded in 1996 by Sergio Capaldo, a veterinarian who grew dismayed at Italy's unfolding farm crisis, in which land prices rose so high that the younger generation no longer wanted to farm. (For one farmer near La Granda, the cost of renting land grew 200 percent.) "He saw these people having trouble—they were leaving the farm," Elena said. "It was a false idea— everything was going to end." So despite having little experience running a business, "he decided he was going to do this right and it would pay off."

Capaldo required farmers to adhere to a strict set of standards (or *statuto*) regarding the quality of the meat they raised. In exchange, he agreed to pay them a price that was not only 32 percent higher than the outside market but that also remained relatively constant throughout the year, varying only with the price of grain.

Before La Granda, farmers lacked the incentive to produce a high-quality product that was also environmentally sustainable. "It's like you go the gym, you work hard, but your muscles aren't as big as the one using chemicals." But with La Granda, they had a reason not to use antibiotics, which pleased Elena. "I am a mother before I am a worker," she said.

Eataly eventually became La Granda's main customer, and Oscar Farinetti purchased a financial stake in the company. Partnering with Eataly in this way "helped out," said Elena, "but it helped out because there is quality behind it."

La Granda has grown from working with six producers to working with one hundred producers, but Elena felt that it had done so in a sustainable way. "You grow your respectability; you have your rules. If you don't respect the rules, you're out."

La Granda also operates on the principle of *trasversalità*, or transversality, in which every link in the chain matters. "We give everyone in the chain the dignity they deserve," Elena said, since all it takes is one mistake to ruin the final product. For example, La Granda has two slaughterhouses, or *macello,* which it monitors closely. "If you go to all this trouble," said Elena, "and then you spoil it at the *macello* . . ." La Granda also tracks each animal as it travels from the farm to the slaughterhouse to their processing facility, and the company labels each cut of meat that leaves its facility, so chefs and consumers will know the exact source of their meat.

Because of restrictions on the importation of raw meat into the United States, Eataly New York uses a Piedmontese breed being raised in Montana. But "the philosophy behind it is the same," said Elena. "It's very clean, very healthy. It's a different kind of agriculture. You can easily export the idea— but the meat is different."

La Granda's experience differs from that of Piero Veglio, who sat down with me, his son Valentino, and my friend and translator Paolo Ferrero one July afternoon on their olive oil farm outside Moncalvo. Nancy, Grace, and I had toured the Veglio farm back in May, when the olives were still just tiny buds on the trees, but now they were starting to look a lot more like the fruits we all know and love. It's still early, however, so they still tasted bitter and astringent.

As we eased into the white resin chairs scattered around his patio, Valentino filled me in on his somewhat tangled relationship with Slow Food and Eataly, while Piedmont's ever-present lizards scurried about the walls.

Given its colder climate, Piedmont does not produce much olive oil compared to other regions of Italy, which makes the Veglio farm somewhat unique. Its oldest trees were planted in 1997, and Valentino produces about three to four liters of oil per tree. (The oil is pressed in Imperia, south of Genoa, before being returned to the farm for bottling.) The Veglios also use integrated pest management and spray only when necessary for the olive fruit fly (*Bactrocera oleae*), so their oil can certainly be considered good, clean, and fair.

The beginnings of Slow Food were good, said Valentino, and the organization still has good ideas. But Slow Food "made the step longer than the leg, as we say in Italian," with the first noticeable changes coming in 2006, when Oscar Farinetti became a major sponsor of the Salone de Gusto. "Farinetti in a sense bought the brand of Slow Food. The warranty of quality is given by the brand of Slow Food," Valentino said.

Valentino was asked to be part of Eataly Lingotto when it first opened, but he did not have enough oil at the time to satisfy the demands of the store. When he eventually amassed enough stock in 2007, he agreed to sell his oil to Eataly, but the relationship soon soured and ended up lasting only a few years. "I'm too bitter, like an olive," he joked.

Part of the problem was price. Valentino's idea of the average Eataly shopper is this: "If I go to Eataly, I can find many brands, but I will buy the cheapest." So when his olive oil is on the shelf for sixteen euros, but the Roi brand (in which Farinetti has an investment) is on the shelf for six euros, he is unable to compete. Also, he said, as a grower, "you don't have any kind of personal relationship" with Eataly, so if you don't have the right turnover, your products don't stay on the shelf. (Another food producer I spoke with felt a similar downward pressure on price from Eataly. "They wanted a Ferrari at the price of a Cinquecento" [a Fiat 500], he said.)

To the average consumer, Eataly "looks like the only container that contains all the good things," but this is not the case, said Valentino. "I grew up without Eataly," he said, "so it is not hard for me to market and sell my oil." He thinks the store resembles nothing less than UniEuro, the electronics chain Farinetti originally ran, whereas he prefers to work with smaller grocers with whom he can have personal relationships. These shop owners come to the farm, he said, and they "teach the customer how to shop." A local grocer also "makes a service to our area, because when he talks about our olive oil, he talks about Moncalvo," as opposed to using the region to promote Eataly. Not surprisingly, he said, many of the smaller shops in Torino did not like Eataly coming in; they thought of Eataly as *diablo*, the devil.

THE LOCAL AND THE GLOBAL

Just as the tensions between the local and the global have only intensified as Eataly has grown beyond its original Lingotto store, so too have they continued to follow Slow Food as the organization has expanded beyond the initial vision of its founders. In the same way that Eataly can now be found in a range of locations around the world, including in a highway rest stop outside of Bologna, Slow Food has grown from a group of a few hundred Italian gastronomes in the mid-1980s to a global organization with more than one hundred thousand members. As Slow Food has sought to create what Petrini has called a form of "virtuous globalization," it has also had to cope with its own growing pains, in a textbook example of what social scientists call the "mainstreaming" of a social movement.

Tracking Slow Food's development through Petrini's writing requires a bit more dedication than trying to understand his approach to "quality" food, which he lays out quite systematically in *Slow Food Nation*. This is because Slow Food's institutional focus has evolved in several ways over the twelve years during which Petrini published his five major books.

In *Slow Food* (2003), Petrini offered a version of the organization's origin story and outlined the projects it pursued throughout the 1980s and 1990s. In *Slow Food Revolution* (2006), he fleshed out that history in interview format and detailed many of the endangered foods Slow Food has been trying to protect. *Terra Madre* (2010) used Slow Food's biennial gathering of international food communities in Turin to reflect on how Slow Food has expanded its focus to address global food sovereignty. And *Food and Freedom* (2015) showed how Slow Food may be preparing to take a humbler role in the network of sustainable food communities it has helped to foster over the last thirty years.

Taken together, all of these books suggest a man and an organization trying to come to terms with the relationship between the local and the global, both in terms of the connection of food communities to globalization and in terms of the role that Slow Food should play in a vibrant international movement.

In *Slow Food: The Economy and Politics of a Global Movement* (2023), Valeria Siniscalchi observes that "we can see the 'Good, Clean, and Fair' triad in a chronological order reflecting the place that these three words occupy inside the movement's evolution" (127).

To start at the beginning, spreading awareness of "good" food—food that requires both taste and knowledge to appreciate—was central to the mission of Slow Food in its early years.

After the formation of ARCI Gola in 1986, much of the organization's early growth was tightly tied to its Italian setting, as well as to its active publishing program. That year the group helped to produce *Gambero Rosso* (Red prawn), a food and wine insert that appeared in *Il Manifesto*, and the following year it published a guide to Italian wine, titled *Vini d'Italia*. These were soon followed, in 1990, by *Osterie d'Italia*, a guide to local eating places that reflect the territories of which they are a part. (Beginning in 2010, Slow Food began publishing its own wine guide, titled *Slow Wine*.) Membership in Arcigola went from five hundred to eight thousand in three years, and by 1989 it had reached eleven thousand (Petrini, *Slow Food* 7–8).

At this point, when Slow Food International was launched at its first meeting in Paris, it may have appeared that the movement was quickly outgrowing its Italian roots. For this reason, says Gigi Padovani, "The choice to keep the phrase 'Slow Food' in its English-language form in Italy was an ingenious twist. Those two words, a reaction to the Big Mac phenomenon, became the best way to spread the group's philosophy" (Petrini and Padovani 73). As Petrini himself has put it, "In taking a stand against McDonald's and Pizza Hut, multinationals that flatten out flavors like steamrollers, we know that we have to fight our battle on their ground, using their weapons: globalization and worldwide reach" (Petrini, *Slow Food* 17).

But many aspects of the organization still remained firmly entrenched in their Italian context. Chapters of the group, for example, are called *convivia*, but as Arthur Lizie points out, "The concept of chapters that meet convivially on a regular basis to enjoy food has more in common with Italian social clubs than with the everyday experience of most non-Italians. It is not a way in which people in other cultures tend to socialize" (4).

And Petrini himself has spoken of the way in which both the Italian origins of the group and its English name were as much a hindrance as a help:

> It was clear from the names of those who signed the manifesto at the
> Opéra Comique that many of our first contacts were Italian expatriates. In
> fact, the launch in Paris was really all about the support that was out there
> for the "made in Italy" brand. But that was not our main interest. In the
> first years, in fact, we made the mistake of defining ourselves too much as
> a movement devoted to promoting the Italian approach to living well. As a
> consequence of that, in Germany and in Switzerland, where our wines and
> our cuisine were much appreciated, we had a fairly easy time of it, and the
> Convivia . . . started coming to life. But it was different in France, where
> they did not completely understand what *"les Italiens,"* as they called us,
> really wanted, and they rejected the English term "Slow" that had opened
> so many doors for us. (Petrini and Padovani 83)

So it is important to recognize that, at least initially, Slow Food arose in part to create a market for Italian food products and to promote Italian tourism, both within Italy and outside of Italy. Yes, it was devoted to "good" food, but it was also—much like Eataly—devoted to good *Italian* food—and, we might even say, good Piedmontese food.

The shift to a focus on "clean" food began in the late 1990s, and with it came a shift from a focus on the consumer to a focus on the producer. The most visible evidence of this shift is Petrini's redefinition of the consumer as a coproducer, which is notable for its attempt to eliminate the idea that individuals should be defined by what they consume and emphasize instead how each person's choices can affect what is produced and how.

The problem with the term "consumer," Petrini stresses, is that it hides the externalities—particularly the environmental ones—involved in the production process, of which the consumer is a critical part. "The *consumer* originates with the consumer society: the consumer consumes," Petrini says.

"But he does not consume only the goods that he buys; he consumes earth, air, and water. This *consumption,* if maintained at its present rate, will lead to destruction of resources. . . . So we must change our attitudes, starting with our terminology. *Consuming* is the final act of the production process; it should be seen as such, and not as extraneous to the process" (*Slow Food Nation* 165)

While Petrini's language seems to suggest a primary concern with consuming—that is, "using up"—resources, his vision is more encompassing than that. He recognizes that "the environment" can be seen not only as a *source* of natural resources but also as a *sink* for human pollution. Thus, he says that *consuming* "no longer manages to conceal its true meaning—that of wearing out, using up, destroying, progressively exhausting" (165).

This change in emphasis heralded the appearance of what Petrini came to call "eco-gastronomy," which he recalls introducing to the Commission on the Future of Food in 2003, in one of the diary entries in *Slow Food Nation.* "To put it plainly," he says, "a gastronome who has no environmental sensibility is a fool; but an ecologist who has no gastronomic sensibility is a sad figure, unable to understand the cultures in which he wants to work. What we need, then, is eco-gastronomy" (50).

These conceptual shifts were accompanied in 1996 by two new initiatives: the first publication of *Slow,* the group's quarterly journal, in Italian, English, and German, and the first staging of the Salone del Gusto (Hall of Tastes) in the Lingotto complex in Turin. The Salone, Petrini says in *Slow Food,* "intended to do more than reproduce the tired formula of a wine and food fair"; it aimed to focus instead on "the territory, its products, and its artisans brought face to face with consumers" (59). Slow Food accomplished this by means of two innovations: "taste workshops," in which attendees learned as much about the production of food and wine products as they did about how these products tasted, and the "Ark of Taste," an evolving catalogue of traditional foods in danger of extinction.

Borrowing the concept of extinction from the natural sciences, along with the biblical language that often accompanies it, Petrini waxed prophetic at the end of the Salone about the need for a Noah's ark for food.

"Since the flood was imminent, as I said at the meeting, our ark could be the only salvation. The incoming storms threatened to inflict genocide. Neither marketing, nor community politics, nor sharp intuitions would have been sufficient. We had to build an ark, I said, based on information and knowing that anybody who worked in this sector was a cultural actor" (Petrini and Padovani 93).

The metaphorical deluge to which Petrini refers is the "flood of standardization" that "threatens to overwhelm all the artisanal food production of Italy and Europe" (Petrini, *Slow Food* 89). This standardization comes in several forms: the spread of high-yield monocultures of rice, corn, and other crops; the disappearance of traditional varieties of food products, as well as the heritage breeds of plants and animals on which they depend; and the enactment of food and agricultural policies designed for the industrial food system rather than the small producers of local, traditional foods.

In some cases, small producers could benefit from such standardized policies, like the European Union's geographical indicators PDO (Protected Designation of Origin) and PGI (Protected Geographical Indication), which were intended to recognize when a product is specifically connected to a region in which it is produced. In other cases, a small producer could be severely harmed, such as by the EU's uniform hygiene standards, known as HACCP (Hazard Analysis and Control of Critical Points), which were primarily intended for large corporations. Since these kinds of regulations can require mountains of paperwork and expensive equipment to meet, they could easily drive a small farmer or food processor out of business.

The Ark was thus in some sense meant to be Slow Food's answer to the list of threatened species maintained by the International Union for Conservation of Nature, commonly known as the IUCN Red List. But determining what constitutes an endangered food is not an easy task, particularly when the concept of "endangerment" is not something normally associated with food.

In *Slow Food*, Petrini outlined the five "indispensable requirements" that Slow Food eventually developed for products to be included in the Ark:

1. they must be of excellent quality;
2. they must be species, varieties, plant ecotypes, and animal populations either indigenous or long adapted to a specific territory, or else made with local ingredients, and prepared and aged following traditional local practices;
3. they must be linked, environmentally, socioeconomically, and historically, to a specific area
4. they must be made in limited quantities in firms of small size;
5. they must be at risk of extinction, real or potential (91)

It is revealing, however, that the "risk of extinction" is only one of the five requirements, while the remainder speak to a host of other values, including quality, indigeneity and tradition, locality, and smallness. This demonstrates that endangered foods are not wholly equivalent to endangered species, in that they involve not merely biodiversity but also economic and cultural diversity. And unlike the IUCN Red List, the Ark of Taste is meant to *encourage* the consumption of these foodstuffs, which (somewhat counterintuitively) can ultimately help to protect them and the various forms of diversity they represent.

Petrini is unapologetic about the accommodation to capitalism this kind of protection can require. "The Ark," he points out in *Slow Food*, "is a place for products with commercial potential" (92). And reflecting on the creation of the Ark in *Slow Food Revolution*, he puts it this way: "Growing an endangered species of bean, raising a particular kind of free-range chicken, producing cheeses made from raw rather than industrially pasteurized milk had to become profitable. It wasn't a question of providing charity to poor exploited farmers, but rather assisting them to obtain proper recognition of their work from discriminating consumers who were willing to spend a bit more in exchange for wholesome, better-tasting food. And it wasn't just an Italian problem; it was a global one" (96).

Slow Food's Presidia project grew out of its Ark of Taste initiative, and in some ways the Presidia project seems to have eclipsed the Ark in its importance to the group.

Although the difference between the two is not as clear as it could be, the Ark is more of a catalogue of endangered foods, whereas the Presidia project actively attempts to save traditional foods at risk of extinction.

Like so many of the terms used in the Slow Food universe, "Presidia" has both a common origin and a specialized meaning, unique to Slow Food. As Petrini explains in *Slow Food*, "the word 'Presidium,' which literally means 'garrison fortress,' raised a few eyebrows at first, since it brings to mind trumpet fanfares and military salutes and seems to imply some sort of armed occupation. But it isn't easy to find another word that signifies the action of safeguarding and protecting as directly as 'Presidium' does, and the Italian verb *presidiare* also bears the meanings 'to protect' and 'to reinforce.' As people got used to the word, it caught on surprisingly fast, and although not everyone likes it, it perfectly conveys the intended notion" (93).

I'm not certain that "presidium" is quite as perfect a term as Petrini believes, particularly given its martial overtones, but his point about its significance is certainly accurate, as the Presidia project is all about *action*. If the Ark is a place for products with commercial potential, the Presidia project is an attempt to actively intervene in the marketplace on behalf of those products. It is "the operational phase of the Ark project," as Slow Food puts it (Slow Food Foundation for Biodiversity, "Ark of Taste FAQs").

The Presidia project developed out of the Slow Food Awards for the Defense of Biodiversity, which were first conferred in 2000, and the project was formally launched at the fourth Salone del Gusto in 2002 (Petrini and Padovani 122–23).

Petrini describes the origins of the Presidia in a diary entry in *Slow Food Nation*, in which he recounts his experience attending one of Piedmont's traditional agricultural fairs. In this case, it was the Fiera del Cappone (Fair of the Capon), devoted to a particularly tasty kind of chicken. (Capons are roosters that are traditionally castrated in late summer and then allowed to fatten up in time for the Christmas feast.)

In Morozzo, where the fair was held, writes Petrini, "the women raise magnificent capons with superior sensory characteristics."

> By 1998, however, the fair had become a depressing occasion. Since the rural economy had completely changed in that area, the tradition of the capon had been dying out. Few women raised them anymore, and the buyers were even fewer—and that, despite the time of year, which should have been one of feasting. In fact, the onerous practice—it took great expertise and passion—of raising these birds was no longer repaid by a just price, and the fair had degenerated to a very sad echo of times past.
>
> After that experience, I became convinced that the only way to keep the tradition of the capons of Morozzo alive was to carry out a commercial operation that guaranteed the women a fair price. (162–63)

"We have to stage a military occupation of the grounds where the capons are bred," Petrini joked in *Slow Food Revolution*. "We have to prevent them from being destroyed by advancing globalization" (109).

And so the Presidia project was born.

Determined to help both the capons and the women of Morozzo survive, Petrini met with the women and proposed that if they would increase their production from three hundred to one thousand capons in the next year, Slow Food would buy the capons at almost double the price.

Petrini's description of this meeting with the farmers is revealing for several reasons: it illustrates the challenges of working across the rural-urban divide, it demonstrates the way in which Slow Food attempts to bridge the traditional and the modern, and it foreshadows the difficulties the organization would encounter in trying to expand the Presidia project to the Global South.

"The atmosphere was somewhat tense," Petrini writes. "I still remember those rustic faces, used to hardship, which had little confidence in me and barely a glimmer of hope. Their incredulity was understandable: the townie's offer must have sounded rather strange. They probably thought I was either trying to swindle them or was a mad philanthropist" (163).

Nevertheless, the Presidia project worked, in part because it involved connecting the local community to distant markets. Slow Food sold many of the capons by subscription, using the community-supported agriculture model, and it sent the rest as Christmas gifts to the Italian prime minister (Petrini and Padovani 109).

"Today the fair is prosperous and well-attended, and I am sure that the scenes I witnessed in 1998 will not be repeated," Petrini writes (164).

The Presidia project is now managed by the Slow Food Foundation for Biodiversity, established in 2003, and it features more than six hundred Presidia and involves more than 2,500 small-scale producers around the world. The Ark of Taste, meanwhile, now includes more than 5,900 at-risk products from more than 150 countries.

Much as Petrini's scheme for saving the capons of Morozzo succeeded in part because Petrini himself was able to vouch for the quality of the product he was promoting, the success of the Presidia at large has depended on Slow Food functioning "as an intermediate regulatory body, operating between the State and the self-regulation of producers," as Valeria Siniscalchi has put it (*Slow Food* 147).

What Presidia actually are, and what Slow Food does to support them, are not easily summarized, given that the whole point of the Presidia project is to preserve the unique characteristics of endangered foods.

"Every product presents its own proper specificity and problems," says Petrini. "Intervening directly might mean something quite different from one case to another" (Petrini, *Slow Food* 93).

In addition, Presidia have expanded to include not only traditional products (such as cheese, seafood, and livestock breeds) but also traditional food processing techniques at risk of extinction (such as small-scale coastal fishing) and endangered agricultural landscapes (such as olive oil groves).

Overall, though, it can be said that Slow Food works with local producers to improve the quality of their products, develop guidelines for production practices, create associations and cooperatives, and help them promote their products, techniques, and landscapes to consumers, chefs, and other retailers.

Do the Presidia work? Slow Food says they do.

In a 2012 study, the Slow Food Foundation for Biodiversity analyzed 47 of the 269 European Presidia at the time (about 17 percent) and found that all of them "significantly improved their position on the total sustainability scale," including improvements in sociocultural, agri-environmental, and economic sustainability (Peano and Sottile 15). The study's most important finding, however, may be that the success of the Presidia depended significantly on the "network of players" that Slow Food helps to facilitate (Peano and Sottile 48). This social element, the study's authors observed, "can be considered a precondition for being able to achieve and, above all, conserve the end results over time" (Peano and Sottile 49).

"Slow Food campaigners are not against globalization per se," notes Carl Honoré in *In Praise of Slowness*. "Many artisanal products, from Parmesan cheese to traditional soya sauce, travel well—and need overseas markets to thrive" (63).

But there are also problems with this approach—or at least complexities and contradictions that deserve our attention.

One of these is a version of what conservationists have come to call "hotspotting," such as when a mainstream media outlet publishes a list of the "top ten secret wilderness areas," resulting in an influx of tourists so large that it destroys the very wilderness the visitors sought to experience.

Michael Veseth describes the Slow Food variety of this problem in his book *Globaloney 2.0*, sharing a concern expressed to him by an Umbrian innkeeper: "When Slow Food identifies an artisanal product, like a cheese or a salami, he explained, then suddenly everyone has to have it precisely because it has been given the Slow Food stamp. It must be the best. So they all rush in to buy this great thing, creating a new demand that the supplier, of course, cannot possibly meet. The producers try, but in doing so they cut corners or make compromises and end up destroying the very qualities they set out to preserve. . . . The flip side of the Presidia, then, is that the 'economic impact' that can save a local product from extinction under one set of circumstances may instead bury it" (153).

Petrini is certainly aware of this danger. "Look what happened to *lardo di Colonnata,* a prized Tuscan cured meat," he writes in *Slow Food,* referencing a product in the Ark of Taste: "gastronomes sang its praises to the point that when tourists flood into Tuscany looking for it, they are fobbed off with mounds of imitations. When a product becomes a status symbol, it draws a horde of profiteers and hustlers, and suckers who are easy to fool" (57).

Another thoughtful critic of the Presidia is Ariane Lotti, the farm manager at Tenuta San Carlo in Tuscany, who examined the initiative in the journal *Agriculture and Human Values.* "By establishing production standards," she wrote, "Slow Food mimics the food system it is trying to oppose and facilitates the commoditization of the products included in its Ark of Taste and Presidia projects. The products become consistent, and can move across scales and through markets. Products identified for their singular characteristics become more like commodities once they are part of Slow Food" (81).

Her critique echoes that of sociologists Federica Davolio and Roberta Sassatelli, who argue that "Slow Food's approach to food production . . . fosters a peculiar ambivalence: it aims at creating alternatives to the mechanisms and distortions of neoliberal food globalisation partially [by] relying on its same tools (from product marketing to large distribution) with results that are at best parallel, at worst encompassed by that economic mainframe that Slow Food aims at fighting" ("Polite Transgressions?" 93).

Alison Leitch has described Slow Food as "a new figuring of cosmopolitanism that seeks to rupture binary oppositions—rural/metropolitan, local/global—refiguring the idea of locality as a kind of 'ethical glocalism'" ("Virtuous Globalization" 60).

That word—glocal—comes up a lot in discussions of Slow Food, but it's not always clear what it means, or even if people are using it in the same way.

Petrini himself seems to use it in two different ways when describing Slow Food's Terra Madre gathering. In *Terra Madre,* he says that the meeting "is a concrete way of putting into practice what has been defined as 'glocalism': a set of actions carried out on a local scale to generate major repercussions on a global scale" (1). But in *Food and Freedom* he claims that Terra Madre "is arguably the only, real and non-virtual, glocal subject that exists, adapting global products to local contexts, connecting, ideally and physically, all the earth's gastronomic diversities" (94).

So, on the one hand, to be glocal means to think locally and act globally, while on the other hand it seems to mean the opposite: think globally and act locally.

Fabio Parasecoli helpfully describes the glocal as "a dimension . . . where the global and the local are intermingled to promote localities within the framework of transnationalism," but he says that Slow Food's desire "to maintain the local by fighting globally" is "a near contradiction in terms." Taking his argument a step further, he notes that "the tension between the global and the local is not an easy matter, since both are socially produced" ("Postrevolutionary" 37).

Of all the critiques of Slow Food's delicate balancing of its "glocalism," this one strikes me as the most insightful, in part because it gives the group—and Petrini—an opening. Once you acknowledge the socially constructed nature of reality, what matters isn't that it's socially constructed; what matters is how you construct it and why.

EATING IN PIEDMONT

It's one thing to read a discussion of Slow Food's ideas in the abstract, but it's another entirely to experience them, and part of what our experience of living in Piedmont—and especially in Monferrato—taught me is that being a coproducer is a lot harder than it looks.

I know that sounds ridiculous; we were living in Italy, after all. How hard could it be to eat delicious food on a regular basis?

But this is Petrini's point, or at least one of them: that being a coproducer really isn't the same as being a consumer. And eating good, clean, and fair food really isn't the same as eating food that just "tastes good," Italian or otherwise.

Instead, being a coproducer means moving away from the *individualistic* model of the consumer to the more *community-oriented* model implied by the word "coproducer."

This shouldn't be a surprising message, coming from a man who has long been associated with the Italian Communist Party, but knowing this doesn't make it any easier to put his message into practice.

Take the Presidia, for instance.

As we were walking around Eataly, we spied signs here and there advertising *la carne e il pesce dei Presìdi* (the meat and fish of the Presidia) and *e dolci dei Presìdi* (the sweets of the Presidia), along with signs and brochures that attempted to explain how products affiliated with a Slow Food Presidium differed from the other products lining Eataly's shelves.

These signs also included a logo that Slow Food Italy created in 2008 at the request of producers who were seeking to further differentiate their products in the marketplace. The logo, which resembles a sort of multicolored cornucopia, is both different from yet reminiscent of the snail symbol that has been Slow Food's logo since the group began. (Initially, the snail symbol could not be used to sell a product, but Slow Food has since changed this policy, and now a new Presidia brand features the familiar snail symbol above the words "Slow Food Presidio.")

Jenn Telfeyan of Eataly admitted, however, that the idea of the Presidia is "not common knowledge," even in Italy, which is home to more than half (about 390) of all the Presidia.

This matched my experience of Italians' awareness of Slow Food generally, which ranged from complete ignorance to passing familiarity to enthusiastic partisanship, either for or against the group. In fact, it is fair to say that despite its deep Italian roots, Slow Food still remains (to use one of Petrini's least favorite words) a "niche" organization in its home country.

According to the brochure I picked up in Eataly, by buying the products

Slow Food logo and the original Slow Food Presidia logo

associated with the Presidia, my purchase "will help to support the custodians of biodiversity" who "adhere to production rules that respect tradition and environmental sustainability."

But this assumes that these values are something I share, and that I want to become a certain kind of coproducer. After all, we're each a coproducer of one kind or another. It's just that some of us recognize our coproduction while others do not, and some of us can afford to support different kinds of production practices with our purchases, if and when we choose to do so.

Assuming I wanted to become Petrini's kind of coproducer, there is still another issue to consider, which is that purchasing Presidia products is only one way for me to participate in a food community—and a relatively shallow means of participation at that.

Consider some of the other ways we attempted to understand our adopted food community during our time in Italy.

For one thing, we went to as many local festivals as possible, each of which showcased distinctive regional foods. Some of these were itinerant festivals of food and wine, such as Golosaria Monferrato and Riso & Rose, in which you travel from place to place over a series of days, sampling local specialties, such as the risotto with rose petals we had during Riso & Rose.

Others were place-based festivals, such as the Fiera di San Marco (Festival of St. Mark) in Cocconato and the Stelle in Stalla (Stars in the Stable) in Tigliole. At the Fiera di San Marco we tasted some robiola di Cocconato, a fresh soft cheese that is recognized as a "traditional agri-food product" (*Prodotto agroalimentare tradizionale,* or PAT), a certification scheme unique to Italy, similar to the European Union's PDO and PGI. And at the Stelle in Stalla we went to see the Razza Piemontese (Fassone), an ancient breed of white cattle that was both the first Presidium and the focus of La Granda's efforts to revive the breed's sagging numbers.

We also went out of our way to understand some of the typical foods of the region, such as the capons that started the Presidia project and the Bue Grasso (or Fat Ox), a particular version of the Razza Piemontese.

To do this, we stopped into Macelleria Fratelli Micco in Moncalvo, one of the finest butcher shops in the region, where we met young Stefano Micco, who was in training to join the family business.

Stefano's parents, Lauro and Marina, own both the shop and the family farm, Azienda Agricola Monfrin, which is located right outside of town. Not only is Lauro one of the few butchers in the area to breed his own cattle, but he has won the title "best butcher in Italy" as a result of his attention to every link in this (very short) chain of production.

After we spent some time admiring the many awards lining the walls of the shop, Stefano graciously hopped in our rental car for the short ride to the farm, where his sister Giulia also lives.

All the cattle on the Micco farm graze freely on the hillsides, and many of them were out and about as we arrived, so naturally we wandered down to say hello.

As we did so, we also spied what appeared to be a chicken coop in the distance.

"Pollo?" I asked.

"Si," Stefano replied. "Galline e cappone." Hens and capons; we were in luck.

We walked over to see the birds, which were roaming around a dusty, fenced-in area.

"Cappone castrato, si?" I asked Stefano, just to make sure I had understood him correctly.

"Si," he replied.

We stood looking at the birds for a few minutes and watching the cattle graze happily on the hillside. The capons also looked about as happy as testes-free birds could look, I thought.

"Cappone castrato, non tu castrato," I said to Stefano at one point, pointing back and forth between the capons and him.

"No!" he replied, laughing and crossing his hands in front of his body. "No castrato, no castrato!"

We understood one another just fine.

Farmers around the world often castrate male animals to reduce aggression, but capons and Bue Grasso are both castrated for their flavor, which tends to be richer and more complex due to the lower levels of testosterone present in the animals. Like the capon, the Bue Grasso is also considered a holiday delicacy: it is castrated after only a few months and then eventually confined to fatten, flavor, and tenderize its meat.

On our way out, we stopped to see the covered, open-air stalls where Stefano and his family were tending to each Bue Grasso with exceptional care, feeding them only with grain produced on the farm itself and preparing them for the next edition of the Fiera del Bue Grasso a Moncalvo, which would be held just up the hill, right in front of the family's butcher shop, come December.

Understanding the food community in and around Villadeati required that we be intentional in two other ways as well—eating out and eating in.

In some sense Slow Food began in restaurants, rather than in the kitchen, so it follows that a lot of what we had to learn about how food is related to place we would learn by eating out.

Petrini himself observes in *Slow Food Nation*, "Even gastronomes—I myself am a good example here—have gradually abandoned the kitchen." He continues: "I myself—I freely admit my deficiencies—am not a good cook. But I am aware of the respect and the scientific interest that culinary skill merits, and I know that I must take this into account if I wish to judge a dish in a restaurant; so I always make a point of asking to meet the chef and his team, of visiting the kitchen and watching the staff at work" (78).

Our two favorite places to eat were each in a neighboring town: Caffe Della Fontana in Murisengo and Restaurante da Maria in Zanco.

Caffe Della Fontana is located at the top of Via Umberto I, directly across from the resellers' market in Piazza della Vittorio, and it is named for the small fountain below the market, which is also home to some colorful carp.

It's a lovely café: clean and bright, painted in shades of ivory and gray, with a marble espresso bar and large wooden tables for sharing a meal or lingering over one of the café's many newspapers. Its shelves are filled with an eclectic collection of local wines, candies, and preserved foods, and when the light hits just right, the sun casts shadows of its window designs onto the walls.

Open since 2006, Caffe Della Fontana is run by Michela Aiassa, its owner and chef, with help from her mother, who can often be found behind the espresso bar. Michela also owns Al Riccio, a bed-and-breakfast in Cocconato, but despite a life in the food industry, and serving some amazing cakes and pastries, she claims she is "not a cook."

"I made a mistake in my life path," she says, "because I got here without having that background."

Her mother hates to cook, she acknowledges, so Michela learned to cook from cookbooks and magazines and now proceeds by "intuition."

Michela's place is not the only café in town, however, and many of the people who frequent it are from outside of Murisengo, and even outside of Italy. Still, when it's possible to promote local products, she does so, and her clientele has developed over time as a result.

What does she think about Slow Food?

"You have to explain to me what you mean by Slow Food," she says.

Not unlike her own café, which caters as much to visitors as it does to locals, she thinks that a lot of Slow Food producers are producing good-quality products to be sold outside Italy, not here.

"The market is not here," she says.

A few miles away, in nearby Zanco, Giorgio and Roberto Penna run Restaurante da Maria, which is about as close to the Slow Food ideal of the *osteria* as you're likely to find.

Not surprisingly in a community this small, Michela is the sister of Giorgio's wife's cousin. Unlike Michela, however, Giorgio comes from a family of cooks. His grandmother, Maria Carbonero, opened the restaurant in 1954, and it passed down to his mother and father in 1977, with his mother doing the cooking. Giorgio inherited the restaurant in 1989, and he's been running it ever since: Giorgio in the kitchen, and Roberto in the front of the house. (Their father died in 2005, their mother two years later.)

Also unlike Michela, Giorgio makes "only typical and historical dishes." But like Michela, he does not use recipes. "You know or you don't know the recipe," he says. Instead, Giorgio says he follows three principles: simplicity in the recipe, a high quality of fresh materials, and experience in the kitchen. (He had been cooking for twenty-four years when we spoke.)

In *Slow Food*, Petrini describes *osterie* as "welcoming places to eat, where you can enjoy the dishes and wines of the territory you are in without being bled dry by overpricing or imprisoned in improbable fantasy settings" (51). They are, he says, "the symbolic locus of traditional cuisine, run as a family business, with simple service, a welcoming atmosphere, good-quality wine, and moderate prices" (51).

This is surely the profile of Restaurante da Maria. With its red tile floor, yellow stucco walls, and ladder-back rush-seat chairs, the space is rustic without being kitschy, and the food matches the decor in its elegance and simplicity.

Grace says the food "tastes awesome"—high praise from an eight-year-old—so we arrived early one night for dinner, to give us time with Giorgio in the kitchen.

As we walk around the restaurant, Giorgio informs us that Piedmont has the highest number of recipes and the highest number of cheeses in Italy, and he notes the hybrid nature of Piedmontese cuisine, which has been influenced not only by the peasant traditions of the rural poor but also the aristocratic tastes of the urban Torinese, who themselves were highly influenced by the French. (From the fifteenth century until 1861, Piedmont was part of the royal House of Savoy, whose lands stretched from Monferrato in the east to the western side of the French Alps near Chambéry.)

"In the last century," Giorgio says, "the king, the marquis, change the cook like the football player."

Reeling off a list of his favorite foods, Giorgio might just as well be reading the contents of a Piedmontese cookbook: *carne cruda* (raw meat salad), *bagna cauda* (raw vegetables served with a dipping sauce of olive oil, garlic, and anchovies), *agnolotti* (Petrini's favorite), *finanziera* (a meat dish made from offal), *fritto misto* (a platter of fried foods), and *bianco mangiare* (a milk-based pudding).

To take just one of these, for the *bianco mangiare* Giorgio uses fresh milk cream, orange flower water, almonds, two spoonfuls of peach cream, and raspberries. He offers it as a seasonal dish, because he can only find good almonds in the winter. "You can find a similar plate in Paris," he notes, referring to blancmange and underscoring the French influence on Piedmontese cooking.

As we step into the kitchen, Giorgio schools us on how he prepares his *carne cruda*. (The first time we ate this, we misheard Roberto describe it as "romaine salad"—quite a different beast, so to speak, than the "raw meat salad" we received.)

"The quality of this plate is only one thing," Giorgio says: "the quality of the meat."

He uses the same Razza Piemontese raised by La Granda and the Micco family, but Giorgio gets his meat fresh every other day from Macelleria Rosso di Rosso Gilberto—"the best butcher in Murisengo," he declares—which is also located on Piazza della Vittorio, right across from Michela's.

The dish could not be simpler, and we watch as he chops the beef by hand and then seasons it with freshly ground pepper and white salt flakes (both from Cyprus), extra virgin olive oil from Ardoino (based in Liguria), and a splash of white wine from Gotto D'oro (based outside of Rome). In Piedmont, he tells us, *carne cruda* is made not with lemon juice but with wine: white in spring and summer (we are here in May), and Barbera in fall and winter.

After a quick stir with a fork, he then gently places some of the meat into a ramekin, upends it into the center of a sparkling white plate, and garnishes the plate with three large dots of aged balsamic vinegar, three small lettuce leaves, and a sprinkling of black salt flakes (again from Cyprus). It is, not to oversell things, a masterpiece of simplicity.

What this dish, and the rest of Giorgio's cooking, tells us is not easily reduced to a catchphrase or a stereotype, even one as innocuous as an *osteria*. Rather, it is a complicated reality composed of tradition and modernity, the local and the global, and the individual and the community.

Slow Food, says Giorgio, "is fantastic," and Oscar Farinetti is "a great businessman, a great intelligence, like Carlo Petrini." Yet much of what Giorgio uses is hyperlocal: he buys his chicken "*only* from Artuffo," he stresses, referring to a poultry farm a few miles away, and he gets his wine—the lovely Môrej we are drinking—from Enrico Druetto in Alfiano Natta, the next town over.

He believes "it is a sin to use frozen materials," but he makes an exception for large institutions. "I am here from morning until evening, so I have a lot of time" to prepare fresh food, he says. "In my kitchen, there isn't frozen materials," he insists.

Outside are the kennels in which he keeps his truffle-hunting dogs, and recently Giorgio and his cousin found two truffles weighing a total of one kilo, which they sold for three thousand euros, part of a large international market for what have become symbols of haute cuisine.

And while many of his customers are local, others (as with Michela's) come from far away: most from northern Europe, but a few—like us lucky eaters—from the United States.

Does that make us part of this food community or not?

The novelist John Gardner was said to have remarked that there are only two plots in all of literature: either you go on a journey, or the stranger comes to town.

In *Slow Food,* Carlo Petrini pondered a similar dichotomy and came down on the side of travel. "Is it better for people to travel or products to be shipped?" he asked. "It is better for people to travel," he answered, "as long as they move attentively, choosing their route with intelligence and seeking to acquire as much cultural stimulus as possible from the land in which they find themselves" (58).

As much as Slow Food is about the expansion of markets for artisan products, it is also about gastronomic tourism, which raises a host of issues about authenticity and tradition.

Petrini's comments on tourism make this especially clear.

"To savor the special dishes that every land boasts means feeling for the tendons of tradition and interacting with a patrimony made up of people, landscapes, and monuments," he writes in *Slow Food*. "No product can be plucked whole from the context of which it is itself a cultural expression" (57–58). Switching metaphors from flood to drought to describe the process of standardization, he then argues that the value of those traditions is closely tied to their authenticity: "In a world dominated by hegemonic forces that are threatening to turn it into a desert, our agricultural and food heritage has become a significant asset, and we have to actively defend its authenticity and favor the development of the territories in which it is rooted" (58–59).

This poses a challenge for any tourist, whether a short- or long-term visitor, for how is one to know what is a "tradition," and how far back must we go before an activity becomes one? If we shop at the same grocery store every week for a month, does our weekly shopping trip become a "family tradition"?

Likewise, chasing authenticity is a fool's errand, beyond avoiding the most explicit kind of deception that Petrini references in *Slow Food*: thinking you are buying a truffle unearthed by the likes of Giorgio, only to discover that it was imported from China—an increasingly common occurrence (Jacobs).

According to Petrini, "all the truffles in Alba and the surrounding area would not be enough to meet the demand generated in a single day by the mass of tourists that swarm into the capital of the Langhe. So truffles are brought in from foreign countries, deceiving the consumers and doing a great disservice to the quality of the excellent Alba truffles, a genuine local specialty of which only the name now survives" (*Slow Food* 58).

The kitchen is perhaps the best place to make sense of this mass of interconnected issues because it's a place where, by design, things are meant to come together.

During the time we spent in Villadeati, we tried as best as we could to be

Petrini's kind of travelers, to "acquire as much cultural stimulus as possible" from the land in which we found ourselves.

In terms of food, that meant trying to understand this place within the context of Italian, Piedmontese, and Monferrato cuisines, which was no easy task.

In Turin we picked up the British edition of Marcella Hazan's *Essentials of Classic Italian Cooking,* on whose first page we learned that "the cooking of Italy is really the cooking of regions that long antedate the Italian nation, regions that until 1861 were part of sovereign and usually hostile states, sharing few cultural traditions, no common spoken language . . . and practising entirely distinct styles of cooking" (1).

Hazan's observation—that "Italian food" is as much a construction as Italy itself—could and does apply to Italy's regions, as well as to the local communities within those regions. In fact, the closer you look, the more it becomes clear that the traditions that Slow Food intends to protect are inventions, not unlike Fabio Parasecoli's observation that the categories of the global and the local are also socially produced.

There is no question that "tradition" is a core concept for Petrini: the words "tradition" or "traditional" appear 67 times in *Slow Food,* 104 times in *Slow Food Nation,* 45 times in *Terra Madre,* and 66 times in *Food and Freedom.* But what's striking is that Petrini has long acknowledged the constructed nature of tradition.

References to this fact appear throughout his work, but its connection to food communities is perhaps best articulated in *Terra Madre.* There Petrini closely echoes what Piero Rondolino of Acquerello had to say about the false dichotomy between tradition and innovation. According to Petrini,

> A frequent mistake is to view tradition as immobile and static, as a thing of the past. Even people who evoke, describe, and honor tradition often risk viewing it as a non-evolving thing, a singular curiosity that came to a standstill at some point in the past. This is a vision that ultimately cuts us off from our roots, depriving us of the memory of what we were and the history of our people. . . .
>
> We don't have to decide which is better: tradition or progress, past or future. But we do have to avoid generalizing, simplifying, and pitting the two concepts against each other.

Food communities are for the continuity of tradition, and they guard their memory precisely because it guarantees their identity in an increasingly standardized world. But they are also aware that it would be a serious mistake not to exploit the resources that globalization and technology make available. All they ask is to do this responsibly and sensibly. (53)

These few paragraphs quite compactly address the relationship between multiple themes in Petrini's work.

First, a community's identity is closely connected to its food traditions, which are themselves dependent on its environment. As Petrini explains in *Food and Freedom,* food culture "has to be formed in connection with context, with the resources available in a local area, with ecosystems, with one's relations with one's neighbors. In this way, it can be stratified and solidified and transformed into what we call tradition and which ultimately constitutes identity" (92).

Second, the enemy of tradition is not "progress" so much as the homogenization of cultural diversity brought about by industrial modernity. Instead of industrial agriculture, Petrini supports a *diversity* of traditional farming practices; instead of industrial food processing, he promotes a *diversity* of artisanal traditions; and instead of industrialized fast food, he advocates for a *diversity* of regional food traditions.

Third, tradition itself is not the goal but, rather, the long-term health of the community as a whole. "After all," Petrini writes in *Food and Freedom,* "only the naïve or incompetent believe that tradition, just like identity, is fixed and immobile, like an exhibit locked in a showcase in a museum. Everything is in motion; what is important is that it goes in the right direction" (93).

As for authenticity, yes, Petrini did say that we have to actively defend the "authenticity" of our agricultural and food heritage in *Slow Food,* but compared to "tradition," the idea of authenticity receives almost no mention at all in Petrini's books. For this reason, it is a significant misreading on the part of some of Petrini's critics to suggest that authenticity and tradition are somehow equivalent. Charles Lindholm and Siv B. Lie, for example, claim that "by relying on authenticity as its marker for the really real, Slow Food glosses over the ever-changing socio-economic and historical construction of 'tradition'" (63). Yet this is clearly not the case, as Petrini's own words reveal.

Indeed, in one prominent example, Slow Food actively created a Presidium product that did not previously exist—Tibetan yak cheese—so that it could help protect a community and build a local economy. In a collaboration with the Trace Foundation and the Ragya monastery in Qinghai, the Slow Food Foundation for Biodiversity worked to help nomadic herders on the Tibetan plateau earn a livelihood by producing a new cheese using excess yak milk that could be transported and sold to Western markets.

"Since Presidia promote local historic and traditional products, we initially reckoned it would be unthinkable to help produce and promote this type of cheese," observed Serena Milano, director of the Slow Food Foundation. "But the ethical value of the proposal put forward by Trace Foundation prevailed over theoretical correctness: after all, people sometimes die by sticking too rigidly to the rules, while even a small additional income for such disadvantaged populations can change their lives completely" (Milano 76). This unconventional project, Petrini says, is an example of how the Presidia strategy "is not about nostalgia for the past and finding ways to keep it alive at all costs, but is, rather, about creative interventions that seek to combine ancient knowledge and modern advantages, the local dimension at the global level" (*Tibetan Yak Cheese*).

In the rhetoric of Slow Food, therefore, "tradition" is neither a synonym for "authenticity" nor merely a signifier of cultural longevity but a handy watchword for a range of values that sound a lot like "sustainability."

Once we recognize that food traditions are a malleable thing, then what we're doing in the kitchen becomes much more interesting, because it becomes about history—and the stories we tell one another about that history. Why this food, in this way?

One of my favorite passages from all of Petrini's writing gets at precisely this understanding of tradition, in all of its diversity and historical contingency:

> Take a dish of pasta with tomato sauce. Look at it. Try to imagine (unless you are so fortunate as to already *know*) the wheat from which the pasta was made, the tomatoes that make up the sauce, the basil that aromatizes it, the parmesan that makes it more tasty. Imagine the people who sowed and processed the plants, the animals that gave that milk, the people who milked them, the people who reaped the wheat. Think of the places of provenance: traditions, cultures (the wheat was Ukrainian or Canadian;

the tomatoes Spanish; the basil Ligurian; the parmesan . . . well, at least that was traceable), societies, economies. Think of the history: tomatoes brought to Europe from America; the pasta, whose method of production is the result of an exchange between Arabs, Chinese, and Italians. Imagine the journeys, the transport, the processing, the packaging that those products have been subjected to. Think back to your purchases, where you bought them, how you brought them home, and which hands—yours?— cooked that pasta. (*Slow Food Nation* 174–75)

Imagine. Much of the power of this passage comes not only from the depth of Petrini's awareness of food history but also from his direct address through the second-person singular: "you." We are being placed in front of that dish of pasta with tomato sauce (the symbol of Slow Food's first pro- test against McDonald's) and asked to imagine its provenance, the human and animal labor involved its production, and the history of exchange that brought its various elements to our table.

The passage also stands out for its awareness of the *lively materiality* of food and the way these materials themselves contribute to a food commu- nity. These are, after all, *raw materials* Petrini is asking us to consider.

Jane Bennett has faulted Slow Food for failing to fully appreciate the materiality of food, asking, "What would happen if slow food were to incor- porate a greater sense of the active vitality of foodstuff? If I am right that an image of inert matter helps animate our current practice of aggressively wasteful and planet-endangering consumption, then a materiality experi- enced as a lively force with agentic capacity could animate a more ecologi- cally sustainable public." While there is some truth to Bennett's observation, the materiality of food is in fact present in Petrini's work, and not merely as a "resource or means" as Bennett has suggested (51).

The sociologists Roberta Sassatelli and Federica Davolio, who raised questions about Slow Food's approach to globalization, describe its attention to the materiality of food in Marxist terms. Building on Karl Marx's notion of "commodity fetishism," or our convenient forgetting of the human labor involved in the production of commodities, Sassatelli and Davolio describe the work of Slow Food as "de-fetishization," or "the illumination of the pro- duction relations which are embedded in commodities," through its focus on material culture (Sassatelli and Davolio 219).

Whether we think of Slow Food in terms of storytelling or defetishization, it's clear that food is actually more of an active verb—grow, process, cook, eat—than the static noun it appears to be.

If we bring all these pieces back together in the kitchen, they help to explain what we were doing and why. We weren't seeking a rural Italian fantasy of the kind Stephanie Malia Hom rightly criticizes in *The Beautiful Country*. Instead, we were seeking to understand the story of food in this place, the history of its role in the life of this community.

But we didn't always know this.

When we first arrived, I drew a circle around Villadeati on a map of Piedmont, wanting to see what a hundred-mile diet would look like in our temporary home. It stretched past Piacenza in the east, into Switzerland in the north, past the French Alps going west, and south into the Mediterranean Sea.

Yet the more I learned about the diversity of ways food functions here, the less this seemed to be the right interpretive tool.

There is certainly some interest in the notion of "food miles" in this part of Italy, and signs indicating "kilometre zero" produce can sometimes be found in shops and markets. But the more important notion turned out to be food communities, which are enriched—though not defined by—their culinary histories.

Lucy M. Long has described this approach to culinary tourism as shifting the focus from food to foodways, from the product that is consumed to "the total network of activities surrounding food and eating" (9), and this was certainly our experience as we sought to understand this place through food.

The notion of food communities also helped us better appreciate the value of the "typical" foods in the region, such as those Giorgio likes to serve at Restaurante da Maria.

While the term "typical" is not unique to Italy, it is much more widely used here than in the United States, where we might talk instead of "local" or "regional" foods. In fact, the term (*tipici*) is so widely used in Italian that Petrini considers it to be a "worn-out word . . . the equivalent of 'old-fashioned' or 'homemade' in English," and he prefers to describe the products in the Ark of Taste as "historical and localized" rather than typical (*Slow Food* 92).

As Maura Franchi has observed, "The concept of typical is not easy to describe, since it refers to a plurality of dimensions that belong to the product itself and to its characteristics, to the systems of its production (how it is made), and to a specific area" (48). Nevertheless, she posits that there are three key terms associated with the idea: territory, taste, and tradition. But just like the idea of tradition, the idea of the "typical" is a cultural construction, the product of storytelling as much as of the land itself.

Travel guides, tourist pamphlets, magazine articles, websites, encyclopedias—more resources are devoted to Italian food than most of us would ever have time to read (or watch, considering the popularity of Stanley Tucci's *Searching for Italy*). Fortunately, the literature on Piedmontese cooking, though still substantial, is markedly less extensive, and that devoted to Asti and Monferrato even less so.

One of the more interesting sources for information about some of the typical foods of the region is the Touring Club of Italy's guide to *Authentic Piedmont–Aosta Valley*. This is in part because it was the publication of the club's 1931 *Gastronomic Guide to Italy* that first introduced the idea of "typical" products to the Italian public. As Fabio Parasecoli points out, the guide "revealed a new mentality that looked at traditional products as 'specialities' and 'typical products' that could attract tourists and that presupposed mobility, disposable income, and an efficient transportation system" (*Al Dente* 177). That such products appeared alongside the rise of automobility and Italy's national railway system demonstrates that the category of the "local" requires an "other" against which it can be defined: either you go on a journey, or the stranger comes to town. In either case, something new is created.

Food historians Alberto Capatti and Massimo Montanari put it this way:

> In the context of culinary traditions, one might assume as self-evident that identity has to do with *belonging* to a particular place and that it involves the products and recipes of a specific location. Thinking about it like this may cause one to forget that identity may also—and perhaps primarily—be defined as *difference*, that is, difference in relation to others. In the case of gastronomy one thing is quite clear: "local" identity is created as a function of exchange, at the moment when (and to the degree that) a product or recipe is brought into contact with different systems and cultures. The "local" product, if consumed only at a local level, is devoid of geographical identity, since identity comes into play through a process of relocation, of "delocalization." (xiv)

Like I said: being a coproducer is a lot harder than it looks. It's almost like a newfangled kind of recipe: first you defetishize your food, then you delocalize it. Pretty soon, we should have something good to eat!

Another reason the Touring Club guide is interesting is because of how far it drills down to the local level in search of these "typical" foods.

Each section of the chapter on food covers a different category (pasta, hams and salami, cheese, wine, and cakes), and within each section listings are organized first by region, then by province, and then by town. So, for instance, a reader could learn that in the province of Alessandria (in which Villadeati is located), in the town of Casale Monferrato (to which we often traveled) can be found Pasticceria Krumiri Rossi, a pastry shop that sells a delicious shortbread biscuit called *krumiri* (one of our favorites). Moreover, the guide points out that *krumiri* were invented in 1878 to honor King Vittorio Emanuele II of Savoy, whose handlebar mustache the biscuits are said to resemble, and that they contain flour, butter, sugar, fresh eggs, and vanilla (188–89).

Eat a cookie, get a history lesson and a recipe; that's how I like it.

As we stocked our kitchen from around the region, then, we tried to be mindful not only of the foodways that help give these raw materials meaning but also the constructedness of these foodways over time.

And when it came time for dinner, authenticity was not on the menu so much as thoughtfulness: what makes sense in *this* place, for *these* people? How can we best connect the communities of interest around the table— however fleeting and improvisational they may be—with the more durable communities of place from which they derive their sustenance?

One way to do so, of course, is to grow your own food. So Grace planted tomatoes, green beans, and basil in a small garden in back of our house, and near the end of our visit we were able to author a few of our own food stories, half native to this place, half from elsewhere, such as a Caprese salad (from Capri, of course) with the tomatoes or some pesto (from Liguria) with the basil.

Meals with friends—some American, some Italian, some British—were similarly hybrid affairs, at least in the Italian sense of mixing foods from different regions, such as using local flour from Mulino Marino to make focaccia (also from Liguria) or pizza (from Naples).

This wasn't quite fusion cuisine, but it did acknowledge John Dickie's point in *Delizia*, his history of Italian food, that "all food, ultimately, is fusion food" (350).

Dickie took Petrini to task in *Delizia* for not fully acknowledging the value of such mashups, and for leaving unanswered "the question of how Slow Food's 'local economy' can accommodate the Moroccan couscous restaurants in Turin's San Salvario quarter, or the Sri Lankan spice stalls in the piazza Vittorio market in Rome" (349–50).

Petrini does seem to appreciate the value of cultural hybridity; he just thinks it can also go wrong, particularly in a culinary sense. As he explains in *Slow Food Nation*, "fusion cuisine, . . . which blends together different products and culinary traditions purely on the basis of flavors, defying all territorial and cultural boundaries, can either lead to complete chaos (con-fusion), which completely distorts the value of the raw materials, or have the positive effect of introducing new cultural stimuli into the evolution of collective taste, spreading the knowledge of new products by means of respectful and pertinent combinations" (102).

Petrini's thinking thus reflects a concept often cited in discussions of Italian food and culture: that of *campanilismo*, or the pride one takes in one's local community. There's no precise English equivalent for the word, because it comes from the Italian *campanile*, the bell tower that can be found in seemingly every Italian city, town, and village. The idea is a complex one, involving regional identity, local traditions, and loyalty to one's birthplace—all of which still matter far more to Italians than their national identity, given that the nation's regions were not united until the Risorgimento. But *campanilismo*, like food traditions, is also about rivalries between neighboring towns: the "other" against which the local can be defined, the *forestiero* ("stranger" or "outsider," from *fuori*, meaning "outside") who came to town. Like the place-based affection of which Wendell Berry writes so eloquently, this is *campanilismo*'s dark side, the xenophobia it shares with more closed-minded forms of agrarianism.

For this reason more than any, the search for the "authentic" Italy is bound to fail, because it represents a distortion of the history that typicality is meant to signal. As Lucy Long has put it, authenticity "presupposes that there exists an original, pure version of a food culture that has remained static and free of outside influences" (14).

The story of Slow Food is thus about both plots: you go on a journey, *and* the stranger comes to town. It is about gastrotourism focused on typical foods as well as creating markets for those same foods, wherever possible, in distant places. It is about both *osterie* and Eataly: local foods "defined by proximity of consumption," as well as *goût du terroir*, or the taste of place, which "can be meaningfully, if differently, experienced regardless of where a food is consumed," as Heather Paxson has pointed out (209).

Villadeati helped me see how this is the case in a way I could never otherwise have understood.

In fact, the longer we lived there, the more I came to see that my initial impressions of a town in decline might not be wholly accurate.

Yes, the population was now only a fraction of its prewar height, and the industrialization that drove this change was part of the reason Petrini has called for a "new rurality," in which the countryside is no longer "a lifeless place, lacking in basic amenities" (*Slow Food Nation* 137). But stories of change are not always stories of declension; sometimes they are simply stories of change.

Consider Villadeati's own *campanile,* built in 1840 as part of the parish church of San Remigio, which dates to the sixteenth century. Like many churches, its bell rings three times a day (morning, noon, and evening) to summon the faithful to prayer, as well as every hour on the hour to mark the passage of time. Its presence is pervasive, a central part of the sonic environment that defines the town, along with singing birds, barking dogs, chattering neighbors, and humming motors on Via Roma. Catholicism is on the decline here, however, as it is throughout the rest of Italy, making the bell tower seem more a relic of the town's past than a herald of its future.

A similar story might be told of the Marian shrines found all along the roadsides, such as the one on Via Roma, just a few steps down from San Remigio. Here, carved into the stucco high on the side of a building, is a small, glass-covered grotto, housing a vase of plastic flowers and a statue of the Virgin Mary, her head and hands raised heavenward in prayer. A marble plaque beneath the shrine reads: *fermati o passegger scopriti il capo china la fronte pia e di ave maria* (Oh traveller stop, bow reverently and hail Mary).

Despite the story of decline these markers seem to tell, there is something else going on here worth noting: a recognition that values-based tourism is centuries-old in this part of Italy.

It turns out that Villadeati is on the pilgrimage path known as Superga–Vezzolano–Crea, which took travelers on a roughly forty-mile journey from west to east, starting at Turin's Basilica of Superga (about thirty miles to the west), stopping at the Abbey of Vezzolano (fifteen miles closer), and ending at the Sacred Mountain of Crea (about ten miles to the east of here).

This is, in short, a sacred path we are on, but today the nature of the path seems to be changing. In an era of declining interest in the church, food is becoming our new religion.

Our contemporary pilgrimage trails trace new kinds of journeys, such as the Strada del Vino, regional wine roads authorized by the Piedmont region's Department of Agriculture, which provide tourist itineraries linking wineries, restaurants, accommodations, and other sites of gastronomic interest.

So while the forms of gastronomic tourism promoted by Slow Food may be new, the idea of guiding travelers on a place-based path is an ancient one.

One could argue, of course, that the movement from religious pilgrimage to gastronomic tourism is part of the twenty-first-century cult of the self, but I think it's much more complicated than that.

Slow Food is ultimately a story about postsecularism—about the resacralization of food, the land, and its people—much more than it is a story of hedonistic consumption.

In her discussion entitled "Slow Journeys," Daisy Tam maintains that Slow Food "does not merely mark the difference of what we eat or the way we eat. It seeks to situate the individual within a network of local relationships, family ties, economic dependences and relations of patronage and friendship" (215). I could not agree more.

Whether you go on a journey or the stranger comes to town, Slow Food is inherently mixed up with the promotion of gastronomic tourism and economic development, and you can't easily pull these ideas apart. In other words, the sustainable food communities that Carlo Petrini is promoting in Italy are not meant to be only subsistence economies, although Petrini does see a place for these. Rather, they are also meant to be exchange economies built on quality food products, respect for the land, and respect for the people who produce that food and protect that land. That is, they are meant to be good, clean, and fair.

What happens when Slow Food attempts to globalize these Italian ideals is the subject to which we now turn.

GLOBALIZING FOOD COMMUNITIES

If Valeria Siniscalchi is right that the ideals of good, clean, and fair can be also read chronologically, then the creation in 2004 of Terra Madre (Mother Earth), the global network of producers and coproducers, is the central moment that marked Slow Food's engagement with social justice on a global scale. With the arrival of Terra Madre, the full scope of Slow Food's engagement with globalization started to become clear, but Terra Madre also challenged both the movement and the organization to understand its place in the global network it helped to create. Similarly, the increasingly global reach of Slow Food challenged Carlo Petrini's ability to narrate Slow Food's expansion, and potential dissolution, at the same time as he celebrated its achievement in making food not only good and clean but also fair.

Petrini first wrote about Slow Food's global ambitions when discussing the Presidia in *Slow Food*. "Slow Food's aim is to export the idea of the Presidia to other countries," he noted, but he also observed that "outside the Mediterranean basin, it may be necessary to place more emphasis on landscape preservation and organic production than on traditional foods" (97). Other countries, in other words, may not have as long a food history as Italy does, or conceive of local specialty products in quite the same way Italians do.

Petrini also offered evidence that Slow Food might not be as elitist as some of its critics suggest by reflecting thoughtfully on the steps the organization would need to take to help preserve biological diversity in the Global South. In developing nations, Petrini pointed out, Slow Food wanted to do more than just collect funds to help protect traditional foods and foodways. "Charity, no matter how useful, is something Slow Food rejects because it doesn't respect the cultural elements of populations and tends to see them as entities needing 'salvation,' and therefore 'conquest,'" he wrote. Rather than imposing a Western model from above, Petrini wanted to see Slow Food nurture the cultural diversity of less wealthy nations from below. "The goal of future Slow Food Presidia in the underdeveloped areas," he stated, "will be to recuperate and make known traditional knowledges, so that they become motors of development and prosperity" (98).

One restaurateur I spoke with in Italy expressed concern about what he called "the degeneration of Slow Food" since its founding in 1986. Slow Food began as a local reaction to the globalization of taste, he noted, but it has gradually moved away from this focus. "In the beginning, Slow Food talked about food and lifestyle," he said. "Now they talk about economics and sustainability." How did we go from an appreciation of good food and wine, he seemed to be asking, to a focus on economic development in the Global South? How, indeed?

Petrini attempts to tell the story of this evolution in two books, *Terra Madre* and *Food and Freedom,* but unlike *Slow Food* and *Slow Food Nation,* they read a bit too much like inside baseball. Both have a somewhat scattershot organization, and they suffer from being simultaneously too abstract when it comes to articulating Slow Food's vision and too detailed when it comes to explaining its institutional dynamics. All too often I found myself saying, "Wait, what is this book about again?" This is not to say there are not redeeming qualities to each, and Petrini's optimistic outlook certainly shines through both. But as much as I wish I could say otherwise, both books are a bit of a slog, and they have the appearance of being cobbled together from Petrini's various notes and speeches, without the overarching purpose of the first two books.

Some of this, no doubt, is due to Petrini's collaboration with Carlo Bogliotti, who, Petrini says in the acknowledgments to *Food and Freedom,* "has been by my side for more than ten years, elaborating and developing ideas, and putting them down on paper" (240). But another reason has to do with the difficulty of Petrini's subject: how does one tell the story of a network? Another way to think about the challenges involved in such an endeavor is this: What if Slow Food became not about the individual producer or consumer? What if it is instead became about the food community as a whole? How would you even begin to convey such a conceptual leap on a global scale?

The best place to start to appreciate this new stage of Slow Food's evolution is through two places where Petrini attempts to define a "food community": one in *Slow Food Nation* and another in *Terra Madre.*

The first comes immediately following Petrini's memorable discussion of the sources for his dish of pasta with tomato sauce. After asking readers to think of the provenance, history, and labor involved in that meal, he makes clear the full significance of those connections: "Food is a *network*: of men and women, of knowledge, of methods, of environments, of relations. . . . The people who make up the network should in theory all have the same gastronomic aim: that this dish of pasta, for example, be good, clean, and fair. The people who make up the network thus have a common aim, and so they are a community—a virtual one if you like, but a community nonetheless" (174).

Petrini's observation echoes my own distinction between the community of *geography* that is Prairie Farm, Wisconsin, and the community of *values* that is Spring Hill Community Farm. A food community, Petrini continues, "may be made up of people who are united by their work and situated in a particular area, but it may also comprise people united by the fact that they constitute a complete production chain, reaching as far as the consumer, or rather co-producer. They are all concerned to ensure that the distances, physical and psychological, become as short as possible, and that at the same time there is no kind of isolation between the different realities: we are all gastronomes" (176).

Some of the most pointed criticisms of Slow Food—and, by extension, Petrini—have focused on the fuzziness of his use of the term "community." Fabio Parasecoli, for example, argues that the idea of "community" and "natural bonds" as used by both Slow Food and its opponents is "part of a romanticized vision that stubbornly refuses to acknowledge the world's contradictions and fragmentation" ("Postrevolutionary" 35). Likewise, Adrian Peace describes Slow Food's use of the term as a "mystification" that has been "used to constitute a particular kind of rural imaginary based on face-to-face association, feelings of belonging, coherent identity, and moral obligation.... When the term was elevated to the global plane, the level of mystification was yet more pronounced, as 'communityness' became an elementary matter of 'being connected' and of 'networking' in a very loose sense" (38).

The aim of both of these critiques is to push Slow Food to more fully acknowledge and engage with the problematic aspects of both the local and global communities it seeks to idealize. Peace is particularly forceful on this point. Claiming that the mystification of "community" is "inseparable from the fetishism focused on the iconically key figure of the small-scale producer," Peace argues that such producers can never fully separate themselves from either the inequalities involved in global systems of production or the local forms of exploitation that manifest themselves along class, gender, and age lines (38).

Okay, fair enough—none of us is innocent. We can't walk away from the global circulation of commodities any more than we can declare ourselves free of any and all forms of inequality, prejudice, and bias. We're all sinners, to put it in religious terms, whether in the hands of an angry god or not. But where does that leave us? And how are we supposed to distinguish between a "romantic" vision of community and a utopian one that seeks to reduce inequality?

Petrini's second attempt to define a "food community," in *Terra Madre*, suggests some of the ways we might go about answering these questions. Petrini frames his definition in the context of an explanation and celebration of Terra Madre, the international gathering of sustainable food communities that first took place in Turin in 2004. Although this discussion overlaps some with his treatment of the same material in *Slow Food Nation*, it does so in a different context, one devoted to assessing the future of Terra Madre in relation to the organization of Slow Food.

First held alongside (but distinct from) the Salone del Gusto, Terra Madre has been a biennial gathering ever since, although in 2012 the two events were united into a single event. The first event brought about 4,800 delegates from 130 countries to Turin for two days of seminars, workshops, and plenary sessions, including speeches by Vandana Shiva, Alice Waters, and Charles, Prince of Wales (now King Charles III).

The logistics were herculean. With funding from the Italian Ministry of Agriculture and Forestry, the Piedmontese regional authority, and the Turin City Council, Slow Food spent 1.6 million euros to pay the airline tickets of participants who needed assistance (out of a total budget of 4 million euros). Housing was provided by farmers throughout the Piedmont (with funding from Coldiretti, the Italian farmers association), along with other civic and religious groups, and five hundred volunteers were recruited to keep the event running smoothly (Petrini and Padovani 163–74).

To understand the origins of Terra Madre, it helps to know that Petrini has been deeply influenced by the work of Edgar Morin, the French sociologist, whom he cites in three of his four books. In some sense, it could be said that Terra Madre emerged from Morin's idea of a shared "community of destiny." In *Homeland Earth* (first published in France as *Terre-Patrie* in 1993), Morin comments on what he calls the "bizarre phenomenon" of globalization, which he says creates a sense of "planetary teleparticipation" as a result of the pervasiveness of television: "We consume, as mere spectators, the tragedies, hecatombs, and horrors of this world, but we also participate in other people's lives and are moved by their misfortune. . . . Catastrophes that strike our antipodes give rise to fleeting transports of compassion and the feeling of belonging to the same community of destiny, which henceforth is the community of planet Earth. If only for the duration of a news flash, we feel we are part of the planet" (Morin and Kern 23–24). But while Morin declared that "there is henceforth a community of destiny," he admitted that "there is not yet a common consciousness of this *Schicksalgemeinshaft* [common fate]" (25).

Gigi Padovani has documented how, in the years following the first Slow Food Awards for the Defense of Biodiversity in 2000, Petrini and his associates worked to increase public consciousness of this common fate. They started talking about rural communities as being "destiny communities," or "communities that were sharing food-manufacturing processes and were inspired by some common feelings: even if they were separated from each other by great distances or were in different stages of development, they were nevertheless sharing values and purposes" (Petrini and Padovani 167). Slow Food was moving, that is, toward a realization that, whether a community of geography or a community of values, any community committed to the idea of sustainable food might be considered part of Morin's planet-wide "community of destiny," which the organization eventually came to call Terra Madre.

Petrini walks the reader through Slow Food's thought process in *Terra Madre*, noting that the group's first intent when using the term "food community" in 2003 was to find a "common denominator" to describe the various individuals invited to Turin for the gathering. They were all "members of groups that, however heterogenous, shared common values and, above all, shaped their lives around food production" (*Terra Madre* 28).

As the gatherings grew in subsequent years, so did Slow Food's appreciation for the complexity of the idea of a "food community." In 2006, the group invited not merely food producers but cooks and academics, and in 2008 these were joined by rural musicians, youth delegates, and producers of natural fibers (*Terra Madre* 8–9). It was at this time that Petrini began using the term "co-producer" to describe consumers, whom he realized must also be considered a critical part of a food community, alongside growers, breeders, processors, and distributors. Food communities, Petrini eventually concluded, are "highly structured entities, made up of subsystems that, though limited, may be complex," and their members "have an identity that preserves the memory of the past and at the same time expresses a clear idea of what they want for the future" (*Terra Madre* 29).

There is, to be sure, no small amount of haziness here, which is why it's helpful to append Petrini's own welcoming remarks at the first Terra Madre gathering to his more theoretical discussion of these food communities in *Terra Madre*. Speaking directly to the delegates, Petrini emphasized how the gathering embodied Slow Food's new orientation to an economy based on social justice. "We are firmly convinced," he announced, "that food communities, founded on sentiment, fraternity, and the rejection of egotism, will have a strategic importance in the emergence of a new society, a society based on fair trade" (Petrini and Padovani 164).

Audrey Arner, who co-owns Moonstone Farm with her husband, Richard Handeen, attended the first Terra Madre meeting in 2004. She was nominated by the Minnesota-based Land Stewardship Project to represent the Pride of the Prairie, its local-foods initiative, and traveling to Turin was no small feat for a working farmer in the Minnesota River valley.

In the November 2005 newsletter of Slow Food Minnesota, Arner described her experience with exceptional vividness:

> I don't think we've ever worked so hard to be able to leave the farm. October is that pinnacle month at the end of the northern harvest when we prepare livestock systems and tuck in the rest of the farmstead for the Minnesota winter. We were working long days and waking up with long lists of things to do. We left a team of trusted friends and family to care for our home, our market and our cattle.
>
> As we neared the Palazzo del Lavoro, we started to recognize occasional travelers as farmers. We did not all have soil still under our fingernails, but there is an earthiness that emanates from agrarian folks, wherever we are. (5)

Once there, she found a hall filled with people from around the world who shared the values and experiences of her fellow Minnesota community members:

> Terra Madre buzzed with the exchange of information. On-farm dairy processors from New Prague, Minn. talked with cheese makers from northern Scandinavia, Ireland, and Tibet. Vegetable growers from Spring Valley, Minn. exchanged information with Peruvian orchardists and Spanish coastal fishermen. There were no officials from the International Mone-

tary Fund or the World Trade Organization demanding that markets be liberalized, seeds patented or land drenched in chemicals to support the sort of production that multinational corporations love to dominate. Terra Madre was full of good ideas and ferociously inclusive. Whereas most world meetings about agriculture do not include farmers, this gathering was predominantly firsthand food producers. (5)

Of all the things she took away from the meeting, the most important seem to have been a feeling of solidarity with the members of other food communities and a sense that navigating the global food system sustainably would require a complex mixture of independence and interdependence.

Terra Madre's agenda invited us all to think and act differently. Those of us from North America are at one with those from Brazil or Burkina Faso to reclaim agriculture from the suffocating grip of agribusiness. Food communities should address their own food needs first (through sustainable production) and then look at systems of distributing surpluses. Americans should challenge the agriculture that builds up huge commodity surpluses, but leaves some U.S. farmers poor and many of its citizens poorly nourished. (7)

At least from a Minnesota perspective, this doesn't sound much like the sentimentalized or romanticized version of rural communities that Slow Food has been accused of promoting. The vision it is advancing may be idealized, but when that vision is shared by thousands of food communities around the world, all of whom want to participate in marketing their own products in order to improve their well-being, those ideals sure do begin to look a lot like a plan for the future.

"This is not mere utopia," Petrini argues in *Slow Food Nation*, "but political theorization, an intellectual effort to find ways of developing certain human forces which at present are mistreated and undervalued. The network can—and must—work, because it is a means of gradually correcting some macroscopic distortions of our food system and of introducing into the machinery regulating the workings of the world certain values that can easily be translated into everyday practice with the help of the system that we have in mind" (209). A bit of a run-on sentence, but you get the picture:

by establishing the network of food communities that is Terra Madre, Slow Food seeks to put a certain set of values into practice. Or as Petrini puts in succinctly later in the book, "I am convinced that he who sows utopia will reap reality" (240).

Siniscalchi has observed that the term "food community" is "performative," in that it seeks to make real various forms of "imagined economies" that are the local equivalents of the "imagined communities" that Benedict Anderson has identified as being central to the creation of nation-states. "The more utopian and inclusive dimension of Slow Food's message," she notes, "is aimed at bringing the poles of the food chain closer, connecting all the actors of local economies in different parts of the world to try and change the food system" (*Slow Food* 167). Yet this is difficult to achieve because, as she pointed out in an earlier article about the movement, "the connection between producers and consumers does not take place everywhere in the same way or with the same intensity and the reality of the movement is not always coherent with its philosophy" ("Environment" 298).

More than *Terra Madre, Food and Freedom* shows Petrini wrestling with the difficulties of connecting this diversity of food communities around the world—along with their "imagined economies"—on both an organizational and philosophical level.

Let's start with the organizational challenge, since the dominant undercurrent in *Food and Freedom* is, amazingly, the possible dissolution of Slow Food itself. In a sense, *Food and Freedom* reads like a valediction, or at least a summing-up of the organization's evolution over the past three decades. Throughout the book, Petrini repeatedly returns to his experience in Piedmont as a point of reference for understanding not only the other food cultures he profiles but also the distance the organization has come since its founding.

"Change may have taken a long time, decades, in fact, but it always comes eventually if you trust in diversity," he writes. "Now there is no turning back and change sometimes risks overtaking us. This is what the journey in the Langa hills thirty years ago has made us: it has allowed us to embrace all the faces, all the skills, all the foods, all the visions of existence that our friends on every continent bring" (126).

Petrini frames the change he describes in terms of "liberation," and he loosely organizes the book around four different types of liberation: (1) the liberation of gastronomy embodied by Slow Food's gradual formulation of its good, clean, and fair slogan, (2) the liberation that can come from embracing diversity as an organizing principle, (3) the potential liberation of Slow Food into the Terra Madre network, and (4) the liberation that gastronomy can enable, particularly in the Global South.

Using the metaphor of "unpairing the cards," from the Italian card games *scopa* and *scopone*, Petrini describes his effort at "turning things upside down" in the Slow Food offices by supporting three major initiatives to further the gastronomy of liberation. He calls these the "three ten thousands": loading ten thousand foods onto the Ark of Taste, creating ten thousand nodes in the Terra Madre network, and planting ten thousand gardens in Africa.

Of these four forms of liberation and three new initiatives, what stands out the most is Petrini's recognition that Slow Food itself may have to die in order to live. Petrini expresses several versions of this idea throughout *Food and Freedom,* and while it is hard to tell how much of this is rhetorical posturing, it is certainly consistent with the message he has been sending all along. In *Slow Food Nation* he spoke at length about the idea of creating a world network of gastronomes, for which he stressed that Slow Food's role was "mainly that of providing a service" (204–5), and he ended *Terra Madre* by claiming that "Terra Madre has to free itself from itself, from the people who devised and organize it" (152). Thus his statements in *Food and Freedom,* though provocative, are not entirely without precedent.

What's notable, though, is how closely Petrini has linked the organizational future of Slow Food to an ideological stance that is thoroughly decolonial. He observes, for instance, that even the idea of an association may be a form of colonial oppression, as it is "a typically Western phenomenon that does not exist in many cultures round the world" (32). He waves off any attempt to take credit for the successes of the Terra Madre communities, arguing that "what the food communities do is not the merit of Slow Food; the merit belongs to the communities themselves, because they have always been doing it and it is their job to do it" (175). And speaking of the new wave of Latin American chefs and cooks who are connecting eco-gastronomy to social justice, Petrini says that "we have to decolonize our imaginations, exactly as its protagonists have done" (197).

"In short," he writes, "I am not afraid that the association that I preside over, which I founded, and which, insofar as it represents virtually my whole life, I am obviously very attached to, may one day dissolve into the 'liquid' form of the free network: into Terra Madre and, above all, into all the networks and swarms that Terra Madre comes into contact with around the world" (175).

To understand the philosophical challenges involved in Slow Food's attempt to "liberate diversity" around the world, it's helpful to consider the two major critiques of the alternative food movement that Alison Hope Alkon and Julie Guthman have identified in the introduction to *The New Food Activism*.

The first of these is that the movement has not yet fully addressed the issue of food justice, which *Food and Freedom* tackles head-on through its discussion of "food sovereignty," the international variant of food justice.

When Petrini first discussed this term in *Slow Food Nation,* he defined it as a "people's right to choose what kind of agriculture they practice, how they eat, and how much they eat, in accordance with their economic potential and the traditional knowledge they possess" (48). The International Commission on the Future of Food and Agriculture, of which Petrini is a member, further developed this concept in its 2006 Manifesto on the Future of Food, which Petrini quoted in *Terra Madre:* "All local, national and regional entities and communities have the inherent right and obligation to protect, sustain and support all necessary conditions to encourage production of sufficient healthy food in a way that conserves the land, water and ecological integrity of the place, respects and supports producers' livelihoods, and is accessible to all people. No international body or corporation has the right to alter this priority. Neither does any international body have the right to require that a nation accept imports against its will, for any reason" (84; see also Shiva 43–75). The concept of food sovereignty thus dovetails quite nicely with Petrini's long-standing concern for food communities, and it provides an important means for Slow Food to move beyond the politics of consumption and address questions of government regulation and structural change in the global food system.

Until *Food and Freedom,* Petrini had been cautious about getting too deep into the weeds of public policy in his writing, and for good reason: it can quickly deaden one's prose and lead to a book intended more for a policy wonk than a general reader. It's difficult to avoid the subject, though, if your point is to call attention to injustice in the developing world. As Petrini himself writes in *Food and Freedom,* "Any exhaustive gastronomic discourse has to set out from here; if it fails to do so, it will lead nowhere" (209). For this reason, *Food and Freedom* takes readers to struggles for food sovereignty (or "fair" food) all around the world, including Africa, Asia, and Latin America—though the book suffers a bit as a result, at times feeling more like a compilation of Petrini's travel notes than a thoroughgoing exploration of how these different communities are connected.

What strengthens *Food and Freedom*, however, is Petrini's awareness of the ways that food justice is an issue not merely in the United States and the Global South but in Italy as well. Petrini is certainly aware of the challenge of extrapolating from his Italian experience, noting that "speaking about local food products and small farmers in Peru is not the same as speaking about them in Italy, because the two realities are separated by three centuries of colonization" (189). But his discussion of the plight of Italy's migrant farmworkers makes clear that no nation is immune from the injustices that accompany industrial agriculture, no matter its colonial history. Citing figures that four hundred thousand farmworkers are illegally recruited in Italy every year, with sixty thousand of them living in squalor, Petrini implores his readers to open their eyes to the problem, even though it may occur far from city centers. "What the eye can't see, the heart doesn't grieve over," he declares (50).

At the same time, *Food and Freedom* would be enhanced by an even deeper reflection on the continuities between Italy and the rest of the world, even when those continuities may not put Slow Food in the best light. It's a slippery slope, for instance, between protecting traditional Italian foods and what Jason Wilson has called the "darker area of food protectionism" exemplified by Verona's 2016 ban on new "ethnic" restaurants serving kebabs and gyros.

A related complication to Petrini's discussion of food sovereignty comes when traditional food communities turn out not to be quite as "clean" as one might like. What happens, in other words, when the celebrated community food systems in Italy are themselves not ecologically sustainable? In 2015, for example, the mayor of San Vitaliano, just outside of Naples, issued a decree banning the use of wood-fired stoves in bakeries and eateries, including traditional pizzerias, in an attempt to address the town's worsening air pollution ("Town Bans Pizza-making"). And after the European Union issued new regulations about sustainable fishing in 2006, many fishermen, restaurateurs, and foodies protested that such biodiversity protections would threaten their

traditional ways of life, whether it be the small-scale fishing they have practiced for centuries or the typical seafood dishes they have come to know and
love (Necchio).

Petrini says in *Food and Freedom* that "'Good' and 'Clean' may be easy
to understand, partly because great progress has been made on these two
counts, but the 'Fair' element in the triptych is arguably harder to grasp"
(53). As these examples suggest, however, and Petrini makes clear in *Slow
Food Nation*, all three of these elements are "essential and interdependent
prerequisites for a quality product" (143).

The second major critique of the alternative food movement identified in *The
New Food Activism* is that the movement has not yet fully come to terms with
the long arm of neoliberalism, or the profit-driven logic of global capitalism.

Although Petrini is clear about his distaste for neoliberalism in *Food and
Freedom*, this is the first book in which he uses the word explicitly, and I
suspect that a certain level of discomfort with the neoliberal-esque shape
that Slow Food has taken over the years may be partly behind his suggestion
that the organization may ultimately need to die in order for its more radical
vision to live.

In a 2013 film about Slow Food, the poet Folco Portinari, author of the
original Slow Food manifesto, observed that the organization "is taking on
more and more the characteristics of an enterprise, with all the needs, laws,
and rules of an enterprise, and not those of a revolution" (Sardo).

Similar critiques have been offered from many different perspectives: that
Slow Food's cosmopolitan, Western perspective prevents it from accurately
representing the marginalized rural communities it claims to champion; that
its reliance on corporate sponsorship to fund its operations is contradictory
if not hypocritical; and that its own use of capitalist and corporatist practices
constitutes a form of neocolonialism that undermines the values it is trying
to promote.

To give just a few examples, Kelly Donati calls on Slow Food "to recognize
its own heritage of privilege derived from an economic system shaped by
imperialism and to actively resist nostalgic renderings of the 'other,' however well intentioned, which fetishize cultural difference and sentimentalize
struggles for cultural or economic survival" (239). Adrian Peace claims that
Slow Food "essentially reflects the power and mirrors the contradictions of
the system against which it pitches its political and symbolic resources" (39).

And Jeffrey Pilcher argues that "the Slow Food program [in Mexico] . . . bears more than a passing resemblance to the *mission civilisatrice* of nineteenth-century imperialism. While more benign than military intervention, the missionary approach still conceals uneven power relationships that limit the opportunities available to the Mexican people" (78).

Although all of these critics were writing before Slow Food's recent emphasis on social justice, the overall concern they express remains a central tension in the movement: whether to challenge the system or work within it.

At times, Petrini seems to want to have it both ways, as his language veers from revolutionary to reformist, sometimes in the space of two pages. On one page of *Terra Madre*, for instance, he argues that the aim of Slow Food "is not only to adjust the present system [of industrial food], which resembles a train heading for the edge of a cliff. It is vital rather to invert the relationship that we have and are forced to have with what we eat" (114). But on the following page he seems to backtrack, claiming that "deindustrialization doesn't mean waging war on the global food system; on the contrary, it means creating alternatives. It doesn't mean yet another system imposed from above, but rather a way of handing over the initiative to food communities and then supporting and assisting them in every way possible" (115).

While this may not necessarily seem like a contradiction, Alkon and Guthman's argument is that perhaps it should: that "in their focus on creating alternatives—farmers' markets, community-supported agriculture, urban farms, and the like—rather than contesting state and corporate power, many food organizations may produce and reproduce neoliberal forms and spaces of governance" (11). (This was Guthman's point in the second edition of *Agrarian Dreams*, as well.) Creating alternatives, in other words, may not invert our relationship with food in quite the way Petrini thinks it will.

Alkon and Guthman themselves point out an effective countercritique to this argument, which is that seeing neoliberalism everywhere can "make it more difficult to imagine and cultivate alternative ways of being." Such a totalizing critique, they point out, can constitute a "disabling discourse" that forecloses possibilities of transforming food systems (16).

I would take this countercritique a step further and suggest that, as Slow Food enters its fifth decade, the almost dizzying diversity of initiatives it has embarked upon may be the most effective way for the group not to fall prey to a failure of imagination.

Slow Food needn't be, and isn't, just one thing.

When the Slow Food staffer I spoke with in Turin pointed out, "If you ask what Slow Food is, you may get ten different answers," I didn't fully realize the wisdom of his observation, mistaking a range of responses for a lack of focus. I now see it—and I think Carlo Petrini does, too—as a symbol of the diversification of community food activism, as the maturing of a movement.

Slow Food is now involved in an astonishing diversity of initiatives and partnerships around the world, in addition to the core activities of the Ark of Taste, the Presidia, and Terra Madre Salone del Gusto. It supports 1,120 *convivia* in 111 countries and, since 2019, has identified hundreds of "Slow Food Communities" that work in their local areas to achieve a specific objective. It organizes numerous other events, including Cheese in Bra, Slow Fish in Genoa, and a range of regional and national meetings. It has a robust social media presence, and its publishing arm (Slow Food Editore) is now responsible for more than one hundred titles, including food and wine guides, tourist guides, cookbooks, essay collections, and manuals (most in Italian, but many also in English). It has created the Slow Food Foundation for Biodiversity, the University of Gastronomic Sciences, and the Slow Food Cooks' Alliance. It has embarked on campaigns against land-grabbing and GMOs, and in support of Slow Bees and Slow Meat. And it has been involved in a host of other recent initiatives, including the creation of narrative labels on foods, the campaign to create Slow Food Gardens in Africa, and the development of Earth Markets, Slow Food Travel destinations, and Slow Food school gardens around the world.

We shouldn't mistake *more* action for *right* action, of course, but this flurry of activity seems to mirror the way the sustainable food movement in general is now operating on multiple fronts to further the cause of food sovereignty. La Via Campesina, the International Peasants Movement, has been active internationally since 1993, and the Genuino Clandestino network of communities and peasant movements began in Italy in 2010, with the goal of promoting alternatives to capitalist agribusiness.

Is Slow Food perfect? By no means. But is the world a better place because it exists? I think so, and the writing of Carlo Petrini is part of the reason why the idea that our food should be good, clean, and fair is increasingly being referenced as a handy shorthand for how to measure the sustainability of our food system, both locally and globally.

But beyond this valuable yet abstract contribution of Petrini's is something else that has stood out to me in the time I have spent thinking and writing about his work. This is his understanding that, as important as discussions of regional, national, and global food policy may be, it is ultimately our relationships with individual people that matter the most.

Consider the comments he makes near the end of *Food and Freedom*: "What it does not take to make ambitious projects happen is megastructures. What is important is to be conscious of one's limits and allow oneself to be regenerated by the people encountered on one's path. If I look back at our history, the history of Slow Food and Terra Madre, I see an evolution of content but also of many wonderful people, and it is my contention that they have all been fundamental—even if some of them have now moved in different directions. I will always admire the constant efforts of those who have had the courage to continue with us, and even of those who have not, to put themselves on the line" (234).

While Petrini's discussions of food communities may sometimes seem academic, they are nonetheless grounded in an appreciation of and genuine affection for the real people who compose these communities. Which raises the question of Petrini's ultimate commitments, his core values, what he finds most meaningful about the idea of community.

I would put it this way: what do we have if not *connections* to one another? This may seem an obvious or simplistic point, but the deeper these connections go, the richer our lives become. Commodity chains tend toward the shallow, while community relationships tend toward the deep. And by "deep" I mean the way that repeated experiences and shared commitments result in lives rich in meaning, lives worth living.

In *Terra Madre*, Petrini says that community is "where genuine food production, interpersonal relationships, and knowledge transmission still count" (40), a statement that reminds me of Adam Gopnik's conclusion in *The Table Comes First* that a "life lived with a face on our food is a richer life than one lived without it" (183).

Both comments get at the same idea: that sustainability must ultimately be about more than just the environment. Even if industrial food systems turn out to be more efficient in terms of carbon emissions or "feeding the world," can they truly be called sustainable if they foster disconnected, mechanical, and abstracted relationships between people and their food sources? If they suggest that individuals can exist outside of ecological communities? If they fail to foster the development and maintenance of local and regional food cultures?

Another way to think about this is to consider what would be lost if "environmental" considerations became the only ones that mattered—much as the opposite has been true for so long, when all that mattered was taste. Isn't a dinner that is "clean" (say, made from certified organic ingredients) but otherwise generic and unremarkable inherently less interesting than one that is embedded in some kind of culinary, historical, or community context? I think so. Both dinners may be equally "sustainable" in terms of their environmental footprint, but not so in terms of their cultural sustainability—in terms of our relationships with and connections to one another in the places that we live, work, and play each day.

The day before we were set to leave Villadeati, our next-door neighbor Franco, whose wife used to run the grocery store in town, flagged us down as we were coming up our walk, the same gravel path on which we first noticed the Lazarus lizards scattering about.

He had a large paper shopping bag with him, and he held it up to us as he approached.

Throughout the five months we lived there, Franco had been renovating the villa next door for his daughter. It was a beautiful stone house, the same age as our own, and we watched as he worked on it every day except Sunday, serving as his own general contractor. Bright-orange fencing blocked off part of his yard, and piles of bricks and construction debris were perpetually scattered about. Trucks would come and go, and our rural idyll would regularly be interrupted by the sound of drills, concrete mixers, hammers, and bursts of shouted instructions.

Like Petrini's experience in Bra, this was still the beautiful country, but it was also a working landscape, full of people whose daily tasks often required intruding on the aural and visual landscape of their neighbors.

And so Franco had come to say he was sorry.

In the bag were three bottles of *genuino* wine—a Dolcetto, a Barbera, and an unlabeled white—a large jar of Piedmontese honey, another big jar of local chocolate sauce, and a box of *krumiri* from our favorite bakery in Murisengo.

Little did he know that our bags were already packed and carefully weighed, so as to come in just under the fifty-pound limit for an international flight. And everything he gave us, with the exception of the *krumiri*, was a liquid that could not be placed in our carry-on luggage. We would have to repack everything and mail another box home.

And yet, this was undoubtedly the most memorable gift any of us had ever been given.

This was not just any food—it was a symbol of this place, and Franco's pride in living here. We had shared this time with him, and he with us, and it was important that we remembered him, and his home, with fondness. Our relationship mattered, and he expressed its significance in the best way he knew how: through a gift of handcrafted food.

He was sorry, he said, for having disturbed us, but the process of renovating his villa took time. It was slow going, and work like this could not be rushed.

Like Italians throughout history, he was not building something for the moment. He was building something for the ages.

THREE

The Chef

———

Reading Alice Waters in France

I learned everything in France: An aesthetic. The way I serve a meal. The way I think about food. Period.

—ALICE WATERS, interviewed by Jane Black

She is a great democratizer of the ideas of good food and good eating.

—WENDELL BERRY on Alice Waters, in the *New York Review of Books*

TRANSFORMING AMERICAN CUISINE

First, a confession: I can be a complete pain in the ass in the kitchen.

There's really no other way to put it, and to write about Alice Waters and cooking without first acknowledging this fact would make it seem as if all is rosy and bright in my own kitchen, when sometimes it is decidedly not.

Alice Waters at the United States embassy in Berlin, February 2015. (Photo by the U.S. Department of State)

Nancy politely describes me as an "alpha cook," but that really just means I can be difficult. I have a certain way of doing things, I often want to do them myself, and that doesn't always leave a lot of room for other people.

I am working on this, but it is an uphill battle.

I mention this not merely to be honest but also because it illuminates some fundamental aspects of sustainable cooking that interest me, including the roles that gender, authority, and ideals play in the kitchen.

Making sense of Waters's message is thus more than an academic exercise. It is personal, because if building a more sustainable food system means attending not only to how we grow and process our food but also to how we cook it, then we need to pay close attention to what actually happens in our kitchens—in our homes as well as in the institutions that feed us, whether those be restaurants, schools, hospitals, or prisons.

Just as Wendell Berry helped Americans see how agriculture might be more sustainable, and Carlo Petrini explained why food processing and purchasing should be good, clean, and fair, Alice Waters demonstrated what sustainable cooking and eating might look like at a time when industrial products and processes had come to dominate the American kitchen—both in restaurants and at home.

Waters saw another way, and she built on her experience as an exchange student in France to become a champion of fresh, local, and organic ingredients for chefs and home cooks around the world.

Whereas Berry has admitted that he is "by no means a chef" (*Bringing It to the Table* 185), and Petrini has acknowledged that he is "not a good cook" (*Slow Food Nation* 78), Waters never shied away from the culinary arts, maturing from a self-taught cook to the chef and owner of Chez Panisse, which *Gourmet* magazine named the Best Restaurant in America in 2001.

In fact, it is fair to say that Waters may have had more effect on how Americans actually eat on a day-to-day basis than anyone else in the sustainable food movement.

Waters's life is also an example of what the literary critic Sandra Gilbert has called the Tale of American Culinary Transformation—the now-familiar story in which "an eager but gastronomically innocent young person of WASP or WASPish descent" travels to France, is transformed by the food, and returns to the United States "determined to preach the gospel of *la bonne table* far and wide" (12–13).

In *The Culinary Imagination,* Gilbert explores two particularly problematic components of this tale, observing that American food may not have needed as much transformation as has previously been assumed, and that the coherence of this narrative depends in part on ignoring the existing foodways of American immigrant families (12).

Gilbert is certainly right to contest these aspects of the tale, but I was eager to better connect its culinary aspects with the sustainability concerns that distinguish Waters from the other prominent American foodies— including M. F. K. Fisher, James Beard, Craig Claiborne, and Julia Child—to whom the story also applies.

In particular, I wanted to explore how Waters's story illustrates several important, and often underappreciated, features of the movement toward more sustainable cooking and eating. One concerns the role of women in the professional kitchen, and particularly how they have tried to balance their ideals with the need to run a business and make a living. Another involves how advocacy for local food is entwined not only with regional food traditions but also with the French concept of terroir. And a third relates to the way that different genres of food writing (such as the memoir, the recipe, and the cookbook) shape how sustainability is conceived and conveyed (in terms of mindfulness and as a community endeavor).

To do this, I decided to visit two places in France that I thought would help provide a more "enhanced version" of Waters's role in the Tale of American Culinary Transformation: Lyon, the country's "gastronomic capital," and the area around Bandol in Provence, where Waters was nourished and inspired by a host of foodie friends, including Lulu Peyraud, Richard Olney, and Kermit Lynch.

Waters's story, it turns out, becomes considerably more intriguing when viewed from the other side of the Atlantic.

In studying Waters's life and work, I also came to see that her interests intersected with mine in three important ways, which structure my approach in this chapter.

The first is that both of us care a lot about the physical space of the kitchen, which is the setting for so much of Waters's advocacy, not to mention the site of so many people's ideal meals. As a result, I begin this chapter in my own home kitchen, which Nancy and I attempted to renovate as sustainably as possible after we returned from Italy. Pursuing this construction project caused me to investigate the history and ecology of the domestic kitchen, as well as rethink the meaning and purpose of "sustainability" more broadly.

Waters's connections to France also intersected with my own because my father is French Canadian, and my favorite memories of my paternal grandmother all take place in the kitchen, where she would implore me, "Don't be shy—eat, eat!" In traveling to France, therefore, I sought to better understand French cooking not from the perspective of haute cuisine (literally, "high cooking") but in terms of the regional dishes that defined French country cooking—*la cuisine de grand-mère*—and that also shaped what Waters came to believe mattered most in the kitchen. My exploration of this tradition, which I have come to call "elemental cooking," is the subject of the central portion of this chapter.

Most travelers eventually return home, however, and so this chapter closes not in France but back in the United States, where I try to understand the different ways that Waters's messages may have been received by her American readers. To do so, I turn to my mother's side of the family, which is Dutch-Irish, as well as to her own experience as a working woman in the late twentieth century, as she sought to balance her domestic obligations with her professional ones. I end the chapter in the only way I could, in the kitchen again, cooking for those I love.

TOWARD THE SUSTAINABLE KITCHEN

Our adventures in kitchen renovation began soon after we returned from Italy, where we were inspired by the open kitchen and island workspace we had in Villadeati, as well as by Franco's work on his villa next door.

If Franco could renovate a premodern farmhouse, we figured, surely we could handle a midwestern Victorian.

Given the many constraints of our existing kitchen, we decided to embark on a complete overhaul, taking the kitchen back to the studs, expanding the space with a small bump-out, and opening up the resulting kitchen to the outdoors by adding windows.

Having watched—and heard—Franco at work on his own project, we were primed for what we knew would be a major life disruption, not to mention a considerable investment of time and money. But we also knew we were entering an ethical minefield from which we would not emerge unscathed, because to renovate a kitchen mindfully means to ask a simple but immensely complicated question: what makes a kitchen "sustainable"?

One way to begin to answer that question is to ask a more fundamental question: what is a kitchen?

No one likes questions like this because the answer seems so self-evident: it's a place where you cook food, duh.

But we humans cook food in lots of places, and in lots of ways, and we have done so differently throughout our history, so the image that springs to mind when we think "kitchen" depends a great deal on culture and history. "Humans have always cooked," Bee Wilson acknowledges, "but the concept of the 'ideal kitchen' is a very modern invention" (264).

For many of us in the developed world, and especially those of us in the United States, the image that springs to mind is straight out of the 1950s: a thin, white woman in an apron and heels standing alone in a pastel-colored kitchen, happily cooking something from a box. But that is neither the norm throughout history nor a particularly representative image for the time, so we would do well to broaden our perspective.

As the architectural historian Ellen Plante has pointed out, to think about the kitchen in history, particularly in Europe and the United States, is to come full circle, beginning with a central space used by all, moving to a separate space used by one person, and returning to a central space used by all, but with some considerable differences.

That original space is the earliest kitchen, or kitchens, in their many and varied forms before industrialization, and the evolution of the kitchen demonstrates the basic ecological services that remain mainstays of the contemporary kitchen: fuel for fire, metal for pots, air and light for working, and water for hygiene and cooking.

The original kitchen, of course, was an open-air gathering around a bonfire, using wood for fuel and bowls and tools made of stone, clay, wood, and skin. As the kitchen gradually moved indoors, into an atrium-like space or other form of "open house," pots and pans began to be made from a variety of metals, such as bronze, iron, copper, and brass. Cooking fires and their resulting smoke were tamed, at least somewhat, by the use of charcoal in addition to wood, and by the construction of raised hearths, fireplaces, and eventually chimneys. Candles and oil lamps brought light to the darkness, whether from a minimally lit room or the arrival of sunset. And cisterns enabled the collection of rainwater from the surrounding roofs.

By the Middle Ages in Europe, wealthier homes had servants who might lay a tablecloth over a long wooden table before a meal, but the kitchen remained a busy, noisy, smelly destination, especially for the less fortunate. "If we were suddenly taken back to the Middle Ages," writes Molly Harrison, "we should find a most striking lack of domestic amenities. The nostrils of even the wealthiest people must have been accustomed to a stench which the poorest among us could not tolerate today. Bones and scraps from the tables were thrown onto the floor and, if uneaten by the dogs, lay to rot and, mixed with offal and mud, were later covered with a fresh layer of 'sweet smelling herbs' or rushes" (37).

While the kitchens in some abbeys and the homes of noblemen were located away from the main house, in part to reduce the risk of fire, most remained "farmhouse kitchens" or "smoke kitchens," in which food was both prepared and eaten. There, the hearth also served as a source of heat, and smoke was a constant companion.

As Doreen Yarwood points out, some kinds of woods were preferred over others, given their different characteristics: "For instance, the wood from the ash-tree burns with a hot, clear flame, beech gives an even heat, cherry wood is particularly suited to oven cooking. On the other hand, conifer and other resinous woods were avoided because of the dark smoke which they produce when burning and poplar because it gives out an unpleasant smell" (58).

The environment, in other words, was not easily forgotten in early kitchens. And it was also right outside the door, in a little kitchen garden full of herbs and vegetables, which by the sixteenth century in England could be found attached to even the smallest cottage (Harrison 53).

By the seventeenth century, however, new technologies began to distance cooks (usually either housewives or their servants) from the natural environment, such as when pipes connected private residences to the public water supply, and coal started to replace wood in the wealthiest households—in part because the forests had been depleted to clear land for cultivation and make charcoal for iron smelting. By the eighteenth century, the kitchen began to look even more familiar, with the appearance of the cast-iron oven (which burned coal more effectively than the open hearth), the increased use of ice houses for refrigeration, and the publication of popular cookbooks.

There was, however, one notable exception, the "turnspit dog," which easily qualifies as history's most curious and problematic kitchen appliance. Unlike our lounging Labrador retriever, the turnspit dog was a short-legged dog (now extinct), bred to run inside a large wooden wheel mounted above the fireplace, much like a mouse on a treadmill. Below the wheel, in front of the fire, was a large piece of meat on a turning metal rod, known as a "turnspit." As the dog moved, so did its wooden wheel, and so did the turnspit, to which the wheel was connected by an endless chain (Bondeson 149–61).

In use from the sixteenth through the nineteenth century in Britain, turnspit dogs also found their way to America, where they caught the attention of Henry Bergh (1813–1888), founder of the American Society for the Prevention of Cruelty to Animals, who campaigned against their use in New York City's commercial kitchens (Coren 171–72).

A turnspit dog at work in a wooden cooking wheel in an inn at Newcastle, Wales, 1797. (Detail of an engraving from *The Book of Days,* vol. 1, ed. Robert Chambers [W. & R. Chambers, 1863], after an illustration in *Remarks on a Tour to North and South Wales: in the year 1797,* by Henry Wigstead [London: W. Wigstead, 1799])

The turnspit dog may be the most striking symbol of a passing way of life—and the advent of a kitchen powered not by obvious sources of energy (however bizarre they may seem to us today) but by hidden ones (less bizarre, perhaps, but also more pernicious).

Renovating a kitchen in the twenty-first century, especially if you care about sustainability, requires a series of decisions that makes at least some of these hidden energies visible. What kind of appliances should you buy? What kind of lighting is the most efficient? What materials should the countertops be made out of? And so forth.

Philip Schmidt's *Complete Guide to a Green Home* (2008) lays out five principles he says are common to most green home initiatives:

1. Energy efficiency: Reducing energy demands through everyday conservation; energy-efficient appliances; and an airtight, well-insulated thermal envelope.
2. Water conservation: Planning drought-tolerant, low-maintenance landscapes and gardens; using low-flow fixtures and water-saving appliances throughout the house.
3. Smart materials: Choosing construction and finish materials for their low environmental impact, sustainable production, low toxicity, durability, and recyclability.
4. High air quality and minimal pollution: Ensuring healthy indoor air with non-toxic materials and effective ventilation; minimizing outdoor environmental pollution from fertilizers, pesticides, and landscape equipment.
5. Natural systems: Increasing reliance on the sun, winds, and plants for electricity, lighting, heating, cooling, and air quality.

In addition, Schmidt suggests that anyone planning to expand an existing kitchen should try to "minimize site disturbance during excavation" and "reduce waste through efficient construction techniques and building materials" (6).

We're a long way from the turnspit dog.

The path from the nineteenth century to today's "green home" runs through more than just transformations in technology and resource use, however; it also runs through a series of social transformations that accompanied those technological changes—and in fact are inextricably linked to them.

If we turn our attention to the development of kitchens in America, we can see this particularly clearly, given the appearance of popular guides to "domestic economy" in the nineteenth century.

The nineteenth century saw the arrival of a number of technological developments, including the closed-top cast-iron kitchen range and natural gas for lighting and cooking in the early part of the century, and domestic refrigeration and electric cooking equipment in the latter part of the century.

But the most notable influence on the kitchen was arguably not a technology but a text: namely Catharine Beecher's *Treatise on Domestic Economy,* which first appeared in 1843 and was later reissued in a revised and enlarged version as *The American Woman's Home,* coauthored with her sister, Harriet Beecher Stowe, in 1869.

Beecher's *Treatise* was the foremost domestic advice manual of its day, and Beecher developed it for a singular purpose: to ennoble domestic pursuits by aligning them with Christian morality and positioning them as the foundation for national unity (Sklar). As Beecher put it in *The American Woman's Home* (the source of all the quotations that follow), "It is the aim of this volume to elevate both the honor and the remuneration of all the employments that sustain the many difficult and sacred duties of the family state, and thus to render each department of woman's true profession as much desired and respected as are the most honored professions of men" (13).

Yet the volume's popularity was likely due as much to the wealth of practical tips it offered as it was to the ideological ends to which those tips were being put. This more limited aim Beecher described as "to exhibit modes of economizing labor, time, and expenses, so as to secure health, thrift, and domestic happiness to persons of limited means, in a measure rarely attained even by those who possess wealth" (24).

For example, Beecher argues for the value of a compact kitchen, much like a cook's galley in a steamship, "so arranged that with one or two steps the cook can reach all he uses." In contrast, she observes, "in most large houses, the table furniture, the cooking materials and utensils, the sink, and the eating-room, are at such distances apart, that half the time and strength is employed in walking back and forth to collect and return the articles used" (34).

As June Freeman has pointed out, Beecher's idea of efficiency is focused more on "the achievement of order than economy of effort" (28). Many of Beecher's suggestions concern what objects the housewife should purchase or have on hand and how these objects should be arranged and employed to secure "a neat and cheerful kitchen" (*American Woman's Home* 371). Nevertheless, Beecher's dedication to what she called "habits of system and order" (220) presaged a growing interest in the professionalization of the domestic sphere that would reshape twentieth-century kitchen design—and ultimately contemporary ideas about how a sustainable kitchen should look and operate.

One of the more unexpected aspects of Beecher's kitchen advice is not her obsession with organization but her reliance on French cuisine as a benchmark for what American women should seek to accomplish in their well-ordered kitchens. "The abundance of splendid material we have in America is in great contrast with the style of cooking most prevalent in our country," Beecher writes. "Considering that our resources are greater than that of any other civilized people, our results are comparatively poorer" (167).

In her chapter "Good Cooking," Beecher instructs her readers on the superiority of the European table generally, but France comes in for special praise. Speaking of the butchering of meat, for instance, Beecher argues against the stereotype that the French attention to aesthetics is impractical, claiming instead that "the French mode of doing almost all practical things is based on that true philosophy and utilitarian good sense which characterizes that seemingly thoughtless people. Nowhere is economy a more careful study, and their market is artistically arranged to this end." Compared to what she calls "the dead waste of our clumsy, coarse way of cutting meats," the French rule is "to cut their meats that no portion designed to be cooked in a certain manner shall have wasteful appendages which that mode of cooking will spoil" (179).

Beecher's attention to French methods of food preparation is remarkable in two ways: not only does it predate Alice Waters's enthusiasm for all things French by a hundred years, but it also calls attention to the same connection between shopping and cooking that Waters emphasized. "In a French market is a little portion for every purse, and the far-famed and delicately flavored soups and stews which have arisen out of French economy are a study worth a housekeeper's attention," Beecher observes. "Not one atom of food is wasted in the French modes of preparation" (180).

Beecher knew she faced an uphill battle in getting American cooks to adopt French methods. "Whether this careful, economical, practical style of meat-cooking can ever to any great extent be introduced into our kitchens now is a question," she admitted, noting that "our butchers are against it" and "our servants are wedded to the old wholesale wasteful ways." But she saw an opening in the education of her female readers, if only they could be convinced to surrender their prejudices against "foreign foppery" and seek the same refinements in cooking as they were eager to acquire in other aspects of the domestic sphere (190). "If such things are to be done," writes Beecher, "it must be primarily through the educated brain of cultivated women who do not scorn to turn their culture and refinement upon domestic problems" (180–81).

Beecher's emphasis on efficiency in kitchen design thus matched her enthusiasm for efficiency in food preparation—and both forms of efficiency should sound strikingly contemporary to anyone who's been paying attention to sustainable food these past few years. That Beecher proposed these new forms of household economy as part of a best-selling domestic advice manual should also make us perk up our ears, because, as Sarah Leavitt has wisely observed, there's a straight line from Beecher to Martha Stewart. And, as Leavitt has also noted, "Domestic-advice manuals have always been the stuff of fantasy. Their historical value lies in uncovering the ways certain women understood the connections between their homes and the larger world" (5).

One place I would not have thought to look for domestic advice is an art museum, but the world continues to amaze me, so I recently made my way to the Minneapolis Institute of Art (Mia) to see an installation of the Frankfurt Kitchen, the first completely built-in or "fitted" kitchen, designed by the Austrian architect Margarete (Grete) Schütte-Lihotzky in 1926.

To get there I walked through the museum's courtyard to the entrance of the Target Wing, part of an addition to the museum designed by Michael Graves that opened in 2006. From there I took the stairs to the third floor, where the galleries devoted to modernism are located, and there, just to the left of the atrium, is Gallery 378, where the Frankfurt Kitchen is housed.

One of only two Frankfurt Kitchens in museum collections (the other is in the Museum of Modern Art in New York), Mia's kitchen was added to its permanent collection in 2004, and it quickly became a favorite of the public.

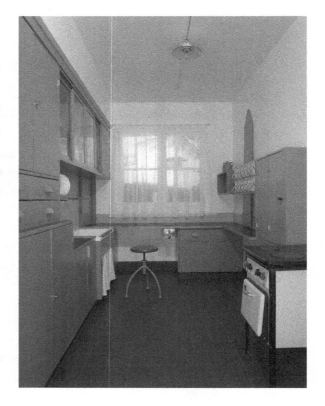

The Frankfurt Kitchen, by Margarete Schütte-Lihotzky, 1926–30. (Minneapolis Institute of Art, gift of funds from Regis Foundation, accession no. 2004.195; photo, Minneapolis Institute of Art)

Tucked into its own nook, the kitchen is one of the museum's popular "period rooms," which attempt to showcase the decorative arts in context. These include a Tudor room from seventeenth-century England, a drawing room from eighteenth-century Charleston, South Carolina, and a living room from 1906 Duluth—all of which were disassembled in their original locations, moved, and then reassembled in the museum.

With its sky-blue cabinets and clean white walls, it's easy to see why so many visitors are charmed by the Frankfurt Kitchen. Not only is it recognizably modern—it resembles a contemporary galley kitchen—but it is also noticeably small: only about 6 feet wide by 11 feet long. Its counters are also less than 3 feet tall, designed to be used by a person seated on an adjustable stool, leading the *Star Tribune,* our local paper, to deem the kitchen "an overgrown playhouse" (Abbe).

Other details jumped out at me the closer I looked. The stove is electric rather than cast-iron, and its enameled white surfaces seem designed to distinguish it from any appliance that would require blacking. The light fixture on the ceiling is movable, sliding back-and-forth along a rod, so it can reach whatever part of the kitchen you are in. A fold-down ironing board (also painted blue) is integrated into the design, and twelve aluminum storage bins with easy-to-grip handles look like something right out of Catharine Beecher's handbook—or smaller versions of the bulk bins at my local co-op. (The bins at the museum are labeled, in German: coffee, salt, semolina, dried fruit, rice, oats, flour, baking ingredients, fine sugar, noodles, barley, and sugar.) A similar bin under the counter sits ready to receive your kitchen scraps, while a drying rack above the sink keeps dishes out of the way before they are returned to the cupboards for storage.

In all, it *does* look like a fun kitchen to play in, but its charm hides both the significance of its innovations and the mixed messages it sends about sustainability nearly a century after its creation.

That the Frankfurt Kitchen has "issues" can be seen most clearly from a revealing comment Grete Schütte-Lihotzky made later in her life: "The truth of the matter was, I'd never run a household before designing the Frankfurt Kitchen, I'd never cooked, and had no idea about cooking" (Kinchin and O'Connor). File this under: Things that make you go, "hmmm."

What Schütte-Lihotzky did have was a curious mind and a talent for design, and the Frankfurt Kitchen reflects the rapid changes in technology and society that had occurred since the mid-nineteenth century in both Europe and the United States.

In addition to the widespread adoption of such conveniences as indoor plumbing, iceboxes, hot-water heaters, and gas stoves, the late Victorian era also saw the mass production of packaged goods, which changed how people (especially women) interacted with their kitchens—and thus their environment. The appearance of commercially canned fruits and vegetables, for instance, not only made the time-consuming task of home canning seem obsolete, but it also meant that the modern family "no longer had to dine according to what was in season," according to Ellen Plante (145). The arrival of branded prepared foods such as Shredded Wheat, Grape Nuts, and Jell-O gelatin further helped to change the identity of middle-class women from "homemakers" into "consumers," and the kitchen increasingly became less a space to produce food from scratch and more a place to store prepared food prior to its consumption.

Although "convenience" became a, well, convenient explanation for these changes, they were driven by a host of interacting factors, for which convenience was as much justification as it was description. Technological innovation and social change went hand in hand, as we have seen, and markets for new consumer products both drove and responded to the appearance of those products. To take just one example, the introduction of the Hoosier cabinet, or freestanding kitchen cupboard, occurred alongside increasing numbers of women working outside the home in the United States, and each development affected the other. As Ellen Plante points out, "Massive advertising campaigns promoted these products as 'helpmates' and 'servants' during a period when employing domestic help was on the decline and, indeed, women were told they'd no longer require help in the kitchen if this room was outfitted with the latest modern furnishing, appliances and tools" (207–8). Particularly during World War I, when women were recruited to fill the jobs of men engaged in the war effort, the "servantless" kitchen increasingly became the norm, and the Hoosier cabinet helped to make this transition possible. With its all-in-one design, the cabinet combined the storage space of a traditional baker's cabinet (repurposed to house packaged goods) with pull-out work surfaces and built-in racks for dishware and a host of newfangled kitchen gadgets—all intended to eliminate trips to the pantry and make life easier for the modern housewife, whether she worked outside the home or not.

The impulse toward efficiency embodied by the Hoosier cabinet was manifested in other ways as well, particularly in the development of the field of domestic science, or "home economics," as it eventually came to be called. Among the leading proponents of this movement was Christine Frederick, whose ideas had a large effect on Grete Schütte-Lihotzky's plans for the Frankfurt Kitchen. Frederick was herself influenced by the time and motion studies of efficiency expert Frederick Winslow Taylor, to whose work she was introduced by her husband, George Frederick (that's a lot of Fredericks, I know). What George Frederick saw as useful for his business, Christine Frederick saw as equally applicable to the domestic sphere: namely, the principles of "scientific management," which sought to optimize productivity through the careful study of workflows. In her 1919 book *Household Engineering: Scientific Management in the Home*, Frederick recounts her enthusiasm upon first learning of Taylorist methods: "Couldn't we perhaps standardize dishwashing by raising the height of the sink and changing other conditions? Did we not waste time and needless walking in poorly arranged kitchens— taking twenty steps to get the egg-beater when it could have been hung over my table, just as efficiency insisted the workman's tools must be grouped?" (14). The result was what Frederick called the "labor-saving kitchen," which differed from Catharine Beecher's compact kitchen not so much in its design as in its purpose: gone are the religious and nationalistic arguments for efficiency, and in their place is "the splendid aim of putting housework on a standardized, professional basis" (17).

Having read Frederick's work in German translation, Schütte-Lihotzky imported many of her recommendations directly into the Frankfurt Kitchen (Heßler 169). In *Household Engineering,* for example, Frederick calls for "a kitchen small and compact" (19), "cupboards and shelves built into the kitchen itself" in place of a pantry (20), the "scientific grouping of equipment" (28), "a comfortable height for all working surfaces and equipment" (37); "a high stool (preferably with an adjustable seat) [for] . . . washing dishes, peeling vegetables, preparing pastry, and many other tasks" (39); and "bins of various sizes for holding flour, sugar, etc. in quantity" (48). That the Frankfurt Kitchen's built-in cupboards and continuous countertops barely register as distinctive today may in fact be the greatest testament to Schütte-Lihotzky's achievement, as these were among the most innovative of all the kitchen's features—a marked step up from the stand-alone Hoosier cabinet.

Frederick also insisted on windows "preferably placed high in the walls" so they can provide ventilation and light the working surfaces, without the curtains getting soiled or the windowsill collecting clutter. Notably, the Frankfurt Kitchen at Mia features a trompe l'oeil window at the rear of the kitchen, fitted with a sheer curtain, through which the visitor can view a photo transparency of the housing complex from which this kitchen was taken: the Ginnheim-Höhenblick Housing Estate in Frankfurt am Main, Germany. In all, the Frankfurt Kitchen was eventually installed in ten thousand new working-class apartments built to help address the city's housing shortage following World War I.

Ironically, while Frederick's goal was to encourage women to stay home (an objective that aligned her with the previous century's domestic ideology), Frederick herself embodied the role of the modern, professional woman, and the Frankfurt Kitchen she helped to shape was primarily designed not for housewives but for women who worked, as Schütte-Lihotzky herself did. In her later writings, Frederick also served as a cheerleader for consumerism, styling herself "Mrs. Consumer" and authoring the book *Selling Mrs. Consumer* (1929), which sought to help companies effectively market their products to women, as well as help women become better consumers. She even coined the term "creative waste" to describe the need to discard a functioning consumer good with a new model to keep the economy running (Rutherford 150). The legacy of the Frankfurt Kitchen is thus as mixed as that of its principal inspiration, Christine Frederick—a fact that became even more clear to me when I turned to leave the museum and took one last look out the "window" at the back of the kitchen, which frames not a kitchen garden but the outside of the housing complex, looking a bit more like a prison than I suspect Ernst May, the project's architect, may have intended.

We live in an older home (by Minnesota standards, at least), built in 1888 and last renovated in the 1970s—a bad decade for lots of things but especially for home design. We made some aesthetic changes to the house when we first moved in—taking up the wall-to-wall carpet and refinishing the floors, pulling down the wallpaper and repainting, and removing the popcorn ceilings, among other things—but we didn't make any major structural changes, given the disruptions these entail, not to mention our limited budget.

Over the course of several years of living in the house, though, we became more and more aware of the limitations of our existing kitchen, as well as more and more intrigued by an interesting possibility. If we were to add a small bump-out to the rear of the house, it would allow us to reconfigure the entire first floor, changing the location of a mudroom and bathroom and opening up the kitchen to better connect with the family room and dining room.

Although our kitchen was not quite as compact as the Frankfurt Kitchen, it shared many of its characteristics: it was a galley kitchen, with access to the dining room through a narrow passage on the south side, and a doorway to a small mudroom (and eventually the back door) on the north side. Like lots of kitchens built since World War II, many of which were influenced by the Frankfurt Kitchen, ours had continuous countertops and built-in cabinets, but the cabinets were made of particle board and had seen better days. The cabinets also stopped well short of the ceiling and were topped by large soffits, which meant that the storage space was more limited than it had to be—forcing us to keep much of our food in the stairwell to the basement and many of our cookbooks on shelves in other rooms. The kitchen was also dark, with only a single window over the sink, and it had so little counter space that we often ended up having to use our dining room as an auxiliary counter. In short, this was not a kitchen conducive to cooking, much less one that invited guests to linger and enjoy the company of the cooks.

Our kitchen also shared other flaws with the Frankfurt Kitchen. As Martina Heßler has documented, once residents began to use the Frankfurt Kitchen, they quickly discovered additional drawbacks to its design. Not only did residents complain that the kitchen was too small, but they also said they felt isolated from the rest of the family, and the kitchen prevented them from keeping an eye on their children. Others unsuccessfully "tried to squeeze their big old kitchen tables into the kitchen's six square meters," likely craving additional prep space as well as a place for family to gather (176). Rather than adapting the kitchen to its users, the design team responded to these complaints with an "educating program" to get residents to adapt to the kitchen, seeing the problem as the failure of "traditional human beings" instead of a failure of architectural design (177).

Being traditional human beings ourselves, we decided to do the opposite and adapt our kitchen to our needs. If the space was too small, we would expand it; if it felt isolated from the rest of the house, we would connect it; and if it didn't fit a kitchen table (it didn't), we would find a way to include one.

Like almost all renovation projects, ours had certain constraints, including the location of our home's foundation and load-bearing walls, our desire to preserve as much of our small backyard as possible by minimizing the footprint of the addition, and, of course, money. But with some creative thinking and the help of a skilled architect, we were also able to find a solution to the kitchen-table problem: by moving our basement stairway, we could widen the kitchen just enough to fit a long and narrow island, including space for seating.

We could, in other words, no longer feel like we were cooking in prison.

It's one thing to see a kitchen in a museum, but it's another entirely to see one in real life, and so as we were on our way to France, Nancy and I stopped in Frankfurt with this finely crafted plan: we would make our way to the Ginnheim-Höhenblick Housing Estate and see if anyone would let us look at their kitchen.

Amazingly, this plan actually worked—with the first person we met!

On a cloudy day in May, with thunder rumbling overhead and light rain in the forecast, we hopped on the U2 U-Bahn line in downtown Frankfurt and rode eight stops north to Hügelstraße. From there, we walked a short distance through the Ginnheim neighborhood to the Ginnheim-Höhenblick Housing Estate.

All in all, it was a surprisingly easy trip.

There, we found Lars Nightingale chatting with his neighbor Annka in their front gardens, and we could not have asked to meet a nicer, friendlier set of people.

The Ginnheim-Höhenblick Housing Estate consists of about one hundred three-story, single-family homes that share walls, and Lars and Annka live right next door to one another.

Annka pointed up and down the street and told us that the orientation of all the houses next to each other are flipped—"it changes right and left, right and left; it's like a mirror"—something we would not have immediately noticed.

What we did observe right away, however, is that the same blue color used in the original Frankfurt Kitchen had also been used on the exterior trim of some of the houses, a subtle indication of what lay within.

That Lars was wearing a Boston Red Sox baseball cap when we stopped by suggested he might be sympathetic to some curious Americans inquiring about his kitchen, and it turned out we were right. After chatting a bit about how almost all the original Frankfurt Kitchens had been ripped out, with only a few placed in museums such as Mia, Lars generously invited us in to see his.

Lars, his wife, and his three children had been living at Höhenblick for about ten years, but the previous owner of their home had done all the renovations.

Originally, the entry hall led straight into the kitchen, with the dining and living spaces in separate rooms off the same hall, and this is what the previous owner had changed.

"In these houses it's more practical to remove the original kitchens," Lars pointed out, "and a lot of these houses have also changed the room concept. It was very tiny rooms."

As soon as we walked in the front door we could see what he meant, as the entry to the original kitchen had been blocked off, and the entire first floor had been made into a single, continuous space.

As if to illustrate how much more welcoming this newly connected space was, Lars's children were playing a game at the dining room table when we visited, within easy reach of the kitchen and two steps away from the living room.

The Frankfurt Kitchen was full of great ideas, Lars noted—"the ironing board, for example"—"but it was too small, and the counters were too short. For me, I've been at the ironing board, and I've had to go like this," he said, squatting down.

Lars says that his new kitchen is still not very big, which is true, but with one entire wall removed, it is now bright, airy, and full of natural light. In a kind of homage to Grete Schütte-Lihotzky, it maintains her continuous countertops and built-in cabinets, but the countertops are now made of butcher block and the cabinets faced with crisp white Formica. A small peninsula houses the oven and stove, and there is still space for a full-size dishwasher and refrigerator.

Best of all, photos of his children line the wall, and a row of colorful pottery sits atop the cabinets. Clearly, this is a kitchen that is lived in, and loved, and which has become an integral part of family life.

Seeing Lars's kitchen helped me to understand that the problems with both the original Frankfurt Kitchen and our kitchen are more than just design problems. A better way to say this may be that the design problems with these kitchens reveal that sustainability is about more than just using "green" materials or energy-efficient appliances. It's also about longevity, relationships, and joy—something Alice Waters clearly values, too.

Think about it this way: if the reductio ad absurdum of environmentalism is the Church of Euthanasia's slogan, "Save the Planet, Kill Yourself," we should be cautious about becoming overly focused on resource use as the sole criterion of sustainability. Yes, we want to limit our environmental footprint, but we also want to create things that will last, that will foster extensive relationships, and that will "spark joy" (to borrow a phrase from the organizational maven Marie Kondo).

The problems with the Frankfurt Kitchen were exactly these. Built with the idea that scientific rationality was the only way, they neglected how people actually used the space. By making it so that only one person could work in the kitchen at a time, by isolating that space from the rest of the house, and by designing the kitchen with an eye toward processed food, the kitchen disconnected people from one another and from the sources of their food. Perhaps worst of all, while at first glance the kitchen may indeed seem like "an overgrown playhouse," the closer you look, the more its focus on efficiency doesn't seem very fun. In fact, it seems more like working in a factory—the domestic equivalent of Wendell Berry's "industrial food."

At the other end of the spectrum, of course, is not the Church of Euthanasia, but the "trophy kitchen" of the 1980s—the gastronomic pleasure palace designed to impress your friends, display your wealth, and make you the envy of all your neighbors. An outgrowth of the gradual transformation of the kitchen from a site of domestic production to a site of conspicuous consumption, the trophy kitchen not only reflected the greed and vanity of America in the Reagan years but also the development of new kitchen technologies (such as the food processor, microwave oven, and vegetable juicer) and the accessibility of high-status brands (such as Cuisinart, Braun, and Krups) to middle-class consumers, thanks to the booming economy (Gdula 176–82). However, the trophy kitchen was decidedly *not* the look we were after.

What we did hope to achieve, however, was the intermediate step of Lars's "open kitchen," which—beginning in the 1960s—returned the kitchen to its rightful place as what Steven Gdula calls "the warmest room in the house." And that concept, it turns out, also has a history.

In his examination of privacy and the Canadian home, Peter Ward observes that "studies of the traditional French-Canadian home don't identify a *cuisine* until the end of the eighteenth century. They refer instead to a *salle commune* (common room), the central space in the home where most daily activities unfolded—cooking included—even when the house had several rooms. This room was usually large, often the largest in the dwelling. By the beginning of the nineteenth century a somewhat smaller kitchen, perhaps with a narrower range of functions, began to emerge in rural houses, as well as a summer kitchen located in an annex" (71). And by the end of the nineteenth century, no matter the size of the house, "the kitchen almost invariably stood apart from the rest of the dwelling, separated at least by a wall and usually by its location at the rear of the house" (73).

What was true for Canada was also true for the United States, until the social and economic changes of the 1950s began to transform how homeowners, architects, and developers thought about the relationship between cooking and eating in the home, or what Elizabeth Cromley calls the "food axis." Specifically, says Cromley, they began to ask, "Where should the family eat—in a separate dining room? That seemed so old-fashioned. In the kitchen? Could the working-class history of kitchen meals be superseded to make kitchen eating pleasant for all classes? Or should meals take place in the living room?" (177). What eventually emerged in the 1960s were new "kitchen-dining-living areas," made possible by a range of domestic transformations, including "technological advances such as better electric refrigerators and more reliable plumbing fixtures (which improved kitchen cleanliness and reduced offensive smells), the new availability of prepared foods from grocery shops, the disappearance of servants from all but the wealthiest households, and a popular redefinition of kitchen work as public, pleasurable, and sociable—to the point at which some men were willing to take up cooking themselves" (Ward 74). As Ward puts it, echoing Ellen Plante, "Absorbed once again into the spaces used for everyday family life, the kitchen had come full-circle" (74).

My point is not that opening up the kitchen is the key to sustainability but rather that unless we make the spaces in which we prepare food inviting, collaborative, connected, and pleasurable, food preparation will seem more like a chore than a joy, and the kitchen more like a prison than a playhouse. Fortunately, reenvisioning this spatial design of the kitchen can go hand in hand with more traditional understandings of environmentally friendly design, such as those that appear in Philip Schmidt's *Complete Guide to a Green Home*.

Calls to "green the kitchen" in this way first began to enter mainstream consciousness in the late 1980s and early 1990s, following the publication of *Our Common Future* (1987), also known as the Brundtland Report, in which the World Commission on Environment and Development (chaired by Gro Harlem Brundtland, former prime minister of Norway) defined sustainable development as "development that meets the needs of the present without compromising the ability of future generations to meet their own needs" (World Commission 43).

As if in response (though more likely a case of convergence), architects and designers began to rethink the kitchen as an organic space, one whose inputs and outputs resemble the functioning of an organism more than the Frankfurt Kitchen's model of a "food factory."

In *The Bathroom, the Kitchen, and the Aesthetics of Waste: A Process of Elimination*, the catalogue of a fascinating 1992 exhibition at the MIT List

Visual Arts Center, Ellen Lupton and J. Abbott Miller explore how *bodily* consumption and *economic* consumption became intertwined in the twentieth century—and how late twentieth-century designers attempted to move from seeing waste "as a form of positive production" (à la Christine Frederick) to one in which trash functions "as a site for struggles over power" (71). At the beginning of the twentieth century, they note, "the kitchen became a site not only for preparing food but for directing household consumption at large; the kitchen door is the chief entryway for purchased goods, and the main exit point for vegetable parings, empty packages, leftover meals, outmoded appliances, and other discarded products" (1). By the end of the century, however, environmental concerns signaled "a new activism of waste, a politics of garbage," which called for "informed consumers, responsive designers, and manufacturers, and rigorous public policy, considered on global as well as local scales" (71).

Two examples Upton and Miller provide of this new attitude toward waste are William (Bill) Stumpf's proposal for a "Metabolic House" and David Goldbeck's development of the "Smart Kitchen," both of which appeared in 1989.

Bill Stumpf was a legendary Minneapolis industrial designer, whose 1994 Aeron chair for Herman Miller exemplified his interest in the connections between the human body and its environment. Prompted by the *New York Times* to fashion a home that would "respond directly to ecological needs," Stumpf developed an outline for what he called the Metabolic House, in which the home functions much like a body in tune with its environment. "Our bodies do a good job of taking in oxygen, food and water, getting nutrition and dispelling waste," Stumpf observed. "Our houses don't do that very well. They should have a digestive system just like we do" (P. L. Brown C12). His visionary proposal for a home tried to better acknowledge its relationship to the surrounding world through a series of chutes, pipes, and conveyor belts that bring groceries and other heavy items into the house and send recyclables, compost, and filtered air out. Designed in an era prior to the ubiquity of home composting and single-stream recycling, his kitchen features a built-in composter for organic wastes, a prominent recycling cabinet, and under-the-counter bins for sorting glass, paper and aluminum. While some of his innovations are now commonplace, such as bulk delivery of biodegradable detergent (think Amazon.com) and a carbonated-water tap to cut down on packaging (think SodaStream), others remain niche features for

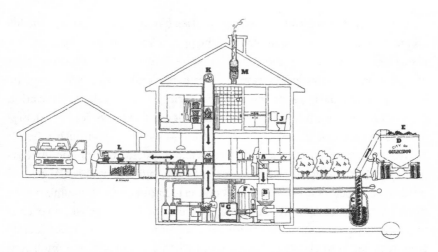

The Metabolic House, by William Stumpf, 1989. (From *The Bathroom, the Kitchen, and the Aesthetics of Waste: A Process of Elimination,* by Ellen Lupton and J. Abbott Miller [Cambridge, MA: MIT List Visual Arts Center, 1992]; courtesy of Ellen Lupton)

most Americans, including a residential waste-to-energy furnace and a bidet-like paperless toilet (P. L. Brown C12).

David Goldbeck's *The Smart Kitchen* shares many of the same assumptions of Stumpf's proposal for the Metabolic House, but as a book-length guide for homeowners, designers, and builders, it goes into far more detail and provides many more practical suggestions. Anticipating the arguments of sustainable food advocates like Waters two decades later, Goldbeck writes: "I believe that one of the reasons for the declining interest in cooking is that our kitchens have not kept up with changes in life-style. This is one of the reasons for the success of the microwave oven: At least they reflect, for better or worse, that people are beginning to view the preparation of food in a different light. If real cooking is to survive, kitchen design and appliances must be improved. Unless we adapt this workspace to contemporary needs, we will abdicate to mass producers one of the true pleasures of life and one of our most important sources of health: fresh food. We will be condemned to a 'boil 'n bag' and 'slit 'n serve' future" (2). While some aspects of Goldbeck's vision now seem dated—he advocates building an under-sink sprout tray, for instance, and provides detailed instructions for adding extra insulation to the *outside* of your refrigerator—his overall approach has aged well, and it is in fact remarkable how many of his concerns remain current today.

Fortunately, more and more communities have access to the knowledge and materials they need to implement the principles of green design without resorting to some of the more outlandish or homegrown "solutions" that characterized this first generation of sustainability advocates. When it came time for us to make the seemingly endless series of choices that a renovation project requires, we had it easy: we could choose from a variety of energy-efficient appliances at Sears, purchase a high-efficiency dual-flush toilet at Lowe's, and order sinks made from recycled stainless steel online. At Natural Built Home, a local source for eco-friendly building materials, we had our choice of colors for our Richlite countertops (made from a combination of 65 percent Forest Stewardship Council–certified or recycled paper content and 35 percent phenolic resin); our bathroom vanity top (made locally from recycled auto glass); and the floor tile for our bathroom and mudroom (made from recycled porcelain by a "Green Squared"–certified company). And to match the rest of the house, we selected a kitchen floor made from ash trees, of which tens of millions have been felled thanks to the emerald ash borer.

That we could do any of this at all reflects a degree of economic privilege not shared by much of the world, and that fact remains a central sticking point for any advocate of sustainability. (As Don DeLillo remarked in *Zero K*, "Half the world is redoing its kitchens, the other half is starving" [70].) But just as the Church of Euthanasia's idea of environmentalism is extreme to say the least, so too is the idea that sustainability must consist of only the purest of actions, free from any moral compromises or less-than-saintly responses to the considerable environmental, economic, and social challenges before us. None of our choices in this project was perfect, and almost all involved some degree of give-and-take, but we certainly tried hard to avoid outright hypocrisy and rationalization—such as installing granite countertops from halfway around the world in the name of more "sustainable" living. Sustainability, as we quickly came to discover, calls us to think creatively and stretch our imaginations in an attempt to live humbly in an already compromised world, all while not making the problem worse by trying to do better.

This is a challenge, needless to say, but also an opportunity. With ten million kitchens being remodeled annually in the United States (Hunter), we have the opportunity to make sustainable food mean more than just buying organic produce, shopping at the local farmers' market, or supporting farm-to-table restaurants. We have the opportunity to literally build it into the structure of our houses, our apartments, and our condominiums. Sustainability shouldn't stop at the kitchen counter, in other words; it should start there.

THE COOK AND THE WRITER

In his *History of Cookbooks,* Henry Notaker draws a distinction between two different roles that are helpful to remember when reading the work of Alice Waters through the lens of the sustainable kitchen. These two roles are the cook and the writer: "The role of the cook demands creativity and intuition in the preparation of food; a sense of balance between different ingredients; and understanding of the nuances of taste; and, to reach the desired result, experience with the choice of temperature and cooking times. The writer transforms the food into words, names the culinary processes and dishes, and makes the cooking techniques understood and accessible" (6).

Waters's role as a cook can best be seen through the series of kitchens she has occupied and engaged with over the years: particularly the four most important kitchens of her adult life: her Chez Panisse kitchen, Lulu Peyraud's kitchen in Provence, her own home kitchen in Berkeley, and the kitchen at the Edible Schoolyard she helped to create.

But it's also important to recognize how the public face of those kitchens has been filtered through the range of texts she has authored, including a memoir, a manifesto, several cookbooks identified with the restaurant, occasional essays on her philosophy of ethical sourcing, two children's books, and her forewords to many other writers' books. The kitchens, and Waters's life itself, thus have as much textuality as they have materiality—they are as much constructions tied to the genres of Waters's various writings as they are forms that take physical shape in the world.

Waters's relationship with both cooking and writing, however, is—how shall I put this?—complicated.

To take the two most prominent examples, it is often said that when devotees of French cuisine would visit Chez Panisse in the early days, they would sometimes proclaim, "That's not cooking; that's *shopping!*"—the implication being that Waters and her crew may have had good ingredients but they lacked technique. (A critique not unlike Truman Capote's response to Jack Kerouac: "That's not writing. It's typing.") In short, the critics said, Waters & Co. didn't know how to cook.

Similarly, when Waters's first cookbook—the *Chez Panisse Menu Cookbook*—was published in 1982, it set off a minor uproar among some collaborators who felt that they had not been fully credited for their contributions. Linda Guenzel, for instance, who had transcribed her interviews with Waters and drafted key parts of the book, was hurt that she was not named as a coauthor. Waters thanked her generously in the acknowledgments and listed her as a collaborator on the title page, but Guenzel's name did not appear on the copyright page, nor was she included in the book contract (McNamee 177).

Jeremiah Tower, the controversial chef who worked at Chez Panisse throughout the mid-1970s, excoriated Waters in his tell-all memoir, *California Dish* (2003), for failing to fully credit both Guenzel and himself in the book, particularly in its first draft. Waters did eventually acknowledge Tower's many contributions, noting that "his innovative and adventurous menus gave the restaurant its reputation for ambitious experimentation and exploration" (239). But she nonetheless opened the book by saying, "For some years now, every Thursday I have faced the weekly dilemma of planning a different five-course meal for each evening of the following week" (15), a claim that Tower calls "unconscionable," given how many of these menus were his own (213). Twisting the knife, he calls Guenzel "the woman who actually wrote" Waters's book (214).

Since those days, Waters has been more careful to indicate the scope of her contributions as both a cook and a writer, but the complicated nature of her relationships to the kitchen and her coauthors needs to be front and center in any examination of her role in advancing the movement toward more sustainable cooking and eating.

Rather than making her story less compelling, this actually makes it more so, because attending to Waters's *collaborative process* illuminates a central feature of everything she does and says: she works together with others to get things done, and she includes the nonhuman world as an active participant in that process, much like Bill Stumpf and David Goldbeck attempted to do with their plans for more "organic" kitchens.

Does that make her wholly without ego? Of course not. But it does give us a richer understanding of her significance, beyond simply identifying her as the "mother of modern American cooking."

Waters's most thorough exploration of the sources and characteristics of her achievements is her 2017 memoir, *Coming to My Senses: The Making of a Counterculture Cook*.

The title and subtitle of the book are revealing in both of their double meanings: *Coming to My Senses* of course refers to the process of waking up to one's situation and thinking reasonably and sensibly instead of foolishly. But since Waters seems never to have lost the "foolishness" of her idealism, the title instead refers to the process—begun in France—of her becoming aware of her physical senses, especially taste and smell. Likewise, while the subtitle refers to *The Making of a Counterculture Cook* in the straightforward sense of Waters's coming of age during the 1960s, it also has the more specific reference to her offering an alternative to the products and methods of industrialized food culture—a counterculture, if you will, to the reigning food culture of the time (Belasco, *Appetite*). In both of these meanings, therefore, the title and subtitle seem to promise nothing short of a book-length version of the Tale of American Culinary Transformation.

Like me, Waters grew up in suburban New Jersey, but readers looking for insights into the deep psychological roots of her success from these early years will likely come away disappointed. If anything, the first few chapters show her youth to be largely unexceptional: her parents seem to have been well adjusted, she appears to have gotten along well enough with her three sisters, and no major tragedy befell the family while she was growing up. Like lots of middle-class American families, hers moved (from New Jersey to Chicago and then to Los Angeles), but Waters appears to have emerged mostly unscathed, thanks in part to her natural extroversion. She drank, chased boys, went to parties—overall, she seems to have had a pretty good childhood.

Things pick up once Waters transfers from UC–Santa Barbara to Berkeley in the spring of her sophomore year and decides to spend the following spring in France with her friend Sara Flanders. Waters describes it as "our unofficial, self-created junior year abroad," but it was really just the spring and summer of 1965 (95). Nevertheless, it's clear that the experience was transformative, and this is where things get interesting, for all manner of reasons, textual as well as culinary.

If all of Carlo Petrini's writings can be read as a kind of intellectual autobiography, *Coming to My Senses* is unambiguously a work of autobiography—or, more precisely, a memoir.

William Zinsser clarifies the difference in the introduction to *Inventing the Truth: The Art and Craft of Memoir*: "Unlike autobiography, which moves in a dutiful line from birth to fame, memoir narrows the lens, focusing on a time in the writer's life that was unusually vivid" (15). Yet there is clearly overlap between the two genres, with memoir merely being a more concentrated form of autobiography.

Zinsser's title also reminds us that any autobiographical act involves "inventing the truth" in a multitude of ways. Like all of Waters's cookbooks, for example, *Coming to My Senses* was collaboratively written. The title page says the book was written "with Cristina Mueller and Bob Carrau," and the acknowledgments clarify just how significant a role they played in its creation. "Over the course of two years," Waters says, "they were variously my interviewers, interlocutors, interrogators, transcribers, and fine-tuners, challenging and guiding me to tell my story the best way I could" (308). While the life may not be theirs, in other words, the story partly is.

It helps, too, to distinguish between Waters the person, Waters the narrator, and Waters the protagonist, since these distinctions point to another central feature of the memoir, which is that it is both remembered and narrated. The word "memoir" comes from the French *mémoire,* or "memory," and the memoir form necessarily interweaves memory and imagination, as authors must make choices about how to structure their stories (and thus their lives) at every level.

For instance, while the main narrative of *Coming to My Senses* proceeds chronologically, Waters and her coauthors use italicized passages throughout the text to set off reflections that do not occur in strict chronological order. Although this is likely the result of the oral nature of Waters's remembrances, it also has the effect of enabling Waters the narrator to reflect at greater length about the subjects and themes that Waters the protagonist is living out in the pages of her memoir.

Structural considerations such as these are not merely academic musings about the form and shape of the memoir genre; they get to the heart of how we narrate the truth of our own lives. As the literary scholar James Olney (and brother of Richard Olney, who greatly influenced Waters) has written, "the act of autobiography is at once a discovery, a creation, and an imitation of the self" (19). Olney argues that the fascination with self-fashioning that has captured readers' imaginations in recent years has also been accompanied by "an anxiety about the self, and anxiety about the dimness and vulnerability of that entity that no one has ever seen or touched or tasted" (23).

What's especially interesting about *Coming to My Senses* is the way the text bypasses such anxieties by dwelling on what *can* be seen, touched, and tasted—namely, food.

Waters is hardly alone in her desire to narrate her sensory engagement with food, which a host of other female authors of food memoirs have also attempted to do. Whether written by celebrity chefs, cookbook authors, food writers, or amateur cooks, these food memoirs have all sought to convey something of the immediacy of each woman's encounters with food in its diverse forms and contexts.

Every memoir is unique, of course, but critics of autobiographical writing have also identified some common features that have distinguished the life writing of men and women over the years, even as less dichotomous understandings of gender have challenged and complicated these generalizations.

If male autobiographies have frequently exhibited the characteristics of the hero's journey—which include narrative continuity, an emphasis on individual experience, and the eventual acquisition of power—those of women have often exhibited the opposite features, including narrative discontinuity, the establishment of one's identity in relationship to others, and the challenges of acquiring and expressing one's agency.

In *Lives of Their Own: Rhetorical Dimensions in Autobiographies of Women Activists,* for example, Martha Watson examines the autobiographies of five women who lived at the turn of the twentieth century and finds that their stories all shared some distinctive elements. "Taken as a whole," she writes, "these women leaders develop a model of the feminine hero. Some of her virtues—loyalty to home and family, perseverance in the face of obstacles, strength of character, and concern for others—differ from the characteristics typical of most male leaders. And, perhaps most significantly, the feminine hero's virtues represent revisions of and notable deviations from the characteristics associated with the 'True Woman' ideal of the nineteenth century: piety, purity, domesticity, and submissiveness" (111).

Although Waters could certainly be seen as part of this lineage of the feminine hero, what is most striking about *Coming to My Senses* is that it ultimately directs our attention away from Waters herself and onto the communities of which she is a part: the living communities of people and the biological communities represented by the liveliness of food she so values. In her narrative construction of identity, in other words, Waters ultimately sides with those who see the self primarily as "relational"—that is, shaped, formed, and lived in relationship to other beings.

LUCY AND THE MÈRES

Everybody has a story. The question is how it gets told.

For Waters, the story turns on her visit to France in the spring of 1965.

"It all went back to France," she says in *Coming to My Senses*, describing her attempt to write a newspaper column about cooking in the years after her return. "I had been awakened to taste there, and I wanted everybody to be awakened the way I had been" (139).

Her first meal in Paris? *Soupe de légumes* in the hotel restaurant. "I'd never tasted anything like it before. The soup had tiny cubed vegetables floating in a clear amber broth, delicate and simple and delicious" (97).

A defining food experience? Living in a house at the bottom of Rue Mouffetard, one of Paris's legendary market streets. "Every day we walked up this winding cobblestone street lined with open stalls of fruits and vegetables on our way into the center of the Latin Quarter" (98).

Her culinary guides? Two French boys named Jean-Didier and Ambroise, who brought Waters and her roommate Sara to a new restaurant each night. "I'd never eaten like that before, and to eat with such discernment made it so much more delicious" (101).

Her most significant meal? Dining with Sara at a little restaurant overlooking the river in Pont-Aven in Brittany. "That meal made a *very* big impression on both of us" (111).

But watch as the magic of memoir transforms that memorable meal into something even more meaningful. What clearly mattered to Waters at the time becomes more significant in retrospect, as Waters the narrator reflects on how Waters the protagonist processed this event later in life.

"I realized later," she says, "that the food tasted so good because the trout probably came from the stream we could see outside the window, the melons came from their garden, and the owners likely made their own jambon. It was one of those perfect little meals. Years later when I opened Chez Panisse, I looked back on that experience as a blueprint" (111).

Even more rich is the way that this meal takes on greater significance to Waters the narrator, and thus Waters the person, as she processes the memory of that meal while recounting it:

> The dining room was filled with French gastronomes—or at least, they seemed that way to me, because they were so clearly enjoying the food. Everyone in the dining room was saying, "*Oh! C'est si bon!*" In other restaurants, the Frenchmen would normally just shrug and say, "*Eh, c'est bien.*" They *never* said anything about any meal, even if it was fantastic— just "*C'est bien,*" in that blasé way. And here they were, exclaiming! Sara and I had never seen anything like it. It was the first time we'd seen the French be overtly enthusiastic about a meal. The men even asked the chef to come out so they could pay their compliments—to *her.* I just remembered: the chef was a woman. (111)

In the *Chez Panisse Menu Cookbook,* Waters had recounted this same origin story, saying that she has "remembered this dinner a thousand times" but only noting in passing that the chef was a woman (x). But in the version of this story in *Coming to My Senses,* Waters emphasizes the gender of the chef. What could have possibly changed between 1982 and 2017?

When #MeToo came to the kitchen, the reckoning was long overdue.

Women had long complained about sexism in the restaurant industry, perhaps best chronicled by Anthony Bourdain in *Kitchen Confidential: Adventures in the Culinary Underbelly* (2000).

So when sexual harassment accusations were made against the celebrity chefs Mario Batali, John Besh, Michael Chiarello, and Paul Qui, along with the restaurateur Ken Friedman, it did not come as a surprise to many in the industry.

"I would rather have a pretty woman in my bed than behind a stove in a restaurant," the legendary chef Paul Bocuse told *People* magazine in 1976. "I prefer my women to smell of Dior and Chanel than of cooking fat. . . . Women are good cooks, but they are not good chefs. Women who systematically want to do what men do just end by losing their femininity, and what I adore most of all is a feminine woman" (Chelminski).

If you were looking to understand the role of Alice Waters in the sustainable food movement, therefore, particularly in the context of women in the food industry, a good place to start might be Paul Bocuse's hometown of Lyon, and a good person to talk to might be Lucy Vanel.

Nancy, Grace, and I first visited Lyon when we were living in Italy, and we liked it so much we returned three more times, including for a month-long stay when I was serving as a visiting professor at the École Normale Supérieure, or ENS.

I first met Lucy when the three of us signed up for a French pastry workshop she was offering through her Plum Lyon Teaching Kitchen, where we learned the basics of pâte à choux and made our own éclairs, profiteroles, and choquettes. A more delicious learning experience would be hard to find!

But while Lucy is a French-certified pâtissier, she is much more than that, and I ended up taking two more classes with her, including a market cooking class in which we created dishes from whatever ingredients we found at the Croix-Rousse outdoor market.

Over the course of two November mornings, Lucy shared her story with me at La Boîte à Café, just up the street from Plum Lyon. As we spoke, we both sipped espresso drinks (quite tasty ones, I might add) and munched on some French pastries that were *almost* as good as the ones she had taught me how to make a few days prior.

One of the unintended consequences of studying life writing is that you tend to look for turning points in a story—the streamside meal that ends up shaping everything else you do, for example.

For Lucy, there were at least three of these: when she found the market, when she found her calling, and when she found her kitchen. In between, there was this little thing called life, which for Lucy happens to have been especially rich.

Born in Nashville, Tennessee, but raised in upstate New York, Lucy studied art at Syracuse University, after which she decided to enlist in the army so she could save money, practice her art, and travel to Europe.

Initially, the army had other plans for her, sending her to the Defense Language Institute in Monterey, California, for a year to learn Chinese. But Lucy had the foresight to put into her contract that she wanted to go to Europe, and so the army eventually relented and posted her to Frankfurt, Germany, where she spent four years at the Ninety-Seventh General Hospital, the Seventh Medical Command, which served the European theater. (The Frankfurt Kitchen, I suspect, was not on her radar.)

Still, the year in Monterey stayed with her, and after ending her tour of duty, she decided to move to China, where she worked for four more years at a Swiss commodities trading company.

"It was a very glamorous, wonderful life, but I was obsessed with the cuisine, because everywhere I went there was a different, wonderful cuisine. People see China in black and white, but there are hundreds of different cultures all brought together in this one country. So everywhere you go they are doing a different kind of cuisine. And this was fascinating to me. I was seeking out people to teach me how to cook."

Seeking to rekindle her passion for art, Lucy returned to the States to enroll in an MFA program in sculpture at UNC–Chapel Hill, and it was there that met her husband, Loïc, a physicist from France, who was at Duke for ten days, doing an experiment.

"Next thing you know, I'd signed up for a semester at La Sorbonne, and then we're engaged, and the whole thing just kind of quickly turned around that way."

After deciding to get married, the couple agreed to live in the United States for a year, and that was when Lucy really started beginning to cook French.

"Because we were living together, and he was missing these things. He's the kind of person who just couldn't function without certain things: he needed to eat French."

When Loïc finally received a job offer to be a *maître de conférences* (or assistant professor) at the ENS in Lyon in 2000, they were ready to pack their bags. Still, it was a big transition for Lucy, despite having lived as an expat before.

"I went through this whole period of trying to adjust and learn how the system works. It looks the same—it's very European and very Western—and I was thinking, 'Oh, the expat experience. This is going to be pretty easy.' But the ways things work is completely different, like you have to go to a certain store to get a certain thing. You can't just go to a big store and buy whatever you need. That doesn't work here."

After what she describes as "a couple of traumatizing experiences" at the big supermarkets, Lucy discovered the outdoor market a few blocks down from where she lived, and that became her place.

"Once I realized that I could find everything I needed in my little neighborhood market, I didn't want to go to the supermarket anymore. And that was when the rhythm of the seasons started setting in. I realized that things are going to come back in season. Morels appear for three weeks in April, then you've got your zucchini flowers . . . things just come in and go, come in and go. At every moment, every point in the year, you've got a different kind of dish that's natural to make, that you don't have to seek out."

Lucy became very animated at this point in our conversation, and it was clear that seasonality was, and remains, a hugely important aspect of her cooking.

"The supermarket," she said, "is about out-of-season, imported stuff."

Lucy describes her awakening to market-based cooking as "a shift from seeking products to cook, in order to execute a recipe I had decided to do, into cooking what was there with the recipes I had. I realized then that I had everything I needed. Going through the entire season I could always find a recipe for something that I found at the market."

One of Lucy's main references to French food in the United States had been Richard Olney, as was also true for Waters, but Lucy quickly realized that it was much easier to cook with his recipes in France, since so much of his approach depends on the quality of the ingredients. "Trying to execute his recipes in the U.S. is not the same," she says.

"Keep it seasonal," Waters wrote in the "Seasonal Menus" section of the *Chez Panisse Menu Cookbook*. "There is nothing simpler or more economical than buying what is in season—if you know what is in season. Unfortunately, going to the supermarket, which tries to supply all of the produce all of the time, and looking at all the waxed and treated fruit will not give you the answer; learning comes from critically tasting and evaluating the produce on a month-to-month basis" (53).

At the time, Lucy had a day job as an executive assistant at a business school in Lyon, but food continued to be her true passion. So in her spare time she took up writing for the food website eGullet and started a blog called *Lucy's Kitchen Notebook*. In 2007, she began giving cooking classes at the Emile Henry store on Presqu'île (in the heart of the city), as well as teaching out of her small home kitchen, and soon after, she quit her day job to teach cooking full-time.

Once her son Ian was born, things became more difficult, as often happens for women working in the food industry. Lucy recalls one transformative moment, after she had just dropped Ian off at day care and rushed over to the Saint-Antoine outdoor market to get supplies.

"I remember running down the Quai de la Pêcherie, with a stroller full of food. I was late for the class, my day was not going well, and I realized I was missing an ingredient. At that point I said, 'Something's got to change here.' We started thinking about the teaching kitchen at that time. That was when I realized it was going to happen, that we were going to build the kitchen."

With Loïc's encouragement, Lucy started to look for commercial properties where her family could also live, and she focused her search on the Croix-Rousse, a hilly neighborhood where Lyon's silk industry once flourished.

"Because the Croix-Rousse was originally an artisan district, it was built into the rules of the property that the artisans can live on the site," Lucy observes.

Walking with a friend one morning, Lucy saw a former bakery for sale, and the price was right.

"The problem was it was in ruins," says Lucy. "Everything was horrible. The place was a mess. But I was very excited about it, and the agent was really convincing. He was like, 'Underneath this ceiling there are wood beams. Behind this wall, you will find. . . .' And I brought Loïc up there and he was like, 'Are you crazy? No, we're not going to do this. No, I cannot handle that.'"

But Lucy's neighbor, who was an interior architect, said that it could be renovated for the amount they were able to pay, and so they bought it.

What followed—and one of the reasons I feel a special bond with Lucy—was the mother of all kitchen renovations. They discovered that what the architect thought was a sewage connection was not, and they had to dig for that. And they realized that there was no toilet and had to find a way to install one. All in all, it took about a year, and they did a complete remodel.

"It was a total catastrophe," says Lucy, "and we turned it into the kitchen, and I would never do that again. Even now I have a little traumatic stress from that project."

What resulted, though, was well worth the effort in my opinion, and I suspect in Lucy's as well.

The kitchen is bright and airy—no Frankfurt Kitchen this—with a large bank of windows facing the street and a huge marble island at its center. Two cooktops—one gas, one induction—line one wall, while the other holds the double sink, fridge, and microwave. A painted chalkboard fills the back wall, on which Lucy writes the menu as each class progresses. And a library and dining room at the back of the space offers a space for students to drop bags and coats and, when the class is complete, to eat.

It helps, of course, to have an instructor who not only knows what she is doing but loves her work.

"For the first time in my whole life I feel like I'm doing what I was meant to do," she says. "And that makes me happy. I don't feel like I'm still searching. I feel like I've found it. I never get tired of it."

"Here is how I cook," Waters writes in the preface to *Coming to My Senses*.

> First I'm at the farmers' market, buying a bunch of French breakfast radishes, the purple-fringed lettuces, the spring garlic—I'm thinking about the state of the Blenheim apricots and the Santa Rosa plums. I'm looking for fruits and vegetables that are perfectly ripe, things that just came out of the ground or were just picked. I'm not necessarily thinking about how the ingredients will go together—I'm just responding to what I'm finding. It's a lot about aliveness, a lot about color, the smell of things, the look. . . . I'm listening to what the farmer has to say about what's going on in the fields. I think we forget sometimes that food is alive and that we have to follow that intuition and treat food as a living thing. (ix)

This is what a food revolution is built on?

In a word, yes.

There's a lot wrapped up in the seemingly simple idea that freshness equals liveliness, but its centrality to Waters's philosophy could not be more clear, as it is one of the key insights that appears throughout her memoir. She praises the fresh salads made by her friend Martine Labro, noting that "the aliveness of something that had just been picked transformed the dish" (161). While traveling in Turkey, she marvels at the hospitality of complete strangers, who feed her and her friends a breakfast of warm goat's milk, whose "freshness and aliveness . . . was incredible" (193). And when planning what became Chez Panisse, she says she wanted to have a *prix fixe* menu instead of an *à la carte* menu, because "I wanted the food to be alive and perfect every night, and I didn't want to have to keep food over from one day to the next" (246).

Freshness is what is not easily found at the supermarket but is everywhere at the local farmers' market. Freshness is not "old food from far away," but newly harvested lettuce, whose cell walls are bursting with crispness and flavor. Freshness is the unmistakable aroma of the ripe peach, the tomato that still smells like the vine, the mint leaves whose bright scent lingers on your fingers long after they have been picked.

But freshness is not merely about "coming to your senses" in terms of taste; it is also about the good sense that links freshness back to the farm, as Waters knows so well. It is about supporting the local farmers who care for the places in which they live and work, and about knowing what is going on in those places yourself. Not least of all, it is about remembering what Wendell Berry called "the dewy first light of morning," that moment when Patty Wright walks outside, the sun hits her, and she says, "Oh, it's gonna be a good day."

I may seem like Captain Obvious to say that "food is alive," but Waters is dead right that we forget this sometimes—usually most times. We open a box or a can or a bag and eat what comes out of it, with little thought to where it came from, who was involved in its production, or what it cost beyond the price on the package.

Yet the *liveliness* of food is absolutely critical to remember, as it is the key upon which the whole sustainable food movement rests. The liveliness of food is its connection to the rest of our blooming and buzzing world, ourselves included.

It is why one of my favorite signs is the one that hangs in some French bathrooms: *Ici tombent en ruine les merveilles de la cuisine* (Here fall in ruin the wonders of the kitchen).

Liveliness keeps us humble; it keeps us grounded; it keeps us human.

We gathered at 9:00 a.m. on a Tuesday in May for "Plum Tuesdays: La Cuisine du Marché," one of Lucy's market table classes. The idea was that we would visit the Croix-Rousse market, see what looks good, and then build a meal around that. We would do *cuisine du marché*, or market cooking.

As Waters says of her own philosophy in *Coming to My Senses*, "I'm improvising, trying to capture and express that moment in time. I'm letting my senses lead me" (x).

This moment in time begins with an unexpected coincidence, which is that all the other people in the class happen to live within thirty miles or so of each other outside Los Angeles: in Huntington Beach, Irvine, and San Clemente. So I will be thinking about a California cookbook author with five people from California. Who could have planned that?

As we go around the room, I learn that Tammy loves to bake, and her husband, Eddie, especially likes her slow-cooked lamb. Laura says she is a desserts and salads person, and Emily has recently just fallen back in love with cooking. To laughs all around, Emily's daughter Amy says, "My boyfriend is the cook, so I am here to be the better cook."

Lucy tells her, "Edge your way in there, because sometimes when people are really into cooking, they just don't want anybody else in there." (Lucy is onto us alpha cooks.)

"Oh, he's willing to share the responsibilities, if I was capable," Amy replies to more laughter.

From the teaching kitchen, we make our way toward the market up the Montée de la Grande-Côte, a pedestrian street with staircases and gardens that culminates in a lovely esplanade overlooking the city.

As delivery vehicles zoom by on the cross-streets, and dollies rattle over the cobblestones, Lucy narrates the culinary history of Lyon, bringing us closer and closer to the present with every step we take.

She begins with the Romans, who called the city Lugdunum and chose its location for strategic reasons: Lyon exists at the confluence of the Rhône and Saône Rivers and offers a straight path down to the Mediterranean. They then cut roads in all directions, to reach the variety of landscapes that surrounded it.

"To the west of here," Lucy says, "once you get through the Beaujolais hills, in Roman times they were growing wheat. North of here is Burgundy, and they were already making wine there to supply the capital. There's traditional hunting ground in Bresse country, which also evolved into a place where they specialize in cream-fed poultry, so today we have the Poulet de Bresse. East of here are the Alps; the Romans were voracious mushroom eaters. This place was created to be the center, to be the provincial capital. The roads were created right at the beginning to bring everything here."

It's hard not to think of Jared Diamond's book *Collapse: How Societies Choose to Fail or Succeed,* in which Diamond describes the Anasazi settlement of Chaco Canyon, which grew too large to support itself and had to be subsidized by the outlying countryside. Like Lyon and many other metropolitan areas, it was connected to the surrounding landscape by a radiating network of roads. "Chaco Canyon became a black hole into which goods were imported but from which nothing tangible was exported," writes Diamond, and the society "turned into a mini-empire, divided between a well-fed elite living in luxury and a less well-fed peasantry doing the work and raising the food" (149). It's a model known as the "center-periphery," in which the periphery feeds the center, and in Diamond's view it leads to collapse when environmental conditions can no longer support the extractive relationship. (Wendell Berry made a similar point.)

There was certainly some of this happening in Lyon, but like other modern cities, the story here is more complicated, since Lyon became a center of banking, trade, and industry while its residents experienced deepening inequalities. In the Middle Ages, the Roman Catholic Church grew in power, and its need for silk helped to fuel the development of the silk industry during the Renaissance. By the end of the eighteenth century, almost thirty thousand people worked in the silk business, with wealthy trading families living very well and eating legendary feasts.

"They were still bringing everything in along those Roman roads," says Lucy, as we continue to make our way up the hill. "So they had all the beautiful veal, and the Charolais and Limousin beef, and the cheeses coming from Auvergne, and then of course the wine was flowing from Burgundy and the northern Côte du Rhone, and the Beaujolais. And we had just all kinds of wonderful things available here, from places as far as Provence and the Mediterranean, because of these roads that had been established so early."

As the Industrial Revolution introduced new weaving technologies, however, and the workers began to revolt, many of those well-established trading families had to start liquidating their assets to stay afloat, and that included laying off their domestic staff.

"Think Downton Abbey in Lyon," says Lucy. "The housekeepers and the cooks were the most vulnerable. They were the women running these households. They had a lot of power in their original roles, and suddenly they were looking for work. It was a difficult time for them."

"Necessity being the mother of invention, there were a couple of women who opened up their own restaurants, and they were trained in a cuisine that was much more elaborate than your average restaurant meal. They had their long-standing sources for the best ingredients. They were adept at getting all the good stuff—the truffles, the fois gras—it was all flowing in through these channels, and they used that in order to adapt their cuisine to restaurant cuisine. So they would take the local specialties and then transform it into their own dish."

"They were building a tradition of women running restaurants," Lucy explains. "This was unique in France. At the time, you didn't have women in urban restaurant environments."

They became known as the Mères Lyonnaises, the Mothers of Lyon.

Despite being France's second-largest urban area, Lyon remains relatively unknown among Americans, which may be one of the reasons Anthony Bourdain chose to profile the city in his *Parts Unknown* television series in 2014 (season 3, episode 4).

Before his 2018 suicide, Bourdain publicly voiced his support for the #MeToo movement and began the difficult work of reckoning with his past behavior, which includes his work on shows like *Parts Unknown*.

In a 2017 interview with Isaac Chotiner of *Slate*, Bourdain said: "I am a guy on TV who sexualizes food. Who uses bad language. Who thinks our discomfort, our squeamishness, fear and discomfort around matters sexual is funny. I have done stupid offensive shit. And because I was a guy in a guy's world who had celebrated a system—I was very proud of the fact that I had endured that, that I found myself in this very old, very, frankly, phallocentric, very oppressive system and I was proud of myself for surviving it. And I celebrated that rather enthusiastically" (Chotiner).

Unfortunately, Bourdain's treatment of Lyon and the Mères suffers from exactly the kind of bro culture Bourdain since came to repudiate.

Bourdain traveled to Lyon with chef and restaurateur Daniel Boulud, who grew up on a farm outside the city, and the episode spends much of the time glorifying the city's own celebrity chef, Paul Bocuse.

At the Institut Paul Bocuse, Bourdain at first seems to celebrate the influence of Eugénie Brazier, the most famous of the Mères, for whom Bocuse worked as an apprentice.

"The at times brutal world of the Michelin star kitchen looks much of the time like a boys' club," Bourdain observes. "But where did they come from? If we track back a bit to where it all began for Lyon and for many of the chefs whose names we now know and look up to, it all goes back to here: *La Mère Brazier*, the godmother, the original master. Teacher, chef, force. Two restaurants with three Michelin stars. An achievement no one, male or female, had ever attained and for many years, Lyon's most famous chef. Her influence runs right through every kitchen that's come since and her graduates carry on her recipes and her traditions."

But when he sits down to dinner with Boulud and Bocuse at Bocuse's legendary restaurant, L'Auberge du Pont de Collonges, there is little appreciation for Brazier's many achievements. Instead, Bocuse reduces her to only one feature: her fiery temper.

"She was such a screamer," Bocuse says, as translated by Boulud. "You would fall on your ass, she was screaming so hard. She was the first up in the morning and the last one to go to bed. She would go to the market with three cooks in the back of the truck and she would put the case of green beans or something and the cook will be sitting down making the beans, not to waste time, for the rest of the *mise en place*."

"Truly a terrifying figure," Bourdain observes.

The rest of the episode does little to counter the perception that women have no place in the professional kitchen, as Bourdain interviews young men working as apprentices, visits with men making *saucisson*, describes "the mysterious, fabulous, goofy, wonderful bro-fests" of Lyonnaise eating societies, and goes hunting with Bocuse himself at "the weekend getaway, the hang-out with the guys." (The one exception is when Bourdain meets Marie, who runs a school cafeteria, whose food he praises.)

By the end of the episode, the Mères have all but disappeared, and Bourdain asks: "Who cooks in the great restaurants? Farm boys, basically. That's who always cooked."

Lucy, not surprisingly, has a different take on La Mère Brazier, whose namesake restaurant—now run by the acclaimed (male) chef Mathieu Vianny—is only a few blocks away from Plum Lyon. (Bill Buford recounts his time working for Vianny, among many other Lyonnaise culinary adventures, in *Dirt*.)

La Mère Brazier "had very high standards in terms of freshness," Lucy notes, as we reach the esplanade and look down on the city stretching out before us.

"You didn't have this whole concept of market-based cuisine. It was more about her doing her rendition of the local specialties. But she was very serious about her suppliers, and she insisted that everything be at the height of freshness. This was the main thing that she transmitted to Paul Bocuse."

"When people referred to her as 'Chef Brazier,'" Lucy continues, "she would correct them, and say, 'No, cuisinière. I'm but a cuisinière.' Was it false modesty? I don't know. But when Paul Bocuse passed away, the full-page obituary in Le Progres, Lyon's local paper, ended with, 'Paul Bocuse, cuisinier,'" using the masculine form of the word.

"Why are there no great women chefs?" asked Charlotte Druckman in the pages of Gastronomica in 2010. "In theory, we've come a long way from the notion that a woman's place is in the domestic kitchen, and that the only kitchen appropriate for a man is the professional one. But in practice, things can be pared down to the following equation: woman: man as cook: chef" (24).

As Ann Cooper has pointed out, the difference between a "chef" and a "cook" is rooted in the French culinary hierarchy: "In the French language, the word chef means 'head' or 'chief' and is a masculine term that actually is specific to men only. The closest feminine equivalent is cuisinière, which refers to a woman who prepares and cooks food" (28).

And the distinction is not merely semantic. In Kitchens: The Culture of Restaurant Work, Gary Alan Fine puts it this way: "The chef must be a generalist while the lower-status cook may be a specialist. The cook may specialize in frying food, broiling steaks, or making salads; the chef should be able to do everything: keep a food budget, repair stoves, hire personnel, provide counseling, and know about food" (88).

Druckman interviewed Alice Waters for Skirt Steak, her follow-up book about women chefs, and Waters herself was reluctant to accept the title of chef, despite the urging of Jacques Pépin:

I had myself corrected by Jacques Pépin one time when I refused to consider myself a chef, and he said, "If you are in the kitchen and you are organizing people to produce a meal, you may not be the most accomplished in terms of cooking, but you are, in fact, doing that job, which is the main one in the kitchen, and you can't think of yourself as a cook." But, for me, a chef has always come with a lot of fanfare and a lot of authority and experience in the kitchen; and I never went to cooking school, and I've always relied on other people coming in who knew more than I did. And yes, I did dream up menus, and certainly have been a critical taster, and I'm pretty good on the grill, but we work more in collaboration. (30)

Perhaps for this reason, the subtitle of *Coming to My Senses* is "the making of a counterculture *cook*" rather than "the making of a counterculture *chef*."

But ultimately, I side with Jacques Pépin, and out of respect for all that Waters has achieved—including her collaborative ethos—I think she deserves the title of chef.

Lucy ended our walk up the hill by describing the emergence of the nouvelle cuisine movement of the 1960s, in which Paul Bocuse was a central figure.

"This insistence on freshness had evolved into concentrating on the ingredient itself," Lucy says. "This is the basis of what we consider to be French cuisine today, although it was always there in the restaurants."

In nouvelle cuisine, says Lucy, laughing, "the food got smaller, and the plates got bigger."

To understand the impact of nouvelle cuisine, it helps to know what it was reacting against, which is the haute cuisine that developed to serve the privileged classes in seventeenth-century France. In particular, it marked a break from the *cuisine classique* of Georges Auguste Escoffier (1846–1935), who modernized the techniques of Marie-Antoine Carême (1784–1883), one of the codifiers of haute cuisine. Whereas *cuisine classique* relied on heavy stocks and sauces, a formalized set of techniques and methods, and a regimented series of dishes, nouvelle cuisine called for lighter seasonings, shorter cooking times, simplified menus and techniques, greater attention to regional specialties, and, of course, an insistence on the freshest possible ingredients.

Both of these styles of cooking are distinct from that practiced by the Mères, but the roots of nouvelle cuisine can nevertheless be seen in the influence of La Mère Brazier on Paul Bocuse. As Rachel Black has pointed out, "Women's cuisine in small *bouchons* and bistros had a deep sense of place that came from cooking a repertoire of codified dishes derived from *cuisine bourgeoise*, the food domestic cooks prepared in private, well-to-do households in nineteenth-century France. Generally, this consisted of slow-cooked dishes with rich sauces." But because this food drew heavily on local, seasonal ingredients, it was the antithesis of the haute cuisine that dominated the great hotel restaurants of the time, according to Black: "Critics complained that the internationalized French food served in these lavish hotel palaces all tasted the same and lacked a sense of place" (30).

Compare Alice Waters talking about her approach to cooking in the *Chez Panisse Menu Cookbook*: "I would like the cooking at Chez Panisse to be perceived as straightforward and basically unsauced because I believe that it is a very healthful way of cooking and eating. I find it to be more visually and aesthetically pleasing than the heavier 'classic' *haute cuisine* which abounds in many French restaurants in this country" (165).

Yet while the impact of nouvelle cuisine on Chez Panisse and its "California cuisine" has often been noted, its deeper connection to the regional and seasonal cooking of the Mères constitutes a hidden history to Waters' cooking that even she may not realize exists.

LA CUISINE DU MARCHÉ

"Allez, trois pour dix euros, trois pour dix euros, trois pour dix euros, allez!"

So sings the woman selling *saucisson*, three for ten euros, at the Croix-Rousse market, where we have just arrived.

"Bonjour, Madame. Exactement quatre euros. Voila, merci," says the vendor next to her, his brightly colored vegetables dazzling the senses.

Lyon has more than forty markets in the city center, but the Croix-Rousse market is the biggest, with one hundred–plus vendors. And this big market is especially busy this morning, bustling with the sights and sounds of commerce, the voices of exchange overlapping with the noises of buses, trucks, and scooters zipping by on the boulevard. The smell of fresh meats and fish mingles with the fragrances of fennel and flowers, and my salivary glands react accordingly. Let's eat!

The seven of us do our best to navigate the crowded sidewalk, pushing past the roadblocks created by the most popular vendors. Fortunately, Lucy has already prepped us about what to look for and how to tell a producer (*productor*) from a reseller.

Back in the 1980s, Lucy tells us, the outdoor market traditions were under threat from the supermarkets. While the offerings at the outdoor markets might be limited to seasonal produce (cabbage, leeks, and potatoes in winter, for example), the supermarkets were able to ship in hydroponically farmed, hothouse-grown, and out-of-season produce (such as strawberries in February, exotic fruits, and produce from far away). In order to allow the outdoor markets to compete and still preserve their traditions, France changed its national system of rules and began to allow warehouse resellers—who buy from the same warehouses that supply grocery stores—to sell at the outdoor markets.

Not all resellers are to be avoided, Lucy clarifies, but we are looking for the freshest products from the producers themselves.

By the time we reach the end of the market, we are ready to decide what to buy, and what to do with it.

"Well, we have to do something with cherries," someone says. "Cherries, potatoes, and garlic . . . but not all together!" "Zucchini flowers," another chimes in.

Lucy suggests veal sweetbreads, "the gateway offal," in a cream sauce, with new potatoes and stuffed zucchini flowers. She also floats another option, duck with cherries.

"I eat all food," says Amy. "I just like food. I can't lose."

Being adventurous eaters, we decide to go with the sweetbreads, and we follow our market adventure with trips to the nearby bakery, butcher, and cheesemonger. We are ready to cook.

"In cooking classes we once gave at the restaurant," Waters writes in the "Uncomplicated Menus" section of the *Chez Panisse Menu Cookbook,* "I was face to face with people's expectations of intricately involved and lengthy recipes. I sometimes felt foolish saying that good cooking meant having the freshest ingredients you could find, and then doing as little as possible to them; it seemed so obvious" (164).

"Not wanting the class participants to be disappointed," she continues, "I nonetheless realized that I had to be true to myself. I found that it required a tremendous interchange of information and lots of experience in order to convey what it takes to make simple foods succeed" (164–65).

Back in the kitchen, Lucy passes out aprons, asks us to wash our hands, and helps us carefully unpack our purchases and place them on the counter. She then turns on her iPod, and Edith Piaf begins to get us in the spirit.

"Smell the savory—ooh, la, la!" Lucy exclaims, as we take turns washing the herbs and vegetables. "It's so tender—this is the first savory we've seen this year."

Today we'll be making a four-course meal based on what we found at the market: an *entrée* (or appetizer), *plat* (main course), *fromage* (cheese course), and dessert.

For our appetizer, Lucy has directed us toward *céleri en rémoulade* (celery root in a mayonnaise sauce) and *radis-beurre* (radishes with butter and salt), accompanied by a variety of artisan-made treats. These include *pâté en croûte Provençal* (pâté baked in a pastry) and *saucisson* Colette (a dry-cured sausage) from Charcuterie Sibilia, *apéro* cheeses from a farm in Montagny (southwest of Lyon), and a selection of cherries, strawberries, Lucques olives, and tartine spreads.

For the main course, we're making *ris de veau aux champignons* (sweetbread with mushrooms), which will sit on a *confit d'oignon* (onion confit) with *pomme de terres nouvelle* (new potatoes). These will be joined on the plate by *tomates confites* (tomato confit), *fleurs de courgettes a la vapeur* (steamed zucchini flowers), and a side of asparagus and fresh peas.

For dessert, a *tarte aux fruits rouges d'été* (a summer berry tart), with a *coulis de verveine* (verbena coulis).

I include the French names of these dishes not to be pretentious (honest!) but simply to indicate that most of them are distinctively French—either classic French preparations or Lyonnaise specialties. But the idea is for us to make them in a way that is far from classically heavy, and one that instead lets the ingredients speak for themselves.

"We try to interfere as little as possible with the transition of good and pure ingredients from their origins to the tables at Chez Panisse," Waters wrote in the *Chez Panisse Menu Cookbook* (165). Or, as the French gastronome Curnonsky (Maurice Edmond Sailland) memorably put it, *"La cuisine! C'est quand les choses ont le goût de ce qu'elles sont"* ("La Cuisine! That's when things taste like themselves") (R. Olney, *Simple French Food* 10).

We've barely begun and I'm already feeling inadequate: Lucy heard someone (ahem, *me*) scrape the diced onions off the cutting board and into a bowl with the edge of the knife, and she reminds us all to use the back of our knives to scrape, so as not to dull the blades. Damn. It feels like I'm back in school again and just got called out by the teacher.

Really, though, this is why I came here.

"In the beginning," Lucy told me when we spoke earlier, "I was a little bit unclear about what I wanted people to take away. But it all became clear when I started teaching people of a lot of different levels. Some people came in and they didn't know how to hold a knife or cut an onion. And other people came in with project-oriented, foodie projects galore under the belt. And I had some professionals coming in, which was intimidating at first. But then I thought, well, everybody is going to take something from a class."

I'm learning already.

As soon as we get the onions on the stove to start slowly becoming confit, we turn our attention to the mayonnaise for our remoulade, into which we will later add the grated celery root.

Lucy tells us a story:

Before my husband and I were engaged, he took me home for Christmas. The word had spread around the family: "He is bringing an American girl." We went to his grandmother's house on Christmas day, and she was in the kitchen—you know, the typical French kitchen is not like this. It's more like a small, boxed-in little room, maybe with one window in the corner, with a big sink and a table, in addition to her freestanding stove. That's it. There were no cabinets, there were no knick-knacks, there were no beautiful decorations. She was in this bare room, with her fancy dress, in a little apron. She was making a slow "clopetty-clopetty-clop" sound in a bowl . . . she was making mayonnaise. I thought, "How is this possible? She's not even using a whisk." You need a machine to make mayonnaise, right? That's what I thought at the time. It's not true. It was an epiphany for me. All you need is a bowl and a fork.

She proceeds to demonstrate by combining the egg yolks, salt, pepper, and mustard and then gradually adding the vegetable oil.

"We're just going to put a little dollop in here, and watch what happens. You see, it's already starting to emulsify, just by stirring it gently. The whole thing is *stirring gently,* that's the point."

Laura stares in disbelief. "I can't believe you made mayonnaise with a fork," she says. "That is so cool."

"I had to make mayonnaise many times before I got the emulsion right," Waters writes in *Coming to My Senses*, "and finally succeeded by sticking half a raw potato on the end of a fork and whisking the mayonnaise with it—somebody's grandmother had told me about that trick. Amazingly, it worked. . . . That's truly how I made mayonnaise every time, at least until I got to Chez Panisse. Crazy" (140).

It wasn't the potato, I want to tell her; it was that the potato slowed down the fork.

Watching Lucy work, I am reminded of the times I tried to teach people how to make pasta after we returned from Italy—a pedagogical experience that is more difficult than it sounds. There's a lot to juggle: the recipes, the explanations, the questions, the order of operations, the ingredients, and so on.

Yet Lucy is amazingly calm—mindful, even—as she goes about her tasks.

Sometimes she needs to go it alone, of course. "We've got a lot of things happening right now, so I'll just quickly boil our potatoes," she says at one point.

And sometimes things go wrong, like when the brown butter gets burned because all of our attentions were elsewhere.

But throughout it all, Lucy remains calm in response.

I confess that I also have a secret agenda in this class, which is to learn a little bit more about salt.

Before I arrived I had done some genealogical research and discovered that my earliest ancestor—as far back as I could find—was born in the town of Flesselles, just north of Amiens, in northeastern France.

Living during the reign of King Louis XV (1715–74), Pierre Philippon was only in his twenties when he was exiled to New France for the crime of *faux sauniers* (salt smuggling) in 1731. Once in Quebec, he became a carpenter, and some of his descendants eventually moved to Maine, where my father was born and raised.

Salt smuggling . . . seriously? I'm descended from a salt smuggler? And why were you smuggling salt in the first place? I want to ask Pierre.

It's not that there aren't good histories of the salt trade in eighteenth-century France; Mark Kurlanksy devotes a whole chapter to the gabelle, or salt tax, in his *Salt: A World History*. But what I want to know can't be found in a history book.

What I want to know is whether Pierre was simply trying to make a buck (or some eighteenth-century *livre*), or was he after something else? Was he only interested in commerce, in other words, or was he also interested in taste?

"Using good sea salt is one of the easiest things you can do to make your food taste better," according to *The Art of Simple Food* (2007), Waters's basic handbook for the home cook. "Sea salt contains trace minerals that give it a stronger, saltier, more complex flavor than ordinary table salt, which contains chemicals to keep it from clumping that affect the flavor of everything you use it on.

"I keep two kinds of sea salt close by: a very coarse one sold in bulk (the gray kind, with its high mineral content, is especially good) for salting boiling water and brine, and a finer, flakier one for seasoning and finishing dishes.

"Perhaps the biggest 'secret' to good cooking is knowing how to season with salt. Too much makes food taste salty, of course, but undersalted food tastes bland. Salt brings out the flavor of whatever is being cooked, but it also gets concentrated if you are boiling something down. Keep tasting, learn how salt works with flavor, and use it to get the most out of what you are cooking" (13).

Throughout our class I pepper (ha-ha) Lucy with questions about salt.

When making the onion confit, she says, "When you have a recipe that says add salt at the beginning, ask yourself why they're doing that. It's pulling the juices out. We're going to see a lot of juice released by these onions."

When we start work on the fruit tart, she notes that "the salt in a shortbread really matters—more than the flour—because there is so little of it. So every change magnifies the ratios."

And we're tasting throughout. "It needs something, don't you think? Some salt, maybe?"

Samin Nosrat, who learned to cook at Chez Panisse and became Michael Pollan's teacher in *Cooked*, writes of her awakening to salt's potential in her book *Salt, Fat, Acid, Heat: Mastering the Elements of Good Cooking*.

After Cal Peternell, the chef at Chez Panisse, threw three enormous palmfuls of kosher salt into her polenta, Nosrat writes, "It was as if I'd been struck by lightning. It'd never occurred to me that salt was anything more than pepper's sidekick. But now, having experienced the transformative power of salt for myself, I wanted to learn how to get that *zing!* every time I cooked. I thought about all of the foods I'd loved to eat growing up—and that bite of seaside cucumber and feta, in particular. I realized then why it had tasted so good. It was properly seasoned, with salt" (19).

The world is full of flavor, and so the goal of the cook is not to create flavor but to allow those flavors to attain their fullest expression through cooking.

This is the principal lesson I learned from Lucy, and from Waters, cooking with the bounty from the market.

I could taste it in the radishes we sprinkled with fleur de sel before eating, in the cherry tomatoes we salted before roasting, in the sweetbreads whose impurities were drawn out by the salted water we boiled them in.

And Amy, taking a bite of our completed dessert, said she could even taste it in the tart dough.

FEMME D'AFFAIRES

The story of Chez Panisse has been told many times, not only by Alice Waters but also by a host of other people, including Waters's biographer Thomas McNamee, the culinary historians Joan Reardon and Paul Freedman, and the journalists and authors David Kamp, Andrea Barnet, and Andrew Friedman. Waters herself has written about it in many places, including *Coming to My Senses*, the *Chez Panisse Menu Cookbook*, the children's book *Fanny at Chez Panisse* (1992), and the photographic history *Forty Years of Chez Panisse* (2011).

Taken together, these accounts provide a rich portrait of one of the most important restaurants in America in terms of both gastronomy and sustainability. But living in Lyon gave me a fuller and richer picture of Waters's achievement in running the restaurant than any written account could provide, while it also illuminated one of the principal features of her own writing about Chez Panisse: namely, the tension between trying to balance her ideals related to sustainable food with the pressure of keeping a business afloat.

To put it another way: if the Mères can help us understand Waters's philosophy of cooking, their modern-day equivalents in the food industry can help us remember that ideal meals don't just happen—they require a ton of hard work, often by women, to bring to fruition.

When Waters returned from France in the fall of 1965, campaigning for the midterm elections of 1966 was underway, and Californians were preparing to elect a governor and all their congressional representatives. Ronald Reagan was running for governor against former San Francisco mayor George Christopher in the Republican primary, and in the Democratic primary Robert Scheer was challenging the incumbent Jeffrey Cohelan to represent the Seventh Congressional District, which at the time included Berkeley. A writer for the New Left magazine *Ramparts*, Scheer was strongly opposed to the Vietnam War, whereas Cohelan supported it.

Although Waters had not been especially active in the Free Speech Movement that had rocked Berkeley's campus in the year before she left, she threw herself into politics upon her return, joining Scheer's campaign and eventually becoming his assistant. When Scheer lost the primary, Waters was devastated.

"I remember abandoning all my faith in the democratic process after that—I didn't believe change could happen anymore," she wrote in *Coming to My Senses*. "I mean, I really lost hope" (136).

That fall, Reagan was elected governor, vowing to "clean up the mess at Berkeley" (Kahn).

A case could be made that Waters's subsequent interest in food was somehow a retreat from politics.

Reviewing *The Chez Panisse Menu Cookbook* in *The Nation* in 1982, David Sundelson wrote that "the triumph of Chez Panisse represents a new privatism, a sad turn inward, away from public issues and commitments. The counterculture has become a Counter Culture—the counter at the gourmet butcher, the pastry shop, the charcuterie" (277).

But David Kamp disagrees, and so do I.

Kamp puts it this way: "Chez Panisse wasn't a retreat from politics—it *was* politics, a representation of what American food could be if people weren't complacent about gassed, flavorless tomatoes and frozen TV dinners" (142).

Like Carlo Petrini, who fought with his fellow Communists over whether food was inherently political, Waters rejected the idea that it was somehow virtuous for leftists to eat bad food, to forsake pleasure, or to ignore food altogether.

Chez Panisse ended up being the physical embodiment of that belief, but it took a village to make it so.

One thing that stands out about *Coming to My Senses* is that it is just chock-full of people. Waters is the central thread connecting them all, but readers would be forgiven if they had trouble keeping them all straight. Which boy-friend was that again? And was he a staff member at the restaurant, or one of the investors, or maybe both?

Susan Stanford Friedman proposed the term "relational life-writing" in 1984 to emphasize the "fluid boundaries" that she felt women's autobi-ographical writing demonstrated between women and other individuals and their community. Since that time, subsequent critics have argued that "rela-tionality" is not unique to women's life-writing but an inherent part of all autobiographical texts, for how do we define ourselves, if not in relationship to others?

The Russian literary theorist Mikhail Bakhtin famously described lan-guage itself as relational, claiming that all utterances acquire their mean-ing in dialogue with others—other words, other people, and other places. He called this relationality "dialogism" and argued that if our language is dialogic, so our consciousness must be, too. All writing thus contains what Bakhtin called "heteroglossia," or the speech of others, and could be seen as "polyphonic," or "many-voiced," to a greater or lesser degree. That Bakh-tin borrowed the concept of polyphony from the field of music is itself an example of dialogism, in which our understanding of one thing develops in relationship to another (Bakhtin).

An even more substantive version of relationality can be found in Sta-cey Alaimo's concept of "trans-corporeality," or the idea that "the human is always intermeshed with the more-than-human world" (2). Alaimo's neol-ogism, which she first used in 2007, is helpful in identifying a concept that had previously gone unnamed, but it is important to remember that Alaimo was not the first to discuss the idea. In a 1991 interview with Vince Penning-ton, for example, Wendell Berry had this to say about the concept of "the environment": "'Environment' is based on that dualism, the idea that you can separate the human interests from the interests of everything else. You *cannot* do it. We eat the environment. It passes through our bodies every day, it passes in and out our bodies. There is no distinction between ourselves and the so-called environment. What we live in and from and with doesn't *surround* us—it's part of us. We're *of* it, and it's *of* us, and the relationship is unspeakably intimate" (Pennington 41).

My point in developing this notion of relationality is to suggest that the interest in sustainability that Waters develops later in her career is not separate from the relationships with other people that mark her memoir and the early life it narrates. Rather, they are continuous with one another, just as our human relationships are continuous with "the environment" that gives them life.

One of the most important of Waters's early relationships is with the British food writer Elizabeth David, whose work she first encountered in the Kitchen bookshop in Berkeley. *French Provincial Cooking* (1960), David's finest and most influential cookbook, was "a ray of sunshine," Waters writes in *Coming to My Senses*. David was "another Francophile who had been transformed after a visit to France" (142).

Where Julia Child provided detailed instructions about how to prepare *cuisine bourgeoise* in *Mastering the Art of French Cooking* (1961), David offered a more improvisational approach to *cuisine régionale* in *French Provincial Cooking*. Like Waters, David valued simplicity, seasonality, and above all the finest regional ingredients.

"A flourishing tradition of local cookery implies also genuine local products; the cooks and the housewives must be backed up by the dairy farmers, the pig breeders and pork butchers, the market gardeners and the fruit growers," David emphasized in her introduction (13).

Waters ended up cooking her way straight through *French Provincial Cooking* beginning in the fall of 1966, and she cooked from it and David's other books while she attended a Montessori teacher training program in Hampstead, north of London, from 1968 to 1969 (McNamee 28; *Coming to My Senses* 176).

David began her book with an introductory survey of the French provinces, starting in Provence, a region for which she had special affection, which no doubt rubbed off on Waters. But she also devoted many pages to Lyonnaise cuisine, noting that its "world-wide fame . . . is largely due to a whole generation of women restaurateurs who flourished during the early years of the twentieth century" (50).

David admits that she finds much of Lyonnaise cooking not to her taste, though she calls out La Mère Brazier for special mention, as well as La Mère Brazier's mentor, La Mère Fillioux. Still, David observes, "the fact is that pigs' trotters and sausages, steak and large quantities of potatoes, boiled chicken, pike *quenelles,* and crayfish in one form or another soon become monotonous, however well cooked" (49).

She does, however, praise three distinctively Lyonnaise dishes: *la salade lyonnaise, tablier de sapeur* (a breaded and fried slice of tripe, similar to a German *Schnitzel*), and a *gratinée.*

Of the *gratinée,* David writes, it is "a clear consommé in which a slice of bread sprinkled with cheese is browned in the oven, the whole being finally enriched with a mixture of beaten egg and port—a restorative soup of the same nature as the Parisian *soupe à l'oignon,* in this case without the onion which is generally but wrongly supposed to figure in every Lyonnais dish" (53).

When you stop to think about it, the idea of "going out to eat" is really quite strange. Let's leave wherever we live and go to some other place, where we will pay someone else to make our food for us (assuming we have a kitchen, of course, which is by no means a universal assumption, either now or in the past). Maybe they can make it better than we can, or in a different style or culinary tradition, or at a different speed (faster or slower), or for a different price (cheaper or more expensive), or with different ingredients, or in some new and exciting way. What links all of these variations is that they are public: eating out means eating in public, whereas staying home means eating in private, relatively speaking. Or so it seems.

The modern restaurant as we know it in the West developed at a particular time and place—specifically, in eighteenth-century Paris. Although Europeans had been eating in public since ancient times, they did so primarily in taverns and inns designed for travelers, or from street vendors serving inexpensive food to urban residents. What changed in the late eighteenth century was the emergence of the "restaurant"—a specific type of eatery that served rich meat broths to help restore (*restaurer*) the health of delicate or weak diners. As Rebecca L. Spang explains in *The Invention of the Restaurant: Paris and Modern Gastronomic Culture,* the need for such "restoratives" could not be met by Parisians' version of a tavern, called a *table d'hôte*, which served a set menu to a common table at fixed mealtimes. So these new *restaurateurs* developed what are the now-familiar features of the restaurant: sitting at private tables, eating at flexible times, ordering from a menu of choices (*à la carte*), getting table service from a waiter, and being shielded from the noises and smells of the kitchen.

What's most interesting about Spang's account, however, is her observation about the way these early restaurants existed at the boundary of public and private life, and how that boundary changed over time. What began as a "semi-public" space prior to the French Revolution became a "semi-private" space during the Restoration—a public space in which you could have a private experience. Indeed, throughout its history, the place of restaurants in the public imagination has been a process of ongoing negotiation. "In the past 230 years," Sprang observes, "the restaurant has changed from a sort of urban spa into a 'political' public forum, and then into an explicitly and actively depoliticized refuge" (3).

As much as I have come to love Lyon, the city can take on a somewhat dreary appearance in the winter, given its routinely overcast skies. The Rhône and the Saône start to feel cold and gray, and when that happens I want nothing so much as a restorative broth to help boost my spirits and revive my flagging mood.

The city's *bouchons*, which serve the traditional food of the Mères, are warming in their own way, but as Elizabeth David observed, their food can become a bit monotonous, not to mention quite heavy, thanks to their origins as canteens for the silk workers.

So I am looking for something lighter, which is why Nancy, Grace, and I have come to Yomogi, a Japanese noodle bar, on this November day, seeking refuge from the cold and damp.

Inside, we meet the co-owners, Jennifer Gilbert and Tamiko Kobayashi, along with Jenny's husband, Harvey de Souza, and settle in for a delicious meal and some good conversation.

Yomogi is not just any restaurant, and as its noodle bar name suggests, it's not really a restaurant at all, at least not in the traditional sense. Rather, it's a ramen shop—plenty common throughout Japan and in most large American cities, but still very much a rarity in Lyon. In fact, when it opened in September 2010, Yomogi was Lyon's first and only ramen shop.

Located on Place Sathonay, a charming square at the bottom of Croix-Rousse, Yomogi is an intimate space, with ten bar stools facing an open kitchen, a handful of two-tops scattered about, and a large common table, which can accommodate from eight to ten people. On warmer days, the tall glass doors facing the street are flung open, and the restaurant spills out onto the sidewalk, making room for another ten or so diners seated on bright-red folding chairs.

Yomogi is the name of a plant (mugwort) that grows wild throughout Japan, and the bright-green color it contributes to rice cakes seems to embody the restaurant's fresh aesthetic especially well. There's something that just feels *right* about the space, some kind of feng shui that makes it warm and welcoming—its clean lines, perhaps, or unadorned walls, reflecting a Japanese minimalism that allows the food, rather than the decor, to take center stage.

At Jenny's urging, we order the ramen (of course), with Nancy and Grace sharing a bowl of ramen with pork and soy sauce, while I try the vegetarian ramen, a favorite of Harvey's.

As we wait for our food to arrive, Jenny tells us about the origins of the restaurant.

Both she and Tamiko are violinists at the Orchestre National de Lyon (Jenny serves as concertmaster), and from time to time they would ask each other the question, "If we don't play anymore, what would we do?"

"We've had this conversation more than once," she says, but about five years ago, "for some reason this conversation went somewhere."

They also asked themselves, "What's missing in Lyon for us?"

"Since Lyon is a traditional city, and a food city, what's missing was a casual Japanese noodle bar, open all the time, where you can eat fast," Jenny says. "It was a combination of those two things: 'What's missing in Lyon?' and 'What could we do that would be fun and—supposedly—lucrative?'" At this she lets out a knowing laugh.

After partnering with a chef, and spending about six months looking for a site, they landed on this storefront, which was originally two spaces that they then combined into one.

"We were thinking, 'Well, if we sell twenty bowls of noodles a day, we'll be fine.' And the second day was full. People really pass by here, and they saw that something was happening and kind of got interested over the time that the work was being done. So it went really well from the beginning, in terms of turnover."

The challenges, however, started soon after that, when they realized that they had more demand than they could handle.

"We were novices—at best. We've had lots of problems, actually. It's been tough," Jenny admits.

For one thing, both she and Tamiko have other jobs, so that makes it difficult to be on the premises all the time. And while their chef had worked in a restaurant before, "running a restaurant is not the same as working in one," Jenny stresses.

In addition, because nobody on the staff had stock in the restaurant's success, motivation became a major issue, and turnover was higher than expected. This might be acceptable if you're a big conglomerate with a management team in Paris, Jenny observes, or if you're a mom-and-pop operation, but such high turnover is tricky for their in-between category of restaurant.

"Also in France the social charges are really high," Jenny says, referring to the *prélèvement social,* used to finance social security. "That's just an issue for everyone. So I think it was a combined thing: being amateurs, not in the business, not having ever worked in a kitchen, plus being foreign, plus being women. In a certain way, I wouldn't beat ourselves up, because the statistics are that 50 percent of restaurants close within the first year of opening. So we survived. But it was close, I have to say."

Our ramen arrives, steaming, a veritable umami bomb of restorative broth, complete with bamboo shoots, soy sprouts, dried seaweed, and handmade noodles. I alternate slurps of broth with mouthfuls of noodles, while Harvey tells me what he thinks of his wife's latest venture.

Like Jenny, Harvey is also a concertmaster (with the Academy of St. Martin in the Fields), so naturally he turns to a musical analogy.

"It's kind of an odd thing," he says, "not dissimilar to learning an instrument. If you took a kid who was so enthusiastic about playing an instrument, and if you sat them down and spent days telling them how much they had to practice every day, you've killed the enthusiasm. I think the same thing is true of these young entrepreneurs when they start their businesses, and mostly it's the enthusiasm, and they may not know all the internal aspects, but sometimes you wish that they did."

"If we did, we wouldn't have opened a restaurant," Jenny says without hesitation. "No way. Never ever. Ever ever ever ever."

Yet Jenny, too, finds similarities between restaurants and orchestras.

"I don't think it's an accident that the vocabulary of a kitchen is very similar to the vocabulary of an orchestra," she says. "Certainly in terms of dealing with people I've found lots of similarities: even in an orchestra, it's not just music. There are also relationships to handle. When you're trying to do anything well, there are similarities."

Jenny and Harvey just recently became parents, and it was clear that the burdens of parenthood were weighing on them in a way neither had expected.

You make choices, Jenny says, but you don't realize the implications of those choices until it's too late.

"When I made the choice to open Yomogi, we were together but we didn't have a child, and I never had it in my head, 'Oh this could affect Harvey or a future child.' But when we started having issues with the restaurant, I was so freaked out by the idea that the choice I made could negatively affect them, it just overwhelmed me completely. I thought, 'My god, what have I done?' I think it's going to be okay, but that was kind of a big eye-opener."

Hearing the conversation turn to children, Grace pipes up as if on cue and asks Jenny the most important question of the day: "Which dessert do you recommend?"

After informing us that there's actually no dessert in traditional Japanese cuisine—who knew?—Jenny nevertheless treats us to a sampling of Yomogi's desserts of the day: tiramisu with green tea, chocolate mousse with Japanese curry, and lemon cheesecake, along with scoops of chocolate and vanilla ice cream for Grace.

Like providing desserts for a sweet-toothed clientele, Jenny and Tamiko have had to make other adjustments to their vision as well, such as closing the restaurant in the afternoon, because most Lyonnaise residents don't go out to eat between 3:00 and 7:00 p.m.

"We started with ideals," Jenny says, "and we've lost some of them in the process."

Nevertheless, she believes strongly in what the restaurant is trying to achieve.

"There are troubles in France—social and economic troubles—and one of the points that just remains positive and vibrant and happy is food. So it's something that's necessary—food—but unites people. It's where you go after working, it's where you find your family again."

"A lot of why Chez Panisse succeeded was because it *didn't* feel like just another restaurant," Waters writes in *Coming to My Senses.* "We were a family—or at least an eccentric, tight-knit tribe. None of us had ever been trained as cooks or gone to cooking school. As James Beard said later, 'It's like you're eating dinner in somebody's home.' I wanted it to feel like that" (304).

When Chez Panisse opened for business on 28 August 1971, it was the result of a wide network of relationships Waters had developed over the seven years since she had first arrived in Berkeley as a transfer student in 1964. And this cooperative style of relationship building continued on—not only throughout her time at the restaurant but throughout her career as a writer and advocate for a more sustainable food system.

Waters gives much of the credit for her initial networking success to her boyfriend at the time, Tom Luddy, who ran the Telegraph Repertory Theater, an art house cinema.

She writes admiringly of him in *Coming to My Senses:*

He was like an enzyme, forever making connections between his friends, bringing people together, making reactions happen, then getting out of the way. It was selfless—he never did it for his personal gain, just for the joy of watching new relationships form. . . . I didn't know I was learning about how to make those sorts of connections from Tom . . . but as we were together, I got some of that through osmosis. Up until that time, I had been much more self-absorbed. But Tom showed me how much happiness you can get out of bringing a diverse group of people together and starting conversations—and what good can come from it. (209–12)

Waters's comment illustrates why some critics have contested claims that relationality is distinctive to women's life-writing—namely, that such an assertion assumes an essentialist model of female identity, in which women have more "flexible or permeable ego boundaries" than men, as Nancy Chodorow has argued (S. S. Friedman 77).

One need not accept such gender essentialism to acknowledge how, for Waters, relationality overlapped significantly with the empowerment of women in the kitchen at Chez Panisse. Yet doing so also requires an acknowledgment of the gender differences that were pervasive throughout the food industry in the 1970s, and that remain so today.

In her detailed examination of the rise of California cuisine, for example, Joyce Goldstein describes a distinction between "boy food" and "girl food" common throughout the industry. Those cooking "boy food," she says, are generally competitive, eager to display their technical and creative prowess, and willing to open multiple locations to promote their "culinary brands." Those cooking "girl food," however, "tend to measure their success and satisfaction in the happiness of their staff and the looks on the faces of their patrons when they taste their food." They are less interested in the latest techniques and more focused on the quality of the ingredients. These cooks also tend to remain at a single restaurant, because they consider that restaurant an extension of their home (96–97).

Goldstein is aware that these distinctions are not wholly based on gender and likely also reflect each chef's personality and philosophy, but the contrast she draws is instructive: "Setting gender aside," she says, "it would be safe to say that there are two types of chefs: those who aim to nurture, and those who aspire to awe" (97).

If this dichotomy sounds familiar, it should, as it recalls Wendell Berry's dichotomy between the exploiter and nurturer, or the industrial and the agrarian. This is not to say that chefs who seek to awe are exploitative or industrial in their approach by any means, but it does suggest that nurturing is a common characteristic in both sustainable agriculture and a more collaborative style of cooking.

Needless to say, Waters—without question—is a nurturer, and it was her nurturing approach that made her a pioneer of what Goldstein terms the "collaborative kitchen."

Most professional French kitchens employ a hierarchical system, developed by Escoffier, called *brigade de cuisine* (kitchen brigade), in which the *chef de cuisine* (head chef) supervises the *sous chef* (subchef), who manages the *chef de partie* (the line cooks who work at particular stations), who then control the *commis* (junior cook).

Waters had no experience with this system, however, so she simply hired her friends and other fellow amateurs—many of whom were women—and collaborated with them to develop and execute her vision.

"The fact that Alice Waters hired so many women at Chez Panisse was pioneering," notes Goldstein, "and her kitchen setup was also iconoclastic. She abandoned the hierarchical titles of the *brigade de cuisine* and referred to all the members of her staff simply and democratically as cooks. They rotated and did all the jobs in the kitchen. Men and women worked together and equally in the kitchen, and the women were not segregated in pastry. This was revolutionary" (98).

Waters's decision to build a changing daily menu, based on the best available ingredients, also required a more collaborative approach. Because Goldstein worked as a chef at Chez Panisse Café from 1980 to 1983, she has insider knowledge of exactly what this entailed: "Each day brought different ingredients, and they in turn brought their own questions: How did they taste today as opposed to last week? How were they going to be handled? What if the ingredients the chef had planned to cook did not come in? Everyone talked about the food, tasted together, and arrived at food and flavor decisions through consensus, as opposed to a dictatorship where the chef mandated the standards and delegated the work" (102–3).

Understanding the nuts and bolts of running a restaurant, particularly one owned by women, is helpful in interpreting two other aspects of Waters's self-presentation in *Coming to My Senses*.

The first is Waters's representation of her agency as a woman in the success of Chez Panisse, which is manifested most vividly in the idea of *seduction*.

The intersection of sexuality and power is present throughout Waters's memoir, most notably in the narration of her attempted rape. Although the incident occurred when Waters was living in Berkeley in the 1970s, it appears out of chronological order in *Coming to My Senses*, in one of the italicized sections, at the end of a chapter partly devoted to her sexual awakening in high school—a chapter that also includes a previous incident of attempted date rape. Most of this italicized section consists of a matter-of-fact narration of how one night a man broke into Waters's apartment and tried to rape her but she was able to escape by jumping out a window. The final two paragraphs, however, constitute Waters taking control of the narrative, turning it from a story of two dueling protagonists to one of a solo, reflective, and ultimately successful narrator.

278 • THE FARMER, THE GASTRONOME, AND THE CHEF

"The whole experience shocked me," she writes at the section's conclusion, "but I also couldn't believe I had that resistance in me, that I was willing to risk my life to keep that from happening. I never, ever imagined that. In the end, I felt empowered because I'd been able to think of a way out" (74).

Waters also makes clear that her newfound power included maintaining control of her own sexuality and not allowing her rapist to dictate who and what she loved.

"Oddly enough," she writes, "it didn't affect my passion for men. I had a new sense of my physical weakness in that circumstance, and I was terrified that someone might break into my house. But my fear absolutely did not extend to all men. It was about power and violence, not about all men" (73–74).

Her use of the word "absolutely" in this case, as well as her classification of the incident as one of "power and violence," allows her to reclaim the connection between power and sensuality (which is at the heart of seduction) as her own.

Watching Mark Donskoy's *Gorky* film trilogy with Tom Luddy later in her life, Waters marvels at "how powerful—and how sensual—film could be," an observation that applies equally well to her relationship to food (216).

Even as a high school student, Waters says, "seduction was my modus operandi" (79), and she admits to being just as easily seduced by others, especially when it involves food—although this does not always work out as planned.

During her semester abroad, she recalls, "I met a blond expat who tried to seduce me by feeding me whole shrimp with their shells on, and I *was* seduced; I went home with him. Then I got hideously sick from eating those shrimp—it felt like a nightmare" (115).

It almost seems like everything is a seduction for Waters: she wants her cookbooks to seduce her readers with their illustrations (132); she believes that the Montessori method involves "preparing the classroom in a seductive way" (174); and she says that the men selling pomegranates at a market in the Caucasus were "hawking them in the most seductive ways" (219). She even dreams of seducing President Clinton with a peach!

"I wanted him to be seduced by it, to be awakened and say, 'I've never had anything like this!' I felt Clinton could be changed if he tasted the perfect peach, that he would get this idea about terroir and varietal and biodiversity without words—words are too limiting. I wanted to get to him through all his senses" (253).

A fascinating concept with multiple meanings, seduction involves a powerful attraction that can have both positive and negative connotations: appealing to someone through the senses with the aim of liberating them from their fears and preconceptions, as well as leading someone astray from their duties and responsibilities. (The word derives from the Latin *seducere*, to lead aside or away.)

The other aspect of running a restaurant that helps illuminate Waters's identity in *Coming to My Senses* is in some ways the *least* seductive, and for this reason the least present in her memoir: that is, the business side of things. These are the duties and responsibilities from which seduction leads you astray.

This is illustrated particularly well in *Marius,* the first film of Marcel Pagnol's Marseille Trilogy, from which Chez Panisse gets its name. When Cesar, the bartender, sees his son Marius attempting to seduce Fanny with a free cup of coffee, he becomes increasingly upset.

"You're treating her to coffee?" Cesar asks Marius. "It's a matter of principle . . . you don't drink the profits. . . . Because if we drink it all for free, what do we sell to the customers?"

Making a restaurant sustainable in terms of the environment and social equity is not possible if the restaurant is not sustainable in the economic sense, and Chez Panisse has had more than its share of economic problems.

Before she decided on the concept for Chez Panisse, Waters had considered opening a *crêperie* but was dissuaded by a businessman friend.

"You can't make enough money off of crêpes, he told me, because they're too affordable," she writes in *Coming to My Senses.* "And plus, I wanted an environment where people would sit around, hang out, and talk—so there would be no turnover! I was planning to sell something for nothing, then ask people to hang around and never leave—that's how keen my business sense was," Waters admits (240).

Because Waters's memoir ends with the story of the first meal served at Chez Panisse (an excerpt of which appeared in the *New Yorker* in 2017), few of the day-to-day challenges of running a restaurant appear in the book. Fortunately, other accounts of the restaurant's financial challenges round out the picture of what happened when Waters's ideals met the realities of the balance book.

Thomas McNamee provides the most detailed accounting of this side of the restaurant's early life, noting that Waters "knew nothing about business and didn't give a damn" (49). She was uncompromising about using the best ingredients, no matter the cost, and often gave away meals, desserts, and drinks in exchange for locally grown produce. She kept menu prices low but spent extravagantly on flower arrangements. No one was keeping track of the bills, suppliers were going unpaid, and the staff was drinking heavily from the wine list (48–75). In 1972, "less than a year after the restaurant's opening, thirty thousand dollars' worth of wine was unaccounted for," writes McNamee (54). That year, David Kamp concludes, Chez Panisse "seemed destined to be another failed let's-open-our-own-place fantasy, albeit a quirkier and more hirsute one than most" (145).

Over the years, the restaurant gradually found its financial feet, due in part to a series of practical business managers who tried to reign in Waters's free-spending idealism. Gilbert Pilgram, who became general manager in 2000, describes the struggle this way: "It was difficult for me to get across the idea of sustainability. I say we have to take care of ourselves. . . . We've got to be profitable enough to pay a living wage. Alice likes to keep the restaurant as affordable as possible, and so one of the things I need to point out to her every now and then is that we need to generate enough income that we can pay everybody well" (McNamee 289).

That focus on including employee well-being in the restaurant's quest for sustainability has also brought Waters full circle in considering the place of parents—and especially mothers—in the kitchen.

Julia Moskin recounts how Waters "pioneered job-sharing programs between parents, instituted a six-months-off furlough system for head chefs and put time and money into building a deep bench of cooks, which allows employees to move in and out of her kitchens as their lives change" (Moskin). In summer, Waters began giving priority for time off to people who have kids, and the restaurant also developed a rotation system in which the staff work two lunch and three dinner services a week, instead of five nights in a row (Druckman, *Skirt Steak* 191).

Motherhood, though, remains one of the biggest challenges for Chez Panisse—and for restaurants generally.

"I think that's the greatest impediment to women's careers in the kitchen,"

Waters told Charlotte Druckman. "Unless you have a completely understanding husband who's willing to participate and you share the raising of the child, and the work that you're doing. I'm just beginning to understand the kinds of things we can do to facilitate that. A whole lot more has to be learned . . . You have to leave room for picking up children, for kids being sick—things that aren't issues for men. So men are thought of as more reliable. We have to figure out how to make room for children" (*Skirt Steak* 186).

And not every restaurant has been able to do that.

When Nancy and I returned to Lyon on a recent trip, we stopped by Yomogi to see if Jenny and Tamiko might be around and to enjoy another bowl of their restorative soup. Alas, we were confronted with only the shell of a restaurant, as Yomogi had closed only a few months before we arrived.

"Why did they close?" I asked a woman named Leticia, who worked at the Café de la Place across the street.

"They closed because they were done," she said.

THE TERROIR OF PROVENCE

It says something about the place of Provence in the French imagination that the A6 and A7 highways connecting Paris to Marseille via Lyon are collectively known as l'autoroute du Soleil (the Motorway of the Sun), as the name naturally assumes that the traveler is moving north to south—not to mention that "the Motorway of the Partly Cloudy" does not have quite the same ring to it.

Completed in 1971, the same year Chez Panisse served its first meal, l'autoroute du Soleil follows roughly the same Roman roads that brought delicacies from the provinces into Lyon and led Curnonsky to dub the city the gastronomic capital of France in 1934.

To the working-class denizens of Marcel Pagnol's Marseille Trilogy, however, Lyon was hardly a city worth admiring. Throughout all three films—*Marius* (1931), *Fanny* (1932), and *César* (1936)—Monsieur Brun, a customs inspector from Lyon, serves as a comic foil for the rest of the characters, enduring gibe after gibe for being much too bourgeois for the salt-of-the-earth people who frequent César's bar.

In this small moment from a set of films so dear to Alice Waters we can see the appeal of Provence writ large, as well as the tension between a metropolitan capital and a fiercely regional outpost—indeed, one might say, *the* most important regional embodiment of France.

Discussing Pagnol's trilogy in *Coming to My Senses,* Waters acknowledges that the movies are "parables about country values versus city values and a dying way of life: cards in the afternoon, a game of *pétanque.* I wanted to live in those films," she says (263). Even though she admits that she hadn't been to Provence at the time she opened Chez Panisse, she says she connected to Pagnol's vision of "a bar where people would gather, connect to each other, and live a life with a spirit of camaraderie around the table" (263–64).

It is this Provence of myth and memory that interests me the most, because a case could be made that it is the terroir of Provence, more than anything, that sharpened Waters's understanding of what she wanted Chez Panisse to become—and eventually led her to develop the network of local and organic producers that helped to change the face of American cuisine forever.

One of the most remarkable aspects of *Coming to My Senses* is how little the physical environment actually appears in the book. For a cook whose star has risen largely on the basis of her advocacy for local food, this might at first seem strange.

The reason for the omission, however, is that the environment *didn't* matter much to Waters in the period covered by *Coming to My Senses.* All of this came after Chez Panisse first opened. And where the environment does appear, it appears out of chronological order, in several italicized portions near the end of the book.

Tellingly, the most important of these are devoted not to California but to Provence, in a chapter titled, simply, "Terroir."

I'm thinking of Elizabeth David as Nancy and I are sitting in our rented Toyota C-HR in Le Beausset, while I'm on the phone with our credit card company, because our card was just declined at the gas station, the pumps only take credit, and the station is now closed for the night.

It turns out there is nothing wrong, just some glitch in the system, despite my having called ahead to notify the card company that we would be traveling abroad. But it brings home a central point worth remembering: stuff like this never makes it into the tourist brochures—or the recipe books, for that matter.

"Provence is a country to which I am always returning, next week, next year, any day now, as soon as I can get on a train," Elizabeth David writes in *French Provincial Cooking*. "Here in London it is an effort of will to believe in the existence of such a place at all. But now and again the vision of golden tiles on a round southern roof, or of some warm, stony, herb-scented hillside will rise out of my kitchen pots with the smell of a piece of orange peel scenting a beef stew. The picture flickers into focus again" (23).

I wonder if the romance would have been this strong had she rented a car.

There is plenty to admire in Provence, to be sure, and some of it can even be seen through the windshield.

Kermit Lynch, who opened his Berkeley wine shop just a year after Chez Panisse opened, begins his chapter on Provence in *Adventures on the Wine Route* this way:

> As one enters Provence from the north, there is a place that never fails to have a magical effect on my spirits. After Montélimar, the road passes through a gorge that pinches right up to the shoulder of the autoroute, then opens out upon a vast, vine-covered plain. The effect is emotionally exhilarating, like the untying of a mental knot, a release and a shock of open space within that mirrors the widening landscape without. Shortly afterward, a large road sign announces: VOUS ÊTES EN PROVENCE.
>
> Provence is good for the psyche. By the time I approach Cassis and that first breathtaking view of the glistening Mediterranean, I am singing, I am happy, I am *chez moi*. (82)

What accounts for the magical hold Provence seems to have had on its American visitors, many of whom—like both Lynch and Richard Olney—eventually came to call it their home?

The sun certainly has something to do with it, along with the warmth that accompanies such abundant sunshine, but so does its relative dryness and the particular mix of plant and animal species such a climate supports, from its stereotypical lavender fields and olive groves to the incessant hum of its cicadas. Add to this the landscape itself, which varies from the rugged Alps in the north down to the Côte d'Azur (the French Riviera) in the south, and it's clear that the physical environment is a large part of the region's charm.

But as Patricia Wells, another American transplant, has written, "It is more than sunshine that draws us to Provence: We come because life here seems more real, less modern, more slowly paced, more personal, and more richly human than almost any other place we know on earth" (Horowitz 2).

At the same time, as the cultural historian Helen Lefkowitz Horowitz has documented, Americans also came to Provence precisely because it *was* modernizing—because early postwar travel restrictions eased, transatlantic transportation improved, and a complicated touristic infrastructure developed, including the availability of long-term accommodations and the completion of roads such as l'autoroute du Soleil (7).

We had driven the autoroute to Le Beausset in part to visit Kermit Lynch, who is now retired and divides his time between Berkeley and Provence. A close friend of Waters, he played a central role in both her life and her memoir.

In the 1970s, Waters writes in *Coming to My Senses,* "Kermit taught me all about terroir, growing the right varietal of grape in the right place, and trying not to get too much in the way of winemaking. Terroir was about allowing the grape to be all it could be, bringing out the character of the place where it was grown, not trying to manipulate the wine too much by blending it. It was about letting the ingredients speak. That idea really influenced me in my thinking about organic farming later, too" (242).

Lynch also happens to be an exceptionally kind and generous man, graced with a healthy sense of humor, and he was an absolute delight to talk with, as Nancy and I looked out over the rolling hills of Provence's Var region from the veranda of his home in Le Beausset.

"I think she started Chez Panisse about the same time as I started my wine shop," Lynch said of Waters. "We didn't know each other. And it was sort of natural to go to Chez Panisse. There was such a small world of restaurants in Berkeley. Just in the small circle of wine people, Chez Panisse was mentioned as a place where you could get a good French meal. And I wasn't selling to restaurants then; I just had a little retail, cubbyhole shop. So I started going, and I met Alice, and we became friendly, because I was going to Chez Panisse a lot."

What followed was a friendship that has lasted fifty years, spanned two continents, and become entwined with the two other people who have loomed large in Waters's experience of Provence: the cookbook writer Richard Olney and the vineyard owner and cook Lulu Peyraud.

Olney's influence on Waters began with *The French Menu Cookbook*, published in 1970, the year before Chez Panisse opened.

Originally from the small town of Marathon in northwestern Iowa, Olney attended the University of Iowa and then moved to New York to study painting at the Brooklyn Museum Art School. After waiting tables at a small restaurant in Greenwich Village while he was a student, Olney moved to Paris in 1951, at the age of twenty-four, and immersed himself in the world of French food and wine. Ten years later, on vacation in Provence, he bought a run-down shepherd's cottage in Solliès-Toucas, outside of Toulon, and began writing articles for the journal *Cuisine et Vins de France*. Olney said that the monthly column he eventually wrote, "Un Américain (gourmand) à Paris," began as something of a joke, in which an American would offer a menu, recipes, and wine selections for a French audience. But it gained a loyal readership, due to Olney's extensive culinary knowledge and lively prose style, and in a few years Simon and Schuster offered him a book contract based on the concept, which eventually became *The French Menu Cookbook* (Ochoa).

Although Olney was virtually unknown to American readers before 1970, *The French Menu Cookbook* changed all that, and it had a profound influence on how Waters approached what she called "composing a menu" in *The Chez Panisse Menu Cookbook*, the title and concept of which were directly inspired by Olney's book. As Waters recounts in her introduction to *Reflexions* (1999), Olney's memoirs, one of her partners gave her a copy of *The French Menu Cookbook* soon after the restaurant had opened, and reading it "was like receiving unexpected validation" in her decision to offer "one meal only, at a fixed price, composed of four or five courses, using only the best ingredients we could find" (7).

But it was the publication of Olney's second book, *Simple French Food* (1974), that had the most direct effect on Waters's connection to Provence.

Waters first met Olney in the spring of 1975 at Williams Sonoma in San Francisco, while he was on a book tour to support *Simple French Food*. The two clicked, and later that August Waters visited him at his home in Solliès-Toucas.

Her description of the visit in her introduction to *Reflexions* offers as good a window as any into the appeal of Olney's version of Provence for Waters:

> My first visit to Solliès-Toucas began in that state of extreme self-consciousness and absorbent, heightened awareness that sometimes accompanies a first visit to the house of someone who is very important to you. I remember every detail: the climb up the steep hill to his little house set amid terraces of ancient olive trees; the clicking of the cicadas, the rustle of the leaves in the wind, the aroma of the wild herbs all around us, mixed with the smell of Richard's Gauloise.
>
> Richard received us wearing nothing but an open shirt, his skimpy bathing suit, a kitchen towel at his waist, and a pair of worn espadrilles. He invited us into his house, which consists basically of one room in which he works, eats, and entertains when weather prohibits dining on his idyllic terrace. I can close my eyes and see the boulders with which Richard and his brothers had built the fireplace at the head of the house, the copper pots hanging above, the marble mortars on the mantlepiece, the column by the table papered with wine labels, the lovely platters and tureens displayed on hard-to-reach shelves, the windows out to the garden where the table under the grape arbor had been laid with beautiful linens. He served us a spectacular salad, full of Provençal greens that were new to me— rocket, anise, hyssop—with perfectly tender green beans and bright nasturtium flowers tossed in, and dressed with the vinegar he makes himself from the ends of bottles of great wine. (That salad was a revelation, and inspired countless *salades composées* in the years to come.) My first visit ended, many hours later, in the same way all my subsequent visits have ended: in a kind of ecstatic paralysis brought on by extraordinary food, astonishing wines, and dancing until dawn to seventy-eights of Edith Piaf and *bal musette* music. (8–9)

Like a seeker visiting a mountain top guru, Waters crafts her account around the motif of her gastronomic education. She begins by emphasizing her heightened sensory awareness: we see the olive trees, hear the cicadas and the rustling leaves, and smell the mixture of herbs and cigarette smoke. Next we become aware of Olney's own curious mixture of monkishness and uninhibited sexuality, his rural retreat a model of rustic simplicity, while his exposed chest and skimpy bathing suit symbolize his sybaritic lifestyle as an openly gay man in 1970s France, where he counted the writer James Baldwin among his friends and the Chez Panisse chef Jeremiah Tower among his lovers. Waters then recounts the features of Olney's kitchen as if she were in a Provençal version of a Nancy Meyers film, complete with copper pots, marble mortars, and beautiful linens. By describing the composed salad in religious terms—a "revelation" that "inspired" her own signature salads—Waters not only honors and celebrates Olney's culinary skills and knowledge, but she does two other things: she demonstrates her belief that the pleasure of food itself cannot easily be distinguished from the context of its consumption, and she positions herself as a rightful heir to Olney's legacy of devotion to the finest ingredients. Like so many accounts of enlightenment, Waters's ends with her reaching a state of "ecstatic paralysis," similar to the trance of a whirling dervish whose dance both embodies and points beyond the ineffable.

A year after Kermit Lynch started his shop, an importer invited Lynch to go with him on a buying trip to Burgundy, and the following year Lynch started to take his own trips to France. His French was rudimentary, however, and by his fourth buying trip in 1976 Lynch knew he needed the help of a translator. The French cooking teacher Lydie Marshall suggested that he contact Richard Olney.

"I mentioned it to Alice: 'His name is Richard Olney.' And she was like, 'Kermit, pack your suitcase.' Those very words, I never forgot. 'Pack your suitcase right now.'"

In the description of his own initial visit to Solliès-Toucas in *Adventures on the Wine Route*, Lynch demonstrates little of Waters's sense of pilgrimage or attention to interior design, but he does share her appreciation for Olney's exceptional taste and ability to teach by example.

Like Waters, Lynch admits to being "astonished" by Olney's pairing of wine and cheese, especially by his first taste of a 1969 Bandol red paired with some mild *chèvres*, so that the Bandol becomes "one of the most fantastically delicious wines I had ever tasted" (14).

And Lynch pays Olney the ultimate compliment, claiming that "he changed the way I tasted, judged, and selected wine. He did not instruct me. I observed him tasting, observed him matching wine to food and food to wine in restaurants, listened to his appreciations in the cellars as he searched for whatever distinguished each wine. He did not taste with a fixed idea of 'the perfect wine' in mind. He valued finesse, balance, personality, and originality. If a wine had something to say, he listened. If a wine was a cliché, he had little interest. If it was different, apart from the rest, he appreciated it more" (14–16).

As Lynch put it on his veranda in Le Beausset, a half-hour's drive from Solliès-Toucas, "The most important thing was that Richard didn't give lessons. Just being with him and hearing what he had to say about things was a teaching experience."

When Waters says that her first visit with Olney ended with them dancing until dawn, she is alluding to a passage that appears later in *Reflexions,* in which Olney describes his introduction of Waters to Lucien and Lulu Peyraud, the proprietors of Domaine Tempier. Theirs was to become a memorable friendship (also illustrated in Waters's *Fanny in France*).

As Olney recounts: "Alice Waters arrived in Solliès. I had spoken to the Peyrauds of her and of Chez Panisse, where Domaine Tempier (then imported by Gerald Asher) was a favorite wine. Lulu invited us to dinner, but we were to taste in the cellars in the afternoon. After sampling all the new wines in the wood, we moved back through vintage after vintage. Alice and I danced (that is to say, we whirled with wild abandon—Alice assured me that we were dancing the tango) until we collapsed on the cellar floor. Alice fell in love with the Peyraud family" (191).

After Kermit Lynch met the Peyrauds on his first trip with Olney in 1976 (the year after Waters's initial visit), he eventually became like an adopted son to the family, as Olney notes in his preface to the 1988 edition of *Adventures on the Wine Road:* "He has been absorbed into the Peyraud family, and to Lucien Peyraud he is *mon fils.*"

For this reason, I wanted to get Lynch's perspective on the mythology that has developed around those early visits, especially the radical hospitality Lulu seems to have shown to everyone who visited the winery—and still does.

"Lulu did it because she loved every minute of it," Lynch says. "But she was in it for the business, too. Lulu and Lucien were very aware that their wine was unknown. It was word of mouth, in those days; there was no wine media to speak of. Lulu was legendary in France for her open-door policy:

if you came by at ten o'clock in the morning, you were still tasting at noon. Even if she already had thirty people invited, you were welcome."

Meanwhile, what was Waters doing in Berkeley?

"Overbooking, mainly," said Willy Bishop, the prep cook at Chez Panisse (Kamp 157). "Sometimes we'd run out of food because Alice would overbook," Bishop told her biographer. "She couldn't say no" (McNamee 81).

To understand the importance of Lulu Peyraud to Alice Waters, we first have to understand something about the concept of *terroir*, which underlies the work of Slow Food, too, as we have seen, but which appears much less frequently in the writing of Carlo Petrini, given his preference for Italian terms over French ones.

And the best way to do that, of course, is over a glass of wine.

About halfway through our visit with Kermit Lynch, which began over glasses of water, Lynch ducked into his wine cellar and returned with a 2007 Chablis Premier Cru "Forêt" from Domaine François Raveneau.

"It's got some age on it—ten years old," he said. "Usually they age well."

Lynch poured glasses for Nancy and me, and together we took a moment to savor this particular vintage.

At this point I could tell you that the wine looked like orange blossom honey in the sun, and that a few swirls revealed a nutty, chalky, lemony nose. On the palate, it was rich and round, with notes of pear, peach, and butterscotch, supported by an undercurrent of saline minerality. It also had a long finish, with hints of ripe pineapple, which nicely showcased the wine's balance of acidity and fruitiness.

But Lynch would argue that this would be a mistake.

"I can't stand American tasting notes; it's vulgar to me. And anti-wine!" he exclaimed. "Nobody tastes like that; no real person can taste like that. I can imagine people reading ten things that are in the aroma, like 'peach gum bark from Polynesian canoes,' and thinking, 'I must not have a palate; I don't get that. I'm never drinking another wine.'"

In contrast, he says, "I love the way that the old French winemakers talked about wine. Wine was always a man or a woman—or sometimes a gay man or a woman, depending on what character. It was always a sexual person. And I loved that, because all of a sudden the wine has a meaning that you can relate to your life, and not berries and cherries."

For this reason, he says, "I try to personalize wines"—which gets to the

290 • THE FARMER, THE GASTRONOME, AND THE CHEF

heart of *terroir* for him. Wines, in other words, can have as much personality as a person, and just like a person they reflect a complicated fusion of nature and nurture.

Lynch puts it this way:

> *Terroir* doesn't mean *terre*; it doesn't mean "earth." *Terroir* is a combination of things. One of them is the soil. One of them is the climate—microclimate, like in Burgundy, where you've got these little parcels, carefully defined for centuries. And you find out, why is that, it's because the wind comes through this valley right here, and this vineyard gets sunlight ten minutes less than its neighbor here, and the wind cools the grapes so they ripen later and they have more elegance with less chewiness . . . these kinds of things. And to me the tradition is an important part of it, and that's being lost now. The enologists go to school in Bordeaux or in Dijon, and all of them learn how to make wine the same way. And it used to be every wine maker had little differences that he liked to do, and he would pass on to his kids who would maybe reject them and add their own. But the tradition of how certain things were done is being lost.

Terroir isn't the same thing as the Italian notion of "quality," to be sure. As Lynch told Daniel Duane, "Look, there's great *terroir* and there's lousy *terroir*. A wine showing *terroir* doesn't mean it's good" (Duane).

But Lynch's concern about losing "the tradition of how certain things were done" is clearly in line with Petrini's repeated invocation of the value of traditional foodways—which, again, is not so much a celebration of "authenticity" so much as it is a defense of biological and cultural diversity in the face of the homogenizing forces of modern life.

Where *this* soil and *this* climate once resulted in *this* technique being used to vinify wine—the ice-cold cellars of Chablis resulting in the use of *feuillette* (small, 132-liter barrels), for example, as opposed to the *foudres* (large oak vats) used in the warmer climates of Provence—Lynch feels that modern enologists (scientific winemakers) have stripped the soul out of winemaking, turning what was once a local art form into a technologically driven industry.

Today, most Chablis is aged in glass-lined or stainless-steel tanks, which Lynch admits in *Adventures on the Wine Route* can produce good wine. "There is a freshness to it that is not bad," he says. "But I have never tasted one that possessed the depth of character, the profoundness, if you will, of the old style, which is aged in wood. Chablis, from that rough soil and climate, needs that respiration, that exchange with the atmosphere that glass and stainless cannot provide. Barrel aging refines the wine while slowly liberating its character. Even when well done, the new vinification in tanks inhibits this evolution toward a certain kind of maturity, resulting in a good rather than a great wine" (222).

Is there an element of agristalgia to Lynch's critique? No doubt. But as with Berry and Petrini, it is nostalgia for more than just an "old style" of winemaking; it is nostalgia for an entire approach to the interaction of land and people, an entire way of life and being that is rapidly disappearing.

Which returns us to our 2007 Chablis from Domaine Raveneau.

Raveneau is not just any Chablis for Lynch, but *the* Chablis, and the reason has everything to do with *goût du terroir,* or the taste of place, as manifested through the choices made by François Raveneau and his children in response to their environment. (François died in 2000, but his sons, Bernard and Jean-Marie, and daughter, Isabelle, continue their father's legacy today.) The Raveneaus harvest the grapes by hand, use only indigenous yeasts, and age their wines for eighteen months in oak barrels and *feuillette.* As Lynch describes in *Adventures on the Wine Route,* because their wine is a natural wine, which undergoes no treatment whatsoever to stabilize it, Lynch spent years convincing François to let him ship it to the United States. He finally managed to do so, in part because Lynch was the first importer to use refrigerated shipping containers, so the wine would not be damaged by heat during its long sea voyage to the West Coast.

In *Inspiring Thirst* (2004), a collection of entries from Lynch's monthly wine brochures over the years, Lynch puts his love for Raveneau Chablis in context. "Outside Chablis and Bandol, I've not claimed to have the best wine of any appellation," he admits (94). But Raveneau, he says, is "the finest winemaker in Chablis" (96), and "the greatest Chablis is Raveneau" (265). "Every time I uncork one, it is an event, especially when they hit 8 to 10 years of age" (376).

To have shared this event with him was a pleasure, not least because he compares his quest for the finest example of an appellation to Alice Waters's own search for the best produce she can find. He recalled one moment in the early days of Chez Panisse when he watched Waters preparing a salad: "She had a big bunch of boxes full of lettuces. And she had a worktable spread out, and so help would put the lettuces in front of her, and there was a garbage can there, and she would go, 'pshut, pshut,' and maybe save one out of five. We would open it up and look, and maybe 90 percent of the lettuces were going into the garbage. And I had that approach buying wines. I'm not looking for a Pommard; I'm looking for *the* Pommard."

The only other "best" wine of an appellation he claims to have found—a Bandol—is from Domaine Tempier, home of the indomitable Lulu Peyraud.

Although the reputation of Domaine Tempier's Bandol wines grew throughout the 1970s and 1980s, it was the publication of *Lulu's Provençal Table* in 1994 that brought the vineyard the widespread name-recognition the Peyrauds had been seeking.

Written by Richard Olney, with a foreword by Alice Waters, the book is not a promotional effort on behalf of the Peyrauds so much as a celebration of one woman's ability to capture the rhythms and traditions of the vineyard in her cooking.

What makes the book special, in my view, is the way it perfectly captures what I have come to call "elemental cooking"—something that Olney, Waters, and Lulu all practice and that has come to embody the core principles of sustainable food in the kitchen.

In fact, I think it's fair to say that if you were searching for the heart of the sustainable food movement, as manifested in the kitchen, you could do a whole lot worse than *Lulu's Provençal Table*.

In *Reflexions,* Richard Olney describes the genesis of the book as follows: "Alice and Kermit were dreaming of a book about Domaine Tempier and Lulu's cuisine, to be written by Alice and illustrated by Gail. I agreed to write the wine chapter. They sent a proposal to Alice's agent, Susan Lescher, and were told that publishers found it too sketchy. Alice said, 'You have to write the book, Richard'" (331).

Sketchy as it is, that original proposal reveals a lot about the way Waters envisioned the book, as well as how Olney's development of that vision helped to mythologize Provence as the native home of elemental cooking.

Originally titled "The Domaine Tempier Cookbook," the book was to consist of three alternating sections. The first was to be a series of conversations between Waters and Lulu while they shopped at the local markets and cooked together. (Waters acknowledged that "a French-speaking assistant will be necessary to tape and help translate.") These dialogues were to "be of varying length and open to whatever subject arises which captures Lulu's spirit and philosophy of cuisine: give and take with fishermen, selecting produce, composing menus, preparing techniques, jokes, anecdotes, memories, etc." The second section was to consist of recipes explaining what Waters and Lulu ended up cooking as a result of these conversations. And the third was to feature comments on wine by Lucien Peyraud, to follow each recipe section, as taped and transcribed by Kermit Lynch. The topics for the wine section were to include "the wine of Bandol, history of Domaine Tempier, the Mourvedre grape, vinification, aging wine, tasting and judging wine, food and wine alliances, etc." Finally, the book was to be illustrated with photographs by Gail Skoff (Lynch's wife), as well as with old wine labels, Chez Panisse menus, and family snapshots ("Book Proposal").

The book that resulted—once Olney agreed not only to write the wine chapter but to author the entire volume—is structured somewhat differently, with a foreword by Waters, a prose portrait of Domaine Tempier and the Peyrauds, an explanation of the seasonal rhythms in the vineyard (accompanied by menus created by Olney), and a section of Lulu's recipes, followed by some brief wine-tasting notes. (The first edition featured Skoff's photographs, but these were omitted from subsequent reprints.)

As cookbooks go, it is a decidedly personal volume, as much family biography and natural history as culinary instruction manual. Compared, for instance, to Nancy Harmon Jenkins's *Mediterranean Diet Cookbook,* published the same year, *Lulu's Provençal Table* has no nutritional data, no scientific guidelines, no dietary agenda, and certainly no Mediterranean Diet Pyramid. Its recipes are also intentionally imprecise, unlike Jenkins's detailed instructions, which are meant to lead American readers through what were then still novel ingredients and techniques. (Despite their different approaches, Jenkins knew both Olney and Lulu.)

Olney retained the conversational aspect of Waters's proposal, noting in *Reflexions* that for two years Lulu "drove to Solliès twice a week for three-hour sessions of culinary stream-of-consciousness conversation, punctuated by questions, while I took notes" (331). (Olney himself did not drive.) But the book reflects Olney's vision as much as it does Lulu's—and may even represent a kind of culinary mind-meld that occurred over the course of those biweekly visits.

In introducing the recipes, for instance, Olney says, "I often feel guilty when writing recipes. To capture what one can of elusive, changing experience—a fabric of habit, intuition, and inspiration of the moment—and imprison it in a chilly formula, composed of cups, tablespoons, inches, and oven temperatures, is like robbing a bird of flight." Improvisation resembles the warmth and freedom of Provence in Olney's vision, while precise measurements equate to mechanical coldness (Olney, *Lulu's*).

Lulu, he says, feels the same way. "Lulu doesn't measure," he observes. "When describing liquid quantity, she speaks in terms of ladles, but, of course, she doesn't count out ladlefuls—she simply pours in liquid until it looks about right. When I ask what she means by 'lots of garlic', the answer is, 'Well, at least a head! But, naturally, when new garlic, which is crisp and fresh and sweet, comes into season, I use lots more than at the end of the season'" (Olney, *Lulu's*).

By "elemental cooking" I mean to indicate a collection of practices—such as Olney's distaste for detailed recipes—that seem to me to reflect a culinary philosophy shared by many of the practitioners of sustainable food. Not every sustainable food advocate embraces every aspect of elemental cooking, of course, but many of them take an approach similar to that of Olney, Waters, and Lulu.

In *The Art of Simple Food* (2007), Waters outlines what she calls "the underlying principles of good cooking," which are as good a summary of these practices as any. They are:

1. Eat locally and sustainably.
2. Eat seasonally.
3. Shop at farmers' markets.
4. Plant a garden.
5. Conserve, compost, and recycle.
6. Cook simply, engaging all your senses.
7. Cook together.
8. Eat together.
9. Remember food is precious. (6–7)

These seem so basic as to hardly require comment, but they are in fact a remarkably compact articulation of the essential elements of sustainable food in the kitchen.

What took Michael Pollan sixty-four rules in *Food Rules: An Eater's Manual*

(2009), Waters does in nine. Yes, Pollan stated his philosophy of eating even more simply in his previous book, *In Defense of Food: An Eater's Manifesto*: "Eat food. Not too much. Mostly plants" (1). But this shorter formulation omits many of the aspects of cooking that are so central to the experiences Waters had in Provence.

Under "Cook simply, engaging all your senses," for example, Waters writes: "Plan uncomplicated meals. Let things taste of what they are. Enjoy cooking as a sensory pleasure: touch, listen, watch, smell, and above all, taste. Taste as you go. Keep tasting and keep practicing and discovering" (*Art of Simple Food* 7). Surely this is what both Olney and Lulu sought to convey in *Lulu's Provençal Table*.

Compare Waters in *Coming to My Senses* to Olney in *Lulu's Provençal Table*: "Something can be lost in writing down a recipe. People can become so focused on measuring ingredients that they're not tasting as they go along, and at the end of it, they don't have the confidence to cook without a recipe" (144).

Jeffrey Cohen and Lowell Duckert have used the term "elemental" to describe a form of ecocriticism focused on the four elements of the material world (*Elemental Ecocriticism: Thinking with Earth, Air, Water, and Fire*), and Michael Pollan has used these same four elements to organize his understanding of the process of cooking (*Cooked: A Natural History of Transformation*). Similarly, Samin Nosrat has identified a form of elemental cooking based on what she sees as the four elements of good cooking (*Salt, Fat, Acid, Heat: Mastering the Elements of Good Cooking*).

In my usage, "elemental cooking" refers to a different quartet of elements, based on those outlined by Waters, that to me define sustainable cooking from farm to table and everything in between. These include: the elements of the *ingredients* (grown locally and sustainably on a small scale), the elements of their *provision* (purchased in season from farmers, for a fair price, or grown yourself), the elements of their *preparation* (used and cooked with care, preferably in a social context), and the elements of their *consumption* (eaten together, whenever possible).

Lulu's Provençal Table offers an illustration of all of these.

Olney's opening chapter, for example, acknowledges the environment from which the elements of good cooking arise, "the natural amphitheatre that describes the Bandol microclimate—a basin of terraced hillsides facing the sea and surrounded by a belt of mountains. The vines receive a maximum of sun and, at the same time, are protected from spring frosts and excessive summer heat, both by the proximity of the sea and by the mountainous barrier. The soil is arid, stony, and chalky, with a high clay content, more or less sandy—hopeless for other crops but typical of the soils that produce great wine."

The second chapter then shows how the Peyrauds are as tightly knit to the seasonal work of the vineyard as they are to one another, demonstrating Kermit Lynch's point that the terroir consists of a combination of soil, climate, and tradition.

Finally, the recipes themselves show Lulu preparing food from local and seasonal ingredients, shopping at the farmers' markets in Bandol and nearby towns, using the bounty of her garden, wasting little, cooking and eating with friends and family, and generally appreciating both the food itself and the way it brings people together in the kitchen.

Waters clearly appreciates this, as she indicates in her introduction.

"The Peyraud family's example has been helping us find our balance at Chez Panisse for years," she writes. "Like them, we try to live close to the earth and treat it with respect; always look first to the garden and the vineyard for inspiration; rejoice in our families and friends; and let the food and wine speak for themselves at the table" (R. Olney, *Lulu's*).

One need not own a vineyard to connect to the earth in this way, though obviously it helps.

In a 1997 review of Olney's *Simple French Food*, among other cookbooks, Alexander Cockburn argued that cookbooks "usually . . . become versions of pastoral, with the urban masticator being whisked into a world where kitchen and garden co-exist in harmonious union instead of being mediated by the Safeway, the can, the freezer, and the poison list on the back of every package." Provence, Cockburn proclaimed, is "the heartland of cookbook pastoral" ("Gastro-Porn").

With its invocation of simplicity and insistence on using only the best ingredients, *Lulu's Provençal Table* would seem to fall squarely into the cookbook pastoral mode, and there is no question that Olney presents Provence as an idealized countryside, the signature feature of the pastoral.

We could go even further and observe that what Olney, Waters, and Elizabeth David all seem to value about Provence is in fact a fantasy: the pre–World War II world of Marcel Pagnol's films, fictional and highly romanticized, "a scratchy black-and-white world where men in cafes amuse themselves by hiding rocks under hats and waiting for someone to come along and kick them," as Ruth Reichl memorably put it, alluding to a particularly comic scene in *César* ("My Year in Provence Last August").

Yet this seems as reductive a way to read these writers as it is to dismiss the terroir that Kermit Lynch values in a Raveneau Chablis.

I say this because to fully appreciate what Olney was trying to capture in *Lulu's Provençal Table* (the last cookbook he authored before his death in 1999), and to fully understand the appeal of Domaine Tempier for Waters, I decided there was only one thing left to do: go meet Lulu myself.

It's hard to sustain a fantasy when the reality is sitting right in front of you. So it seemed early one Sunday morning in June when Nancy and I found ourselves in the drawing room of Domaine Tempier, talking with Lulu and her daughter Laurance, the sixth of Lulu's seven children.

There is an aspect of pilgrimage to any visit to Domaine Tempier, especially to meet Lulu, given that the writer Jim Harrison made annual trips there from 1994 to 2000 (sixteen years, if you're counting), and several food journalists (including David Tanis, Sarah Jay, and Steve Hoffmann) have also paid their respects over the years. And all of these visits are in addition to the regular visits made by Waters, Olney, and Lynch.

The Domaine lies about seven kilometers north of the port city of Bandol, on the Mediterranean, and four kilometers southwest of Le Beausset, where Kermit Lynch lives and where our Airbnb was located. From Le Plan du Castellet, just to the south, it is a short drive up a narrow road until you turn into the main entry, a gravel path lined with arching plane trees that leads you to the house.

Built in 1834 by Lulu's great-great-grandparents, the house is a typical Provençal farmhouse, with a tile roof and light-blue shutters, which are closed today to block the sun. The vineyards surrounding the house are planted mainly in Mourvèdre grapes (called Monastrell in Spain), a notoriously finicky grape to grow, but one that the Peyrauds have more than mastered.

The previous Friday we had stopped in for a tasting with Véronique Peyraud Rougeot, Lulu's youngest daughter, who noted the significance of the terroir as we sipped our way from the Domaine's Bandol white through its celebrated Bandol rosé to several of its Bandol reds.

The vineyard is at the end of the Alps, she noted, pointing toward Gros-Cerveau (Big Brain), the mountain to the southeast, as she poured the first of our glasses.

"In this area, the soil is sand and shell. And my father said all the time, 'It's a very beautiful area for white wine.' Sometimes you can smell the salt of the sea in the wine; it has good acidity."

Her father, Lucien, married Lulu in 1936, and three children quickly followed: Fleurine in 1938, Jean-Marie in 1939, and François in 1940. Around the time François was born, Lulu's father offered the young couple the Domaine Tempier, and they soon became skillful growers of Mourvèdre and vigorous promoters of Bandol wine.

Most notably, Lucien was instrumental in getting Bandol certified AOC (*appellation d'origine contrôlée*), a system that guarantees the ingredients, geographical origins, and modes of preparation for foods and wines—a formalized indicator of terroir.

Although Mourvèdre was the most widely planted grape in Bandol during the eighteenth and early nineteenth centuries, many Bandol producers chose not to replant it after the *phylloxera* aphid destroyed France's vineyards in the mid-nineteenth century, because of the grape's low yield. As a result, Lucien also had to convince the certifying body to gradually raise the percentage of Mourvèdre that must be included in Bandol red from 10 to 50 percent, as growers slowly increased the acreage devoted to the grape. Today, the minimum percentage remains at 50 percent, although many producers use much larger amounts in their Bandol reds.

Thus, while the 2015 Bandol rosè Véronique poured next was 55 percent Mourvèdre, 25 percent Grenache, and 20 percent Cinsault, the 2014 Bandol red that followed was 75 percent Mourvèdre, 14 percent Grenache, 9 percent Cinsault, and 2 percent Carignan.

The minimum amount of Mourvèdre allowed in Bandol rosé is 20 percent, Véronique said, while the maximum allowed in both rosé and red is 95 percent. Mourvèdre is "never alone," she added.

Why is it never alone? I asked.

"It's more interesting with a variety of grapes and can give the good acidity with the grenache," she said. "It's very important for that."

There are other features to the AOC regulations for Bandol—thirteen pages of them, to be precise—including such things as the age of the vines, the amount of time the wine spends in wood, minimum planting density, and maximum yields.

But even these strictures cannot easily account for the changes coming to the region's climate.

The 2014 vintage had 30 percent less production because of hail, Véronique pointed out, while the 2015, 2016, and 2017 growing seasons all shortened because of the heat. In 2017, she noted, "we started in 22 August for the harvest and finished in 12 September," an early close to the season because of the very high temperatures.

The consequences of such changes range from the serious to the subtle, although they are not always for the worse.

"It's more easy for the taste of the red wine now, when it's very young," Véronique observed. "When I remember the red wine I drank with my father, it was very strong. The tannin take your mouth very, very particular. And now it's more easy. We don't change really the vinification, or the soil—we are all biodynamic—but the structure is more easy" because of climate change.

"We are the mosaic of all this," she says, gesturing around to encompass the world in her outstretched arms.

Like Waters, Véronique ran a restaurant in Bandol—named L'oulivo (The Olive Tree)—for fourteen years, until her husband had a heart attack several years ago and they decided to quit the business.

"We were working a lot, it was very intense," she said of that time in her life. "But we couldn't stop it. We loved the people, and we loved the cooking also."

For all the attention the wines of Domaine Tempier have received, it's fair to say that their fame is now overshadowed by that of Lulu's cooking, thanks largely to the work of Olney, Waters, and Lynch (who, now that I think about it, sound like some sort of powerhouse public relations firm).

Having already tried to understand Waters from the perspective of women working in the professional food industry in Lyon, I was curious to see a different side of Waters's interests in Lulu—namely, a woman who cooked at home.

Clearly, Lulu was not just any home cook, but I had a sneaky suspicion that part of her appeal was due to her lack of pretension. Kermit Lynch's portrayal of her in *Adventures on the Wine Route* likely helped to shape my expectations: "It is my experience that when anybody makes the acquaintance of the Peyrauds and Domaine Tempier, he or she tends to mythologize them. Everything seems so down-to-earth and wonderful and perfect. Even the names: Lucie and Lucien. And the setting contributes, too; the rugged hillsides, the sea, and the enormous blue sky create a landscape of divine dimension. And one's glass is never empty; reverie is natural. Then, when you get to know the Peyrauds better and you see how human they are, 'mad and wonderful' according to their friend Richard Olney, you love them and their wine even more" (92).

Lulu—born Lucie Tempier (another Lucy!) in 1917—had recently turned one hundred years old, but she easily seemed twenty years younger when we met. Her legendary sparkle seemed hardly to have dimmed, and she looked as lively as I expected in a sharp white skirt, pink jacket, and matching scarf.

How, I wondered, had she learned to cook?

"My mother was my first teacher, because she was the one who produced the menus for a family of five children," Lulu said, with Laurance translating.

Had she ever considered opening a restaurant like Véronique?

"I got married at eighteen, and I had children every year, so I never considered this," she said with a laugh.

Four more daughters followed François in 1940—Marion in 1943, Colette in 1945, Laurance in 1947, and Véronique in 1956—for a total of two sons and five daughters, so in a sense Lulu ran her own private restaurant for more than forty years, not counting her many guests.

"Their idea of getting known was to entertain people here," Laurance added, "so this was where she had different menus, this is how she was like a chef. The whole lamb roasted, and sardines grilled on branches of vines for 25 to 30 people."

It is easy to see why Waters so admires Lulu, as they both share a vision for extending the hospitality of the home to a widening circle of friends and acquaintances.

"In Français, we call it *convivialité*," said Laurance. "Feeding people is sharing something with them. You want to please them."

Nancy and I experienced some of that *convivialité* as Laurance and Lulu shared family photographs with us while reminiscing about Richard Olney's influence on the family.

"Lulu became famous because of that book," Laurance observed, speaking of *Lulu's Provençal Table*. "During the book tour, she went to New York, Washington, San Francisco, Berkeley, Los Angeles."

Yet Olney's portrait of Lulu makes it seem as if she was entirely self-taught, which is not quite true.

Lulu showed us a bilingual French and Provençal cookbook that she used regularly throughout the years she knew Olney: *Vieii receto de cousino prouvençalo/Vieilles recettes de cuisine provençale*. (Lulu owns the third edition, published in 1972, and Olney clearly knew the book, as he cites it in several of his own cookbooks.) Originally self-published in 1966, the book is the work of Calixtine Chanot-Bullier, the wife of Jean-Baptiste Amable Chanot, who was a mayor of Marseille in the early twentieth century. Featuring traditional recipes of Provençale cuisine, on facing pages of French and Provençal text, the book is "one of the best cookbooks ever written," according to the food writer Edward Behr. "What makes it special are its combinations of flavors and clear presentation of tradition," Behr says in his *Art of Eating Cookbook*— although he adds that "its old-fashioned scarcity of measurements and limited instructions" make it seem decades older (104).

It's no surprise that Lulu would admire this book, since she grew up in Marseille, some fifty kilometers to the west of Le Plan du Castellet. After her marriage, Lulu said, she would come to Domaine Tempier for the holidays, because it was a country house, before moving here permanently in 1940.

Having spoken with Véronique about the changing climate, I was curious what changes the family had seen to the countryside since that time.

"In the beginning, in 1940, there was nothing imported; no food was imported. So that's the big change," Laurance said. "Getting grapes from Chile now is a big change over the years."

Laurance also noted other changes: more drought because of climate change; fewer cherry trees and almond trees; and more houses and concrete in place of the grapevines, because of a law that villages have to build low-income housing.

Further changes that have come to the Domaine since 1940 have less to do with the environment and more to do with the process of modernization. Initially, the house did not have running water, electricity, or telephone service, which puts Lulu's culinary achievements in sharper focus, as she had to feed four children before these conveniences arrived.

And this, more than anything, may be the key to understanding the appeal of Lulu's story not only for Olney and Waters, but for readers around the world.

"One way to tell the history of cooking," writes Michael Pollan, "is as the story of the taming of the cooking fire followed by its gradual disappearance from our lives. Contained first in stone fireplaces and brought indoors, it was then encased in iron and steel, and in our time replaced altogether by invisible electric currents and radio waves confined to a box of glass and plastic. The microwave oven, which stands at the precise opposite end of the culinary (and imaginative) spectrum from the cook fire, exerts a kind of *anti*-gravity, its flameless, smokeless, antisensory cold heat giving us a mild case of the willies. The microwave is as antisocial as the cook fire is communal" (*Cooked* 111).

When Grace was in elementary school, she asked to have a camping-themed birthday party, complete with s'mores, but when bad weather forced the festivities inside, we were compelled to improvise. We cut flame-shaped pieces out of colored construction paper and taped them to the front of our microwave to resemble a campfire, which we then used to melt the marshmallows and chocolate squares for the s'mores. It was a valiant attempt, and the kids didn't seem to know any better, but it just wasn't the same. (Waters, notably, does not own a microwave.)

As Pollan's observations attest, and my own experiences confirm, cooking with fire is something primal—elemental, really—and a large part of Lulu's appeal can be traced to her fireplace, which occupies the entire north wall of her kitchen.

"Alice just loves the fireplace," said Laurance.

Lulu's kitchen *is* something to behold, no question. Thick wood beams fill the ceiling, and the floor is tiled in a blue-and-white checkerboard pattern, matching the colors of the shutters. A large worktable fills the center of the space, much like the island in our own kitchen, and a huge antique buffet fills the wall opposite the fireplace, holding plates, bowls, serving trays, and sundry other items, including—of course—several bottles of wine. A large green tagine sits atop it, evidence of the Moroccan influence on Provençal cuisine. A door on the far wall leads to the outside, and to the left of that is a large farmhouse-style sink and countertop, made of a single, impressively thick block of stone.

Dominating the kitchen, though, is the fireplace, which in its current incarnation stands waist high.

"When Lulu was a child," Laurance said, translating, "the hearth was on the ground. And then they put a stove in that space. Later, her dad had this installed at this level. Lulu saw in a restaurant in Sainte-Maxime where there were all these little compartments on the side, so she had it made like this."

The result is a large brick fireplace, framed on both sides by built-in wooden cabinets. Above it, on the mantelpiece, are various metal racks for grilling meats and fish and keeping pots raised above the coals. Underneath are the cubbies Lulu had installed, which hold her pots and cast-iron skillets, cutting boards, mortars and pestles, and assorted other cooking implements.

The caption to a sunlit-photograph of the kitchen in *Saveur* is typical of visitors to this space: "To cook in Lulu Peyraud's Provençal kitchen is to cook not just in a centuries-old room but also with centuries-old traditions. Electricity is shunned in favor of a fireplace, antique iron tools, marble mortars, and wooden pestles" (Tanis).

The hearth in the kitchen of Lulu Peyraud, June 2018. (Photo by Nancy Dilts)

The only problem is, this isn't quite true. Lulu's kitchen has certainly been home to many memorable feasts cooked over the fire, but to imagine that the Peyrauds live in the past is to fall victim to a romantic stereotype that doesn't do anyone any favors.

"We don't cook on that; we cook on the gas stove," Laurance points out. "We use the hearth only to grill, or to heat on the side."

When we spoke, of course, Lulu's days of hosting dozens of guests at a time were behind her. She cooked until 2015, but she doesn't cook any longer, said Laurance. "But if there is a sauce blanche, or an omelet, she will do it."

The real appeal of Lulu's kitchen, to my mind, is the tiny closet in which most of the cooking actually takes place.

"That kitchen!" exclaimed Kermit Lynch, when we later talked about my visit. "You can't turn around, you can't have two people at once where the stove and the refrigerator are; it's one person at a time."

Inside is a modern, four-burner Electrolux gas stove and a full-size Bosch refrigerator, tucked into a closet the size of a pantry. Outside, relegated to a small shelf next to the pantry, are a range of other electric appliances: a toaster, coffeemaker, kettle, juicer, and food processor. It's an elegant solution to a difficult problem: how to preserve the charms of an old-fashioned kitchen while still making space for the modern tools most cooks use every day.

To me, then, the realities of the Lulu's Provençal kitchen are far more interesting than the somewhat mythical portrait we get in *Lulu's Provençal Table*. But at the same time, what charmed me most about Lulu was the lack of pretension that the writings of Olney, Waters, and Lynch had prepared me to expect.

When I asked Lulu if she ever had a memorable failure in the kitchen, she paused for a moment to think, and then gave a definitive "no"—followed immediately by a sly smile and a statement of deniability that had us all in stitches.

"I poisoned no one," she said.

In *The Last Days of Haute Cuisine*, Patric Kuh observes that at precisely the same time that Olney's *Simple French Food* "conjured up a France that was swiftly disappearing," Waters and her friends "were determined to re-create it" (134).

Yet this seems to me to tell only half the story—and miss the most important part.

Kuh sees Olney as the primary influence on Chez Panisse's adoption of grilling as "the restaurant's cooking technique of choice" (136), particularly through Olney's inclusion of a diagram of his own kitchen fireplace in *The French Menu Cookbook*.

Not only was Olney only (say that five times fast!) one of the influences on Waters's interest in grilling, but the reason for her enthusiasm has less to do with agristalgia and more to do with fire as a principal component of elemental cooking—a visible and tactile means to restore our connection to the fundamental building blocks of our environment.

Where microwaved s'mores happen as if by magic (yet remain mediocre), marshmallows toasted over a campfire require patience, skill, and care (and also happen to taste incredible).

Olney himself makes this clear in *The French Menu Cookbook*, noting that people who choose to install a fireplace in their home kitchens "have no desire to recapture living patterns of the past with all of the attendant discomforts. They simply understand that the superiority of a roast on a turnspit before an open fire or of fish and meats grilled over fruitwood embers is pertinently real and not merely part of a past mythology" (54).

No turnspit dog needed, thankfully.

Waters writes extensively about cooking with fire in *Coming to My Senses*, referencing both Olney and Lulu. "The place I feel most comfortable cooking now is over the fire—I've always had a fascination with it," she says. Olney's hearth was a "dream fireplace," but it was really Lulu's fireplace that inspired the one she installed in her own kitchen (198–99).

In the early years of Chez Panisse, the cooks would use a small lava-rock grill in the kitchen or set up some grills in the alley outside the restaurant. In 1978, however, Waters installed a large wood-burning oven and grill in the restaurant's kitchen, and in 1982, she installed a similar fireplace in her own home kitchen, just a few blocks north of Chez Panisse (Goldstein 177; McNamee 139; Whitaker 80–82).

Neither fireplace, though, could match the renown of Lulu's, which Waters herself helped to cultivate at a conference on Mediterranean food hosted by the American Institute of Wine and Food in 1988. The institute flew Lulu, Laurance, and Jean-Marie Peyraud to New York, along with Richard Olney, for a Provence-themed reception that featured a blow-up photo of Lulu's hearth along one wall (Olney, *Reflexions* 308–9).

Ironically, in her quest to cultivate the simplicity of the hearth, Waters not only unwittingly contributed toward the trend of exhibition kitchens (Pearlman 73), but she also raised the ire of her most fervent critic: Anthony Bourdain.

The month was January 2009, and Waters had recently been in the news, trying to persuade the newly elected President Obama to select a White House chef who would be a powerful advocate for sustainability, as well as to plant a vegetable garden on the White House grounds—a dream she had been pursuing since the Clinton administration. She had already campaigned for Obama during the election, and now she was hosting a series of preinaugural dinners with celebrity chefs, such as Rick Bayless, Dan Barber, and Nancy Silverton.

"Alice Waters annoys the living shit out of me," Bourdain told a Washington, D.C., interviewer just before the inauguration. "We're all in the middle of a recession, like we're all going to start buying expensive organic food and running to the green market. There's something very Khmer Rouge about Alice Waters that has become unrealistic" (Eater Staff).

Later that fall, after *60 Minutes* aired a segment on Waters in which she cooked an egg for Lesley Stahl in the fireplace of her home kitchen, using a large iron spoon, Bourdain went ballistic.

"She's Pol Pot in a muumuu," he said at the New York City Wine and Food Festival in October. "I saw her on *60 Minutes*. She used six cords of wood to cook one egg for Lesley Stahl" (Yoo).

The squabble that followed inspired Bourdain to devote an entire chapter to Waters in his 2010 book, *Medium Raw*. While Bourdain admits in that chapter (entitled "Go Ask Alice") that "it was excessive and bombastic of me to compare Alice to 'Pol Pot in a muumuu,'" he sticks to his position that "there is a whiff of the jackboot" in "Waters's fondness for buzzwords like 'purity' and 'wholesomeness'" (130).

Bourdain's indictment of Waters comes down to two essential things.

First, *labor*. Bourdain sees Waters's vision of "small, thriving, family-run farms growing organic, seasonable, and sustainable fruits and vegetables" and asks, *"Who will work these fields?"* (129–30). His answer? "Either enormous numbers of people who've never farmed before are suddenly convinced that waking up at five a.m. and feeding chickens and then working the soil all day is a desirable thing. Or, in the far more likely case, we'll revert to the traditional method: importing huge numbers of desperately poor brown people from elsewhere—to grow those tasty, crunchy vegetables for more comfortable white masters" (131). Waters's vision, in other words, is a pastoral fantasy, and one with racist implications.

Second, *class*. Eating local, organic, and seasonal produce is fine if you're a well-to-do chef in Berkeley, says Bourdain. "But what about the Upper Peninsula of Michigan? Or somewhere on the margins of Detroit? What if I were an out-of-work auto worker, living on public assistance or a part time job? . . . Basically you can eat like a fucking Russian peasant, is what she's saying" (131–32).

These are, as we have seen, two common complaints about the sustainable food movement, and in the years since *Medium Raw* appeared, environmental justice advocates around the world have worked to call attention to the plight of migrant agricultural workers and to address the inequalities in access to healthy food that Bourdain bemoans.

But just as Bourdain's treatment of Lyon failed to do justice to the city's rich history of female chefs, his criticism of Waters's cooking is tinged with an equal amount of sexism. As Kim Severson has documented, the food writers Kat Kinsman and Samin Nosrat have both commented on the bias that attacks such as Bourdain's contain. According to Severson, "Cooking an egg in an iron spoon over open fire is really no more precious and probably a lot less elitist than cooking an egg in a \$300 sous-vide machine, Nosrat said in a recent interview—except that women tend to do the former and men the latter."

Equally important, Bourdain fails to ask why Waters might have had a fireplace in her kitchen in the first place. Focusing on the restrictions on wood fires in metropolitan areas, as well as their carbon emissions—this from a man who spent his career flying all over the world—Bourdain repeats his initial critique, using hyperbole and vulgarity to take Waters to task: "I don't know about you, but burning up a couple cords of firewood for a single fucking egg doesn't exactly send a message of sustainability to me" (135).

Severson rightly observes that "only people who are very rich or very poor have fireplaces in their kitchens." But the point is not where the fire is located but what you do with it.

The night before we were to leave Provence, we knew we needed to do one last thing: come to terms with the outdoor fireplace in the rustic villa we had rented through Airbnb.

Inspired by the recipe for Grilled Lamb Skewers (Brochettes à la Provençale) in *Lulu's Provençal Table,* we stopped at a butcher shop in Saint-Cyr-sur-Mer earlier in the day and picked up some lamb brochettes, which had been marinated (à la Lulu) with red onions, garlic, thyme, and bay leaves. (The lamb, from Le Diamandin's "Red Label," was certified throughout the supply chain for good breeding, feeding, and animal welfare practices, as well as meat quality. It cost 19.80 euros per kilogram, or about ten dollars a pound, and we bought two kebabs for about five dollars total.)

While we were there, we also spied some green beans we liked at the weekly farmers' market, and we decided to pair those with some small new potatoes we brought with us from another farmers' market in Bourg-en-Bresse, north of Lyon, which is home to the Poulet de Bresse that Lucy referenced. Add a baguette from Maison Chenavier in Le Beausset, and a 2017 Bandol rosé from Domaine Tempier, and we had what sounded like a meal worthy of Lulu herself, or at least her PR representatives in Olney, Waters, and Lynch.

All that stood between us and that meal was one thing: the fire.

"With the grill," says Waters in *Coming to My Senses,* "you learn by doing it over and over again, and it becomes second nature, like making bread: you just do it and do it and do it and do it—pretty soon you can just press on the skin and say, *Ah, that's done.* I'm always manipulating the fire under the meat—I know when certain parts of the meat are thicker than others, so I'm moving both the meat and the fire underneath. You learn how long it takes for a loin of pork to grill, for instance. I figured out it would take about half an hour and would need to rest for ten minutes, but there were all these variables in between" (200).

For us, "all these variables" included damp matches, an unfamiliar kitchen, the rapid onset of nightfall, and a grill rack that had exactly one setting: the height of a brick laid on its side.

As a former boy scout, I like to think I know my way around a campfire, but getting this fire started before sunset took some doing, even with old grapevines for kindling and olive tree cuttings for fuel. (Could there be a more Provençal fire imaginable? I think not.)

Meanwhile, Nancy and I were tag-teaming the meal, as this was no place for an alpha cook.

"How long do you think the kebabs will take?" she asked from the kitchen, as we did our best to time the various components of the meal to arrive together.

"I'm not sure," I hollered back. "Olney says ten minutes, but that doesn't seem like enough time to me."

According to his recipe, I was supposed to: "Preheat an iron grill over a solid bed of wood embers and grill the brochettes, at about 10 cm (4-inch) distance from the coals, for 10 minutes in all, turning them every 2 or 3 minutes."

Four inches was right on target for the height of my bricks, but getting "a solid bed of wood embers" was easier said than done. Too thin a bed of embers and I would lose the heat; too thick and I would burn the meat. Plus we decided to grill the potatoes after we had parboiled them for a few minutes, and we wanted to warm the baguette on the grill as well, so I soon had three different kinds of food over the fire, all needing different kinds of heat.

"Tell me when I should start the beans," came a voice from the kitchen, as I worried over when to turn the brochettes.

I thought of Lucy back in Lyon, who urged us to cook with our noses, paying more attention to smell than to time, but my American obsession with food safety constantly had me wondering, "Are they done?"

I wished I had brought my instant-read thermometer, so I could get that precise 145-degree Fahrenheit temperature, and no more, to ensure that our skewers were thoroughly cooked but still juicy. That I was now grilling in the dark, using the flashlight on my phone to see the meat, wasn't helping, either.

After about fifteen minutes, I finally decided the kebabs were cooked enough that we wouldn't die a painful, lamb-induced death, and the potatoes had a nice char on them, so it was time to move inside to complete the meal. Nancy tossed the potatoes with a chunk of butter, a handful of freshly chopped parsley and chives, and a scattering of Fleur de Sel de Guérande, in honor of Pierre, my salt-smuggling ancestor. A squeeze of lemon juice on the beans, along with a dash of salt and pepper, and we were ready to go.

I won't say this was the best meal we've ever prepared, but I do have some obligation to tell the truth. And the truth is it was pretty damn good. Top five for sure, maybe even top three.

Even Anthony Bourdain would have to admit, as he eventually did in *Medium Raw*, Alice was right. Grilling really is elemental.

Lulu, by the way, is a fan of the egg spoon—but only in its latest incarnation.

"We totally agree with the new egg spoon, which is less shallow than the previous ones," Laurance told us, speaking of the egg spoons Waters brought Lulu on her annual visits to Provence.

"The first egg spoons, we just spilled the eggs in the fire, many times."

As for me, no kebabs or potatoes ended up in the ashes. So I got that going for me, which is nice.

THE KITCHEN OF THE WORLD

Having gone to France in part to understand the culinary heritage of my father's side of the family, I hadn't thought much about how Alice Waters might relate to my mother and her side of the family—those Dutch and Irish ancestors—until it was almost too late.

My great-grandparents immigrated from Ireland in the mid-nineteenth century and eventually settled in Montezuma, New York, on the north end of Cayuga Lake, where they bought a farm, since my great-grandfather had grown up on a farm in Ireland. My grandmother followed in their footsteps, marrying a man who raised Holstein cows, pigs, chickens, ducks, hay, wheat, and corn on more than a hundred acres of rolling hills just down the road from her parents. Wendell Berry, not to mention Patty and Mike, would have approved.

My mother, on the other hand, left Montezuma as soon as she could, attending college in Rochester and eventually leaving rural New York for suburban New Jersey, where she spent thirty-six years as a public high school teacher.

When I asked my mom about her family's food traditions, I was surprised by just how much she knew, as food was never a big part of her life when I was growing up.

Here's what she told me:

"My grandparents were very self-reliant people. Living in the countryside did not provide an opportunity for the family to go to the local store, co-op, or farmers' market to purchase food. They *were* the farmers' market.

"My grandparents planted and harvested all of their own vegetables and slaughtered pigs and cows for meat products. Having their own root cellar provided them with the means for storing vegetables and fruits grown during the summer months. Fruit trees were plentiful on the farm.

"My grandmother was a wonderful cook and enjoyed having a house full of relatives. This was not a trait passed to my own mother. My grandmother made all of her breads from scratch, and her cinnamon bread seemed to be a favorite. Cabbage was one of the most used vegetables in the home and accompanied the Sunday ham along with the homemade baked beans. Creamed cabbage, cold slaw, and cabbage soup were staples. My Irish grandmother did not fry foods—ever! She mostly prepared 'boiled' dinners or prepared food in the oven. This seemed to be the Irish tradition. Roast pork, of course, was prepared in the oven.

"Potatoes were prepared every day. Potato soup was served often in the wintertime. Turnips, carrots, parsnips, and apples were also plentiful from the root cellar. She always had the ingredients ready for a simple Irish stew, and it was a dish served often in the wintertime. Creamed soups and vegetable soups were also made often and stored.

"My grandmother had large crocks in the cellar of the house and brined pork. She also prepared canned beef. This was prepared in the manner similar to how she and my mother canned tomatoes. The beef was cut into chunks, seasoned, placed in quart jars, and placed in the canner on top of the stove. Many, many quarts were prepared for winter. The beef was then used for many types of meals including the stew. Corned beef was also prepared. Pork was canned in a similar way. With their own pork, beef, and chicken (raised on the farm), vegetables from the garden, and fruits from the fruit trees, the family had all that was needed for meals year-round. Ingredients for making bread had to be purchased, but butter was churned at home.

"One of the desserts made was a one-egg cake. During wartime, waste was not an option, and thus the one-egg cake. Homemade cookies (molasses, oatmeal, and sugar—no chocolate ever) were stored in a large copper tin and always available with lots of milk. Coffee was not the drink—tea was it.

"It is disappointing to me that I have none of these recipes. My sister feels that most of the dishes were prepared by my grandmother from memory, and she does not remember seeing a written recipe. I know my mother cooked without recipes. Maybe we just never asked and did not know what we were missing until now."

I cite these memories at length because they say something important about what Alice Waters learned from her time in France and how and why she came to share them with her American readers. My mom's memories also speak to the complicated way in which Waters's message was received by a changing readership for food writing, a readership that continues to evolve and diversify to this day.

What they remind me most of all is that Waters's interest in seasonal, organic, and local ingredients is less about "cookbook pastoral," some sort of mythologized landscape, than it is about real communities that are intimately connected to their agricultural roots, a much more expansive understanding of *terroir* than is commonly assumed in France.

In *The Taste of Place: A Cultural Journey into Terroir*, Amy Trubek argues that "the French taste of place remains primarily essentialist, a fundamentalist rally for the importance of 'location, location, location'" (247). But Trubek ultimately argues that those of us in the United States should "take back an original definition of terroir, the earth from the point of view of agriculture" and "rescue terroir from the prison of essentialism, a highly problematic endeavor as seen in the nationalistic and fundamentalist movements of the past century" (248).

This, it seems to me, is exactly what Waters has been trying to do at Chez Panisse and the Edible Schoolyard Project, both of which have been the subjects of her writing over the years.

Waters has written about her agriculture-based vision for Chez Panisse in a number of different venues, including *Forty Years of Chez Panisse: The Power of Gathering* (2011) and *We Are What We Eat: A Slow Food Manifesto* (2021). But to my mind the clearest articulation of her vision, as well as the most thorough recounting of her halting progress at achieving it, is still "The Farm–Restaurant Connection," which was first published in 1989 as part of a special issue of *The Journal of Gastronomy.* (The issue was republished in book form the next year as *Our Sustainable Table.*)

The opening of the essay is as good a summary as any of what Waters had hoped to achieve in the restaurant's early years:

> I have always believed that a restaurant can be no better than the ingredients it has to work with. As much as by any other factor, Chez Panisse has been defined by the search for ingredients. That search and what we have found along the way have shaped what we cook and ultimately who we are. The search has made us become part of a community—a community that has grown from markets, gardens, and suppliers and has gradually come to include farmers, ranchers, and fishermen. It has also made us realize that, as a restaurant, we are utterly dependent on the health of the land, the sea, and the planet as a whole, and that this search for good ingredients is pointless without a healthy agriculture and a healthy environment. (113)

This opening paragraph also suggests some of the many features that make this short essay so effective. For one thing, Waters is telling a story of the evolution of Chez Panisse's efforts, and not simply making an argument. She takes readers from the first meal served at the restaurant through the many attempts—some successful, others less so—at finding reliable sources for ingredients that would help replicate "the simple wholesome good food of Provence" she had come to love (122). In so doing, she's also illustrating the importance of improvisation and experimentation, a "utopia of process," which necessarily has to allow for failure. In 1977, for example, when one of Waters's partners acquired some land in Amador County, in the foothills of the Sierra Nevada, the restaurant tried to farm its own produce, "but we knew even less about farming than we thought we did," Waters admits, "and the experiment proved a failure" (116). A second farm attempt in 1980 and 1981 was more successful but inconsistent, and the restaurant had to rely upon other producers to meet their produce needs. This attempt, Waters notes, "finally disabused us of any illusion that we were farmers" (117). There was no cookbook for how to do this, in other words, no recipe for success. As Thomas McNamee observes, "This was something that no American restaurant had ever done" at the time, though now it has become commonplace (59).

In the course of telling the story of Chez Panisse's halting search for ingredients, "The Farm–Restaurant Connection" also does something else important: it maps a network of foragers, gardeners, farmers, ranchers, fishermen, and other specialty producers that has grown over time and on which the restaurant has come to rely. Waters is highly particular in this essay, talking not just in general terms but of many specific individuals who work at the restaurant, many specific producers up and down the West Coast, and many specific lands and waters in which they work. The essay functions inductively, then, making general observations about why these specific people and places matter only near its end: "fresh, locally grown, seasonal foodstuffs are more than an attractive fashion or a quaint, romantic notion," Waters concludes: "They are a fundamental part of a sustainable economy and agriculture—and they taste better, too" (121). Waters use of the first-person plural throughout the essay accentuates this theme of community-building, demonstrating that this is not an ego-driven narrative but a story of the power of togetherness—a "we" that extends the restaurant kitchen to encompass the kitchen of the world. "This isn't a matter of idealism or altruism but rather one of self-interest and survival," Waters insists. "Restaurateurs have a very real stake in the health of the planet, in the source of the foodstuffs we depend on, and in the future of farmers, fishermen, and other producers" (120).

"The Farm–Restaurant Connection" does one other thing so obvious that it risks being overlooked: it broadens the conversation about farm-to-table cooking from individual household kitchens like mine and my grandmother's to the kitchens present in our institutions, which have a significantly larger collective impact on our planetary health. Waters moves the conversation out of the realm of agristalgia and gets readers thinking about the food provisioning systems that supply not only our restaurants but also our schools, our hospitals, our prisons, and every other large institution that houses a kitchen.

Institutional change is hard, which is one of the reasons first-person food writing has tended to appear under the guise of either the farm memoir (such as in Wendell Berry's essays) or the kitchen memoir (such as in *Coming to My Senses*), rather than as stories about, say, "how I got my work colleagues to use more local produce in our company cafeteria." There are exceptions, of course, such as Will Allen's *The Good Food Revolution* (2012), in which Allen tells how he built "Growing Power," his now-defunct urban farm and community center in Milwaukee, which served as a model for other such efforts around the country. But endless committee meetings tend not to make for the most dramatic storylines, unless you are Aaron Sorkin—and even Sorkin doesn't write screenplays about his *own* committee meetings.

Perhaps this is why Waters's *Edible Schoolyard: A Universal Idea* (2008) is one of her lesser-known books, although it's also one of her most significant. In it, Waters explains how she expanded her advocacy for sustainable food to the Martin Luther King Jr. Middle School in Berkeley, beginning in 1995, when an offhand comment she made to a journalist about the school sparked a lifetime of involvement in food-based public education.

Edible Schoolyard is not a big book—only about twenty-five pages of text, with the remainder of its eighty large-format pages devoted to photographs and a handful of recipes—but the story it tells is important for several reasons, and the first of these brings me back to my mom.

When my mom left home after high school, she also left her rural community behind, just as so many Americans did after World War II, thanks to the expansion of industrial agriculture, as Wendell Berry has so eloquently explained. But when my mom became a public school teacher, she left the farm behind a second time, so to speak, since the suburban schools in which she taught had no place for food or agriculture in the curriculum.

This is why Trauger Groh, the CSA advocate, wrote in 1990 that "every school, public or private, needs a farm or a group of farms to give students the opportunity for practical training in nature" (16).

For Waters, this was another difference between her experience in France and her time teaching at the Berkeley Montessori School in her early twenties.

"French food, and the way it anchored French family life to an agricultural community and even to the seasons, was a revelation to me," Waters wrote in the foreword to *Edible Schoolyard*.

French agriculture was also modernizing after World War II, of course, and the same economic and technological forces that drove the rural exodus in the United States and Italy also emptied out the French countryside in favor of city living. But the French, like the Italians, had long-standing food traditions to preserve their connections to the land, whereas many Americans were more than happy to embrace both industrial agriculture and the industrial forms of eating it enabled.

With the Edible Schoolyard, Waters saw an opportunity to restore the connections to agriculture that the students in Berkeley had lost, as well as to continue to cultivate the kind of local food networks she was already building at Chez Panisse.

Making all of this happen, however, was far from easy.

Edible Schoolyard, the book, does a fine job illustrating, in both words and photographs, the challenges Waters and her crew needed to overcome, and like "The Farm–Restaurant Connection," it doesn't try to sugarcoat their missteps. It turns out, for example, that middle-schoolers aren't that fond of peach fuzz, even though Waters brought them a box of "the most glorious peaches on earth, the kind that can change your life with a bite" (23). After an unsuccessful attempt to share the fruit with the students, Waters ultimately admits defeat. "I went home that day with a lot of uneaten food and a broadened perspective," she says (24).

Yet what's ultimately inspiring about the book is that Waters *means* for it to inspire. "I'm going to tell a positive story, here," she says at the start, "shaped from my own memories of the next several years—about how a public school principal and a British gardener, a cook named Esther, and a lot of teachers, students, and parents made something beautiful happen in a blighted place" (10).

Read in isolation, Waters's diction appears to evoke the racialized image of "urban blight," and a critical reader might be tempted to classify her story as another iteration of the "white savior" complex in education. But this is not that kind of story.

Instead, *Edible Schoolyard* offers a far more complex accounting of the kind of community-building Waters describes in "The Farm–Restaurant Connection," with the added dimensions of age (what middle-schooler would want to eat at Chez Panisse, after all?) and cultural diversity (an early fundraiser featured "recent Thai immigrants and UC Berkeley professors, second-generation Indian families and African Americans whose grandparents had moved out west during the Second World War to work in the naval shipyards" [13]).

In fact, Waters's recounting of the pressures faced by the teachers and administrators at King (as the school is commonly known), and their skepticism about the project's viability, reminds me of nothing more than the many conversations I had with my mom over the years, as she would come home exhausted and frustrated at the barriers to change she faced on a daily basis in the public schools. What made the Edible Schoolyard succeed, however, in addition to the cultural and financial resources that Waters was able to draw upon, was that it was more than just a school garden.

"From the beginning," Waters told an interviewer in 1996, "what interested me was putting the kitchen *and* the garden together" (Ford 17).

While the first half of *Edible Schoolyard* mainly concerns the process of turning an empty two-acre lot (known as the "Back Forty") into a flourishing fruit and vegetable garden, the second half emphasizes the reopening of King's cafeteria and kitchen, which had been abandoned when they became too small to accommodate the school's growing population. Eventually, Waters's team moved the kitchen to be closer to the garden, and in the renovation of this new space Waters's philosophy starts to become clear:

> Determined to make the place utterly unlike an institutional kitchen, we had a local artisan fashion magnificent tabletops from poured concrete, and we mounted them on heavy timbers. Another local craftsman painted the walls in soft, soothing colors, and we built open storage spaces for every kitchen tool, so the eye could wander from a worn stone mortar and pestle, to a hand-press for making tortillas, to an apple press. Old French illustrations, framed and hung between the big, sun-flooded windows, showed ancient heirloom fruits and vegetables; and Esther [the first kitchen director] hung colorful prayer flags over the dishwashing area and let the teachers inscribe them with encouraging thoughts for the students. Most of all, we used this place to express a core belief: Beauty is not a luxury; it is a means of lifting the human spirit and of giving richness to everyday life. (33–34)

Two notable things come together in this passage. The first is Waters's insistence that institutions need not be *institutional*. They can instead be personal spaces, where individuals are not just permitted but encouraged to express themselves, and where creativity can thrive as in a garden. The second is the larger point this personal approach exemplifies. Waters here describes it as the process of cultivating *beauty*, which she explains is "a means" of accomplishing the broader goals of "lifting the human spirit" and "giving richness to everyday life." But a few pages later Waters refines this concept further, as one of the Principles of Edible Education, which over the years has come to be encapsulated by the phrase "beauty is the language of care" (43).

The phrase "beauty is the language of care" is reminiscent of *A Pattern Language: Towns, Buildings, Construction* (1977), the influential book on architecture and urban design authored by Christopher Alexander (1936–2022), to whom Waters turned when restoring Chez Panisse after a devastating fire struck the restaurant in 1982. A professor of architecture at UC Berkeley, Alexander founded the Center for Environmental Structure, and he coauthored *A Pattern Language* with his students there.

"That book was my bible," Waters told Thomas McNamee, her biographer. Alexander was a friend of Waters's collaborators at the restaurant, "and because I admired him so much, we met," Waters recounted. "And we talked for quite a long time about how to translate my ideas into the reconstruction of the downstairs" (McNamee 170–71).

A Pattern Language proposes that the problems and solutions in our world occur in patterns, and that the relationships between these patterns constitute an "extremely practical" language that can be used to plan, design, and construct buildings, towns, and neighborhoods (x). The worldview this approach entails sounds a lot like Waters's own philosophy for the Edible Schoolyard. According to Alexander, "It says that when you build a thing you cannot merely build that thing in isolation, but must also repair the world around it, and within it, so that the larger world at that one place becomes more coherent, and more whole; and the thing which you make takes its place in the web of nature, as you make it" (xiii). The hope, he says, is to "make people feel alive and human" (xvii).

A Pattern Language echoes the kind of advice offered by Bill Stumpf and David Goldbeck for more sustainable ways of living, particularly for how gardens, kitchens, and other places for eating and cooking should be arranged. "The isolated kitchen, separate from the family and considered as an efficient but unpleasant factory for food is a hangover from the days of servants; and from the more recent days when women willingly took over the servants' role," Alexander explains (661). Such kitchens rely on the supposition "that cooking is a chore and that eating is a pleasure." The solution, he suggests, "lies in the pattern of the old farmhouse kitchen," in which "kitchen work and family activity were completely integrated in one big room" (662).

Prior to the fire at Chez Panisse, the kitchen and the dining room were separate, connected by only a single narrow door. But when the fire took out both the door and the wall between the rooms, Waters decided not to restore them, thus creating the restaurant's now distinctive open kitchen.

"I had always wanted to be connected, cooking and serving the customer in one room," Waters said. "So when that wall went down in the fire, I just said, 'Let it be'" (McNamee 171).

In addition to specific design guidance such as this, *A Pattern Language* also offers more general reflections on the direction that modern society should take. Alexander makes the case, for instance, for a "network of learning" to connect communities to one another. Building on Ivan Illich's notion of "de-schooling," Alexander recommends a decentralized process of learning, in which students are enriched through "contact with many places and people all over the city: workshops, teachers at home or walking through the city, professionals willing to take on the young as helpers, older children teaching younger children, museums, youth groups traveling, scholarly seminars, industrial workshops, old people, and so on. . . . Build new educational facilities in a way which extends and enriches this network" (102).

The Edible Schoolyard may not quite live up to Alexander's ideal in practice, but it certainly comes close in philosophy. Waters's belief that "beauty is the language of care" resembles nothing if not Alexander's attempt to articulate the principles of beautiful living in *A Pattern Language*, as well as his more philosophical discussion of "the power to make buildings beautiful" in *The Timeless Way of Building* (1979), its companion volume (14). Waters puts the principle this way: "A beautifully prepared environment, where deliberate thought has gone into everything from the garden paths to the plates on the tables, communicates to children that we care about them" (43). Both Waters and Alexander may be guilty of overreach, in assuming that their subjective perceptions of beauty are indeed objective facts (case in point: peach fuzz), but neither can be accused of not caring. Both, in fact, care passionately about the environments they attempted to create, and the success of the Edible Schoolyard suggests that Waters's willingness to care about the children of the King school ultimately matters much more than the particular language of beauty in which that care is articulated.

In her memoir *Always Home* (2020), Waters's daughter, Fanny Singer, puts it this way: "It's not really about beauty in the end, but about care. If food is plated carefully, it will almost always be beautiful. If a child is surrounded by lush color, by growing places, by the variegated plumage of the chickens that run wild across her schoolyard, that child, I would wager, feels and registers that care on a profound, if subconscious level" (12).

In her thirty-six years as a high school teacher, my mom gradually worked her way up the administrative ladder, beginning as a teacher of business, then rising to become department chair, and for the last ten years of her career serving as the supervisor of five departments: business, technology, science, industrial arts, and art. She taught accounting, economics, and word processing; she advised student groups, often late into the evening; she served as president of her local professional association; she attended conferences, evaluated other high school programs, wrote teacher's guides, reviewed textbooks, and built computer labs.

I mention this because she did what I think most people assume teachers should do in public education: prepare students to succeed in our modern, technological world.

This is certainly what Caitlin Flanagan thinks they should do, as evidenced by her evisceration of Waters and the Edible Schoolyard program in *The Atlantic* in 2010.

Waters, Flanagan argues, has fallen prey to "a vacuous if well-meaning ideology that is responsible for robbing an increasing number of American schoolchildren of hours they might otherwise have spent reading important books or learning higher math (attaining the cultural achievements, in other words, that have lifted uncounted generations of human beings out of the desperate daily scrabble to wrest sustenance from dirt)."

It's not that Waters doesn't care, Flanagan suggests; it's just that she cares about the wrong things—namely, tomatillos instead of test scores.

Interestingly, Flanagan's critique gets at the heart of what makes the Edible Schoolyard program so distinct: that it is not simply a school garden but an entire curriculum built around the production, processing, and consumption of food. School gardens have been around since the Nature Study movement of the late nineteenth century, when Progressive Era reformers felt that such gardens could solve many of the ills of modern life: they could help students acquire practical skills, foster their spiritual growth, inspire further scientific study, and encourage their active citizenship, among other goals (Armitage). The Edible Schoolyard is Nature Study for the twenty-first century, integrating the growing of fruits and vegetables into every aspect of the curriculum, from reading, writing, and social studies to science, art, and math.

But Flanagan doesn't buy it.

"What evidence do we have that participation in one of these programs— so enthusiastically supported, so uncritically championed—improves a child's chances of doing well on the state tests that will determine his or her future (especially the all-important high-school exit exam) and passing Algebra I, which is becoming the make-or-break class for California high-school students?" she asks.

Flanagan's critique is misguided, I think, and the apparent glee she takes in provoking the supporters of school gardens suggests she may be more interested in starting a fight than solving the problems that plague our public education systems.

Melanie Okamoto, the program supervisor for the Berkeley Unified School District's Garden and Cooking program, responded to Flanagan this way: "Flanagan's claim that garden-based education fails to help our students achieve academically takes an incredibly narrow view of how garden-based programs have been used around the country to support student learning and achievement. So often it's a teacher who reports how a student was able to grasp a key concept within a hands-on context in the garden, or how another student who had not participated at all in class joined in on the discussion once in the cooking class. While these stories might seem fluffy or trite to Flanagan, they are very real to the teachers and students in the program" (Kummer, "School Gardeners Strike Back").

I suspect my mom would have been as skeptical as Flanagan about the value of the Edible Schoolyard, since I grew up hearing about state standards and "scope and sequence" around the dinner table. But I think she would ultimately have been persuaded by Okamoto's point, since she knew that standardized testing was only one way—and a limited one at that—of assessing student learning.

A better question we might ask of the Edible Schoolyard, in the end, is not whether it is effective, since by most accounts it is, but how we might replicate its success more broadly.

Waters has continued to create allied programs elsewhere, including the Yale Sustainable Food Project (which she began when her daughter, Fanny, was a freshman in New Haven), the Rome Sustainable Food Project at the American Academy, and "Edible Education 101" at UC Berkeley.

But *Edible Schoolyard*, the book, is not meant to be an instruction manual for how to accomplish a similar project, and it fails to address how another school might fund such a project without a celebrity chef to attract donations. Still, it can be done, as evidenced by the many Edible Schoolyards now in place at schools all around the world, including two right here in Saint Paul.

Christopher Alexander, I think, would be impressed, as would my mom.

COOKING IN TIMES OF CHANGE

One commonality between how my great-grandmother, my grandmother, and my mother all cooked was that none of them used recipes. I hadn't known this about my grandparents until my mom pointed it out, and I never paid much attention to how my mom cooked while I was growing up. But after I left home and began to cook for myself, it occurred to me that she owned very few cookbooks and rarely used the ones she did own.

When I asked my dad why we had so few cookbooks in the house, his answer instantly made sense: "the recipe was on the side of the box."

"If you live and cook the same way your grandmother did, you'll probably never open a cookbook," the writer John Lanchester smartly observed. "Cookbooks, and everything they symbolize, are for people who don't live the way their grandparents did. Once upon a time, food was about where you came from. Now, for many of us, it is about where we want to go—about who we want to be, how we choose to live" (37).

Like most Americans, my mother didn't live the way her grandparents did, and this was unquestionably by choice. She was the youngest of eight children from that Dutch-Irish farming family, and she often spoke of the hardships of rural living.

"My father's life was work," she wrote me a few years ago. "He once told me that anyone who had a suntan that was not from riding a tractor was not good for much. We never took a vacation—never heard of summer vacation, skiing, or going to the beach (although they were all around us).

"For the small farmer to succeed," she continued, "it took lots of hard work and cooperative weather. One good rainy season and a long, cold winter with electricity costs could be devastating. A damaged crop meant not much in the silos (we had two), or a dry season meant buying water for the cattle if the creek dried up. One season we had to pay for water for the house and water for the animals—no profit. My sister tells me that when she was in school she had two skirts and two tops. I have to say—I did not have much more. Shoes (one pair) were bought at the beginning of the school year for each and that was it. I wore brown oxfords (tie ups) for many years."

It would be difficult to argue that my mom should have stayed in her hometown and toughed it out for the sake of some romanticized version of rural life, when the reality was nothing short of punishing. In fact, five of her six brothers made the same choice as she did and left home as soon as they could, to avoid having to work on the farm.

"When I left there were three stores, hotel, post office, and the church," my mom reported. "Now—no church, no stores, no hotel—just the P.O. in a house and the firehouse."

It's possible, certainly, that my mom could have become an early version of an "urban homesteader," planting a garden, canning vegetables, and baking her own bread from scratch (Coyne and Knutzen). But that would have been difficult to do in suburban New Jersey, especially for someone with a full-time job in the professional middle class. Instead, she did what so many late twentieth-century women did: she let corporations cook for her instead.

In bringing the lessons of France home to the United States, Alice Waters gradually moved from applying these lessons at Chez Panisse to sharing them with a broader readership, which included not only children (in the form of her children's books and the Edible Schoolyard) but also adults (in the form of cookbooks for amateur adult cooks).

Since the first *Chez Panisse Menu Cookbook* was published in 1982, the restaurant has been a veritable cookbook-making machine, pumping out volumes on almost every aspect of food preparation. Each of these have involved Waters in some capacity, although several were written principally by others who worked at the restaurant, including Paul Bertolli, who wrote *Chez Panisse Cooking* (1994), and Lindsey Shere, who authored *Chez Panisse Desserts* (1994).

In addition to these, there have been *Chez Panisse Pasta, Pizza, and Calzone* (1984), the *Chez Panisse Café Cookbook* (1999), *Chez Panisse Vegetables* (2014), and *Chez Panisse Fruit* (2014). And many Chez Panisse alumni—including Deborah Madison, David Lebovitz, Judy Rodgers, and Samin Nosrat, among others—have gone on to write their own award-winning cookbooks as chefs, restaurateurs, and prominent figures in the food business.

None of these books, however, were owned by my mom. What she did own, and what now sits on my kitchen bookshelf, is a hardcover first edition of *The French Chef Cookbook* (1968), by Julia Child, which collects almost all of the recipes Child used on the black-and-white seasons of her popular television series, *The French Chef,* which ran from 1963 to 1966 on PBS. (The show returned for four more seasons, in color, from 1970 to 1973.) With its distinctive red-and-white cover, *The French Chef Cookbook* is a more accessible condensation of *Mastering the Art of French Cooking,* since it includes many of the most popular recipes Child wrote for the first volume, which appeared in 1961, as well as many of the recipes she was testing for the second volume, published in 1970.

It's helpful, I think, to compare Child's cookbooks to those of Richard Olney, since Olney had such an influence on Alice Waters. John Birdsall puts it this way: "Julia's *Mastering the Art of French Cooking* reads like a technical manual you prop open when obliged to cook for your husband's boss; *Simple French Food* is a manifesto for living. In 1974, you couldn't just drive to the A&P and buy a bunch of ingredients to start cooking like Olney. You had to begin by changing your life" (Birdsall).

Paging through *The French Chef Cookbook,* I can't think of a single dish from it that I was served when I was younger, and the book itself appears spotless, unlike the pages of my own sauce-splattered cookbooks. Perhaps this was because my mom was never obliged to cook for her husband's boss, since she was too busy working for her own. Still, Birdsall's point is well taken: Child and Olney—and by extension, Waters—were very different kinds of cooks.

Just as Waters democratized the expansive understanding of *terroir* she acquired in France through Chez Panisse and the Edible Schoolyard, her cookbooks helped to democratize what I have been calling her style of "elemental cooking"—though this did not happen all at once. Like any evolutionary process, it happened slowly over time, but we can mark its progress through moments in two key texts: *The Chez Panisse Menu Cookbook* and *The Art of Simple Food.*

For all its debts to Olney, *The Chez Panisse Menu Cookbook* is significant in its own right for documenting the development of California cuisine, or the application of French and, later, Italian techniques to California ingredients. The cookbook chronicles the first decade of Chez Panisse, from its opening in 1971 to the book's publication in 1982, a period that roughly overlaps with my first decade as well.

One reason my mom did not own a copy of *The Chez Panisse Menu Cookbook* is that it was not written for someone like her. She did, however, own another cookbook published that same year—*The Silver Palate Cookbook*—and the differences between the two books are revealing.

Named after the celebrated food shop on Manhattan's Upper West Side, *The Silver Palate* was written for the home cook, with the goal of bringing "gourmet" food to the masses. Coauthored by Sheila Lukins and Julee Rosso (Lukins was the primary cook, while Rosso ran the business), *The Silver Palate* quickly became the culinary bible for a new generation of working women in the 1980s. Where Julia Child encouraged cooks to replicate the exhaustive, and exhausting, methods of the French kitchen, and Molly Katzen's *Moosewood Cookbook* (1977) popularized a style of vegetarian cooking that was heavy on both the palate and the waistline, *The Silver Palate* offered a third way, something lighter, easier, and more accessible. "We hope our approach will encourage you to entertain more often and show you how it can be done beautifully as well as simply," the authors wrote in their preface (vii). The strategy worked, with millions of copies of the book in print and their signature chicken Marbella (with its then-bold flavors of prunes, olives, and capers) served at fashionable dinner parties across the country during the Reagan years.

The Chez Panisse Menu Cookbook was after something different, more an attempt to cement the restaurant's legacy than a West Coast competitor to the *Joy of Cooking*. (Compare *The New Basics Cookbook*, which Lukins and Rosso published in 1989 and which became the go-to gift for Gen X weddings and graduations.) Although the *Silver Palate* included occasional menus ("First Day of Spring Buffet," "Fourth of July Picnic," etc.), these were more an afterthought, suggestions printed in the sidebars rather than the organizing principle of the book. *The Chez Panisse Menu Cookbook,* in contrast, was a menu-driven affair, reflecting not only the influence of Richard Olney on the restaurant but also the fact that this was a cookbook shaped by a *restaurant*. Menus might be useful for home entertaining, but my mom was not interested in planning a multicourse meal after a long day at work. *The Silver Palate*'s "chicken with lemon and herbs," however, she could handle.

The frequency with which citrus, fresh herbs, and garlic appear in *The Silver Palate* is itself testament to the way California cuisine had begun to infiltrate dishes across the country, including on the East Coast. And few restaurants were as influential in driving that trend as Chez Panisse. Yet *The Chez Panisse Menu Cookbook* is not so much a handbook to this style of cooking as it is an aestheticized portrait of its rough birth.

The central tension at the heart of the book is between the restaurant's early interest in French techniques and methods and the *terroir* on which French regional cooking relied. Which is more important—the method or the ingredients—and how much should cooks adapt to the ingredients found in their own backyards? That the ingredients eventually won, along with the style of elemental cooking they enabled, was not a foregone conclusion but one born of practical necessity.

"The plans to make our own culinary region was [*sic*] not so much then a conscious movement as a race to have quality fresh ingredients available in enough quantity to keep up with more and more ambitious menus," claimed Jeremiah Tower, the restaurant's legendary early chef, in his self-aggrandizing memoir, *California Dish* (96–97).

Tower joined Chez Panisse in 1973, and he quickly came to exert his influence over the restaurant, pushing it away from its original roots in French provincial cooking toward more and more ambitious dishes in the style of Escoffier. Yet he was also deeply influenced by Richard Olney, and on a memorable trip to Provence in October of 1975 (following Waters's own trip there in August), Tower discovered just how important local ingredients can be. While visiting Olney in Sollies-Toucas, where the two became lovers, Tower was shocked to find that a fishmonger would not sell Olney a fish because the fish were "foreign"—that is, caught more than twelve kilometers from the shop (97–98). Olney later took Tower to Domaine Tempier, where they feasted on "sea bass cooked on a fire of dried vine cuttings served with a sauce of its roe made in a huge marble mortar, spit-roasted leg of lamb, and a deeply ripe and perfect apricot tart" (98). Tower recounts how in 1976, after his return from Provence, he then "realized I had been improvising for years, so why fret any longer about the authenticity of 'French' ingredients for French regional food? Why not just go shopping in Northern California and call that the region?" (107).

This evolution in Tower's thinking eventually culminated in the celebrated menu for "The Northern California Regional Dinner" on October 7, 1976, which is reprinted in *The Chez Panisse Menu Cookbook* (260). In a style that has now become cliché, the menu indicates the sourcing of local ingredients for almost every course, including the California wines that were served throughout:

- Tomales Bay Bluepoint Oysters on Ice
- Cream of Fresh Corn Soup, Mendocino Style, with Crayfish Butter
- Big Sur Garrapata Creek Smoked Trout Steamed over California Bay Leaves
- Monterey Bay Prawns Sautéed with Garlic, Parsley, and Butter
- Preserved California-Grown Geese from Sebastopol
- Vela Dry Monterey Jack Cheese from Sonoma
- Fresh Caramelized Figs
- Walnuts, Almonds, and Mountain Pears from the San Francisco Farmers' Market

Waters annotates the menu this way: "This regional dinner, conceived and prepared by Jeremiah Tower, marked a turning point in the restaurant's focus. This was the first time we made a really concerted effort to serve the ingredients available to us here in the Northern California area, and it truly set a precedent which has been followed since then. It was an extremely well composed and executed meal, and was successful from the point of the reception it received. I can say that with some authority, since I actually sat in the dining room and ate this meal, a rare experience for me at my own restaurant!" (260).

Many of the dishes that have now come to be associated with California cuisine were the result not of Chez Panisse proper in the 1970s, however, but the Chez Panisse Café, which opened above the more formal restaurant in

1980 and offered service à la carte rather than from a set menu. "It was at Chez Panisse Café that California cuisine got a focus in the nomenclature," said Clark Wolf, a former manager of the San Francisco Oakville Grocery, in conversation with Joyce Goldstein. "Downstairs was experimental and emotional and metaphorical; it was too intellectual, it was university. It was based on French structure and codification. At the Café, cooks thought, 'I'm going to make a simple salad but every time I touch these leaves, they will be special.' Upstairs worked from the produce sheet, whereas downstairs worked from a concept of French food" (Goldstein 28).

Wolf exaggerates, to be sure, but the influence of the Café on the restaurant's reputation—and menus—is unquestionable. Throughout the late 1970s and early 1980s, the introduction of pizza, pasta, and other Italian dishes gradually loosened the grip of haute cuisine on the restaurant (Tower left Chez Panisse in 1978). Notably, those shifting interests were also symbolized by a shift in language, with bilingual menus being replaced with English-only menus for a time (Freedman 395–96).

Most accounts of California cuisine focus on whether Waters or Tower should ultimately be credited for its development, as well as the conflicts that resulted from their growing celebrity. But both chefs agree that "California cuisine" is not really a *cuisine* at all, at least not in the strictest sense of the term.

"For me, a *cuisine* takes the test of time," Waters told Andrew Friedman. "When you talk about Chinese cuisine or even Italian cuisine, we're talking hundreds, thousands of years. It's sort of presumptuous to think that we could define a kind of cooking in California that has these qualities about it that are enduring. I think what I was thinking about, that's been confused with California cuisine, is a *philosophy* of food. And that's what is enduring, and that is what certainly we've tried to express. It's about what is found locally, what is cooked simply, what is seasonal and ripe, what is pure and grown correctly—that's all part of a philosophy of food and can be applied to any food" (A. Friedman 300–301).

Tower made much the same point: "*California cuisine* is not the right term because it wasn't a cuisine; it was a mind-set which was the only one I knew because I grew up in Europe, which is that the menu is done from the marketplace. . . . So it was really restating what was completely obvious to every

French grandmother for the last five hundred years. It was an *approach* to cooking" (A. Friedman 301).

Waters's eventual interest in organic ingredients emerged out of this focus on the restaurant's local environment, yet "local" and "organic" are decidedly not the same thing. If the Northern California Regional Dinner was the result of French country cooking techniques applied in a North American context, concern about organic production practices was the result of trying to practice this kind of elemental cooking in an increasingly compromised world.

Warnings about the problems of industrial agriculture had been growing more and more common in the 1960s and 1970s, through the influence of Rachel Carson's *Silent Spring,* Frances Moore Lappé's *Diet for a Small Planet,* and Wendell Berry's *The Unsettling of America,* as we have seen. And Waters certainly embraced the organic movement's calls for food grown without synthetic pesticides, herbicides, and fertilizers. But like Berry, Waters championed a more expansive understanding of "organic" food, which resulted directly from her passion for regional French cooking and the concept of *terroir.*

Trying to explain why the organic movement had not taken off in France in the same way it did in the United States, former Chez Panisse pastry chef David Lebovitz speculates, "Maybe it's because the French never strayed that much from their agricultural roots to begin with. Farmhouse cheeses and good breads are easily available, even in supermarkets, and wine is chosen based on the region, not by the grape variety (which is changing, in a rare nod to globalization). Most French chefs seem primarily interested in the *terroir,* that vaguely-translatable term that means that the product is a sum of the elements from where it's grown; the soil, the climate, the cultivation techniques . . . the 'territory' of origin, gives food its certain *'Je ne sais quoi'*" ("Paris Organics").

If French country cooking is elemental cooking, then elemental cooking is ultimately *cuisine du terroir*—a concept that the term "local food" doesn't quite capture. It's the difference between an obsession with distance, travel time, and freshness—and *flavor.* In this sense, the celebration of *terroir* is a reaction against industrialization, standardization, and the quantification of quality; it is about particularities over generalizations, and specificity over homogeneity. *Terroir* is not only about place, however, but also about the people and the culture in that place. It is an "expression of landscape and the way that people make a living in it," as the food historian Ursula Heinzelmann said at a conference in Munich. As a result, she observed, "terroir can travel." In an American context, *terroir* thus represents a reaction against the uniformity of the American landscape and the American way of eating. That the term "California cuisine" has become shorthand for "New American cooking" more generally is an irony not lost on me.

It's worth pausing for a moment to consider the form and function of the cookbook, particularly in the age of the Internet, when millions of recipes (some divine, some atrocious) are a mere Google search away. Of what value is a cookbook in such a world?

Cookbooks begin life as collections of menu items, of course, whether those be found in Lucy's kitchen notebook, Lulu's menu diary, or the menu notebook Waters kept throughout her time in the kitchen at Chez Panisse.

Yet as Susan J. Leonardi has observed, "a cookbook that consisted of nothing but rules for various dishes would be an unpopular cookbook indeed. Even the root of *recipe*—the Latin *recipere*—implies an exchange, a giver and a receiver. Like a story, a recipe needs a recommendation, a context, a point, a reason to be. A recipe is, then, an embedded discourse, and like other embedded discourses, it can have a variety of relationships with its frame, or its bed" (340).

All cookbooks, in other words, are flights of fantasy—offering page after page of ideal meals, their variations dependent on their ideals. Dinner in thirty minutes or less? A northern Italian feast? A menu of low-fat favorites? Whatever your desires, cookbooks can help you satisfy them, whether in imagination or in practice. They dangle the prospect of status, of health, of togetherness, of seduction. They offer inspiration and aspiration in a single volume. They are the ultimate how-to books for the domestic striver.

For this reason, reports of their demise have been greatly exaggerated. As Laura Shapiro put it, "Printed cookbooks have been defying their own death notices for years now, probably because they don't just offer recipes, they offer relationships. There's a person inside those covers—someone whose voice is appealing, whose guidance is reliable and whose food evokes the world you wish you lived in" (Shapiro).

Waters's cookbooks are also part of a subgenre of cookbooks written by celebrity chefs, which Waters herself helped to shape. According to Megan J. Elias in *Food on the Page: Cookbooks and American Culture*, "Although famous chefs and personalities like Duncan Hines had written popular cookbooks in the 1940s and 1950s, Waters introduced a new style in which the chef's personal philosophy was central to the engagement between reader and book. The book was possible because the restaurant had been successful and the restaurant had been successful because of one woman's vision of what food should be" (178).

Whether celebrity or not, every cookbook author must consider a host of questions about themselves and their readers, about the visions animating their work, and about the frames in which their recipes will be embedded, if they wish their book to be successful. For instance:

- For whom should the cookbook be written, and how much knowledge can its author assume this imagined reader may have?
- How should the book be organized, how much narrative should it contain, and how many recipes?
- How detailed, how systematic, and how standardized should those recipes be? How faithfully should it follow the format, standard since the nineteenth century, of a list of ingredients followed by the method of preparation, all using exact measurements?
- What ingredients should it assume a reader has on hand, and how expensive or exotic should any specialized ingredients be?
- Should it be chatty or formal, evocative or encyclopedic? Should it include or omit nutritional information? Should it feature photographs, line drawings, or other illustrations? Should all the recipes be original, or may some be versions of other authors' visions?

Women who write cookbooks have even more questions to consider about how the frame for their recipes might function. In *Eat My Words: Reading Women's Lives through the Cookbooks They Wrote*, Janet Theophano offers a feminist reading of women's cookbooks, for example, describing how these works can function as acts of community (11–48), collective memory and identity (49–84), and autobiography (117–54). Women's cookbooks, she says, "can be maps of the social and cultural worlds they inhabit" (13), can help women to "define themselves and their cultural groups, to preserve the past, and to shape the future" (51–52), and can function as acts of "autobiographical writing and self-representation" in which women write themselves into being (121). The cookbook form has also allowed women "to probe issues of social and cultural identity" (228) and has enabled recipes to operate as a "feminine discourse" (343).

As Theophano observes, Waters's cookbooks fulfill many of these functions as well, but I want to focus on three interrelated things I think they accomplish in the context of sustainability: I think Waters's cookbooks (1) convey an ethic and an aesthetic, (2) foster community, and (3) promote cooking as a practice.

If you could draw a straight line from Richard Olney's *French Menu Cookbook* to *The Chez Panisse Menu Cookbook*, a similar line might extend from Olney's *Simple French Food* to *The Art of Simple Food*, which appeared in 2007.

Unlike *The French Menu Cookbook*, Olney's *Simple French Food* concerned itself less with the harmonies of multicourse meals and more with the ingredients required of each individual dish. While the organization roughly follows the progression of the French menu, the focus is on the basics of French country cooking and the fundamental kitchen wisdom such cooking requires rather than on the experience of assembling a complete meal. Creating menus, cooking dishes, and mastering techniques are not mutually exclusive, of course, but Olney's two best-known cookbooks differ in the emphasis they place on each of these activities.

The same could be said of how *The Chez Panisse Menu Cookbook* differs from *The Art of Simple Food*. Where the *Menu Cookbook* is high-concept, *Simple Food* is the most democratic of all of Waters's cookbooks. It consciously pursues accessibility, and it defines quality food in terms of taste as a sensation rather than taste as a marker of class—a limitation from which the *Menu Cookbook* surely suffers.

That Waters would eventually follow *The Silver Palate*'s Lukins and Rosso in publishing her own version of *The New Basics* is not all that surprising, considering that she herself learned to cook from reading cookbooks and opened Chez Panisse in a converted house. Writing an instruction manual for the beginning home cook must have seemed the inevitable next step, even though doing so upended the expert-novice model of much culinary literature at the time, in which trained chefs shared their professional techniques with the unskilled masses.

Given the attention Waters pays to every last aspect of food preparation, it is also likely no accident that her title not only echoes Olney's *Simple French Food* but also clarifies that simplicity is often accompanied by, and sometimes even requires, artistry. We might ask, therefore, is Waters's food really that "simple"? And what does it mean to describe the process of creating it as an "art"?

Interestingly, one important difference between *The Chez Panisse Menu Cookbook* and *The Art of Simple Food* is the amount of time each book spends trying to answer such questions. As one of the first published cookbooks to contest the creeping industrialization of food and flavor, the *Menu Cookbook* included a five-page manifesto by Waters, "What I Believe about Cooking," which followed a shorter, separate introduction, also written by her. In the opening sentences of the manifesto, Waters offered a critique of mindless consumption that echoed nothing if not "Economy," the opening chapter of *Walden,* in which Thoreau excoriated his neighbors for living lives of "quiet desperation": "My approach to cooking is not radical or unconventional. It may seem so simply because we as a nation are so removed from any real involvement with the food we buy, cook, and consume. We have become alienated by the frozen and hygienically sealed foods. I want to stand in the supermarket aisles and implore the shoppers, their carts piled high with mass-produced artificiality, 'Please . . . look at what you are buying!'" (3).

Today we might call this "blaming the victim" and place the responsibility for poor eating habits more at the feet of corporations than consumers—not to mention acknowledging that flash-frozen vegetables can often be tasty, handy, and inexpensive substitutes for fresh produce. But in fact, it quickly became clear that the true target of Waters's critique was not consumers but "the alienation we suffer at the hands of the fast-food giants," whom she saw as responsible for "the distance they create and emphasize between the food and the diners" (3). In place of this alienation, Waters wanted to see *connection*—between people and their food, and between one another. How to do that? Through "the opening up of the senses on the part of the diners," which Waters hoped to re-create through her cookbook (4).

The Art of Simple Food builds on this premise, but it does so with a much lighter touch: a brief introduction that consists of three pages of text, followed by a two-page spread of Waters's nine "principles of good cooking," which I discussed earlier when defining "elemental cooking." These are Waters's ideals, which she began to articulate from her early years at the restaurant, as she described in the introduction to the *Menu Cookbook:* "We all believed in community and personal commitment and quality. Chez Panisse was born out of these ideals. Profit was always secondary" (x).

What becomes clear in *The Art of Simple Food* is that ethics and aesthetics cannot easily be separated for Waters, no more than they could for Wendell Berry. Food does not just have utilitarian value, as it offers more than mere sustenance. When we cook at home, especially, we are not concerned about making money: we do not cook to make a profit but to make something beautiful—sometimes for ourselves, but usually for the people we love. Food also has an aesthetic value, as expressed through gastronomy, which is connected to its intrinsic value as a part of our wider, living world. This was one of the key lessons Waters took away from her time in France: that cooking and eating are about much more than just food.

One way Waters expresses her appreciation for aesthetics is in the design of the books themselves, which stand out in a sea of competing volumes for their elegance and simplicity. The *Menu Cookbook* was designed and illustrated by David Goines, a talented artist, calligrapher, and printer who had been a member of the Chez Panisse family from the start, including as one of Waters's lovers. *Simple Food* features illustrations by Patricia (Patty) Curtan, who also illustrated *Chez Panisse Fruit* and *Chez Panisse Vegetables*. Waters discussed the importance of the design of her books in *Coming to My Senses*, noting that "the way you communicate is almost as important as *what* you're communicating. It's what Marshall McLuhan said: the medium is the message" (131). The cookbooks, she added, "come from a place of trying to inform rather than to indoctrinate—not shouting at people, the way advertisements do, but inviting them in, seducing them with illustrations. You don't want to overdesign—you want to maintain clarity and simplicity. It's hard for me to read something that's cluttered, with loud colors. It gets too confusing" (131–32). Again with the seduction!

Like its design, *Simple Food* aims for its recipes to be simple as well, certainly compared to the four pages of instructions for bouillabaisse found in the *Menu Cookbook* (176–79). In fact, as a book for beginning cooks, it is likely *too* simple for more experienced hands in the kitchen, and its competition is closer to Mark Bittman's *How to Cook Everything: Simple Recipes for Great Food* (1998) than to more specialized volumes devoted to particular ingredients or culinary traditions. The first part of the book, for example, includes instructions on how to build a basic pantry, select kitchen equipment, plan a menu, and even pack a lunch. It also includes recipes for a number of foundational dishes—such as risotto, roast chicken, and an omelet—which illustrate essential cooking techniques, while the second part features additional recipes that build on these techniques.

Nevertheless, the simplicity of the title is not so much opposed to complexity as it is aligned with authenticity and democracy. As Waters puts it, "When you have the best and tastiest ingredients, you can cook very simply and the food will be extraordinary because it tastes like what it is. . . . But food like this is not just the privilege of a restaurant like ours. The same local producers sell the same fresh food down the street at the farmer's market. And anyone can buy it" (3–4). The "art" of simple food is similarly available to all: "You don't need years of culinary training, or rare and costly foodstuffs, or an encyclopedic knowledge of world cuisines. You need only your five senses" (5). In short, by focusing on "simple" food, Waters is articulating two essential aspects of her food philosophy: that simple food allows the original flavors of the food to manifest themselves, and that simple food is accessible to anyone. And all without preaching.

The second thing Waters's cookbooks accomplish is to foster community, although this value may be less visible to the reader than the obvious aesthetics of each text.

This community takes at least three different forms.

First, there is the fact that writing the cookbook is itself a community effort. As Waters explained to Danika Worthington, "I do it with a lot of people. A *lot* of people. So I'm out all the time, trying to think of an idea and I'm just kind of canvassing everybody I know and asking them how they cooked the kale or how they make the Brussels sprouts. I find the person who can illustrate it really well. I have somebody who tests the recipes. I have someone who writes narratively really well. And somebody who's very good at organization. We do it as a whole group." While this social context is often minimized in the cookbooks themselves, in favor of strong first-person narration by Waters, the effect is nevertheless to mimic the back-and-forth of in-person recipe-sharing from which cookbooks first emerged and to extend *La famille Panisse* (the network of Chez Panisse) to everyday cooks. In the introduction to *Simple Food,* for instance, Waters describes her food philosophy using the first-person plural—"This is what we've learned at Chez Panisse after years of sourcing, preparing, and tasting food" (3)—and explains that "By choosing to buy food grown locally and sustainably, in ways that are healthy and humane, I had woven myself into a community that cares about the same things" (4).

Waters's cookbooks thus attempt to put her ideas about community into practice, adapting the communal experiences in her restaurants for the home kitchen, along with her ideas about ethical sourcing. In so doing, she illustrates a second idea about community: that it requires specificity, fostering relationships and connecting with people in a particular place. Sharing additional resources for readers to consult at the end of *Simple Food*, Waters writes, "Don't forget . . . that the benefits of shopping locally at farmers' markets include learning about the agriculture of your own locality directly from the farmer—not to mention participating in a real community rather than a virtual one" (389). There is an *intimacy* to Waters's approach to cooking that her belief in the power of seduction also reveals. "It's not that I *can't* eat a meal by myself. I can," she writes in *Coming to My Senses*. "But I really like to sit down to a meal with a friend. There's something about having that enjoyment reflected back at you, when you can feel that mutualism, that shared understanding" (16).

A challenge for Waters, however, concerns the third aspect of community her cookbooks seek to foster, which is the larger nonhuman community of which our kitchens and restaurants are a part. Despite her best intentions, it is difficult to "scale up" the intimacies she values to address the web of relationships between people and the rest of the living world on a global level. In one of her more memorable statements, Waters once told Marian Burros that "when you eat and care about [people's] nourishment around the table, . . . the bigger table is the community," and it's clear that for Waters this community also encompasses the nonhuman world. The companion volume to *Simple Food*—*The Art of Simple Food II*, published in 2013—attempts to address this wider community more directly, but it mostly limits itself to guidelines for the creation and maintenance of a kitchen garden. Nevertheless, a glimmer of what could be comes in the form of Waters's description of the "most fascinating and important fact" she has learned from Bob Cannard, who has supplied Chez Panisse with its produce for decades. This fact is "that well-tended garden soil is filled with a vast, teeming underground ecosystem of tiny creatures that work together to create the nutrient-rich conditions in which his delicious produce grows" (361).

These are cookbooks, after all, and not postmodern novels or treatises on natural history or political economy, so it may be too much to ask that they feature "ecological storytelling," "multispecies storytelling," or "networked narratives." Still, considering that the kitchen is ultimately a site of transformation, they could likely do more to reflect the *influence* of the non-human world in making that transformation possible, to show the *animacy* of California and other environments in a meaningful way, and to illustrate how cooks everywhere might work in *partnership* with those environments and other humans in building a more sustainable world. Despite these limitations, Waters's cookbooks still constitute a kind of instruction manual for the sustainable kitchen (à la Catharine Beecher), and it is clear that their publication can influence consumption choices, and thus purchasing practices, and ultimately production and distribution decisions. Like building a market for recycled paper one ream at a time, Waters's cookbooks can help to foster a community that values organic produce, local foods, and maybe even that "underground ecosystem of tiny creatures" around the world.

To accomplish any of this, however, people first must cook, and then cook some more, and then continue to cook until it becomes second nature. They must engage directly with the diversity of the living world as represented by food, and they must experience it through all their senses. This is the third, and possibly most important, function of Waters's cookbooks: to promote cooking as a practice.

To understand cooking as an art means to see it as a skill attained through practice: through repeated exercise to attain proficiency. "Ideas of what to cook come from [thinking about food] and from practice," Waters says in *Simple Food;* "certainly, you have to spend time in the kitchen before your own ideas come easily and before putting together a menu becomes instinctive. The way I think about food and cooking comes from years of experience; by now it's second nature" (9).

Practice reflects another key component of Waters's philosophy: valuing *process* (the process of running a restaurant or cooking at home) at least as much as *product* (the food itself). Seeing cooking as a process with which to engage, rather than a task to be accomplished, is certainly more accurate, as cooking is not a single activity but a series of actions that are repeated meal after meal: chopping onions, braising meat, kneading dough. The French term *mise en place* (putting in place), or the practice of preparing one's ingredients before cooking, also suggests the importance of seeing cooking as a process with multiple components.

Focusing on cooking as a process also helps illustrate how the grammatical status of "food" may be part of the problem with the term "sustainable food." Whereas *food* is a noun, *cook* is a verb, which aligns much better with what the idea of *terroir* is trying to capture. Not just a marketing tool or way to distinguish "authenticity," *terroir* is instead an attempt to emphasize the *activity* of the soil: "the conditions in which a food is grown or produced and that give the food its unique characteristics" (dictionary.com). The point, in other words, is that the environment is the active agent: *it* produces the flavor, not us.

Seeing cooking as a practice helps reorient our ideas about food in other ways as well. For one thing, seeing cooking as a practice teaches you to be present and mindful, which in turn makes you a better cook. When Lucy Vanel instructs you to tell the doneness of a dish by smell rather than by time, you know you had better be *present* in the kitchen if this is going to work. Likewise, when Waters tells you to let taste be your guide—"Taste as you go. Keep tasting and practicing and discovering" (7)—you know you won't be able to just "set it and forget it." Living in the moment can not only keep one's mind from obsessing over the past or worrying about the future; it can also create the conditions for being in community. As Edward Espe Brown observes in *No Recipe: Cooking as Spiritual Practice*: "Entering the sacred space of the kitchen, we don't know what will happen. We shift from the preoccupation of being in control to the focus of being in connection" (6).

Acting mindfully in the kitchen can also return a degree of imprecision and spontaneity to food preparation, which aligns with Waters's disdain for many of the so-called "improvements" that modern kitchen gadgets have introduced into cooking. "My friends tease me and call me a Luddite because I don't particularly like even small electrical appliances," she admits in *Simple Food*. "Instead, I love to use a mortar and pestle and have hands-on contact with the food" (22).

Notably, Waters's antimodernism has its roots in an important transition in French home cooking, which Luce Giard documented in *The Practice of Everyday Life*, her landmark work of French sociology, which she coauthored with Michel de Certeau and Pierre Mayol. Generalizing from a series of twelve interviews conducted across the country in the 1970s, Giard observed how both French cooking and recipe-writing were changing as a result of industrialization:

> The entrance of these [modern] appliances into kitchens has changed
> the procedures of preparation, cooking, and preserving; it has thus had
> a direct effect on the language of recipes. It has introduced the quanti-
> fication and unification of measures (weight and volume), as well as the
> precision of cooking times and temperatures. Hence, a certain impoverish-
> ment of vocabulary and the erasing of numerous small procedures (how
> to know how hot an oven is, how to avoid having mayonnaise turn, how to
> successfully make whipped cream) whose secret will disappear along with
> the memory of the older generation. . . . The generalization of a written
> transmission in place of oral communication entails a profound reworking
> of culinary knowledge, a distancing of tradition, just as pronounced as the
> movement from the soup pot in a hearth or on the wood stove to electric
> or gas appliances. (Certeau, Giard, and Mayol 220–21)

What is especially inspiring is Giard's observation of how her interview-
ees actively resisted the advent of consumer society through the creative
activity involved in their everyday practices. As Giard explained, "There is
a profound pleasure in achieving by oneself what one offers to one's guests,
in practicing a modest inventiveness, in ephemeral results, but whose subtle
combination silently defines a *lifestyle,* circumscribes one's *own space*" (Certeau, Giard, and Mayol 213). Seeing cooking as a practice thus has the potential to return a degree of control to the individual, to empower each person to
make their own decisions about what to cook, rather than to let corporations
cook for us. Attending to "kitchen craft" can certainly save money and time,
as Tom Philpott has pointed out, but it can also make us better citizens, as
Michael Pollan has observed (Philpott, "Recipes"; Pollan, *Cooked*). It's not
just that you can't eat farm-to-table if you can't cook; it's that you regain
some of your own autonomy if you do.

Like my dad, my mom was a member of the "Silent Generation" that grew up
during World War II and came of age during the postwar period. As a group,
she and her peers were described as hardworking, thrifty, and conformist in
their outlook, and this generalization certainly fit my mom's behavior.

After she retired, however, my mom realized that she had lost something
by outsourcing much of her food preparation to others, and that cooking
need not be an all-or-nothing endeavor. There was a space, in other words,

between cooking three meals a day for a large farm family, like her mother did, and taking pleasure, and even a little bit of pride, in baking a halfway-decent apple crisp to bring to a church potluck.

By the end of her life, my mom had developed her own modest collection of cookbooks (including a shiny new copy of *The Joy of Cooking*), and she saved many more recipes from the pages of women's magazines, including *Good Housekeeping, Family Circle,* and *Martha Stewart Living.*

After she died of ovarian cancer at age seventy-nine, I knew I couldn't keep all her recipes and cookbooks, so I chose a few that had either practical or sentimental value and donated the rest.

The most meaningful, of course, were the Christmas cookie recipes she had baked with my daughter: Dorie Greenspan's celebrated "World Peace Cookies," a gingerbread recipe from *Cook's Illustrated,* and a recipe for cranberry-pistachio lace cookies from *Good Housekeeping,* which they made in addition to traditional rolled sugar cookies.

Another valuable book I retained was her church cookbook, in which she had bookmarked her favorite recipes for apple cake (by her friend Doris Singer), marbled fudge bars (by her friend Phyllis Hughes), and pumpkin bars (by fellow churchgoer Evelyn Pallas). "Good," my mom wrote in the margin of the pumpkin bar recipe, circling the word for emphasis.

What my mom didn't have, even though she knew of my interest in them, were any cookbooks by Alice Waters. Why was that, I wonder, and what might my grandmother or great-grandmother have made of Waters's cookbooks? Would they have found them useful, pointless, precious, or absurd?

My mother, I suspect, simply wanted something more mainstream, more straight-ahead, guides to the kind of respectable upper-middle-class table she sought to set more than anything having to do with sustainability. As for what my grandmother or great-grandmother might have thought, I truly don't know.

But thinking about Waters's cookbooks in the context of my mom made me wonder: If Waters' cookbooks didn't appeal to her, who else might they not appeal to? And what might this say about the way Waters's arguments are received more generally?

One of the more important concepts to emerge from legal studies in the last few decades is the idea of "intersectionality," a term Kimberlé Crenshaw coined in 1989 to describe how race, class, gender, and other markers of human identity "intersect" to create more complex dynamics that might otherwise not be recognized if these same characteristics were viewed in isolation from one another (Crenshaw).

Gender does not exist apart from other features of identity, in other words, so we would do well to remember that Alice Waters is also cooking *white* food and promoting an *aspirational class identity*. Some of the strongest critiques of Waters come from these two perspectives, and it is worth considering why.

Julie Guthman's critique of "The Unbearable Whiteness of Alternative Food" (2011), for example, could be applied as much to Waters as it was to Wendell Berry, given that Waters's texts assume a largely white readership. Guthman puts the problem this way: "many of the discourses of alternative food hail a white subject and thereby code the practices and spaces of alternative food as white. Insofar as this coding has a chilling effect on people of color, it not only works as an exclusionary practice, it also colors the character of food politics more broadly and thus may work against a more transformative politics" (264). We need to take "a less messianic approach to food politics," she suggests, and "do something different than 'invite others to the table,' an increasingly common phrase in considering the ways to address diversity in alternative food movements" (264). Acknowledging intersectionality, she continues, will be a vital part of the solution. "My underlying concern is that because alternative food tends to attract whites more than others, whites continue to define the rhetoric, spaces, and broader projects of agrifood transformation. . . . The current menu reflects a fairly delimited conception of the politics of the possible, with a tremendous emphasis on market-driven alternatives, which often take root in the most well-resourced localities" (277).

Peter Naccarato and Kathleen LeBesco lodge a similar critique against Julia Child in *Culinary Capital,* arguing that Child promotes an aspirational class identity much like Waters appears to do. While they admit that Child functions as a "gender outlaw" (237), they claim that she provides consumers "with an illusion of access that contradicts the reality of their class position" (224). It may be, they argue, "that consumers of food culture are seduced less by recipes, and more by the imagined status that food culture claims to confer," and they claim that "food culture offers those consumers illusory access to 'culinary capital' as they use food and food practices as vehicles for performing an imagined class identity" (224). Examining multiple examples from Child's cookbooks, television shows, and life, they suggest that this evidence contradicts what others have seen as her apparent democratizing of food, not unlike what Waters has attempted to do.

Both of these critiques get at something fundamental: you can't eat farm-to-table if you can't afford it, or if you live in a food desert, or if the structure of the food system prevents it. It's not about choice, in other words, but about the *constraints* on choice. It's about who holds power in the food system to shape individual decisions about consumption (Patel).

Two more recent critiques of sustainable food discourse could also be applied to Waters, as she is one of the leading figures in what she calls the "delicious revolution."

One comes from S. Margot Finn, who argues in "Food Injustice: What the Food Movement Misses about Poverty and Inequality" that the kind of work Waters has done with the Edible Schoolyard might actually be making things worse. As Finn puts it, "demands for food justice are too often based on assumptions about health, sustainability, and equity that actually *reinforce* inequality while doing little to meaningfully improve health outcomes for low-income communities of color or reduce damage to the environment. A food justice movement that takes seriously the problems of equity, health, and sustainability will need to start asking harder questions about what counts as good food, and who should get to define what counts as *goodness* and *justice* when it comes to food for low-income communities of color." (This claim builds on the argument she made in *Discriminating Taste*, that class anxiety created the food revolution, which I think somewhat simplifies the complex dynamics at work in the movement and undervalues the sustainability concerns driving many of its adherents.)

Another comes from the authors of *Pressure Cooker: Why Home Cooking Won't Solve Our Problems and What We Can Do about It*, who are critical of claims that returning to the kitchen will solve our social problems, especially those that relate to gender and class. Summarizing an early version of their argument in "The Joy of Cooking?" they question "why the frontline in reforming the food system has to be in someone's kitchen. The emphasis on home cooking ignores the time pressures, financial constraints, and feeding challenges that shape the family meal. Yet this is the widely promoted standard to which all mothers are held. Our conversations with mothers of young children show us that this emerging standard is a tasty illusion, one that is moralistic, and rather elitist, instead of a realistic vision of cooking today.

Intentionally or not, it places the burden of a healthy home-cooked meal on women" (25).

The kitchen, in short, is not the panacea that people like Waters seem to think it is.

What are we to make of such critiques?

Waters has at least as many defenders as she does critics, and some of them suggest that at least a few of these critiques may be asking too much of someone who has already contributed a great deal to the movement for a more sustainable way of eating.

David Lebovitz, for example, writing on his blog in 2007, affirms that:

> Alice is an idealist, which is someone who imagines things that are . . .
> "ideal." We need people like that. If no one imagined anything but what
> already existed, or nixed any new ideas, we wouldn't have telephones,
> electricity, flour, tires, espresso makers, and the Spice Girls reunion. . . .
> So when Alice goes on television and presides over a display of gorgeous
> produce, or celebrates the glory of farm-fresh produce at the Greenmarket,
> why the criticism? Would we all be better off if she hadn't spent the past
> thirty years advocating for better-quality and safer foods? . . . Should we
> simply throw up our hands and say, "*Oh, she's so out of touch with reality!*"
> and simply accept rock-hard strawberries in January, pesticide-laden veg-
> etables, corn syrup injected dinners, or factory-raised beef slaughtered in
> the most inhumane, filthy conditions imaginable? . . . Should we give up?
> Or maybe can we perhaps incorporate her ideas and work towards making
> them a reality and within reach of everyone, no matter what their income
> level, instead of squabbling about them and criticizing someone's effort
> at making the positive changes which have and will continue to positively
> affect our food supply. ("My View")

In her memoir *Spoon Fed: How Eight Cooks Saved My Life*, Kim Severson likewise declares that much criticism of Waters "seems unfair. Alice is quite aware that she runs a restaurant where the food costs a lot of money and that her worldview is that of a privileged white woman, but she works hard to broaden her perspective. She thinks quite a bit about how to get good food to people without the means to eat at places like Chez Panisse. And I have never heard her claim to be responsible for the food revolution" (69).

Finally, Josée Johnston urges us to reject the stereotype of the "foodie" as "an oblivious, white bourgeois jerk," who "assumes that all people have access to fresh food, a decent kitchen, an appreciation for farmers' markets and fresh herbs, and hold an undue faith in the transformative power of home cooking." Yes, Johnston admits, "these kinds of people exist. But foodie culture is complex and diverse, and also includes people of color, eaters with limited financial resources, men who value home cooking, and consumers who are deeply critical of the social and ecological injustices of the mainstream food system" (97). Though she may fit some aspects of the foodie stereotype, Waters has also worked hard to combat this image and diversify the movement, and she certainly deserves credit for those efforts.

Besides, writes Johnston, "food pleasures can serve as an entry point into food politics. This is certainly not an automatic pathway, but sometimes the pleasures of eating and cooking connect to critical, collective approaches—newcomer kitchens and community gardens, food gleaning projects and canning workshops, public school cooking classes and incubator kitchens. Home cooking certainly won't solve all of our problems, but maybe, just maybe, food can be an element of collective strategies that mobilize joy, build off of foodie passions, and give people a sense of hope in politically dark times" (97).

The kitchen, in short, may still be our best way forward.

My mom died a few years ago, just before Christmas, after living with ovarian cancer for six years, and in a brutal twist of fate, she was diagnosed with a complication known as MBO, or malignant bowel obstruction. She had not digested food since before Thanksgiving, and as a result she was literally dying of hunger.

At the side of her bed hung a gastrostomy bag, which was connected to a tube that emerged from her stomach. The tube allowed her to savor the pleasure of food without vomiting, since her intestines were blocked in multiple places by the cancer. Without the tube, any food she consumed had only one place to go: up and out.

Much of what she ate was by necessity prepared food, first in the hospital, and then at home, where I was living with my parents to care for my mom during her final weeks of life. She especially liked pureed tomato soup from a box—organic, but still industrial—and because the soup could easily fit through the tube, that was what I made her, along with the strong drip coffee she had consumed throughout her life.

One night, however, I decided to bake banana bread, as my dad had purchased bananas just before my mom's hospice began, and the fruit had been sitting uneaten on the counter ever since.

In a kind of tribute to my mom's cooking preferences, I found Martha Stewart's recipe for banana bread and collected the wet ingredients from the refrigerator: a stick of butter, two eggs, and some sour cream. I then gathered the dry ingredients from her baking cabinet: sugar, flour, baking soda, and salt.

The vanilla extract was nearby, but the chopped walnuts required some searching, since they were in another cabinet with a different set of supplies, including the cookie cutters my mom had used to bake Christmas cookies with my daughter the previous year.

As I worked, I looked in on my mom every few minutes to see how she was doing. Her cheeks were sunken, her eyelids closed, and her breathing had slowed into apnea. She was clearly growing weaker.

I buttered her bread pan—a beautiful blue stoneware dish—and lined it with parchment paper. I then preheated the oven, creamed the butter and sugar, and added the eggs.

When I put the mixing bowl down for the second time, however, something seemed off. The labored breathing that had been in the background of everything over the past few days was no more. The house, already quiet, had grown still.

Even before I went to check in on her again, I knew what I would find. My mom was gone.

After the prayers, the phone calls, the visit from the hospice nurse, and the departure of the funeral directors, my dad and I returned to the kitchen, which seemed frozen in time.

There was the mixing bowl, with its sugar and butter suspension, still glistening from the added eggs. There were the walnuts, chopped and ready to be added to the batter. And there was the sour cream, having reached room temperature after two hours had passed.

"What should I do?" I asked my dad.

"You should keep going," he said.

And so I did.

Conclusion

—

Practice Makes the World

There is no theoretical or ideal *practice*. Practical advice or
direction from people who have no practice may have some
value, but its value is questionable and is limited.

—WENDELL BERRY, *The Gift of Good Land*

I believe that we learn by practice. Whether it means to learn
to dance by practicing dancing or to learn to live by practicing
living, the principles are the same.

—MARTHA GRAHAM, *"An Athlete of God"*

A few months after my mom died, much of the world shut down because of
the COVID-19 pandemic, including many of the people and organizations
featured in these pages.

In the summer of 2020, Patty and Mike changed the member delivery system
at Spring Hill Community Farm so that members no longer traveled to the
farm to harvest vegetables, and they instituted new pickup site protocols,
including masking, hand-sanitizing, and social distancing. It was a rough
season, and at the end of it they found themselves exhausted.

"This season challenged us in ways we could not have imagined," they told the CSA's members in their fall 2020 letter. "The combination of COVID, climate change, and simply getting older all converged in a way that had us stepping back and asking new questions of the farm and of ourselves."

Eventually, they made the difficult decision to transition away from the full-time community-supported agriculture model they had practiced for almost thirty years and instead institute a more modest program in which members could order plants to grow themselves, purchase vegetables at pop-up markets, and support the cultivation of produce for local food shelves.

"In the broadest sense," they wrote, "what we hope for and believe is that there are opportunities ahead for us and the Spring Hill Community that will look different but can still hold the same values of sustainability, steward-ship, and community."

Slow Food's Terra Madre Salone del Gusto went mostly virtual in 2020, with a mix of physical and digital events that ran from October 2020 to April 2021.

"In a historical moment like the one we are going through," Carlo Petrini wrote in *La Stampa* in May 2020, "it is difficult to imagine the sounds, col-ors, scents, and physical intensity of this gathering, which is expected to fill the Lingotto pavilions again this October. Yet, never before has this move-ment, this network, been so alive and active, strong and compact. The social distancing that is now customary at all latitudes cannot stop the solidarity, determination, and militancy of those who every day struggle to change a food system that destroys the environment and generates exclusion and pov-erty" ("Despite Lockdowns").

Slow Food was responding to the pandemic, he said, in two ways. First, it was continuing much of its work to "ensure the continuity of sustainable economies of proximity, strengthening the relationship between producers and citizens, keeping markets alive through new technologies, creating new services to revitalize local and fair supply chains." But this work of uniting citizens and producers was "not enough," Petrini stressed, "because, as in any period of crisis, it is the poor, ultimately, who pay the highest price." And so the second part of the Slow Food response was to provide "direct and gen-erous assistance to those who need it most," with the organization's mem-bers taking "immediate action to ensure the delivery of local and fresh food to those who do not have the means and tools to get it"—not unlike Mike and Patty's decision to focus their efforts on neighbors facing food insecurity ("Despite Lockdowns").

In Berkeley, Chez Panisse closed its doors in mid-March 2020, furloughing its one hundred staff members and imperiling approximately eighty farms that supplied the restaurant with its meat, fish, and produce.

"If we just close up shop, then we're not buying from, not only our farm [Cannard Family Farm], but also River Dog, Star Route Farms, La Tercera, Mariquita, Dirty Girl," said general manager Varun Mehra (Dubrovsky).

The restaurant's solution, which began in March and evolved throughout the summer, was to institute a Sunday Market, much like a CSA, in which the staff sorted produce from its suppliers into boxes and then sold the boxes in a neighboring parking lot. After finding success offering produce from Cannard Family Farm, the restaurant started including products from other suppliers, eventually selling between 150 and 200 boxes per week.

"The pivot actually resulted in an increase in the amount of produce Chez Panisse ordered from farms—a welcome development for growers who otherwise scrambled to make up for the loss of the restaurant market," according to the *Berkeleyside* (Dubrovsky).

In addition, to retain as many staff members as it could, the restaurant began accepting take-out orders on Fridays in May, and in October 2020 it expanded its take-out service to lunch and dinner, Wednesday through Sunday. À la carte dinners could be ordered five days a week, mirroring the service at the Chez Panisse Café upstairs, while three-course dinners could be ordered Thursday to Saturday, much like service at the downstairs restaurant. By November, staffing levels had increased to fifty employees (Dubrovsky).

Two things stand out to me about these diverse responses to the pandemic: first, the way COVID-19 underlined how all of us are embedded in systems that exceed our ability to understand, much less control; and second, how challenges to the stability of these systems can nonetheless lead to transformative changes based on the values of generosity, kindness, gratitude, and care. At the same time, these responses also raise questions about these systems and the changes they can both promote and sustain: namely, what is the relationship of writing to social change? And what is the relationship of ideas to practice?

In the introduction, I noted that I embarked on this intellectual and physical journey to better understand how Wendell Berry, Carlo Petrini, and Alice Waters sought to make our food systems more sustainable, and I observed that one way these writers helped to create social change was by harnessing the power of nonfictional forms to give shape to their utopian visions.

But the pandemic complicated what was already a difficult question by putting a finer point on it: What happens when the "gastronomic imagination" involved in utopian thinking comes up against the realities of actual places and biological materialities, the lived experience of individuals, and the complexities of local food economies and globalized food systems? In other words, what good does it do to "imagine" new food systems when the realities of the existing systems are so daunting? Literary criticism is rife with reference to how writers "resist" various forms of oppression (such as racism, sexism, imperialism, and colonialism) through their writing, but what does that mean, exactly, especially if such resistance is not paired with explicit political action?

One helpful guide I have found to answering these questions is *How Change Happens,* Duncan Green's thoughtful book on global development and social activism. In it, Green references the analytic framework developed by Gender at Work, an international feminist collaborative, which organizes the domains of change along two axes (in another memorable quadrant chart!): from individual to systemic, and from formal to informal.

On one side of the formal axis are the kind of changes often associated with social movements: changing individuals' access to resources (by reducing food insecurity, for example) and changing the laws and policies that govern systems (such as changing the farm bill to the "food bill" in the United States, as Wendell Berry and others have advocated for years). On the other side are the kind of informal changes that activists often neglect: changing the awareness and confidence of individuals (by informing them about where their food comes from, for example) and changing the social norms of what is and is not acceptable (by normalizing the open kitchen, for example, or listing the sources of produce on restaurant menus).

Seeing these domains of change laid out so clearly reminds me that writing has an *enormously* important role to play in creating social change, even

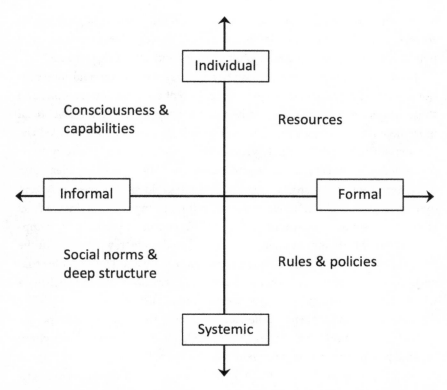

The Gender at Work analytical framework. By Aruna Rao, Joanne Sandler, David Kelleher, and Carol Miller. (From *Gender at Work: Theory and Practice for 21st-Century Organizations* [New York: Routledge, 2016]; courtesy of Aruna Rao and David Kelleher)

if that role sometimes seems indirect and difficult to quantify. It also illustrates, as Green points out, that "change processes will flow between the different quadrants, and activists' attention may move from one to another," as well as that "the many facets of power permeate each quadrant, influencing how change happens" (242). We needn't bemoan the fact that the pandemic underlined how little progress the sustainable food movement had made in reducing individuals' dependence on global supply chains, for example, when it simultaneously occasioned an explosion of interest in home cooking, kitchen gardens, CSA subscriptions, and food justice—all things these writers helped to lay the groundwork for, both literally and figuratively.

It's certainly fair to question the kind of actions readers may have taken after encountering various forms of sustainable food writing: were they moved only to private, individual action (changing their shopping habits, cooking with different ingredients, and so on), or were they moved to more public, collective action (such as joining groups and attending protests)?

No doubt many leverage points they pursued were individual interventions. Writing may change readers' perception of an issue, for example, and those readers may change their values and behaviors as a result. But social movements are emergent systems, and to talk about what I have called the "ecology of influence" is really just another way of talking about systems of influence, how certain ideas and behaviors influence other ideas and behaviors through the stocks, flows, and feedback loops involved in system dynamics (Meadows). It's inaccurate, therefore, to tag the sustainable food movement as *either* consumerist *or* political, as this is yet another symptom of binary thinking that needs to be disrupted. In fact, what many in the food movement are trying to do is to create alternative food economies that exist outside the state and other mainstream institutions, which is neither a wholly individualistic nor wholly systemic kind of change.

Sometimes this happens on the individual level, through particular people acting in ways they find morally responsible, such as opting to purchase organic produce rather than conventionally grown. Sometimes this happens on the collective level, when individuals join a community-supported agriculture farm like Spring Hill, open a community-oriented restaurant like Chez Panisse, or form a food co-operative, as many in the Twin Cities did in the early 1970s (Upright). And sometimes this happens on the organizational level, as when Carlo Petrini and friends formed ARCI Gola in 1986, launching what eventually became Slow Food. Change can happen quickly or slowly, through revolutions or incremental reforms, and it can happen through formal or informal means, as we have seen. But neither individual action nor structural change is primary to the other, and changes to one can occur alongside changes to the other.

Of course, creating social change is difficult, and individuals have limited time and money to invest in collective action that they think may or may not succeed. What may seem like individual food choices are also connected to large-scale processes like colonization through violence and the global structures of inequality that are predicated and dependent on keeping consumers distant from the sources of their food. And many of the problems the food movement is trying to solve will ultimately require public policy solutions, such as reforming the subsidy system. But individual transformation through the written word remains a foundational basis for enacting these and other structural changes, and the personal appeal—in the form of an emotional, accessible story—can make all the difference.

The pandemic—and especially SARS-CoV-2, the virus that causes COVID-19— also raises questions about how idealism is related to materialism, or more broadly, how ideas are related to practice.

To see the entire world upended thanks to a virus only about one hundred nanometers in diameter is to be reminded (lest any of us need reminding) that humans are not the only force at work on Earth and that many of these forces lack consciousness and intentionality.

Food itself is a reminder of this fact, though it is sometimes easy to forget this, so large do the human characters loom in our food systems, especially in the age of the celebrity chef.

In her landmark work *Vibrant Matter*, Jane Bennett claims that "food writing seldom attends to the force of materiality" (43), and she makes the case not only for thinking of food as a system but also for granting the nonhuman world a form of *agency* within that system. She argues for a view of eating "as the formation of an assemblage of human and nonhuman elements, all of which bear some agentic capacity. This capacity involves the negative power to resist or obstruct human projects, but it also includes the more active power to affect and create effects. On this model of eating, human and nonhuman bodies recorporealize in response to each other; both exercise formative power and both offer themselves as matter to be acted upon. Eating appears as a series of mutual transformations in which the border between inside and outside becomes blurry: my meal both is and is not mine; you both are and are not what you eat" (49).

Though I agree with the spirit of Bennett's argument, I hesitate at describing a green pepper, or even a coronavirus, as having "agency" in any formal sense, as such a term seems to imply a purposefulness that is lacking in much of the nonhuman world. Nevertheless, Bennett's emphasis on the power of material formations to shape our world is a significant departure from business as usual, not least because it reminds us of our own embodied materiality, as Berry, Petrini, and Waters have each attempted to do in their own ways.

As Bennett puts it, "Materiality is a rubric that tends to horizontalize the relations between humans, biota, and abiota. It draws human attention sideways, away from an ontologically ranked Great Chain of Being and toward a greater appreciation of the complex entanglements of humans and non-humans" (112).

A focus on materiality, therefore, helps us remember that food is about the transformation of materials and is itself transformational. The key questions in this framework thus become: who and what has the power to transform things, how and why do they transform them in certain ways, who benefits and loses from these transformations, and how do these transformations ultimately transform *us*? It also helps us recall that we are not the only actors in these systems, that our supposed "freedom of choice" is often constrained by forces beyond our control, and that the choices we make frequently have unintended consequences. There is a vibrancy and liveliness to the world, in other words, that we ignore at our peril. (For more on material ecocriticism, see Iovino and Opperman; and Clark 111–36.)

Another way to understand this approach is to consider how, when Geoff Tansey and Tony Worsley define food in a matter-of-fact way as "a part of the environment that we eat," materiality helps illuminate the inherent strangeness of this definition (49).

Materiality has one more implication, which is implicit in Bennett's claim that food has a "productive power . . . to coarsen or refine the imagination" (49). *Vibrant Matter* aims to contest Karl Marx's philosophy of historical materialism, particularly his signature concepts of "base" and "superstructure." Central to Bennett's critique is Marx's claim in the preface to *A Contribution to the Critique of Political Economy* (1859) that "the mode of production of material life conditions the social, political, and intellectual life process in general. It is not the consciousness of men that determines their being, but, on the contrary, their social being that determines their consciousness" (666–67). Whereas Marx defines materialism almost solely in terms of human economic structures (the "mode of production"), Bennett emphasizes "the agentic contributions of nonhuman forces" (xvi). And where Marx argues that all other forms of ideology (legal, political, religious, aesthetic, and philosophical) constitute a "superstructure" shaped by this economic base, Bennett acknowledges that the directionality of influence is more fluid, noting that "ethical political action on the part of humans seems to require not only a vigilant critique of existing institutions but also positive, even utopian alternatives" (xv). The materiality of food, in other words, has the power to shape the imagination of human bodies, just as the human imagination—through both critique and the construction of alternatives—has the power to shape the materiality of food.

Bennett's effort to challenge the anthropocentrism of historical materialism has its corollary in the work of Raymond Williams, whose own revisions to Marx add another valuable perspective on how Berry, Petrini, and Waters remade our relationship with food.

In his landmark essay "Base and Superstructure in Marxist Cultural Theory" (1973), Williams wrote, "We have to revalue 'superstructure' towards a related range of cultural practices, and away from a reflected, reproduced or specifically dependent content. And, crucially, we have to revalue 'the base' away from the notion of a fixed economic or technological abstraction, and towards the specific activities of men in real social and economic relationships, containing fundamental contradictions and variations and therefore always in a state of dynamic process" (1339).

The material world—whether defined as Marx's economic base or Bennett's nonanthropocentric "vital materialism"—is thus shaped and refined by human social practices and activities. (Whatever its origins, for instance, SARS-CoV-2 obviously spread in large part as a result of human activity.) Similarly, as Williams observes, the "superstructure" of ideas consists of cultural practices; ideas are never separate from practices but formed in relationship to and through them. (Williams further distinguishes between what he calls "alternative" and "oppositional" practices, which to some degree correspond to the "individual" and "systemic" axis on Gender at Work's analytic framework—but, he admits, "it is often a very narrow line, in reality, between alternative and oppositional" [1345].)

The most important thing I learned both from the pandemic and from these writers, therefore, could be summed up in a phrase: *practice* makes the world.

What often gets lost in discussions of systems and structures are people—individuals—and the specific historical and cultural contexts of the things they do, the *practices* they engage in. For example, there are the processes of industrialization and modernization, and then there are Wendell Berry and Mike and Patty, trying to keep the soils from washing away on their steeply sloping hillsides. There are the systems of globalization and commodification, and then there are Carlo Petrini and the artisan producers of the Piedmont, seeking quality in everything they do and trying their best to make food that is good, clean, and fair. And there is the economic system of capitalism, and its attendant values of speed, efficiency, and cheapness, and then there are Alice Waters and the women of Lyon and Provence, choosing instead to make food that takes time to produce, reflects its local origins, respects the people and places involved in its production, and builds community.

Growing, producing, processing, distributing, and cooking food are all *practices,* and we miss something important when we focus only on the end product, the dish itself, and fail to appreciate the practices involved in its creation (Peterson; Vogel).

This insight, common to all three authors, actually has four components worth distinguishing.

First, practices are epistemological—they are ways of knowing. Just as Donna Haraway's notion of "situated knowledges" represents "the view from a body," the ideas involved in making our food sustainable cannot be separated from the agricultural, productive, and culinary practices through which they develop. We do not form our values and beliefs *prior* to our practices, in other words, only to apply them to our practices like a balsamic reduction. Nor do we discover them after the fact, the products of reflection upon prior, distinct action. Instead, our ideas about sustainability emerge *within and through* our practices; our ideas and practices arise in concert with one another. Ideas about food, in other words, cannot be separated from their context, just as the content of food writing cannot be separated from its form.

Second, practices are simultaneously social and material. As Michael S. Carolan has put it, "no one eats alone." When we practice sustainable agriculture, artisan production, and what I have been calling "elemental cooking," we connect ourselves to the liveliness of food and the social lives of others. Food joins the community of the body, the community of the table, and the community of the producer into a unified, mutually dependent community of humans and nonhumans, animate and inanimate materials. Food reminds us that we are animals, that eating is a biological process, and that we are related to the nonhuman world in the most intimate of ways, as members of the same extended family. "When we consider food at any length at all," observes Paul Schmidt, "life bursts incredibly and awfully upon our speculation" (184–85). Indeed, even our "last meals" as lively actors are only last meals for "us," as we soon become meals for other creatures, a set of ecological relationships that are always in motion: one meal leading to another, each composed (and decomposed) of another.

Third, practices always take place. Michael Ziser has articulated this eloquently in *Environmental Practice and Early American Literature,* observing that the kind of place bioregionalists talk about is "not so much a region as it is a practice, a craft, a process of bringing-forth. Accordingly, it is preferable to focus not on a geographic place . . . but on a *practice* that incorporates in any human practitioner the specificity of the world to which he belongs. No single practice defines a place entirely, but whatever knowledge of a place there is is knowledge of the practices of the place" (19). Place matters in part because *matter* matters: place-based materials are the source of the food we eat, and the practices of growing and transporting that food generate undesirable materials that pollute places near and far. A practice-based understanding of place and landscape, however, expands the concept of "sense of place" to include a "sense of process," a linkage that acknowledges the global flows of people, information, goods, and capital that define our modern world, but does so without neglecting the foundational understanding that food production and consumption always take place somewhere.

Finally, practice—in its best moments—can become a form of *spiritual* practice. Practice is not only about politics and morality; it is also about spirituality and pleasure, enabling momentary experiences that seem to transcend time. Recall again Patty Wright describing her morning practice at Prairie Farm: "You walk outside in the morning; you kind of really didn't want to get out of bed; but you walk outside, and the sun hits you and it's like, 'Oh, it's gonna be a good day.'" Or Adam Gopnik, who similarly sees cooking as a kind of practice, which he describes as "an escape from consciousness— the nearest thing that the nonspiritual modern man and woman have to Zen meditation; its effect is to reduce us to a state of absolute awareness, where we are here now of necessity" (219). Or as Sam Sifton puts it, "Cooking is a practice, same as Buddhism, CrossFit and sobriety. You just have to do it until that's what you do." In each case, sustainable food practices call us to a kind of mindfulness: they ask us to focus on what is before us in the present moment. To do so is not to abandon politics and ethics but to embed them in the daily work of practice.

In the end, practice doesn't make perfect, and to think so is to miss the point. Instead, practice makes the world. There is, ultimately, no ideal meal, only one in a series of many, many meals, some good, some not so good, some simply "good enough." We may try, again and again, to achieve some vision of perfection—the God Shot, let's call it—but I have finally come to understand what I suspect many of my fellow coffee nerds have secretly known all along: God is not in the shot but in the practice.

Works Cited

Abbe, Mary. "Kitchen Artistry: Designed in 1926, the Minneapolis Institute of Arts' New Frankfurt Kitchen Maximized Efficiency and Hygiene." *Star Tribune* [Minneapolis, MN] 30 July 2006: 3F.

Ackerman-Leist, Philip. *Rebuilding the Foodshed: How to Create Local, Sustainable, and Secure Food Systems.* Foreword by Deborah Madison. White River, VT: Chelsea Green, 2013.

Agnoletti, Mauro. "Italian Historical Rural Landscapes: Dynamics, Data Analysis and Research Findings." *Italian Historical Rural Landscapes: Cultural Values for the Environment and Rural Development.* Ed. Agnoletti. New York: Springer, 2013. 3–87.

Alaimo, Stacey. *Bodily Natures: Science, Environment, and the Material Self.* Bloomington: Indiana University Press, 2010.

Alexander, Christopher. *The Timeless Way of Building.* New York: Oxford University Press, 1979.

Alexander, Christopher, Sara Ishikawa, and Murray Silverstein. *A Pattern Language: Towns, Buildings, Construction.* New York: Oxford University Press, 1977.

Alkon, Alison, and Julie Guthman, eds. *The New Food Activism: Opposition, Cooperation, and Collective Action.* Berkeley: University of California Press, 2017.

Allen, Will. *The Good Food Revolution: Growing Healthy Food, People, and Communities.* With Charles Wilson. Foreword by Eric Schlosser. New York: Gotham, 2012.

Anderson, Benedict R. *Imagined Communities: Reflections on the Origin and Spread of Nationalism.* 2nd ed. New York: Verso, 2006.

Andrews, Geoff. *The Slow Food Story: Politics and Pleasure.* Montreal: McGill-Queen's University Press, 2008.

Armiero, Marco. *A Rugged Nation: Mountains and the Making of Modern Italy.* Cambridge: White Horse, 2011.

Armitage, Kevin C. *The Nature Study Movement: The Forgotten Popularizers of America's Conservation Ethic.* Lawrence: University Press of Kansas, 2009.

Arner, Audrey. "Postcard from Mother Earth: Terra Madre, the World Meeting of Food Communities." *Slow Food Minnesota Newsletter* November 2005: 5–8. slowfoodmn.org.

Bakhtin, Mikhail M. *The Dialogic Imagination: Four Essays.* Ed. Michael Holquist. Trans. Caryl Emerson and Holquist. Austin: University of Texas Press, 1981.

Balbo, Adriano. *Quando inglesi arrivare noi tutti morti: Cronache di lotta partigiana.* Turin: Blu, 2005.

Barbour, Ian G. *When Science Meets Religion: Enemies, Strangers, or Partners?* San Francisco: HarperSanFrancisco, 2000.

Barnet, Andrea. *Visionary Women: How Rachel Carson, Jane Jacobs, Jane Goodall, and Alice Waters Changed Our World.* New York: Ecco, 2018.

Baxter, John. *The Perfect Meal: In Search of the Lost Tastes of France.* New York: Harper Perennial, 2013.

Beecher, Catharine E. *A Treatise on Domestic Economy: For the Use of Young Ladies at Home, and at School.* Boston: Thomas H. Webb, 1843.

Beecher, Catharine E., and Harriet Beecher Stowe. *The American Woman's Home; or, Principles of Domestic Science: Being a Guide to the Formation and Maintenance of Economical, Healthful, Beautiful, and Christian Homes.* New York: J. B. Ford, 1869.

Behr, Edward. *The Art of Eating Cookbook: Essential Recipes from the First 25 Years.* Berkeley: University of California Press, 2011.

Belasco, Warren J. *Appetite for Change: How the Counterculture Took on the Food Industry.* 2nd ed. Ithaca, NY: Cornell University Press, 2007.

———. *Food: The Key Concepts.* New York: Berg, 2008.

Bennett, Jane. *Vibrant Matter: A Political Ecology of Things.* Durham, NC: Duke University Press, 2010.

Benyus, Janine M. *Biomimicry: Innovation Inspired by Nature.* New York: William Morrow, 1997.

Berger, Rose Marie. "Heaven in Henry County: A *Sojourners* Interview with Wendell Berry." *Conversations with Wendell Berry.* Ed. Morris Allen Grubbs. Jackson: University Press of Mississippi, 2007. 164–77.

Berry, Wendell. "An Agricultural Testament." *The Last Whole Earth Catalog: Access to Tools.* New York: Random House, 1971. 46.

———. *The Art of Loading Brush: New Agrarian Writings*. Berkeley, CA: Counterpoint, 2017.

———. "The Big Food Menace." *New York Review of Books* 15 May 2008. nybooks.com

———. *Bringing It to the Table: On Farming and Food*. Intro. Michael Pollan. Berkeley, CA: Counterpoint, 2009.

———. *Citizenship Papers*. Washington, DC: Shoemaker and Hoard, 2003.

———. *A Continuous Harmony: Essays Cultural and Agricultural*. 1972. Washington, DC: Shoemaker and Hoard, 2003.

———. *The Gift of Good Land: Further Essays Cultural and Agricultural*. San Francisco: North Point, 1981.

———. *The Hidden Wound*. Boston: Houghton Mifflin, 1970.

———. *Home Economics: Fourteen Essays*. San Francisco: North Point, 1987.

———. *Imagination in Place: Essays*. Berkeley, CA: Counterpoint, 2010.

———. *It All Turns on Affection: The Jefferson Lecture and Other Essays*. Berkeley, CA: Counterpoint, 2012.

———. *Life Is a Miracle: An Essay against Modern Superstition*. Washington, DC: Counterpoint, 2000.

———. *The Long-Legged House*. 1969. Washington, DC: Shoemaker and Hoard, 2004.

———. "The Making of a Marginal Farm." *Recollected Essays, 1965–1980*. San Francisco: North Point, 1981. 329–40.

———. *The Need to Be Whole: Patriotism and the History of Prejudice*. Berkeley, CA: Shoemaker, 2022.

———. *Our Only World: Ten Essays*. Berkeley, CA: Counterpoint, 2015.

———. *Standing by Words: Essays*. San Francisco: North Point, 1983.

———. "Toward a Healthy Community: An Interview with Wendell Berry." 1997. *Conversations with Wendell Berry*. Ed. Morris Allen Grubbs. Jackson: University Press of Mississippi, 2007. 114–21.

———. *The Unsettling of America: Culture and Agriculture*. 1977. 3rd ed. San Francisco: Sierra Club Books, 1996.

———. *The Way of Ignorance: And Other Essays*. With Contributions by Daniel Kemmis and Courtney White. Berkeley, CA: Counterpoint, 2005.

———. *What Are People For? Essays*. San Francisco: North Point, 1990.

———. "Whose Head Is the Farmer Using? Whose Head Is Using the Farmer?" *Meeting the Expectations of the Land: Essays in Sustainable Agriculture and Stewardship*. Ed. Wes Jackson, Berry, and Bruce Colman. San Francisco: North Point, 1984. 19–30.

Bertolli, Paul. *Chez Panisse Cooking*. With Alice Waters. New York: Random House, 1994.

Bilbro, Jeffrey. *Virtues of Renewal: Wendell Berry's Sustainable Forms*. Lexington: University Press of Kentucky, 2019.

Birdsall, John. "America, Your Food Is So Gay." *Lucky Peach* 13 April 2014. medium.com.

Bittman, Mark. *How to Cook Everything: Simple Recipes for Great Food.* Illus. Alan Witschonke. New York: Macmillan, 1998.

Black, Jane. "Alice Waters Awarded French Legion of Honor." *All We Can Eat* blog. washingtonpost.com. 13 August 2009.

Black, Rachel E. "Cuisine des Femmes: Finding Women in the Kitchen in Lyon, France." *Render: Feminist Food and Culture* 3 (Spring 2015): 30–33.

———. *Porta Palazzo: The Anthropology of an Italian Market.* Philadelphia: University of Pennsylvania Press, 2012.

Bondeson, Jan. *Amazing Dogs: A Cabinet of Canine Curiosities.* Stroud: Amberley Publishing, 2013.

"Book Proposal: The Domaine Tempier Cookbook." Carton 7, folder 31. Chez Panisse, Inc. Records, BANC MSS 2001/148 c. The Bancroft Library, University of California, Berkeley.

Bourdain, Anthony. *A Cook's Tour: In Search of the Perfect Meal.* New York: Bloomsbury, 2001.

———. *Kitchen Confidential: Adventures in the Culinary Underbelly.* New York: Bloomsbury, 2000.

———. "Lyon." *Parts Unknown* (television series). Season 3, episode 4. CNN, 2014.

———. *Medium Raw: A Bloody Valentine to the World of Food and the People Who Cook.* New York: HarperCollins, 2010.

Bourdieu, Pierre. *Distinction: A Social Critique of the Judgement of Taste.* 1979. Trans. Richard Nice. Cambridge, MA: Harvard University Press, 1984.

Bowen, Sarah, Joslyn Brenton, and Sinikka Elliott. "The Joy of Cooking?" *Contexts* (Summer 2014): 20–25.

———. *Pressure Cooker: Why Home Cooking Won't Solve Our Problems and What We Can Do about It.* New York: Oxford University Press, 2019.

Brand, Stewart. "Earl Butz versus Wendell Berry." *News That Stayed News, 1974–1984: Ten Years of CoEvolution Quarterly.* Ed. Art Kleiner and Brand. San Francisco: North Point, 1986. 116–29.

Brown, Dona. *Back to the Land: The Enduring Dream of Self-Sufficiency in Modern America.* Madison: University of Wisconsin Press, 2011.

Brown, Edward Espe. *No Recipe: Cooking as Spiritual Practice.* Boulder, CO: Sounds True, 2018.

Brown, Patricia Leigh. "Space for Trash: A New Design Frontier." *New York Times* 27 July 1989: C1, C12.

Buford, Bill. *Dirt: Adventures in Lyon as a Chef in Training, Father, and Sleuth Looking for the Secret of French Cooking.* New York: Knopf, 2020.

———. *Heat: An Amateur's Adventures as Kitchen Slave, Line Cook, Pasta-Maker, and Apprentice to a Dante-Quoting Butcher in Tuscany.* New York: Vintage, 2006.

Burros, Marian. "Alice Waters: Food Revolutionary." *New York Times* 14 August 1996.

Butz, Earl L. "Agriblunders." *Growth & Change* 9.2 (April 1978): 52.

Calvino, Italo. *Mr Palomar.* 1983. Trans. William Weaver. London: Vintage, 1999.

Capatti, Alberto, and Massimo Montanari. *Italian Cuisine: A Cultural History.* Trans. Aine O'Healy. New York: Columbia University Press. 2003.

Carolan, Michael S. *No One Eats Alone: Food as a Social Enterprise.* Washington, DC: Island, 2017.

Carpenter, Novella. *Farm City: The Education of an Urban Farmer.* New York: Penguin, 2010.

Carruth, Allison. *Global Appetites: American Power and the Literature of Food.* New York: Cambridge University Press, 2013.

Carson, Rachel. *Silent Spring.* 1962. Intro. Linda Lear. Afterword by Edward O. Wilson. New York: Houghton Mifflin, 2002.

Certeau, Michel de, Luce Giard, and Pierre Mayol. *The Practice of Everyday Life.* Vol. 2: *Living & Cooking.* Trans. Timothy J. Tomasik. Minneapolis: University of Minnesota Press, 1998.

Chanot-Bullier, Calixtine. *Vieii receto de cousino prouvençalo/Vieilles recettes de cuisine provençale.* 3rd ed. Marseille: Tacussel, 1972.

Chelminski, Rudi. "The Secrets of France's Super Chef, Paul Bocuse: Cook Quicker Than the Concorde and Butter up the World." *People* 6 September 1976.

Child, Julia. *The French Chef Cookbook.* New York: Knopf, 1968.

Child, Julia, Louisette Bertholle, and Simone Beck. *Mastering the Art of French Cooking.* Vol. 1. 1961. New York: Knopf, 1990.

Chin, Ava. *Eating Wildly: Foraging for Life, Love and the Perfect Meal.* New York: Simon & Schuster, 2014.

Chotiner, Isaac. "Anthony Bourdain Wonders What He Could Have Done." *Slate* 24 October 2017. slate.com.

Clark, Timothy. *The Value of Ecocriticism.* New York: Cambridge University Press, 2019.

Cockburn, Alexander. "Gastro-Porn." *New York Review of Books* 8 December 1977. nybooks.com.

Cohen, Jeffrey Jerome, and Lowell Duckert, eds. *Elemental Ecocriticism: Thinking with Earth, Air, Water, and Fire.* Minneapolis: University of Minnesota Press, 2015.

Conford, Philip. *The Development of the Organic Network: Linking People and Themes, 1945–95.* Edinburgh: Floris, 2011.

———. *The Origins of the Organic Movement.* Edinburgh: Floris, 2001.

Cooper, Ann. *"A Woman's Place Is in the Kitchen": The Evolution of Women Chefs*. New York: Van Nostrand Reinhold, 1998.

Coren, Stanley. *The Pawprints of History: Dogs in the Course of Human Events*. New York: Free Press, 2002.

Cori, Liliana, Annuziata Faustini, and Laura Settimi. "Communication about Pesticide Risks in Italy." *Communicating about Risks to Environment and Health in Europe*. Ed. Philip C. R. Gray, Richard M. Stern, and Marco Biocca. New York: Springer, 1998. 241–56.

Coyne, Kelly, and Erik Knutzen. *The Urban Homestead: Your Guide to Self-Sufficient Living in the Heart of the City*. Rev. ed. Port Townsend, WA: Process Media, 2010.

Crenshaw, Kimberlé. "Demarginalizing the Intersection of Race and Sex: A Black Feminist Critique of Antidiscrimination Doctrine, Feminist Theory and Anti-racist Politics." *University of Chicago Legal Forum* 1 (1989): 139–67.

Cromley, Elizabeth Collins. *The Food Axis: Cooking, Eating, and the Architecture of American Houses*. Charlottesville: University of Virginia Press, 2010.

Daily, Gretchen C., ed. *Nature's Services: Societal Dependence on Natural Ecosystems*. Washington, DC: Island, 1997.

Danbom, David B. "Romantic Agrarianism in Twentieth-Century America." *Agricultural History* 65.4 (Autumn 1991): 1–12.

David, Elizabeth. *French Provincial Cooking*. 1960. Rev. ed. Illus. Juliet Renny. London: Penguin, 1971.

Davolio, Federica, and Roberta Sassatelli. "Polite Transgressions? Pleasure as Economic Device and Ethical Stance in Slow Food." *Critical Food Studies: Food Transgressions: Making Sense of Contemporary Food Politics*. Farnham, UK: Routledge, 2016. 83–107.

De Groot, Roy Andries. *In Search of the Perfect Meal: A Collection of the Best Food Writing of Roy Andries de Groot*. Selected by Lorna J Sass. New York: St. Martin's, 1986.

DeLillo, Don. *Zero K: A Novel*. New York: Scribner, 2016.

DeLind, Laura B. "Considerably More Than Vegetables, a Lot Less Than Community: The Dilemma of Community Supported Agriculture." *Fighting for the Farm: Rural America Transformed*. Ed. Jane Adams. Philadelphia: University of Pennsylvania Press, 2003. 192–208.

Dennis, Spencer. "Lazarus Lizards Now Part of Our Culture." *Cincinnati Enquirer* 23 May 2011. news.cincinnati.com

Diamond, Jared. *Collapse: How Societies Choose to Fail or Succeed*. New York: Penguin, 2005.

Dickie, John. *Delizia! The Epic History of Italians and Their Food*. London: Hodder & Stoughton, 2007.

Donati, Kelly. "The Pleasure of Diversity in Slow Food's Ethics of Taste." *Food, Culture & Society* 8.2 (Fall 2005): 227–42.

Druckman, Charlotte. *Skirt Steak: Women Chefs on Standing the Heat and Staying in the Kitchen*. San Francisco: Chronicle, 2012.

———. "Why Are There No Great Women Chefs?" *Gastronomica* 10.1 (Winter 2010): 24–31.

Duane, Daniel. "Kermit Lynch Knows the Terroir." *New York Times Magazine* 18 October 2013.

Dubrovsky, Amalya. "COVID Changed Chez Panisse, but Alice Waters Is Still Taking Care of Local Farmers." *Berkeleyside* 9 November 2020. berkeleyside.org.

DuPuis, E. Melanie. *Dangerous Digestion: The Politics of American Dietary Advice*. Berkeley: University of California Press, 2015.

Eater Staff. "5 Great Chef Disses." *Eater* 20 November 2009. eater.com.

Elias, Megan J. *Food on the Page: Cookbooks and American Culture*. Philadelphia: University of Pennsylvania Press, 2017.

Felski, Rita. *The Limits of Critique*. Chicago: University of Chicago Press, 2015.

Fine, Gary Alan. *Kitchens: The Culture of Restaurant Work*. Berkeley: University of California Press, 2008.

Fink, Deborah. *Agrarian Women: Wives and Mothers in Rural Nebraska, 1880–1940*. Chapel Hill: University of North Carolina Press, 1992.

Finn, S. Margot. *Discriminating Taste: How Class Anxiety Created the American Food Revolution*. New Brunswick, NJ: Rutgers University Press, 2017.

———. "Food Injustice: What the Food Movement Misses about Poverty and Inequality." *Breakthrough Journal* 11 (Summer 2019). thebreakthrough.org.

Fiskio, Janet. "Unsettling Ecocriticism: Rethinking Agrarianism, Place, and Citizenship." *American Literature* 84.2 (2012): 301–25.

Flanagan, Caitlin. "Cultivating Failure: How School Gardens Are Cheating Our Most Vulnerable Students." *The Atlantic* January/February 2010. theatlantic.com.

Flower, Dean. "Ishmaels All." *Hudson Review* 31.1 (Spring 1978): 170–77.

Ford, Marilyn Wright. "Alice Waters Creates the Edible Schoolyard." *Berkeley Insider* May 1996: 15–19.

Franchi, Maura. "The Contents of Typical Food Products: Tradition, Myth, Memory: Some Notes on Nostalgia Marketing." *Typicality in History: Tradition, Innovation, and Terroir*. Ed. Giovanni Ceccarelli, Alberto Grandi, and Stefano Magagnoli. Brussels: Peter Lang, 2013. 45–68.

Frederick, Christine. *Household Engineering: Scientific Management in the Home*. Chicago: American School of Home Economics, 1919.

Freedman, Paul. *Ten Restaurants That Changed America*. Intro. Danny Meyer. New York: Liveright, 2016.

Freeman, June. *The Making of the Modern Kitchen: A Cultural History.* New York: Berg, 2004.

Freyfogle, Eric T. "The Dilemma of Wendell Berry." *University of Illinois Law Review* 2 (1994): 363–85.

———. *Why Conservation Is Failing and How It Can Regain Ground.* New Haven, CT: Yale University Press, 2006.

Friedman, Andrew. *Chefs, Drugs and Rock & Roll: How Food Lovers, Free Spirits, Misfits and Wanderers Created a New American Profession.* New York: Ecco/HarperCollins, 2018.

Friedman, Susan Stanford. "Women's Autobiographical Selves: Theory and Practice." *Women, Autobiography, Theory: A Reader.* Ed. Sidonie Smith and Julia Watson. Madison: University of Wisconsin Press, 1988. 72–82.

Garrard, Greg. *Ecocriticism.* New York: Routledge, 2004.

Gdula, Steven. *The Warmest Room in the House: How the Kitchen Became the Heart of the Twentieth-Century American Home.* New York: Bloomsbury, 2008.

Gilbert, Sandra M. *The Culinary Imagination: From Myth to Modernity.* New York: Norton, 2014.

Gladwell, Malcolm. *The Tipping Point: How Little Things Can Make a Big Difference.* New York: Little, Brown, 2000.

Goldbeck, David. *The Smart Kitchen: How to Design a Comfortable, Safe, Energy-Efficient, and Environment-Friendly Workspace.* Woodstock, NY: Ceres, 1989.

Goldstein, Joyce. *Inside the California Food Revolution: Thirty Years That Changed Our Culinary Consciousness.* Berkeley: University of California Press, 2013.

Goode, Abby L. *Agrotopias: An American Literary History of Sustainability.* Chapel Hill: University of North Carolina Press, 2022.

Goodrich, Janet. *The Unforeseen Self in the Works of Wendell Berry.* Columbia: University of Missouri Press, 2001.

Gopnik, Adam. *The Table Comes First: Family, France, and the Meaning of Food.* New York: Knopf, 2011.

Gould, Stephen Jay. *Rocks of Ages: Science and Religion in the Fullness of Life.* New York: Ballantine, 2002.

Graham, Martha. "An Athlete of God." Ca. 1953. npr.org.

Green, Duncan. *How Change Happens.* New York: Oxford University Press, 2016.

Groh, Trauger M., and Steven S. H. McFadden. *Farms of Tomorrow: Community Supported Farms, Farm Supported Communities.* Kimberton, PA: Bio-dynamic Farming and Gardening Association, 1990.

Guthman, Julie. *Agrarian Dreams: The Paradox of Organic Farming in California.* Berkeley: University of California Press, 2004.

———. *Agrarian Dreams: The Paradox of Organic Farming in California.* 2nd ed. Berkeley: University of California Press, 2014.

———. "'If They Only Knew': The Unbearable Whiteness of Alternative Food." *Cultivating Food Justice: Race, Class, and Sustainability*. Ed. Alison Hope Alkon and Julian Agyeman. Cambridge, MA: MIT Press, 2011. 263–81.

Hall, Donald. "Back to the Land." *New York Times Book Review* 25 September 1977: 24.

Haraway, Donna. "Situated Knowledges: The Science Question in Feminism and the Privilege of Partial Perspective." *Feminist Studies* 14.3 (Autumn 1988): 575–99.

Harrison, Molly. *The Kitchen in History*. New York: Scribner, 1972.

Hazan, Marcella. *The Essentials of Classic Italian Cooking*. London: Boxtree, 2011.

Heldke, Lisa. "The (Extensive) Pleasures of Eating." *Educated Tastes: Food, Drink & Connoisseur Culture*. Ed. Jeremy Strong. Lincoln: University of Nebraska Press, 2011. 121–57.

Henderson, Elizabeth. *Sharing the Harvest: A Citizen's Guide to Community Supported Agriculture*. With Robyn Van En. Foreword by Joan Dye Gussow. Rev. ed. White River, VT: Chelsea Green, 2007.

Heron, Katrina. *Slow Food Nation's Come to the Table: The Slow Food Way of Living*. Foreword by Alice Waters. San Francisco: Modern Times, 2008.

Hershey, David R. "Sir Albert Howard and the Indore Process." *HortTechnology* 2.2 (April/June 1992): 267–69.

Heßler, Martina. "The Frankfurt Kitchen: The Model of Modernity and the 'Madness' of Traditional Users, 1926 to 1933." *Cold War Kitchen: Americanization, Technology, and European Users*. Ed. Ruth Oldenziel and Karin Zachmann. Cambridge, MA: MIT Press, 2009. 163–84.

Hom, Stephanie Malia. *The Beautiful Country: Tourism and the Impossible State of Destination Italy*. Toronto: University of Toronto Press, 2015.

Honoré, Carl. *In Praise of Slowness: How a Worldwide Movement Is Challenging the Cult of Speed*. New York: HarperSanFrancisco, 2004.

Horowitz, Helen Lefkowitz. *A Taste for Provence*. Chicago: University of Chicago Press, 2016.

Howard, Louise E. *Sir Albert Howard in India*. London: Faber and Faber, 1953.

Howard, Sir Albert. *An Agricultural Testament*. 1940. New York: Oxford University Press, 1943.

———. *The Soil and Health: A Study of Organic Agriculture*. Intro. Wendell Berry. 1945. Lexington: University Press of Kentucky, 2006.

———. *The Waste Products of Agriculture: Their Utilization as Humus*. New York: Oxford University Press, 1931.

Hunter, Brad. *True Cost Report: 2017*. homeadvisor.com.

Imhoff, Dan. "Linking Tables to Farms." *The New Agrarianism: Land, Culture, and the Community of Life*. Ed. Eric T. Freyfogle. Washington, DC: Island, 2001. 17–27.

Iovino, Serenella. *Ecocriticism and Italy: Ecology, Resistance, and Liberation*. New York: Bloomsbury, 2016.

————. "Restoring the Imagination of Place: Narrative Reinhabitation and the Po Valley." *The Bioregional Imagination: Literature, Ecology, and Place.* Ed. Tom Lynch, Cheryll Glotfelty, and Karla Armbruster. Athens: University of Georgia Press, 2012. 100–117.

Iovino, Serenella, and Serpil Opperman, eds. *Material Ecocriticism.* Bloomington: Indiana University Press, 2014.

Jacobs, Ryan. "The Dark Side of the Truffle Trade." *The Atlantic* January 2014. theatlantic.com.

Johnston, Josée. Rev. of *Pressure Cooker: Why Home Cooking Won't Solve Our Problems and What We Can Do about It,* by Sarah Bowen, Joslyn Brenton, and Sinikka Elliott. *Gastronomica: The Journal of Food and Culture* (Fall 2019): 96–97.

Kahn, Jeffery. "Ronald Reagan Launched Political Career Using the Berkeley Campus as a Target." *UC Berkeley News* 8 June 2004. berkeley.edu.

Kamp, David. *The United States of Arugula: The Sun Dried, Cold Pressed, Dark Roasted, Extra Virgin Story of the American Food Revolution.* New York: Broadway, 2006.

Kaufman, Gordon D. *In Face of Mystery: A Constructive Theology.* Cambridge, MA: Harvard University Press, 1995.

Kelley, Margot Anne. *Foodtopia: Communities in Pursuit of Peace, Love, and Homegrown Food.* Boston: Godine, 2022.

Kinchin, Juliet, and Aidan O'Connor. *Counter Space: Design and the Modern Kitchen.* New York: Museum of Modern Art, 2010. moma.org.

King, F. H. *Farmers of Forty Centuries: or, Permanent Agriculture in China, Korea, and Japan.* 1911. Emmaus, PA: Rodale, 1973.

Kline, David. "How Wendell Berry Single-Handedly Preserved Three Hundred Years of Agrarian Wisdom." *Wendell Berry: Life and Work.* Ed. Jason Peters. Lexington: University Press of Kentucky, 2007. 60–65.

Klinkenborg, Verlyn. "Wendell Berry's High Horse." *New York Review of Books* 8 October 2020.

Kuh, Patric. *The Last Days of Haute Cuisine: America's Culinary Revolution.* New York: Viking Penguin, 2001.

Kummer, Corby. *The Pleasures of Slow Food: Celebrating Authentic Traditions, Flavors, and Recipes.* Photographs by Susie Cushner. Preface by Carlo Petrini. Foreword by Eric Schlosser. San Francisco: Chronicle, 2002.

————. "School Gardeners Strike Back." *The Atlantic* 15 January 2010. theatlantic.com.

————. "The Supermarket of the Future." *The Atlantic* May 2007: 128–31.

Kurlanksy, Mark. *Salt: A World History.* New York: Penguin, 2003.

Lanchester, John. "Shut Up and Eat: A Foodie Repents." *New Yorker* 3 November 2014: 36–38.

Lappé, Frances Moore. *Diet for a Small Planet.* Illus. Kathleen Zimmerman and Ralph Iwamoto. New York: Ballantine, 1971.

Laudan, Rachel. "An Italian Critic of Slow Food." 26 May 2009. rachellaudan.com.

———. "Slow Food: The French Terroir Strategy, and Culinary Modernism." *Food, Culture & Society* 7.2 (Fall 2004): 133–44.

Lavin, Chad. *Eating Anxiety: The Perils of Food Politics*. Minneapolis: University of Minnesota Press, 2013.

Leavitt, Sarah. *From Catharine Beecher to Martha Stewart: A Cultural History of Domestic Advice*. Chapel Hill: University of North Carolina Press, 2002.

Lebovitz, David. "My View." 18 October 2007. davidlebovitz.com.

———. "Paris Organics." 22 May 2006. davidlebovitz.com.

Leitch, Alison. "Slow Food and the Politics of Pork Fat: Italian Food and European Identity." *Ethnos* 68.4 (December 2003): 437–62.

———. "Slow Food and the Politics of 'Virtuous Globalization.'" *The Globalization of Food*. Ed. David Inglis and Debra Gimlin. New York: Berg, 2009. 45–64.

Leonardi, Susan J. "Recipes for Reading: Summer Pasta, Lobster à la Riseholme, and Key Lime Pie." *PMLA* 104.3 (May 1989): 340–47.

Leopold, Aldo. *A Sand County Almanac, and Sketches Here and There*. Illus. Charles W. Schwartz. New York: Oxford University Press, 1949.

Levine, Caroline. *Forms: Whole, Rhythm, Hierarchy, Network*. Princeton, NJ: Princeton University Press, 2015.

Lindholm, Charles, and Siv B. Lie. "You Eat What You Are: Cultivated Taste and the Pursuit of Authenticity in the Slow Food Movement." *Culture of the Slow: Social Deceleration in an Accelerated World*. Ed. Nick Osbaldiston. New York: Palgrave Macmillan, 2013.

Lizie, Arthur. "Slow Food." *The SAGE Encyclopedia of Food Issues*. Ed. Ken Albala. Thousand Oaks, CA: Sage, 2015. 1–6.

Logsdon, Gene. "Back to the Land." *Farm Journal* 96.3 (March 1972): 30–32.

Lomborg, Bjørn. *The Skeptical Environmentalist: Measuring the Real State of the World*. New York: Cambridge University Press, 2001.

Long, Lucy M. "Culinary Tourism." *The Oxford Handbook of Food History*. Ed. Jeffrey M. Pilcher. New York: Oxford, 2012. 1–20.

Lorde, Audre. "The Master's Tools Will Never Dismantle the Master's House." 1984. *Sister Outsider: Essays and Speeches*. Berkeley, CA: Crossing Press, 2007. 110–14.

Lotti, Ariane. "The Commoditization of Products and Taste: Slow Food and the Conservation of Agrobiodiversity." *Agriculture and Human Values* 27 (2010): 71–83.

Lupton, Ellen, and J. Abbott Miller. *The Bathroom, the Kitchen, and the Aesthetics of Waste: A Process of Elimination*. Cambridge, MA: MIT List Visual Arts Center, 1992.

Lynch, Kermit. *Adventures on the Wine Route: A Wine Buyer's Tour of France*. 25th Anniversary Edition. New York: Farrar, Straus and Giroux, 2013. Kindle.

————. *Inspiring Thirst: Vintage Selections from the Kermit Lynch Wine Brochure.* Berkeley, CA: Ten Speed, 2004.

Lyon, Janet. *Manifestoes: Provocations of the Modern.* Ithaca, NY: Cornell University Press, 1999.

Madden, Etta M., and Martha L. Finch, eds. *Eating in Eden: Food and American Utopias.* Lincoln: University of Nebraska Press, 2006.

Madison, Deborah. *Vegetarian Cooking for Everyone.* Tenth Anniversary Edition. New York: Broadway, 2007.

Major, William. *Grounded Vision: New Agrarianism and the Academy.* Tuscaloosa: University Alabama Press, 2011.

Marx, Karl. "Preface to *A Contribution to the Critique of Political Economy.*" *The Norton Anthology of Theory and Criticism.* Ed. Vincent B. Leitch. 3rd ed. New York: Norton, 2018. 666–67.

Massa, Silvia, and Stefania Testa. "The Role of Ideology in Brand Strategy: The Case of a Food Retail Company in Italy." *International Journal of Retail & Distribution Management* 40.2 (2012): 109–27.

McCord, Garrett Michael. *Examining the Exclusionary Rhetoric of the Slow Food Movement's Recipes and Literature.* 2011. Master's thesis, California State University, Sacramento.

McFadden, Steven. "Community Farms in the 21st Century: Poised for Another Wave of Growth?" *New Farm.* newfarm.org.

McKibben, Bill. "A Citizen of the Real World." *Wendell Berry: Life and Work.* Ed. Jason Peters. Lexington: University Press of Kentucky, 2007. 113–18.

————. "Prophet in Kentucky." *The Bill McKibben Reader: Pieces from an Active Life.* New York: Henry Holt, 2008. 263–77.

McNamee, Thomas. *Alice Waters and Chez Panisse: The Romantic, Impractical, Often Eccentric, Ultimately Brilliant Making of a Food Revolution.* Foreword by R. W. Apple Jr. New York: Penguin, 2007.

Meadows, Donella H. *Thinking in Systems: A Primer.* Ed. Diana Wright. White River, VT: Chelsea Green, 2008.

Mikulak, Michael. *The Politics of the Pantry: Stories, Food, and Social Change.* Montreal: McGill-Queen's University Press, 2013.

Milano, Serena. "The Right Recipe." *Slow Food Almanac 2008.* Bra, Italy: Slow Food Editore, 2008. 74–79.

Miller, Nancy K. "Getting Personal: Autobiography as Cultural Criticism." *Getting Personal: Feminist Occasions and Other Autobiographical Acts.* New York: Routledge, 1991. 1–30.

Monteiro, Carlos A. "Nutrition and Health: The Issue Is Not Food, Nor Nutrients, So Much as Processing." *Public Health Nutrition* 12.5 (2009): 729–31.

Montmarquet, James A. *The Idea of Agrarianism: From Hunter-Gatherer to Agrarian Radical in Western Culture*. Moscow: University of Idaho Press, 1989.

Morin, Edgar, and Anne Brigitte Kern. *Homeland Earth: A Manifesto for the New Millennium*. Trans. Sean M. Kelly and Roger LaPointe. Cresskill, NJ: Hampton, 1999.

Morozov, Evgeny. "Making It." *New Yorker* 13 January 2014: 69–75.

Moskin, Julia. "A Change in the Kitchen." *New York Times* 21 January 2014.

Moss, David. "Agriculture." *Encyclopedia of Contemporary Italian Culture*. Ed. Gino Moliterno. New York: Routledge, 2005.

Myers, Justin. "The Logic of the Gift: The Possibilities and Limitations of Carlo Petrini's Slow Food Alternative." *Agriculture and Human Values* 30 (2013): 405–15.

Naccarato, Peter, and Kathleen LeBesco. *Culinary Capital*. New York: Berg, 2012.

Necchio, Valeria. "Fishing for Sustainability." *UNISG Newsletter* September 2010. unisg.it.

Nosrat, Samin. *Salt, Fat, Acid, Heat: Mastering the Elements of Good Cooking*. New York: Simon and Schuster, 2017.

Notaker, Henry. *A History of Cookbooks: From Kitchen to Page over Seven Centuries*. Oakland: University of California Press, 2017.

Ochoa, Laurie. "The Olney Table: Richard Olney's Quiet Revolution." *Los Angeles Times* 2 February 1995.

Oliver, Mary. "Wild Geese." *New and Selected Poems*. Vol. 1. Boston: Beacon, 1992. 110.

Olney, James. "Autobiography and the Cultural Moment: A Thematic, Historical, and Bibliographical Introduction." *Autobiography: Essays Theoretical and Critical*. Ed. Olney. Princeton, NJ: Princeton University Press, 1980. 3–27.

Olney, Richard. *The French Menu Cookbook*. Intro. Paul Bertolli. 1970. Berkeley, CA: Ten Speed, 2002.

———. *Lulu's Provençal Table*. Foreword by Alice Waters. Grub Street Cookery. 2013. Kindle.

———. "Preface to the 1988 Edition." *Adventures on the Wine Route: A Wine Buyer's Tour of France*. By Kermit Lynch. 25th Anniversary Edition. Farrar, Straus and Giroux, 1988. Kindle.

———. *Reflexions*. New York: Brick Tower, 1999.

———. *Simple French Food*. 1974. New foreword by Mark Bittman. New York: Houghton Mifflin Harcourt, 2014.

Orr, David W. "The Uses of Prophecy." *The Essential Agrarian Reader: The Future of Culture, Community, and the Land*. Ed. Norman Wirzba. Foreword by Barbara Kingsolver. Washington, DC: Shoemaker and Hoard, 2003. 171–87.

Parasecoli, Fabio. *Al Dente: A History of Food in Italy*. London: Reaktion, 2014.

———. "Postrevolutionary Chowhounds: Food, Globalization, and the Italian Left." *Gastronomica: The Journal of Food and Culture* 3.3 (Summer 2003): 29–39.

Parkins, Wendy, and Geoffrey Craig. *Slow Living.* New York: Berg, 2006.

Patel, Raj. *Stuffed and Starved: The Hidden Battle for the World Food System.* Rev. ed. New York: Melville House, 2012.

Paull, John. "Biodynamic Agriculture: The Journey from Koberwitz to the World, 1924–1938." *Journal of Organic Systems* 6.1 (2011): 27–41.

Paxson, Heather. *The Life of Cheese: Crafting Food and Value in America.* Berkeley: University of California Press, 2012.

Peace, Adrian. "Terra Madre 2006: Political Theater and Ritual Rhetoric in the Slow Food Movement." *Gastronomica: The Journal of Food and Culture* 8.2 (Spring 2008): 31–39.

Peano, Cristiana, and Francesco Sottile, eds. "Slow Food Presidia in Europe: A Model of Sustainability." Bra, Italy: Slow Food Foundation for Biodiversity, 2012. slowfood.com.

Pearlman, Alison. *Smart Casual: The Transformation of Gourmet Restaurant Style in America.* Chicago: University of Chicago Press, 2013.

Pennington, Vince. "Interview with Wendell Berry." 1991. *Conversations with Wendell Berry.* Ed. Morris Allen Grubbs. Jackson: University Press of Mississippi, 2007. 36–49.

Peterson, Anna L. *Works Righteousness: Material Practice in Ethical Theory.* New York: Oxford University Press, 2021.

Petrini, Carlo. "Despite Lockdowns, Slow Food Network Has Never Been So Alive." 19 May 2020. slowfood.com.

———. *Food and Freedom: How the Slow Food Movement Is Changing the World through Gastronomy.* Trans. John Irving. New York: Rizzoli Ex Libris, 2015.

———. Introduction. *Alla Ricerca del Grand Fiume: Atlante dei prodotti agroalimentari del Po.* Pollenzo, Italy: University of Gastronomic Sciences, 2007.

———. *Loving the Earth: Dialogues on the Future of Our Planet.* 2014. Kindle.

———. *Slow Food: The Case for Taste.* Trans. William McCuaig. Foreword by Alice Waters. New York: Columbia University Press, 2003.

———. *Slow Food Nation: Why Our Food Should Be Good, Clean, and Fair.* Trans. Clara Furlan and Jonathan Hunt. New York: Rizzoli, 2007.

———. *Terra Madre: Forging a New Global Network of Sustainable Food Communities.* Foreword by Alice Waters. White River Junction, VT: Chelsea Green, 2010.

Petrini, Carlo, in conversation with Gigi Padovani. *Slow Food: Storia di un'utopia possibile.* Florence and Bra, Italy: Giunti–Slow Food Editore, 2017.

———. *Slow Food Revolution: A New Culture for Eating and Living.* Trans. Francesca Santovetti. New York: Rizzoli, 2006.

Pfeiffer, Ehrenfried. *Bio-Dynamic Farming and Gardening: Soil Fertility Renewal and Preservation*. Trans. Fredrick Heckel. New York: Anthroposophic Press, 1938.

Philippon, Daniel J. *Conserving Words: How American Nature Writers Shaped the Environmental Movement*. Athens: University of Georgia Press, 2005.

Philpott, Tom. "Ruminations on Food, Class, and Carlo Petrini." *Grist* 8 June 2007. grist.org.

———. "You're Using Recipes Wrong." *Mother Jones* 8 March 2017. motherjones.com.

Pilcher, Jeffrey M. "Taco Bell, Maseca, and Slow Food: A Postmodern Apocalypse for Mexico's Peasant Cuisine?" *Fast Food/Slow Food: The Cultural Economy of the Global Food System*. Ed. Richard R. Wilk. Lanham, MD: AltaMira, 2006. 9–81.

Pirsig, Robert. *Zen and the Art of Motorcycle Maintenance*. 1974. New York: HarperTorch, 2006.

Plante, Ellen M. *The American Kitchen 1700 to the Present: From Hearth to Highrise*. New York: Facts on File, 1995.

"Poison Plonk: A Deadly Wine Scandal in Italy." *Time Magazine* 127.14 (7 April 1986): 50.

Pollan, Michael. "Big Food Strikes Back: Why Did the Obamas Fail to Take on Corporate Agriculture?" *New York Times* 5 October 2016.

———. *Cooked: A Natural History of Transformation*. New York: Penguin, 2013.

———. "The Food Movement, Rising." *New York Review of Books* 10 June 2010.

———. *Food Rules: An Eater's Manual*. New York: Penguin, 2009.

———. *In Defense of Food: An Eater's Manifesto*. New York: Penguin, 2008.

———. *The Omnivore's Dilemma: A Natural History of Four Meals*. New York: Penguin, 2006.

Qualset, Calvin O. Rev. of *The Unsettling of America: Culture and Agriculture*, by Wendell Berry. *Science Books and Films* 14.2 (September 1978): 77.

Ransom, John Crowe. "Introduction: A Statement of Principles." *I'll Take My Stand: The South and the Agrarian Tradition*. By Twelve Southerners. 1930. 75th Anniversary Edition. Intro. Susan V. Donaldson. Baton Rouge: Louisiana State University Press. 2006. xli–lii.

Rayner, Jay. *The Man Who Ate the World: In Search of the Perfect Dinner*. New York: Henry Holt, 2008.

Reardon, Joan. *M. F. K. Fisher, Julia Child, and Alice Waters: Celebrating the Pleasures of the Table*. New York: Harmony, 1994.

Reed, Matthew. *Rebels for the Soil: The Rise of the Global Organic Food and Farming Movement*. London: Earthscan, 2010.

Reichl, Ruth. "My Year in Provence Last August." *New York Times* 22 April 1998.

Remer, Nicolaus. *Laws of Life in Agriculture*. 1986. Trans. K. Castelliz and B. Davies. Kimberton, PA: Bio-dynamic Farming and Gardening Association, 1995.

Richards, N[orval]. R[ichard]. Rev. of *The Unsettling of America: Culture and Agriculture,* by Wendell Berry. *Queen's Quarterly* 87.1 (Spring 1980): 137–40.

Ricoeur, Paul. *Freud and Philosophy: An Essay on Interpretation.* New Haven, CT: Yale University Press, 1970.

Riso amaro (Bitter rice). Directed by Giuseppe De Santis. Starring Silvana Mangano, Raf Vallone, Doris Dowling, and Vittorio Gassman. Lux Film, 1949.

Rosso, Julee, and Sheila Lukins. *The New Basics Cookbook.* Illus. Lukins. New York: Workman, 1989.

———. *The Silver Palate Cookbook.* With Michael McLaughlin. Illus. Lukins. New York: Workman, 1982.

Rutherford, Janice Williams. *Selling Mrs. Consumer: Christine Frederick and the Rise of Household Efficiency.* Athens: University of Georgia Press, 2003.

Sanders, Scott. "Back to Earth." *The Progressive* 42 (February 1978): 43–44.

Sando, Steve. "Slow Food versus the Farmers and You and Me, Part 1." May 2007. ranchogordoblog.com.

———. "Slow Food versus the Farmers and You and Me, Part 2." May 2007. ranchogordoblog.com.

Sardo, Stefano, director. *The Slow Food Story.* Indigo Film/TICO Film Company, 2013.

Sassatelli, Roberta, and Federica Davolio. "Consumption, Pleasure and Politics: Slow Food and the Politico-aesthetic Problematization of Food." *Journal of Consumer Culture* 10.2 (2010): 202–32.

Schmidt, Paul. "As if a Cookbook Had Anything to Do with Writing." *Prose* 8 (Spring 1974): 179–203.

Schmidt, Philip. *The Complete Guide to a Green Home: The Good Citizen's Guide to Earth-friendly Remodeling and Home Maintenance.* Minneapolis: Creative Publishing International, 2008.

Sebastiani, Roberta, Francesca Montagnini, and Daniele Dalli. "Ethical Consumption and New Business Models in the Food Industry: Evidence from the Eataly Case." *Journal of Business Ethics* 114 (2013): 473–88.

Sedgwick, Eve Kosofsky. "Paranoid Reading and Reparative Reading, or, You're So Paranoid, You Probably Think This Essay Is about You." *Touching Feeling: Affect, Pedagogy, Performativity.* Durham, NC: Duke University Press, 2003. 123–51.

Sereni, Emilio. *History of the Italian Agricultural Landscape.* 1961. Trans. R. Burr Litchfield. Princeton, NJ: Princeton University Press, 2016.

Severson, Kim. *Spoon Fed: How Eight Cooks Saved My Life.* New York: Riverhead, 2010.

———. "What's Cooking in That Egg Spoon? A Bite-Size Culture War." *New York Times* 26 March 2018. nytimes.com.

Shapiro, Laura. "From Brooklyn to Kentucky to Iran: Cookbooks for Every Taste." *New York Times* 30 November 2016. nytimes.com.

Shattuck, Roger. *Forbidden Knowledge: From Prometheus to Pornography.* New York: St. Martin's Press, 1996.

Shere, Lindsey Remolif. *Chez Panisse Desserts: A Cookbook.* Preface by Alice Waters. New York: Random House, 1994.

Shirk, Adrian. *Heaven Is a Place on Earth: Searching for an American Utopia.* Berkeley, CA: Counterpoint, 2022.

Shiva, Vandana, ed. *Manifestos on the Future of Food and Seed.* Cambridge, MA: South End Press, 2007.

"Showdown at Slow Food." SFGATE 16 May 2007. sfgate.com.

Sifton, Sam. "Just Cook!" *New York Times Cooking Newsletter* 19 September 2016.

Simonetti, Luca. "The Ideology of Slow Food." rachellaudan.com.

———. *Mangi chi può, meglio, meno e piano: l'ideologia di Slow Food.* Florence: Pagliai, 2010.

Singer, Fanny. *Always Home: A Daughter's Recipes and Stories.* Foreword by Alice Waters. Photographs by Brigitte Lacombe. New York: Knopf, 2020.

Singer, Ross, Stephanie Houston Grey, and Jeff Motter. *Rooted Resistance: Agrarian Myth in Modern America.* Fayetteville: University of Arkansas Press, 2020.

Siniscalchi, Valeria. "Environment, Regulation and the Moral Economy of Food in the *Slow Food* Movement." *Journal of Political Ecology* 20 (2013): 295–305.

———. *Slow Food: The Economy and Politics of a Global Movement.* New York: Bloomsbury Academic, 2023.

Sklar, Kathryn Kish. *Catharine Beecher: A Study in American Domesticity.* New Haven, CT: Yale University Press, 1973.

Slotkin, Richard. *The Fatal Environment: The Myth of the Frontier in the Age of Industrialization, 1800–1890.* New York: Atheneum, 1985.

Slovic, Scott. *Seeking Awareness in American Nature Writing: Henry Thoreau, Annie Dillard, Edward Abbey, Wendell Berry, Barry Lopez.* Salt Lake City: University of Utah Press, 1992.

Slow Food. "Our Philosophy." slowfood.com.

Slow Food Foundation for Biodiversity. "Ark of Taste FAQs." fondazioneslowfood.com.

Smart, Ninian. *The World's Religions: Old Traditions and Modern Transformations.* 2nd ed. New York: Cambridge University Press, 1998.

Smith, J. Russell. *Tree Crops: A Permanent Agriculture.* New York: Harcourt, Brace, 1929.

Smith, Kimberly K. "Wendell Berry's Feminist Agrarianism." *Women's Studies* 30.5 (2001): 623–46.

Solnit, Rebecca. "To Break the Story, You Must Break the Status Quo." *Literary Hub* 26 May 2016. lithub.com.

Spang, Rebecca L. *The Invention of the Restaurant: Paris and Modern Gastronomic Culture.* Foreword by Adam Gopnik. Cambridge, MA: Harvard University Press, 2020.

Steiner, Rudolf. *The Agriculture Course.* Trans. George Adams. London: Bio-dynamic Agricultural Association, 1958. wn.rsarchive.org.

Stevens, Stuart. *Feeding Frenzy: Across Europe in Search of the Perfect Meal.* New York: Ballantine, 1997.

Stock, Paul V., Michael Carolan, and Christopher Rosin, eds. *Food Utopias: Reimagining Citizenship, Ethics and Community.* New York: Routledge, 2015.

Sula, Mike. "Carlo Said He's Sorry." *Chicago Reader* 23 May 2007. chicagoreader.com.

Sundelson, David. "After Quiche, What?" *The Nation* 25 September 1982: 277–78.

Suro, Mary Davis. "Chernobyl Cloud Passes, but Chill in Italy Lingers." *New York Times* 27 May 1986.

Syse, Karen Lykke. "Celebrity Chefs, Ethical Food Consumption and the Good Life." *Sustainable Consumption and the Good Life: Interdisciplinary Perspectives.* Ed. Karen Lykke Syse and Martin Lee Mueller. New York: Routledge, 2016. 165–82.

Táíwò, Olúfémi O. *Elite Capture: How the Powerful Took over Identity Politics (and Everything Else).* Chicago: Haymarket, 2022.

Tam, Daisy. "Slow Journeys." *Food, Culture & Society* 11.2 (June 2008): 207–18.

Tanis, David. "Lulu Peyraud, the Cooking Queen of Provence." *Saveur* 14 February 2018. saveur.com.

Tansey, Geoff, and Tony Worsley. *The Food System: A Guide.* London: Earthscan, 1995.

Theophano, Janet. *Eat My Words: Reading Women's Lives through the Cookbooks They Wrote.* New York: Palgrave, 2002.

Thirsk, Joan. *Alternative Agriculture: A History: From the Black Death to the Present Day.* New York: Oxford University Press, 1997.

Thompson, Paul B. *The Agrarian Vision: Sustainability and Environmental Ethics.* Lexington: University Press of Kentucky, 2010.

———. "Land and Water." *A Companion to Environmental Philosophy.* Ed. Dale Jamieson. Malden, MA: Blackwell, 2001. 460–72.

Thoreau, Henry D. *Walden.* 1854. Ed. J. Lyndon Shanley. Intro. Joyce Carol Oates. Princeton, NJ: Princeton University Press, 1989.

The Tibetan Yak Cheese: From the Roof of the World to the Big Apple. Bra, Italy: Slow Food Foundation for Biodiversity, 2007.

Tigner, Amy L., and Allison Carruth. *Literature and Food Studies.* New York: Routledge, 2018.

Tompkins, Jane. "Me and My Shadow." *New Literary History* 19.1 (Autumn 1987): 169–78.

Touring Club of Italy. *Authentic Piedmont-Aosta Valley.* Milan: Touring Club of Italy, 2007.

———. *Guida Gastronomica d'Italia.* Milan: Touring Club of Italy, 1931.

Tower, Jeremiah. *California Dish: What I Saw (and Cooked) at the American Culinary Revolution.* New York: Free Press, 2003.

"Town Bans Pizza-making over Soaring Pollution." BBC.com. 22 December 2015.

Trubek, Amy B. *The Taste of Place: A Cultural Journey into Terroir.* Berkeley: University of California Press, 2009.

Tucker, Rebecca. *A Matter of Taste: A Farmers' Market Devotee's Semi-Reluctant Argument for Inviting Scientific Innovation to the Dinner Table.* Toronto: Coach House, 2018.

Uekötter, Frank. *The Greenest Nation? A New History of German Environmentalism.* Cambridge, MA: MIT Press, 2014.

Upright, Craig B. *Grocery Activism: The Radical History of Food Cooperatives in Minnesota.* Minneapolis: University of Minnesota Press, 2020.

Veseth, Michael. *Globaloney 2.0: The Crash of 2008 and the Future of Globalization.* New York: Rowman and Littlefield, 2010.

Vogel, Steven. *Thinking like a Mall: Environmental Philosophy after the End of Nature.* Cambridge, MA: MIT Press, 2015.

Wald, Sarah D. *The Nature of California: Race, Citizenship, and Farming since the Dust Bowl.* Seattle: University of Washington Press, 2016.

Ward, Peter. *A History of Domestic Space: Privacy and the Canadian Home.* Vancouver: University of British Columbia Press, 1999.

Waters, Alice. *The Art of Simple Food: Notes, Lessons and Recipes from a Delicious Revolution.* With Patricia Curtan, Kelsie Kerr, and Fritz Streiff. Illus. Patricia Curtan. New York: Clarkson Potter, 2007.

———. *The Art of Simple Food II: Recipes, Flavor, and Inspiration from the New Kitchen Garden.* With Kelsie Kerr and Patricia Curtan. Illus. Patricia Curtan. New York: Clarkson Potter, 2013.

———. *Chez Panisse Menu Cookbook.* In collaboration with Linda P. Guenzel. Recipes edited by Carolyn Dille. Designed and illustrated by David Lance Goines. New York: Random House, 1982.

———. *Coming to My Senses: The Making of a Counterculture Cook.* With Christina Mueller and Bob Carrau. New York: Clarkson Potter, 2017.

———. *Edible Schoolyard: A Universal Idea.* With Daniel Duane. Photographs by David Littschwager. San Francisco: Chronicle, 2008.

———. "The Farm–Restaurant Connection." *Our Sustainable Table.* Ed. Robert Clark. San Francisco: North Point, 1990. 113–22.

———. *We Are What We Eat: A Slow Food Manifesto.* New York: Penguin, 2021.

Waters, Alice, and Friends. *Forty Years of Chez Panisse: The Power of Gathering.* Foreword by Calvin Trillin. Afterword by Michael Pollan. New York: Clarkson Potter, 2011.

Waters, Alice, and the Cooks of Chez Panisse. *Chez Panisse Café Cookbook.* In collaboration with David Tanis and Fritz Streiff. Illus. David Lance Goines. New York: William Morrow, 1999.

———. *Chez Panisse Fruit.* In collaboration with Alan Tangren and Fritz Streiff. Illus. Patricia Curtan. New York: HarperCollins, 2002.

———. *Chez Panisse Vegetables.* Illus. Patricia Curtan. New York: William Morrow, 1996.

Waters, Alice, Patricia Curtan, and Martine Labro. *Chez Panisse Pasta, Pizza, and Calzone.* New York: Random House, 1984.

Waters, Alice, with Bob Carrau. *Fanny in France.* Illus. Ann Arnold. New York: Viking, 2016.

Waters, Alice, with Bob Carrau and Patricia Curtan. *Fanny at Chez Panisse.* Illus. Ann Arnold. New York: HarperCollins, 1992.

Watson, Martha. *Lives of Their Own: Rhetorical Dimensions in Autobiographies of Women Activists.* Columbia: University of South Carolina Press, 1999.

Watson, Molly. "Bourdieu's Food Space." gastronomica.org.

Wells, Leigh. "The Food Space." leighwells.com.

Whitaker, Ellen. *Great Kitchens: At Home with America's Top Chefs.* Newtown, CT: Taunton, 1999.

White, Richard. "'Are You an Environmentalist or Do You Work for a Living?': Work and Nature." *Uncommon Ground: Rethinking the Human Place in Nature.* Ed. William Cronon. New York: Norton, 1996. 171–85.

Wilk, Richard. "From Wild Weeds to Artisanal Cheese." *Fast Food/Slow Food: The Cultural Economy of the Global Food System.* Ed. Wilk. New York: Altamira, 2006. 13–27.

Williams, Raymond. "Base and Superstructure in Marxist Cultural Theory." *The Norton Anthology of Theory and Criticism.* Ed. Vincent B. Leitch. 3rd ed. New York: Norton, 2018. 1337–50.

Wilson, Bee. *Consider the Fork: A History of How We Cook and Eat.* New York: Basic, 2012.

Wilson, Edward O. *Consilience: The Unity of Knowledge.* New York: Knopf, 1998.

Wilson, Jason. "Food Is a New Front in Europe's Immigration Struggle." *Slate* 25 July 2016. slate.com.

Wirzba, Norman, ed. *The Art of the Commonplace: The Agrarian Essays of Wendell Berry.* Berkeley, CA: Counterpoint, 2002.

———. *The Essential Agrarian Reader: The Future of Culture, Community, and the Land.* Foreword by Barbara Kingsolver. Washington, DC: Shoemaker and Hoard, 2003.

Wordsworth, William. "The Tables Turned." 1798. *English Romantic Writers.* Ed. David Perkins. New York: Harcourt Brace Jovanovich, 1967. 209.

World Commission on Environment and Development. *Our Common Future.* New York: Oxford University Press, 1987.

Worthington, Danika. "Renowned Chef and Food Philosopher Alice Waters Brings Denver a Message: Slow Down." *Denver Post* 14 July 2017. denverpost.com.

Wright, Wynne, and Gerad Middendorf. "Introduction: Fighting over Food: Change in the Agrifood System." *The Fight over Food: Producers, Consumers, and Activists Challenge the Global Food System.* Ed. Wright and Middendorf. University Park: Pennsylvania State University Press, 2008. 1–26.

Yarwood, Doreen. *The British Kitchen: Housewifery since Roman Times.* London: Batsford, 1981.

Yoo, Aileen. "Bourdain Likens Alice Waters to Cambodian Dictator." *Scavenger* 30 October 2009. blog.sfgate.com.

Zader, Amy. "Understanding Quality Food through Cultural Economy: The 'Politics of Quality' in China's Northeast Japonica Rice." *Agriculture and Human Values* 29.1 (2012): 53–63.

Zinsser, William, ed. *Inventing the Truth: The Art and Craft of Memoir.* Rev. ed. Boston: Houghton Mifflin, 1998.

Ziser, Michael. *Environmental Practice and Early American Literature.* New York: Cambridge University Press, 2013.

Index

Italicized page numbers refer to illustrations.

Printed in the USA
CPSIA information can be obtained
at www.ICGtesting.com
CBHW021956270924
15038CB00002B/10